In Memory
of
Frank S. Mead (1898–1982)

HANDBOOK OF
DENOMINATIONS

HANDBOOK OF DENOMINATIONS

IN THE UNITED STATES

New Tenth Edition

Frank S. Mead

Revised by

Samuel S. Hill

Abingdon Press
NASHVILLE

HANDBOOK OF DENOMINATIONS IN THE UNITED STATES
New Tenth Edition

This book is printed on recycled, acid-free paper.

Library of Congress cataloging-in-Publication Data

Mead, Frank Spencer, 1898-
    Handbook of denominations in the United States / Frank S. Mead.—
New 10th ed. / revised by Samuel S. Hill.
        p.   cm.
    Includes bibliographical references and index.
    ISBN 0-687-01478-6 (alk. paper)
    1. Sects—United States—Dictionaries.   2. United States.—
Religion—1960—Dictionaries.   I. Hill, Samuel S.   II. Title.
BL2525.M425   1995
291'.0973—dc20   95-38528
                                                                               CIP

"Fourteen Kinds of Evangelicalism in America," p. 304, is from *Common Roots: A Call to Evangelical Maturity,* by Robert E. Webber. Copyright © 1978 by Zondervan Publishing House. Reprinted by permission of Robert E. Webber.

"Hunter's Four Traditions of Evangelicalism," p. 306, is from *American Evangelicalism: Conservative Religion and the Quandary of Modernity,* by James D. Hunter. Copyright © 1983 by Rutgers, The State University. Reprinted by permission of Rutgers University Press.

00 01 02 03 04 — 10 9 8 7

MANUFACTURED IN THE UNITED STATES OF AMERICA

CONTENTS

CONTENTS

CONTENTS

CONTENTS

CONTENTS

CONTENTS

CONTENTS

13

CONTENTS

CONTENTS

CONTENTS

PREFACE
to the Tenth Edition

It is now my pleasure for the third time to revise and make available to the public the *Handbook of Denominations in the United States* that the late Frank S. Mead wrote and reedited from the first edition in 1951 through the Seventh Edition in 1980. After his death in 1982, Abingdon Press asked me to continue the pattern that Dr. Mead had carried on for so long.

Producing the Eighth Edition in 1985 and the Ninth in 1990 really brought home to me the fact that this book "has a life of its own." I have sought to revise it by updating it and making some changes and additions, but to do so without intruding upon its uniqueness, in the earlier editions and in this, the Tenth Edition. Ideally, this is the same *Handbook,* but with some improvements.

Of course, any author/editor receives help from many people in putting together a book. I owe a huge debt of gratitude to the contact people of the denominations who responded to my request for assistance. I hope that they and their fellow members read here an accurate reporting of their statistics, history, and beliefs. But more, I hope that the description of their religious body, which means so much to them, elicits pride and celebration.

Specifically, I extend thanks to two professionals who have evaluated and offered suggestions for this revision: Professor Edwin S. Gaustad of the University of California, Riverside, and Mrs. Jeanne Chamberlin of Gainesville, Florida. Professor Allen C. Guelzo of Eastern College, St. Davids, Pennsylvania, provided indispensable assistance as information concerning the "new" Anglican bodies that have been forming in recent years.

The test of this book is its usefulness. I hope it measures up.

Samuel S. Hill,
Gainesville, Florida
December 1994

A WALKING TOUR THROUGH THE RELIGION PAGES OF THE NEWSPAPER

You pick up the city newspaper on Saturday. That day's insert section is entitled "Religion," or two or three pages are devoted to "religion." Glancing at it, you wish it had a bit more snap, some real appeal, were more enticing than any strip of "church ads" can possibly be. But you don't put it down. You'd like information about particular services. Or perhaps you're curious about religion in our society and you view those pages as an opportunity to learn differences among denominations or to gain insight into what is happening on the current religious scene—some of it dangerous, you fear, but also some of it inspiring.

Those blocks, in actuality, only seem to be dull and uninformative. You begin to develop a hunch that each ad tells quite a lot about what that congregation stands for. If it is grouped with other congregations of the same denomination, you sense that even more information is available. That fact, whether it is grouped with other churches or stands alone, is one of the early clues to solving the mystery that religious diversity—confusion, perhaps—can present.

In the special section or on the couple of pages that carry the heading "Religion" or "Churches"—another throw-away distinction that proves to have some significance—you glance at three or four paragraphs of prose, perhaps a column, probably a couple of news stories, and a journalist's summary of religious events for the local community, some reporting, some announcing. That material seems to be, and really is, more commanding of your serious attention, but today you want the information you can gain by scanning. Those somewhat forbidding listings, blocks, and advertisements are your fare.

You note some subsections or large groupings, each with several entries, for "Methodist," "Presbyterian," "Roman Catholic," and "Lutheran," let us say, in your particular newspaper (and probably a few other major groups too). Why are they so clustered? Why are they arranged together like this under these headings? Probably for one of two reasons. The first reason is that each group is a quite organized body, with a local office and officer who goes by some title (itself revealing). Accordingly, the Presbyterian churches in that "presbytery," located in the newspaper's immediate readership area, have faxed or phoned into the newspaper's office information concerning the next Sunday's calendar of events. Not all of them have done so, to be sure, but a good many seize such an opportunity to publicize the times of their worship occasions, perhaps also to announce a ministry they carry on—of music or meals or health care—to the neighborhood.

Almost certainly only the organized denominations with a local judicatory of some kind will gather and coordinate this material. Methodists call them "districts," Catholics the "diocese," and Baptists the "association." But a second possibility exists—namely, that the newspaper on its own will cluster several "Religious Science" bodies or "Evangelical" churches or "Charismatic" services. These are not, by such title, organized denominations, although individual congregations that fall under those headings may have affiliation.

Instead, in such cases as these, particular identity grouping has occurred rather than organizational clustering. You may be sure that a questionable or mistaken placement will not occur more than once or twice. A congregation that is not "evangelical" but is listed that way may be counted on to notify the paper's office of its error—or the other way around. An example: "Grace Evangelical Lutheran Church" is Lutheran, not Evangelical. There the word is traditional (from Luther's era in sixteenth-century Germany) and refers to its commitment to the gospel, the message of and about Christ, for which the Greek word is *euangelion*. A different example: A particular Episcopal church may be "charismatic," emphasizing the "gifts of the Spirit," but its notice will appear in the denominational bloc, not under "Charismatic." Or a congregation that belongs to the Assemblies of God denomination is about as likely to appear in the "Pentecostal" section as in the denomination's, either being acceptable to the Assemblies of God people.

In such ways as these, the existence of groupings, classifications, or common listings is significant. Already the reader has learned something.

But now we are ready to examine the individual items under these headings. Since ministerial (clergy) leadership is important to a congregation's vitality and effectiveness, we look for the name(s) of the clergy, maybe even the sermon title for the coming Sunday. Alas, we discern that in some cases the minister's name is not included. Is that a clue? We may be assured that it is. First, in those settings where the sermon is the central action during the worship period, the name of the minister (one or more) and of the person preaching is likely to be printed. Two settings fitting that description are the two classic Protestant Reformation families, the Lutheran and Presbyterian or Reformed (Calvinist). Finally, one has to say that those are the great preaching traditions within historic Protestantism.

In other cases too the ministerial names may be expected, the Baptist, the Assemblies of God, the Methodist, and the Christian Church (Disciples of Christ) prominent among them. There too the fact of preaching and the particular sermon are basic. But a second major reason compels the listing of the minister's name: The personality of that designated official (ordained) leader is central to the congregation's being and well-being. Here the role is not generic in any sense. Pastor Williams or Preacher Frank or Brother Bill is the point of identification for its very existence in the eyes of many. This is probably at variance with the theology taught and may be quite distasteful to the pious minister, but it is, often at least, simply a fact. Many kinds of assets can "carry" a congregation, of course, causing it to be effective or not. But none surpasses the capacity of the ministerial leadership to "make it go." That person can "make or break" its success. As the most visible single factor, he (sometimes she—another telling clue) had best present some or several of these qualities of leadership: attractive personality, fine speaking ability, gifts for ministering in times of personal need, and skills at organizing and managing membership activities and staff personnel.

But the ministerial personality item is the first factor only in some instances. In Roman Catholic, Orthodox, and Episcopal parishes, it is not—or at least there is no justification for it when it happens. Rarely does an ad from one of these churches show the name of the priest(s). In those settings the official role of the ordained leader centers on the sacraments, especially the sacrament of Holy Communion. Only an ordained person can celebrate Communion and his (by canon law a male in Catholic and Orthodox churches) personal character and conduct do not affect this official role. *Ex opere operato* is the classic phrase for this qualification; the sacrament "works" because "it works," not because of the worthiness of the celebrant or the spiritual state of the recipient. (Of course, clergy should be devout Christians.)

There is no doubt that the leadership qualities of the clergy affect the vitality and direction of a parish's life. Nor is the attractiveness of the homily, or sermon, totally without significance. However, these are not "great preaching traditions." In these liturgical/sacramental churches, the act of worship is all important. The clergy lead the prescribed service and officiate at the altar. Outside the set services (of which there are likely to be a few during the week), the rector's or pastor's capacity for "running" the parish is indeed a crucial factor. Yet, there is considerable difference between an effective-personality kind of leadership and the "generic" kind operating the "catholic" (in the sense of general, universal, or common) churches.

As for worship occasions at other times than Sunday morning, those catholic churches are likely to announce morning prayer a day or two a week and Holy Communion once or twice, perhaps on Wednesday at 5:00 P.M. But the scheduling of gathering occasions at other times is common, and significant, in other types of churches too. Almost certainly evangelical congregations will gather on Wednesday evening. One major form of this combines some kind of dinner fellowship with a devotional period or Bible study hour. People come as family units for the two-part evening, with child care and children's classes a standard component. The adult event may be called "prayer meeting" or "midweek service" or "Bible study." In any case, convening at some time(s) between Sundays takes high priority. These congregations believe in nourishing fellowship, a spirit of community within the membership—for maybe a hundred or two people or even a couple of thousand. Fellowship is an end in itself, but such occasions invariably feature a fostering of discipleship through study or prayer. Just as these kinds of churches—"evangelical" comes closest to classifying them—typically schedule a midweek occasion, so also a similar logic issues in their insistence on a Sunday evening service. Notably in an evangelistic or pentecostal context, it is almost a test of orthodoxy whether the congregation offers two Sunday services. A sizable proportion of members "go to church" three times a week, perhaps more when you include committee, board, or special ministry gatherings. (The more "formal" churches too hold various committee meetings on week nights.)

Frequency of expected attendance, then, is one indicator of the orientation of churches. Two other prominent characteristics appear in the newspaper ads: (1) observance of the Christian calendar, the seasons of the church year, and (2) the name the congregation goes by—its "first name," Such-and-Such Methodist or Church of God or Catholic. With respect to the first, the Christian calendar, the liturgical churches by their very nature observe Advent, Epiphany, Lent, and Easter. That means that the religion pages reader may be fairly certain that any church displaying the season of the Christian year gives order to whatever it does. This includes the Scripture lessons that are studied, the sermons preached, the music selected, and the colors adorning the pulpit, altar, and clergy leader. "Order" is a value and always a determining consideration in Lutheran, Catholic, and Episcopal worship life. Often it is for Methodists, Presbyterians, Disciples, and United Church of Christ congregations. Their study assignments and worship elements trace the life of Jesus from his birth (and just before) to his death and resurrection (and what follows as the Holy Spirit continues Christ's presence). That story is the thread that gives direction and strength to what the worshipers do across the year.

Simply by count, the large majority of American congregations pay no definitive attention to the Christian year. Christmas and Easter are certainly observed, but more as days than as seasons. (Thanksgiving Day attains near-sacred significance, suggesting that popular culture may have as much to do with special-day observances as any inclination to step in accord with historic Christianity.) By these churches' understanding, spontaneity and flexibility outrank "order" for importance. What the minister has on his heart, how he is guided by the Spirit, is a major impetus. Also what the congregation has chosen to take on as a project or campaign or emphasis gives shape and direction. Just as basic is the condition of being oblivious or indifferent to the "Christian calendar." Any recognition of the tradition of the historical church takes a quite secondary place. Their "seasoning" comes from the Spirit's guidance of the minister and congregation and of each Christian in his or her daily walk, all rooted in Bible study. Their investment is in the present and God's future, their grounding in the normative past, the biblical period, especially during Jesus' lifetime and the era of the earliest church.

Second, "first names" of churches reveal a great deal. Probably for more reasons than just being able to refer to themselves clearly, churches call themselves something, not just ———— denomination. One powerful example comes from a fellowship or brotherhood that insists that it is not a denomination—there are only "Churches of Christ" (not a title such as "Baptist" or "Episcopal" or "Pentecostal"). Even these possess a name, "first" and "last," however. There is the "Northeast Church of Christ" or the "Glasgow Church of Christ" or the "Broadway Church of Christ," location namings being the most prominent. So as to clarify its having a "last name" without being a denomination, the sign in front of the building typically says that the "———— Church of Christ Meets Here."

The vast majority of congregations take for granted the matter of having "last names" and "first names." "Take for granted" turns out to be somewhat misleading, however, in that most churches are proud to identify themselves as Orthodox or Mennonite or Friends Meeting (Quaker) or Baptist. While few show a triumphalist spirit, almost all wear their badges in plain view. What those badges stand for provides direction and limits for their choice of "first names"; at least it suggests a range of suitable, appropriate, discriminating choices.

We saw that the nondenominational Churches of Christ lean to location namings. Since what they stand for is restoring (in a sense, duplicating) the primitive church (of the New Testament), all they want to accomplish is showing where their body meets. In almost all other cases, what you call your church, at the corner of Main and East Michigan Avenue or on Route 4, Mason City, accords with your congregation's self-understanding. Let's take three general examples: (1) Christian groups that attach little theological importance to their names—in which location, ordinal numbers, and memorialization are foremost; (2) those denominations that draw on doctrinal or theological titles for their names; (3) those that claim the names of biblical figures and historical stalwarts of the faith.

1. First Baptist, Second Presbyterian, Weaver Memorial Methodist, Greenfield United Church of Christ, Pleasant Ridge Church of God. Denomination-specific this naming pattern is not. What it does point to, wherever it is put to use, is something like: This church is in this place where it has been quite a while and where "many saints have trod." Its reference point is this locale and these people.

2. Grace Lutheran, Trinity Methodist, Reconciliation Presbyterian, Holy Cross Episcopal, and so on in a long list of doctrinal titles that might include Redeemer, Incarnation, Prince of Peace, Emmanuel, Abiding Savior, Good Shepherd. What they preach and teach discloses their theology, needless to say. So intent are they on embodying the Christian message that their very names are teaching devices.

3. St. John the Baptist, St. Paul's, John Calvin Memorial, St. Thomas Aquinas, St. Augustine's, St. Anne's, St. Barnabas's, St. Mary's. Any denominations that follow this plan of name choosing are conscious of Christian history, biblical and subsequent. In the Roman Catholic instance, "canonized" saints, those officially so designated by the church, are especially attractive, but other "saints," biblical and otherwise, are so honored. Still, "honoring" is not all that is involved. Since the church is the people of God over 2,000 years of history, it provides numerous models of the message; this and that mundane person was called and used in God's service by the Lord, and *so can we be too.* In all of the churches where catholicity is

26

integral to church life, the history of the people of God is an available
resource for naming and modeling. "Why not refer to that resource?"
one hears them think. "They are our brothers and sisters in the faith.
We all belong to the same body, and we should claim that heritage of
devotion to God."

Obviously, descriptions provided so far do not cover the entire
sweep of churches or religious organizations that function in American society. Nor do they treat all of those that take out ads on the
Religion pages. Jewish services may or may not be listed. The number
of Jewish temples or synagogues in the newspaper's readership area
may be quite small. A couple of other factors also pertain to the
Jewish case and their publicizing Sabbath services. One is that
Judaism is for Jews (overwhelmingly), and events at its centers,
religious and otherwise, tend to be known, or information is readily
attainable, to the Jewish community. Another is the fact that "Jewish"
activities are as basic as "Judaistic" activities—that is, what Jewish
people do together for the various causes that concern them is
important across the board. Thus educational, fund-raising, so-
cial/recreational, Zionist, and social service activities are as elemen-
tally Jewish as Sabbath (worship) occasions. Comparing Christian
and Jewish Sabbath services facilitates our seeing that "going to
church" is more definitive for Christians than Sabbath attendance is
for Jews.

A particular focus is needed to clarify black church life. In earlier
descriptions of Baptist, Methodist, and Pentecostal characteristics,
patterns in black churches and white churches alike were considered.
At that level, the differences are minor. But we need to note two
singular conditions. The first is the black church's smaller inclination
to advertise religious news in "mainstream" papers. The second is the
probability that the ad will provide more details; black church ads are
veritably packed with information, perhaps with the pastor's picture,
and likely an inventory of several services and meetings during the
ensuing week.

One arrangement somewhat common in large city newspapers
further clarifies the black church situation. Where there is a major
section heading for Methodist or Baptist, a few subheadings may give
specificity. For example, under "Methodist," one may find United
Methodist Church, African Methodist Episcopal Church, and Christian Methodist Episcopal Church, the latter two being black denominations. Similarly, Baptist sections may well include National Baptist
Convention, Inc., and Progressive National Baptist Convention. The
four-million-member Church of God in Christ, a black Pentecostal
communion, when it appears at all is apt to have its own heading. But

sometimes it will be arranged under "Pentecostal." Denominational memberships, after all, are not inherently respecters of persons. Only the particular history of communities of faith determines the degree of involvement in them by racial or ethnic or national or regional groups of people.

Users of the *Handbook of Denominations* may note that some (several dozen) of the bodies described in the entries that follow have not been mentioned in this "walking tour" through the Religion pages. That fact is due in part to the brevity of this guide, but mostly to the fact that many of the "denominations" never advertise. A large number of them are very small. Many congregations in all of them have memberships under 200. In addition, a great many are located in rural areas where those who might want to know what congregations are doing find out by simply living in the community where they are located. On quite another front, thousands of Catholic and Mormon congregations are "parishes" (actual or virtual) that serve designated neighborhoods—although boundaries are not hard and fast. Then, too, the descriptions offered here pertain much more to metropolitan journalism than to small-town or county newspapers.

Even so, your "tour guide" hopes that the issues raised, the clues noted, and the explanations given may serve people throughout the United States, irrespective of community size or region or any other demographic conditions. The trip is a bit complex but also can be rewarding. It offers an interested person a chance to learn about religious bodies and about our society—not a bad afternoon's venture.

HOW TO USE THIS BOOK

Locating the religious body you are seeking information on may be simple. If you know the exact, official name of the body, you will of course turn to the table of contents and be on your way.

But that may not prove to be the case. Religious groups are sometimes known by a kind of nickname or by a secondary title. Mormons, for example, are really Latter-day Saints. While they take no offense at the use of this secondary title, they refer to themselves as "LDS." They are listed here under "L" for their official title, Latter-Day Saints.

The people called Quakers provide us with another example of "How should I look them up?" They are actually members of the "Society of Friends," hence they are most properly referred to as "Friends." In this book that tradition is listed under "F" for their real name, Friends (or Friends, Society of). (It would mislead any user if we placed them under "S" for Society of Friends.)

This suggestion: If your first leads and hunches prove unsuccessful, go straight to the index, which should take you to your goal if the table of contents does not.

Sometimes a seeker will associate a particular group with its family. For instance, the person who wants to learn about a Holiness body, let us say, the Wesleyan Church, may turn to the "H" section. Such an action will frustrate the search; the Wesleyan Church is listed under "W." In reality, few Holiness bodies employ "Holiness" in their name. A different kind of example is the Church of the Nazarene. It belongs to the Holiness family, but that is not how it is known. Note that in this case "Church" comes before "Nazarene," so it appears under "C": the Church of the Nazarene. Members of this body, by the way, will say to you that they belong to the "Church of the Nazarene" more often than they will say that they are "Nazarene."

By contrast, most Pentecostal groups use "Pentecostal" as part of their names, often as the first word; so they are shown here under "P," for the family name, Pentecostal. One of the largest of them, the

Assemblies of God, falls under "P" for the Pentecostal family, but does not make Pentecostal a part of its name.

The Baptist case is similar. Every Baptist group uses "Baptist" in its title. Thus all of the many Baptist bodies are listed in the "B" section, as members of the Baptist family.

The "Church of God" heading is especially complex and confusing. The several groups that call themselves "Church of God" appear here under the general heading "Church of God." But so much variety exists in this naming pattern that this is not a family. Several such bodies are Pentecostal, but one may be Holiness and not at all Pentecostal. In this case, the name is the thing. The various "Churches of God" bodies do not comprise a family. While some of them are kin, many are not.

Another challenging name is "Brethren." I incline to say, "Good luck," but the difficulty actually is not that great. The descriptions of "Brethren" under "B" reveal real diversity, but the generic section at the beginning should afford some clarity. Bear in mind that "Plymouth Brethren" do not fit in the "Brethren" classification at all. One might say that they (and a number of other bodies) are their own classification.

What the average American may refer to as "Eastern Orthodox" is here (appropriately) shown as "Orthodox." (Readers are encouraged to tackle an understanding of this ancient and large branch of Christianity, owing to its great significance in this era following the breakup of the Soviet Union and its bloc of nations in Eastern Europe. It seems that Americans are rediscovering this tradition—and we surely should be.)

Faith communities that we have in the past associated with other, "foreign" societies in the world, very little with our own, are briefly introduced here. Islam's presence in the United States, increasingly significant, is treated under "Muslim." "Black Muslims" make up a major part of that family group. Buddhist Communities and Hindu Communities are so listed. A new entry in this Tenth Edition is the Native American Church.

All membership statistics provided reflect reports from 1991, 1992, or 1993, unless otherwise indicated. In several cases, there appears to be no way to obtain figures that are more recent than the ones given.

The *Handbook of Denominations* is certainly a handbook. Readers wanting more detailed and extensive information are directed to the bibliography. In particular, the large-scale work done by J. Gordon Melton in *The Encyclopedia of American Religions* and by Arthur C. Piepkorn in *Profiles in Belief* are recommended.

Denomination here is a catchall term. Judaism does not use the term, nor is it a felicitous expression to the Orthodox, the Old Catholics, and many Evangelicals. This term may simply be the best available label for the wide-ranging treatment of religious bodies in America that this book aims to provide.

Now better equipped to use this book (as I hope), take advantage of it to your enjoyment and edification.

DENOMINATIONS

ADVENTIST

This family of conservative Protestants has built its theology around a particular theme that always has been part of Christian teaching—the return, or Second Advent ("coming to" our world) of Jesus Christ. Growing from a widely believed message made popular in the 1830s and 1840s, Adventists confronted a crisis, the Great Disappointment, when the predicted return of Christ did not occur in October 1844. Two Adventist bodies were soon organized and still continue.

Great emphasis is placed on the evil nature of the present age. But good—that is, God's righteousness and purpose—will prevail. Thus Adventists are pessimistic about the present but filled with confidence and hope for God's future. In the meantime, they are a devout, disciplined people who practice a wholesome personal and family life, as well as a life of obedience toward God and toward the evangelization of the whole world.

Adventism, in general, is based on the conviction that the Second Advent of Christ is the sole hope of the world. It holds that humanity's nature is fallen because of sin and that on the basis of neglect or rejection of God's plan of salvation, those who rebel against the government of God will be ultimately destroyed, while believers, by God's grace, will be saved. After that cataclysmic event, Jesus Christ will reign in triumph through the thousand-year period, or millennium, of Revelation 20:1-6. The whole Adventist thesis rests heavily upon the prophetic and apocalyptic texts of Daniel and Revelation.

As a religious movement, it began with a widespread "awakening" on the question of the Advent, which developed spontaneously in both the Old World and the New in the early decades of the nineteenth century. It became strongest and most clearly defined in the United States, at first under the leadership of William Miller (1782–1849) of Low Hampton, New York, a veteran of the War of 1812 and respected as a diligent student of the Bible, although he did not have formal college or seminary training.

The movement under Miller was at first an interchurch (or more accurately, *intra*church) development, with many Methodists, Baptists, Presbyterians, Congregationalists, and others among its adherents. It was thus a movement within existing churches, and in the days of its beginnings there was no intention or attempt to organize a separate denomination. So influential was William Miller that for years his followers were known as Millerites. Miller himself became a Baptist in 1816 and at once began a careful study of the Scriptures, concentrating on the prophecies of Daniel and Revelation. Using only the Bible, its marginal references, and Cruden's *Concordance,* Miller came to the same conclusion that many biblical scholars had already reached: The symbolic "day" of Bible prophecy represents one year. He also concluded that the 2,300 "days" of Daniel 8:14 started concurrently with the "seventy weeks of years" of Daniel 9—that is, from 457 B.C., the year of the command to rebuild and restore Jerusalem; he believed that the longer of the two periods would end in or about the year 1843, as calculated by Jewish reckoning. Miller thought that the "sanctuary" mentioned in Daniel 8:14 was the earth (or the church), which would be cleansed by fire at the Second Advent, and that this cleansing would occur sometime between March 21, 1843, and March 21, 1844.

When this expectation failed to materialize by the spring of 1844, many left the movement. Miller's associates, on the basis of meticulous study of Old Testament types, then set a second date, October 22, 1844, as the great antitypical Day of Atonement, confident that the "day of the Lord is near, even at the door." By 1844 there were between 50,000 and 100,000 Adventists in North America. As the day of expectation approached, some disposed of their property, settled all their accounts, and waited prayerfully for the Lord. When October 22 passed with no second coming, vast numbers lost all interest in Adventism and went back to their former churches or abandoned the Christian faith altogether.

Those persons who continued as Adventists formed several smaller bodies. A loosely knit organization came into being at a conference in Albany, New York, in 1845. This group held generally to Miller's positions and theology, emphasizing the personal and premillennial character of the Second Advent, the resurrection of the dead—the faithful to be raised at Christ's coming, the rest a thousand years later—and the renewal of the earth as an eternal abode of the redeemed. Known at first as the American Millennial Association, a portion later came to be called Evangelical Adventist, a church that has dwindled to the point of obscurity. In 1860 another and larger group became known as the Advent Christian Church.

While the general expectation of the Advent had united the disparate groups, the disappointment in 1844 brought their differences to light again. Nearly all Adventists at first agreed that the Second Advent would be premillennial—that is, that Christ's return would *precede* the thousand-year period foretold in Revelation 20. Today, however, many, including the Advent Christian group, hold the amillennial position.

In other areas, also, there were differing viewpoints. Just what is the state of the dead—conscious or unconscious—as they await the resurrection? Who are to arise—the righteous and the wicked both, or only the righteous? Is there to be eternal punishment or ultimate annihilation for the wicked? What is the nature of immortality? Does the cleansing of the sanctuary in Daniel 8 refer to a sanctuary in heaven or to one on earth? When should the sabbath be recognized—on the first day or on the seventh; on Sunday or on Saturday? Over these questions, the Adventists, as organized bodies, became divided into the three major groups we find today.

ADVENT CHRISTIAN CHURCH

Founded in 1860, the Advent Christian Church is one of several denominations that grew out of the Millerite movement of the 1830s and 1840s. While William Miller was not directly involved in the founding of this church, his preaching and teachings concerning the second coming of Christ formed the theological basis for much of Advent Christian theological, biblical, and organizational thinking.

In addition, the doctrine of life only in Jesus Christ, or conditional immortality, as preached by George Storrs and Charles F. Hudson, became a major teaching of the denomination. Dissatisfied with the widespread teaching of a purely Platonic doctrine of the immortality of the human soul, Advent Christians declared valid the unconscious state of all the dead until the resurrection at Christ's return, the extinction (as opposed to eternal torment) of the wicked after their resurrection to final judgment at Christ's return, and the imminent return of Christ.

The first Advent Christian Association was followed closely by the founding of publications and missions societies and of Aurora University. The denomination also maintains missions in Japan, Mexico, India, Nigeria, the Philippines, and Malaysia.

Congregational in polity, the church is composed of approximately 28,000 members in 325 local churches, grouped in five regional districts in the U.S. and Canada, associated under the Advent Christian General Conference of America. The General Conference meets every three years and maintains denominational offices in Charlotte, North Carolina, which house work in missions, urban ministries, church growth, Christian education, publications, administration, women's ministries, and public relations.

The denomination maintains no formal creedal statement, but does have a declaration of principles, adopted by the General Conference in 1900 and revised in 1934, 1964, and 1972. Two sacraments are observed: baptism by immersion and the Lord's Supper. Worship is held on the first day of the week.

In 1964, Advent Christian Church merged with Life and Advent Union, an Adventist group with three churches and 300 members, organized by John T. Walsh in 1848. The Advent Christian Church became a member of the National Association of Evangelicals in 1986.

CHURCH OF GOD GENERAL CONFERENCE

This church is the outgrowth of several independent local groups of similar faith, some in existence as early as 1800; others date their beginnings from the arrival of British immigrants to this country around 1847. Many were organized under the name Church of Christ in Christ Jesus and also carried the name Church of God of the Abrahamic Faith for many years. The corporate name today is Church of God General Conference, Morrow, Georgia.

State and district conferences of these groups were formed as an expression of mutual cooperation. A national organization instituted at Philadelphia in 1888 met again in 1889; however, because of strong convictions on questions of congregational rights and authority, it ceased to function until 1921, when the present general conference was formed at Waterloo, Iowa.

The Bible is accepted as the supreme standard of faith. Adventist in viewpoint, the church strongly emphasizes the premillennial second coming of Christ. The church teaches that the kingdom of God will be literal, beginning in Jerusalem at the return of Christ and extending to all nations. Emphasis is placed on the oneness of God and the Sonship of Christ; it is taught that Jesus did not exist prior to his birth in Bethlehem and that the Holy Ghost is the power and influence of God. Members believe in the restoration of Israel, the time of restitution, the mortality of humans (asleep in death until the resurrection), the literal resurrection of the dead, the reward of the righteous on earth, and the complete destruction of the wicked in a second death. Membership depends on acceptance of doctrinal faith, repentance, and baptism (for the remission of sins) by immersion.

Delegates from each church meet each year to determine denominational plans and policies and elect officers, who serve on a board of directors. A general conference supports Atlanta Bible College for the training of pastors; the Atlanta Bible College Development Foundation, an endowment fund; a Publishing Department to produce church literature and curricula; and an Outreach and Church Development Department, which promotes youth work, Sunday school activity, mission, and evangelism. The work of the general conference is carried on under the direction of the board of directors, which meets as necessary throughout the year. The executive officer is a president who administers the work as a whole. The conference is incorporated as Atlanta Bible College/Church of God General Conference. Because of the congregational nature of the church's government, the general conference exists primarily as a means of mutual cooperation and development of yearly projects and enterprises. There are 5,526 members in 89 churches, in 13 state and district conferences. The church periodical, *The Restitution Herald,* is published bimonthly. Mission stations are located in India, Mexico, the Philippines, Great Britain, and Peru.

SEVENTH-DAY ADVENTIST

By far the largest single Adventist body in number of members, in the U.S. and throughout the world, is the Seventh-day Adventist Church, which traces its beginnings back to the 1840s. It arose in the aftermath of what has been termed the Great Disappointment, the failure of the Millerites' prediction that Christ would return on October 22, 1844.

By April of 1845, Adventists who had unified during the Millerite movement were becoming divided over the relevance of that movement's interpretations. The majority group abandoned its earlier belief and concluded that the 2,300 years in the prophecy of Daniel 8 would end sometime in the future.

Members of a smaller group, who later would become Seventh-day Adventists, continued to study the Scriptures, searching for explanations. They concluded that a significant event had indeed occurred in October of 1844. They believed the event corresponded with a change in Christ's ministry in heaven, from the Holy to the Most Holy Place. As Adventists looked toward the Most Holy Place, the theology of what they termed the Third Angel's Message (Revelation 14) began to form. The group focused on the commandments of God and the faith of Jesus, seeking to show the interrelationship of the Law and the gospel. It was thus that the sabbath of the fourth commandment came to hold great meaning: "Six days shalt thou labor . . . but the seventh day is the sabbath of the Lord thy God."

As early as 1844, a small group of Adventists near Washington, New Hampshire, had begun to observe the sabbath on the seventh day. A pamphlet written by Joseph Bates in 1846 gave the question wide publicity and created great interest. Shortly thereafter, Bates, together with James White, Ellen Harmon (later Mrs. James White, whose writings Seventh-day Adventists hold "in highest esteem . . . accepting them as inspired counsels from the Lord"), Hiram Edson, Frederick Wheeler, and S. W. Rhodes, with the aid of regular publications, set out to champion the seventh-day sabbath, along with the imminence of the advent. Hence the name: Seventh-day Adventist.

The growth of the group around these leaders was slow at first, owing to the general derision in which Adventists were held. By 1855, however, that group was prosperous and numerically strong enough to set up headquarters at Battle Creek, Michigan, with a publishing house, the Seventh-day Adventist Publishing Association. In 1860 the name Seventh-day Adventist was officially adopted, and in 1903 the headquarters was moved to its present location in Washington, D.C.

Doctrinally, Seventh-day Adventists are evangelical conservatives, with a sound Protestant recognition of the authoritative nature of the revelation of God through the inspired writings encompassed in the entire Bible. Their standard statement, appearing annually in their yearbook, declares that they believe in the transcendent, personal, communicating God as revealed in the Father, the Son, and the Holy Spirit, each equally and uniquely divine, personal, and eternal. They believe in creation by divine fiat and recognize the fall of the human race. Humans are by nature mortal, but may receive immortality through divine grace and the redemption offered through the total atoning work of Jesus Christ.

The church holds that the great principles of God's law are embodied in the Ten Commandments and exemplified in the life of Jesus Christ. Their observance of the seventh day as the sabbath stems from the doctrine of creation, the fourth commandment being subsidiary.

The entire support of the ministry of the church consists of the tithe. Beyond their tithes, Seventh-day Adventists give generously to missions, local church expenses, and other church enterprises. In 1992, total per-capita giving amounted to $920.45 in North America; $168.99 in the world field.

The members believe in the gift of prophecy in the church, that the dead awaiting the resurrection are in an unconscious state; that the whole person will be resurrected on the last day, with immortality for the righteous and destruction by fire for the wicked. They seek religious liberty for all and, especially in North America, advocate the complete separation of church and state. The basic teaching has to do with religious liberty, more than with the civil mechanism used to achieve it. They consider the human body the temple of the Holy Spirit; in consequence, they rigidly abstain from the use of alcoholic beverages, tobacco, and drugs. They advocate sound principles of healthful living through diet, exercise, and philanthropic outlook. The church teaches the premillennial, personal, visible return of Christ "at a time unknown but close at hand," with a new earth created out of the ruins of the old, to be the final abode of the redeemed. Immersion is practiced as the biblical form of baptism, and foot washing is a preparatory service for Communion.

The overall administrative body of the church is the executive committee of the general conference, chosen by delegates from the various church groups in the quinquennial sessions. Working under this general conference are three lesser governmental units: (1) 11 divisions, which administer church affairs on different continents; (2) 92 union conferences, which make up the divisional organizations; and (3) 441 local conferences, or missions, the smallest administrative unit.

Each unit has a large amount of autonomy in a highly representative form of government. Local congregations elect lay elders, deacons, and other officers; the local conference office supervises all local pastoral and evangelistic work and pays all pastors and other workers in its territory from a central fund.

The evangelism, publishing, educational, and health and welfare work are outstanding and highly successful. It regards itself not just as another church, but as a movement established in the fulfillment of Bible prophecy, to prepare humankind for the Second Advent and to revive and restore neglected truths of the Reformation and the apostolic church. It carries forward its work in 687 languages and dialects—190 in print and 497 orally. Fifty-seven publishing houses are distributed over the world; four are in the U.S. and Canada.

In the U.S. and abroad, the church supports 594 medical units, 973 colleges and secondary schools, and 4,533 elementary schools. There are 1,558 weekly radio and television broadcasts reaching nearly every country. Approximately 800,000 students are enrolled in Bible correspondence schools. Each week an international broadcast, "The Voice of Prophecy," goes out over approximately 1,600 stations worldwide—459 in the U.S.; and two TV programs are aired—"Faith for Today" and "It Is Written."

Since the Seventh-day Adventists practice adult (age of accountability) baptism, no infants or children are reported in their world membership, listed at 7,724,760 in 36,032 churches.

There are 799,542 Seventh-day Adventists in the U.S. and Canada, in 4,602 churches.

AMANA CHURCH SOCIETY

Officially named Amana Church Society (from the Aramaic for "to remain faithful"), this group stems from the Pietist movement in early eighteenth-century Germany. In 1714, a small company under the leadership of Johann Friedrich Rock and Eberhardt Ludwig Gruber stirred the German people with their pronouncements that the days of direct inspiration from God had not ended and that they and others had the divine gift of inspiration. These leaders established new churches in the province of Hessen, Germany, but were persecuted until 1842, when approximately 800 came to America and settled near Buffalo, New York. There they organized a Christian communal group called the Ebenezer Society.

All property was held collectively; each person did the work for which he or she was fitted and shared equally in the rewards. Each of the six villages had a common school, a meetinghouse, and a store. The settlers farmed the land around them, which had been purchased from the Seneca Indians through an American land syndicate. In 1855 and thereafter, they moved to Iowa, where the villages of Amana (East, South, Middle, High, and West) and Homestead were established. Here the church became a nonprofit religious corporation, taking the name Amana Society in 1859.

In 1932 many communal practices were abandoned, and the Amana Business Society, with its own board of directors, and the Amana Church Society, with a separate board of 13 trustees, were organized. The Amana Church Society remains nonprofit, while the business society operates under a cooperative plan as a pecuniary corporation. It conducts many different enterprises and farms 25,000 acres of land, the stockholders voting for directors in the multimillion dollar corporation. Employees draw salaries or wages.

The purpose of the Amana Church Society is purely religious, based on the salvation of souls in the service of God. The members believe that God can inspire people now as well as in days of old, but no one has been inspired since the historic leaders and two early Americans, Christian Metz and Barbara Landmann, who died in the latter part of the nineteenth century. The Amana Church Society

40

accepts the teachings of a holy universal church, remission of sins, communion of saints, resurrection of the body, punishment of the wicked, and life everlasting. It acknowledges baptism by fire and the Holy Spirit. Young members are confirmed at age 15 and are admitted to the church at 21; children attend both church-sponsored Sunday schools and public schools. There is no ordained ministry; the church services consist of hymns; prayer; readings from the testimonies of Rock, Gruber, Metz, and Landmann; and sermons preached by the elders. The church is separate from the temporal affairs of the community but still has a dominant influence. In 1993 there were 500 members in a single church.

AMERICAN ETHICAL UNION

The Ethical Movement in the U.S. builds its thought and program upon moral philosophy and the ethical traditions of the great religions of humankind. Its main emphasis is on ethics rather than creed or ceremony, and members include both theists and nontheists. A statement of principles declares:

> The search for ethical values and their progressive realization are inherently a religious enterprise. . . . All human beings, however different in their abilities or backgrounds, have an equal right to such fulfillment as encourages the fulfillment of their fellowmen. Such a goal requires diversity in beliefs and practices, and therefore freedom of conscience, thought, and expression. . . . Our attitude toward that which is beyond present knowledge, including questions about cosmic matters, is one of free and cooperative exploration, and respect for individual experience.

Stress is laid on the development of conscience and a sense of responsibility.

There are 21 active Ethical Culture societies in the Ethical Union, the first of which was founded by Felix Adler in 1876. The Union is a founding member of the International Humanist and Ethical Union, which has organizations in some 34 countries around the world. Meetings feature inspirational music, meditation, readings from Scripture or other inspired poetry or prose, and an address on some social, political, philosophical, religious, or ethical subject. Ethical Culture leaders serve as counselors, officiate at weddings and funerals, name children, and perform in general a pastoral function. Programs include Sunday schools, young people's groups, and study groups; very effective work is done in educational, philanthropic, and social projects as well. The New York Society must be given credit for starting urban settlement work in the U.S.; at the time of this writing, societies in New York, Chicago, and Philadelphia still sponsor such programs. Free kindergartens, visiting nurses, the Child Study Movement, the abolition of child labor and capital punishment, model tenements, the inauguration of free legal-aid societies, civil liberties, and interracial adoption practices all constitute Ethical Culture drives.

Outstanding Ethical Culture schools have been developed at Central Park West and Riverdale in New York City and in Washington, D.C., attracting many who are not otherwise identified with the movement. The denomination has approximately 3,200 members.

AMERICAN EVANGELICAL CHRISTIAN CHURCHES

Launched in 1944 and incorporated in Illinois, the A.E.C.C. is described as "an ecclesiastical body or denomination of interdoctrinal character." It seeks to compromise between Calvinistic and Arminian beliefs. Local churches established under its charter are known as American Evangelical Christian Churches. Each church is sovereign in its management but is obliged to cooperate with the national headquarters if it is to retain membership in the body.

Ministerial applicants must subscribe to seven articles of faith: (1) the Bible as the written Word of God; (2) the virgin birth; (3) the deity of Jesus Christ; (4) salvation through the atonement of Christ; (5) the guidance of life through prayer; (6) the return of Christ; and (7) the establishment of the Millennial Kingdom. Upon completion of training, ministerial students are granted licenses enabling them to perform all the functions and offices of the ministry, with the exception of officiating at marriages. Full ordination is withheld until the licentiate has become pastor of a regular congregation or is engaged in full-time evangelistic or missionary work. The present ministerial membership is reported at 200, of whom about half are engaged as full-time pastors.

All ordinations must be performed under the supervision of either regional or national officers; 12 regional offices in the U.S. and one in Canada supervise the work of the organization.

AMERICAN RESCUE WORKERS

Incorporated in 1884 as the Salvation Army and in 1896 as the American Salvation Army, with its name amended when the organizational charter was drawn up in 1913, American Rescue Workers, a religious and charitable movement, is a branch of the Christian Church. Its membership includes officers (clergy), lay members (called soldiers), participants in varied activity groups, and volunteers who serve as advisers. It offers emergency aid (lodging, clothing, food), halfway houses and rehabilitation centers for alcoholics and drug addicts, homeless shelters, workshops and social-service programs for the socially and physically handicapped, and evangelism. The fact that it attempts to perform so many community-service programs does not alter its status as a full-fledged denomination. The rites of baptism and Communion are administered by ministers in charge of local churches (corps), and church and Sunday school services are held in community churches. A minister is ordained after serving three years as an officer and must have graduated from a seminary and/or the study courses of the organization and been approved by it.

The articles of religion include belief in the Trinity, the inspiration of the Scriptures, the Fall, redemption through Christ, and other standard orthodox doctrines.

The motivation of the organization is love of God and a practical concern for the needs of humanity. Its purposes are to preach the gospel, disseminate Christian truths, supply basic human necessities, and undertake the spiritual and moral regeneration and physical rehabilitation of all persons in need, regardless of race, color, creed, sex, or age.

Government is by a board of managers elected by the members of the Grand Field Council. Structure follows a quasi-military pattern, with territorial and divisional commanders in charge, and Paul E. Martin as commander in chief. A periodical, *The Rescue Herald*, is published in Hagerstown, Maryland. There are approximately 2,700 members in 20 churches.

APOSTOLIC CHRISTIAN CHURCH (NAZARENE)

The Apostolic Christian Church (Nazarene) began in the U.S. with the arrival of S. H. Froelich from Switzerland about the year 1850. Froelich went to work immediately among Swiss and German immigrants, founding a number of small churches in the Midwest.

The theology is conservative. The church consists of members who have been converted to Christ, are reborn and baptized, and who strive for sanctification—"and of such friends of the truth who sincerely and earnestly strive to attain adoption to sonship in Christ." Members are required to live "according to the Gospel of Christ, subject to the authorities, strive to be at peace with their fellow men, and fulfill their obligations as good citizens." They refuse to take up arms, since this denies the biblical command to love one's enemies, but they will engage in noncombatant service.

The local churches are independent in polity but united in fundamental organization. Each church is served by elders authorized to baptize, lay on hands, serve the Lord's Supper, and conduct meetings for the exercising of church discipline.

Much of the membership is found in Illinois and Ohio; small bodies are located in nearly all of the northern states, from New England to the West Coast and Canada. With about 50 churches and 3,000 members, there are missionaries in Brazil, Argentina, New Guinea, and Ghana. There is also a nonprofit service organization, the Apostolic Christian Church Foundation.

APOSTOLIC CHRISTIAN CHURCH OF AMERICA

Descending from a movement originated by S. H. Froelich in Switzerland in 1832, the Apostolic Christian Church of America was organized by Benedict Weyeneth, a Swiss who came to America about 1847 and began a number of Swiss-German churches.

The doctrine is based largely on the teaching of salvation by grace through faith in Jesus Christ, aimed "solely at the saving of souls, a change of heart through regeneration, and a life of godliness guided and directed by the Holy Spirit." Members are noted for a life of simplicity, separation from worldliness, and obedience to the Bible, which is embraced as the infallible Word of God. Members serve in the military, but do not bear arms or swear oaths. Discipline of erring members is practiced for their spiritual welfare.

There are no educational institutions for ministers, and they are not paid. Moreover, they are not expected to prepare sermons but depend entirely upon the inspiration of the Holy Spirit. A very closely knit fellowship and strong sense of community exist throughout the denomination. Doctrinal authority and national governance of the church rest with a council of approximately 50 elders (bishops). There are more than 11,000 members and 80 congregations—two in Japan, one in Canada, and the remainder in the U.S.

APOSTOLIC FAITH MISSION
OF PORTLAND, OREGON

Organized in Portland, Oregon, in 1907 by the Reverend Mrs. Florence L. Crawford, "not to promote any new doctrine but rather to reestablish, maintain, and teach all the doctrines as taught by Christ and his apostles in the days of the early church," the Apostolic Faith is "Trinitarian, Fundamental, and Evangelistic." Arminian in theology, it presents the usual doctrines of fundamentalism, stressing especially justification by faith (as taught by Luther), entire sanctification (as taught by Wesley), and the baptism of the Holy Ghost as evidenced at Pentecost. There are 50 churches and 4,100 members in the U.S. (mostly in the South and West). Branches exist in several foreign countries, with more members in Africa than in America.

Shunning "the swelling of numbers," there are baptismal records but no membership reports; a born-again experience and subscription to the doctrines of the group are required for membership. It is "a church without a collection plate" (no offering is taken during services); worldly amusements (dancing, theater, card playing, drinking, smoking) are banned. Members are required to dress conservatively, and there is no marriage with unbelievers.

Governing bodies consist of a board of five trustees, of which the general overseer of the denomination is chair, and a board of 24 elders. The church was incorporated as Apostolic Faith Mission of Portland, Oregon, U.S.A. A headquarter church, a campground, and a publishing house that circulates evangelical literature in more than 60 languages and dialects are located in Portland.

APOSTOLIC OVERCOMING HOLY CHURCH OF GOD

Bishop W. T. Phillips, a former member of The Methodist Church, became deeply concerned with the teaching of the doctrine of holiness and, after four years of study and preaching on the doctrine, organized the Ethiopian Overcoming Holy Church of God in 1916. *Ethiopian* was later changed to *Apostolic*.

Active in 22 states, the West Indies, Haiti, and Africa, the ministers, both men and women, are supported by tithes. Worship includes foot washing and divine healing. Services generally are free emotional affairs, with the participants speaking in tongues and engaging in ecstatic dances.

It is claimed that this church existed "even from the days of Enos," when Christianity was known to be in existence in Abyssinia. Marriage to the unsaved, the use of tobacco, foolish talking, jesting, and use of slang are forbidden.

In doctrine, sanctification and holiness are stressed, along with the tenet of the deity of Christ, the final resurrection of the dead, and the evil to be punished at the time of the last judgment at the second coming of Christ. A special relief fund provides for the needs of orphans, widows, and aged and disabled members. A publishing facility is located in the headquarters building in Birmingham, Alabama. Bishop Jasper Roby is the executive bishop; he and six other bishops supervise the work of the church, which claims more than 12,500 members in 175 local churches.

ARMENIAN CHURCH

Armenia is historically recognized as the first Christian nation. The apostles Thaddeus and Bartholomew brought the message of Christ, and Christianity was adopted as the state religion in A.D. 301. Saint Gregory the Illuminator, preaching in Armenia at the time, became the first head of this national church, with the title Patriarch Catholicos of All Armenians.

The Armenian Church has sustained its people throughout a history marked by tragedy. It suffered in the evitable conflict between the Byzantine Empire and Persia, and sustained persecutions by the Turks, culminating in the genocide of 1915. Thousands escaped to America before World War I, but the bulk of emigration occurred after the war. The first Armenian Church in America was established in Worchester, Massachusetts, in 1891; the Armenian Diocese of America was organized in 1898, headed by a Primate appointed by the Mother See of Holy Etchmiadzin in Armenia, under whose jurisdiction the diocese functioned. In 1933 a political faction effected a split in the church. In 1957, these churches placed themselves under the jurisdiction of the Holy See of Cilicia in Antelias. The Armenian Church of America remained within the jurisdiction of the Mother See of Etchmiadzin.

The dogma and liturgy of the church were not affected by the division. One branch is headed by a Primate; the other, a Prelate. Deacons, priests, bishops, and archbishops are ordained and elevated by the hierarchical authorities of the respective jurisdictions. The Armenian Apostolic Orthodox Church of America has 66 churches; the separated Apostolic Church has 29.

In government, both bodies are democratic in that the lay officials are elected. Each diocese has bylaws adapted to its particular needs, but that must be approved by the Catholicos of its respective jurisdiction.

Doctrine is based on Scripture, the historic writings of the early Church Fathers, and the decisions of the first three Ecumenical Councils. The saints and Virgin Mary are venerated; the Assumption of the Virgin is celebrated but not accepted as a dogma as in the Roman Catholic Church. A translation of the Scriptures by St. Sahag and St. Mesrob and their students is accepted as the authoritative Armenian version of the Bible. There are seven sacraments: baptism by immersion as early as eight days after birth; chrismation immediately following baptism; Holy Communion even for infants; penance; marriage; ordination; and final unction. The principal service is the Holy Sacrifice of the Divine Liturgy; various orders of "hour" liturgies and celebrations of feasts are observed. The Bible is read in classical Armenian at these services. Sunday schools, language schools, cultural programs, and libraries help to disseminate faith and heritage.

BAHA'I

The Baha'i faith aims at a universal community of the human race, the unity of all religions, and peace for the whole world. Its founder, Balla'u'llah (Glory of God), said, "The religion of God is for the sake of love and union; make it not the cause of enmity and conflict." His followers see in his teachings the same spirit that spoke in Moses and Jesus, Krishna and Buddha, Zoroaster and Muhammad; to them he is the "return" of all previous prophets and religious leaders, the Promised One of the world's great religions.

Actually, the Baha'i faith originated with the teachings of Mirza Ali Muhammad, called the Bab (Arabic, for "gate" or "door"), who suffered persecution and was martyred in 1850. It is estimated that 20,000 followers of the faith, then known as Babi, were slain during that persecution. The title Baha'u'llah was given to Mirza Husayn Ali, the Bab's successor, who died in 1892, leaving a vast accumulation of writings that are treasured as the sacred scriptures of Baha'i belief. His eldest son, Abbas Effendi, later known as Abdul-Baha, spent some 40 years in captivity. Released in 1908 at the time of the revolution of the Young Turks, he toured Egypt, Europe, and the U.S. At Wilmette, Illinois, in 1912, he laid the cornerstone of the first Baha'i house of worship in the West. The headquarters of the National Spiritual Assembly, the administrative body in the U.S., is in that vicinity.

The Wilmette temple is a unique structure, in which the number 9, the Baha'i symbol of unity, is repeatedly emphasized: There are 9 concrete piers, 9 pillars, and 9 arches; it is set in a park with 9 sides, 9 avenues, 9 gateways, and 9 fountains. The building was dedicated in 1953 to "the unity of God, the unity of his prophets, the unity of mankind." Worship services are conducted frequently and not restricted to weekly programs. A Baha'i home for the aged was built in Wilmette in 1958.

Coordination and direction of international activities are now vested in the Baha'i Universal House of Justice, a body of nine members elected for terms of five years, located at the World Center in Haifa, Israel. In addition to administrative and judicial functions, this body legislates matters not expressly revealed in Baha'i writings. Another institution, the International Teaching Center, functions through boards of counselors assigned to each continent. Local groups are organized as Spiritual Assemblies, supervised by a National Spiritual Assembly consisting of nine members. Since 1963 there has been marked growth: There are approximately 20,000 local assemblies and 165 national assemblies; followers of the faith now reside in some 7,000 localities in the U.S., with over 120,000 worldwide. Within this world fellowship are people of all races, nationalities, and creeds—former Moslems, Hindus, Christians, Jews—perfect integrations, in recognition of the truth of their founder's statement, "Ye are the fruits of one tree and the leaves of one Branch."

There are central Baha'i temples at Frankfurt; Sydney; Kampala, Uganda; Panama City; Delhi; and Apia, Western Samoa. Publishing trusts have been established at Wilmette, London, Buenos Aires, Rio de Janeiro, New Delhi, Teheran, Kampala, Frankfurt, Brussels, and 16 other locations. The writings of the Baha'i faith have been translated into more than 801 languages.

There is no ritual or clergy, in the belief that each seeker may act upon truth and the Spirit without ecclesiastical aid. Unpaid teachers and "pioneers" give assistance to students. Marriage and funeral services are simple and flexible. Meetings vary from devotional and prayer services to public lectures, study classes, and discussion groups for inquirers, to meetings for the Baha'i community, conventions, and summer and winter schools and institutes. Permanent schools are located in Maine, California, and Michigan, and permanent institutes are in Arizona and South Carolina. Events within the communities are scheduled by a special calendar of 19 months of 19 days each, with the New Year at the vernal equinox. The Baha'i day starts and ends at sunset.

The chief purpose of the Baha'i faith is to unite the world in one religion and one social order; hence, its chief principle is "the oneness and the wholeness of the human race." Among other dominant principles are (1) independent investigation of the truth; (2) essential harmony of science and religion; (3) recognition of the divine foundation of all religions; (4) universal compulsory education; (5) equality of all men and women; (6) spiritual solution of economic problems; (7) need for a universal auxiliary language; (8) universal peace based on a world federation of nations; (9) elimination of all prejudice; and (10) recognition of the essential unity of humanity.

In its effort to develop spiritual qualities of character, Baha'i prescribes monogamy; discourages divorce; emphasizes strict obedience to one's government; condemns idleness; exalts any work performed in the spirit of service; prohibits slavery, asceticism, monasticism, and the use of alcohol and narcotics except for medicinal purposes; and insists on prayer and fasting as means of elevating the soul.

BAPTIST

A third-generation Reformation development that appeared in England about 1610, this devout group wanted to take Protestantism "to its logical conclusion." Convinced that Puritanism needed still further reform, Baptists began to teach that only self-professed believers were eligible for membership in the church and thus that the church is properly made up of only regenerated people. Intensely biblical, Baptists have been evangelistic, helping found the modern missionary movement, and have held high standards for membership, often requiring a notable conversion experience and usually emphasizing purity in personal life and habits. In the U.S., they have been especially strong among Southern whites and in the black population, but are represented through a variety of Baptist groups, ranging from large to quite small. This is now the largest Protestant family in the U.S.

Twenty-seven Baptist denominations reported an approximate membership of 32 million in 1994; there are about 100,000 local Baptist churches, each independent of the others. Members also are completely independent of one another, yet bound together by an amazingly strong "rope of sand," in a great common allegiance to certain principles and doctrines based generally on the competency of each individual in matters of faith.

It is often heard among them that they have no founder but Christ and that Baptists have been preaching and practicing from the days of John the Baptist. This is true in a limited sense; men and women then certainly held what have come to be considered distinctly Baptist principles. But organized Baptist churches first appeared in Holland and England.

With the Reformation early in the sixteenth century, scattered groups began to advocate the convictions of faith that today are the warp and woof of Baptist theology and ideology. We find the name in various forms in Germany and Switzerland: Pedobaptists, who baptized infants and children; Anti-Pedobaptists, who opposed infant baptism; and Anabaptists, who rebaptized adults once baptized as children. The Anabaptists were in the left wing of the Reformation and held to a literal application of the Word of God in social matters; they were communistic and pacifist, opposing capital punishment, oaths in court, the holding of public office, and payment of taxes and interest; they rejected infant baptism as unscriptural. They insisted on the separation of church and state and defended this belief

49

heroically, to the point of fanaticism and martyrdom. Under persecution they spread all over Europe—some to Norway, others to Italy, Poland, Holland, and England.

In Holland a group of Mennonites, followers of the former Anabaptist leader Menno Simons (see MENNONITES), was teaching Anabaptist principles: that the Scriptures were the sole authority for faith and practice; that baptism was a believer's privilege; that church and state should be completely and forever separated; that church discipline should be rigidly enforced in business, family, and personal affairs. These Mennonites met a little group of British Separatists who had taken refuge in Amsterdam from the religious persecutions under James I. Many lived in Mennonite homes, and one of the leaders, John Smyth, was completely captured by the Mennonite argument. He rebaptized himself and his followers in that faith and organized the first English Baptist church in 1609. When he tried to make Mennonites of his people, however, he went too far. Baptist they would be, but not Mennonite, for that meant a threat to their British heritage; they were still English and proposed to remain so. Smyth was excommunicated and died in 1612, leaving behind him, in a "confession," his convictions that the magistrate, by virtue of his office, is not to meddle with religion or matters of conscience, nor to compel persons to any form of religion or doctrine, but to leave the Christian religion to the free conscience of everyone and to meddle only with political matters. Smyth's people drifted back across the channel and, with persecution waning, established yet another Baptist church in London.

These first two churches were General Baptist churches, believing in a general atonement for all. In the course of time there arose a Particular Baptist Church, which held to the predestinarian teachings of John Calvin and preached a limited atonement. The first British Particular church dates back to 1638. A third body, known as Immersion Baptist, broke away and in 1644 wrote a confession that stamped these people popularly for the first time as Baptist.

Those early British Baptists wielded a tremendous influence in their time and on the future; it is claimed that "more than any king or Parliament, they set the heart and mind of England free." John Smyth's teaching that "the magistrate . . . is not to meddle with religion, or matters of conscience" has become one of humankind's great spiritual principles. William Carey was sent to India in 1793 and became the pioneer of modern missions. More than a century earlier, in 1631, Roger Williams had come to America; he was to be the first great champion of freedom for faith and conscience in North America.

Williams was not a Baptist, but a Separatist minister when he arrived. His story is well known: Preaching "new and dangerous opinions against the authority of the magistrates," he organized a Baptist church at Providence, Rhode Island. John Clarke established another Baptist church at Newport at about the same time. The Baptists are still arguing as to which was first; many scholars date the Providence church to 1639, the Newport church to 1641.

These were Particular, or Calvinist, Baptist churches. Their strength was challenged by the rise of interest in Arminian theology during the preaching of George Whitefield, but Calvinism prevailed; it is the theological standard of many, if not most, Baptists in the U.S. today. Their progress was slow; bitter persecution of their church ennobled them and left one of the darkest blots on colonial history.

Following the tour of Whitefield through the American colonies, a dispute arose among Baptists, dividing them into Old Lights, or Regulars, who distrusted revivals and emotionalism, and New Lights, or Separates, who demanded a reborn membership in their churches. Separate Baptists were outstanding in the fight for religious freedom in the new land. The friction died down with the signing of the Constitution, however, and new unity was found in a foreign missions crusade. The first Protestant missionary board in America was the American Board, made up of Baptist, Reformed, Congregational, and Presbyterian church members.

In 1814, Baptists organized their own General Missionary Convention of the Baptist Denomination in the United States of America for Foreign Missions. This convention, representing a national Baptist fellowship, marked the first real denominational consciousness. It was followed eventually by other organizations that welded them firmly together: a general Baptist convention; a general tract society—later called the American Baptist Publication Society; various missionary societies for work at home and abroad; an education society; and the Baptist Young People's Union.

These organizations were on a national scale. Their unity was disrupted first by a feeling that home-missions agencies within the body had failed to evangelize Southern territory and later by the issues of slavery and the Civil War. The great division occurred in 1845, when Southerners formed their own Southern Baptist Convention in order to carry on the work of their churches more effectively. From this point forward there were to be Northern and Southern conventions among white members, but very soon numerous black Baptist congregations emerged and, later, organized denominations.

Actually African Americans had been part of the Baptist community for a long time. The first black Baptist church was organized at Silver Bluff, across the Savannah River, near Augusta, Georgia, in 1773. Other churches followed—in Petersburg, Virginia, 1776; Richmond, Virginia, 1780; Williamsburg, Virginia, 1785; Savannah, Georgia, 1785; and Lexington, Kentucky, 1790. Of notable interest is the fact that Andrew Bryan, a slave, was the first pastor of First African Baptist Church in Savannah and that its organization came about through the efforts of Abraham Marshall (white) and Jesse Peter (black).

As early as 1700, white slaveholders in the South were providing religious teaching and places of worship for their slaves—at least, most owners did little to prevent such activity. Usually, however, slaves sat in the galleries of white churches, identifying with the faith of their owners. White preachers, sometimes assisted by black helpers, moved from one plantation to another, holding services more or less regularly. Occasionally a black preacher was liberated to give full time to religious work among blacks, and these ministers had great influence. They were consulted by white persons as the respected leaders of their people and were a real power until the time of the slave rebellion led by Nat Turner in 1831. For a period following that disturbance, it was illegal in some sections of the South for blacks to become Christian or to build meetinghouses. Almost everywhere slave meetings were monitored by owners, lest unrest be fomented. But slaves conducted their own meetings hidden from sight and sound of the masters in the "invisible institution," privately and secretly. Also there were independent all-black congregations among free blacks in cities.

The great majority of blacks in pre–Civil War days were either Baptist or Methodist. In 1793 there were 73,471 Baptists in the U.S., one-fourth of them black; in 1806, one-third of Baptists of North Carolina were black. When the Battle of Bull Run was fought in 1861, there were 200,000 black members of the Methodist Episcopal Church, South, and 150,000 black Baptists. The lack of formality in Baptist churches, together with the absence of ritual and the freedom and democracy of the local congregation, appealed to blacks more than did the episcopal structure of The Methodist Church. But both denominations practiced Evangelicalism's communal spirit, with interjection and interdependence standard features; this condition joined the ritual and policy factors in making the two denominations compelling to the black population. This was accented at the end of the Civil War; a revival spirit swept through African American society, creating thousands of new churches. Aided by the Freedman's Aid

Society and various Baptist organizations, nearly 1 million black Baptists worshiped in their own churches within 15 years.

The first black Baptist group, the Providence Baptist Association of Ohio, was formed in 1836; the first attempt at national organization occurred in 1880 with the creation of the Foreign Mission Baptist Convention at Montgomery, Alabama. In 1886, the American National Baptist Convention was organized at St. Louis, and in 1893 the Baptist National Educational Convention was begun in the District of Columbia. All three conventions were merged into the National Baptist Convention of America in 1895 at Atlanta.

In 1915 a division arose over the adoption of a charter and the ownership of a publishing house. The group rejecting the charter continued to function as the National Baptist Convention of America; the group that accepted the charter became known as the National Baptist Convention of the U.S.A., Inc. (that is, incorporated under the laws of the District of Columbia). The former is frequently referred to as the "unincorporated" and the latter as the "incorporated" convention, but both trace their beginnings to the Foreign Mission Baptist Convention.

About 87 percent of black Christians in the United States were either Baptist or Methodist in 1965, with Baptists comprising 65 percent of that number. Recent growth in Pentecostal bodies, especially the Church of God in Christ, has reduced the Baptist proportion, but it is still more than half. Its membership is grouped into a large number of denominations, some very large and many quite small. The two oldest and largest—the National Baptist Convention, U.S.A., Inc., and the National Baptist Convention of America, Inc.— have memberships of 7,500,000 and 3,500,000, respectively.

Black Baptist doctrine runs quite parallel to that of white Baptist churches, but is slightly more Calvinistic. The policy of the two larger white conventions prevails; local churches unite in associations, usually along state lines, for the purpose of fellowship and consultation. There are also state conventions concerned with missionary work, often extending beyond state boundaries.

Foreign missionary work is especially strong in Africa, but extensive programs exist also in the Caribbean and Central America. Home missions efforts aim to help needy churches and schools, to provide family support and relief, and to address civil rights concerns and policy matters that most directly affect the lives of African Americans.

The two "National Baptist" bodies have endured some historic enmity, but terms are now more positive. Disagreements within each have given rise to a new and quite large body: the "U.S.A." denomination in 1961 to the Progressive National Baptist Convention of America, with 2,142,000 members.

The formation of new bodies of Baptists has been common within the white (predominantly) denominations as well. Such actions are to be expected in this Protestant tradition, since independence is prized and its expression quite predictable. While they differ in certain minor details, Baptists generally agree on the following principles of faith: the inspiration and trustworthiness of the Bible as the sole rule of life; the Lordship of Jesus Christ; the inherent freedom of persons to approach God for themselves; the granting of salvation through faith by way of grace and contact with the Holy Spirit; two ordinances—the Lord's Supper and the baptism of believers by immersion; the independence of the local church; the church as a group of regenerated believers who are baptized upon confession of faith; infant baptism as unscriptural and not to be practiced; complete separation of church and state; life after death; the unity of humankind; the royal law of God; the need of redemption from sin; and the ultimate triumph of God's kingdom.

These overall doctrines never have been written into any official Baptist creed for all the churches, but they have been incorporated into two important confessions of faith. The Baptist churches of London wrote a Philadelphia Confession in the year 1689, and this was enlarged by the Philadelphia Association in 1742. The New Hampshire State Baptist Convention drew up another confession in 1832. The Philadelphia Confession is strongly Calvinist, the New Hampshire Confession only moderately so.

Baptists have insisted on freedom of thought and expression in pulpit and pew. This has made them one of the most democratic religious bodies in America—with the result that a wide variety of interpretations and applications is found and, usually, respected.

They have insisted, too, on the absolute autonomy of the local congregation; each church arranges its own worship and examines and baptizes its own members. There is no age requirement for membership, but the candidate is usually of an age to understand and accept the teachings of Christ. Candidates for the ministry are licensed by local churches and ordained upon recommendation of a group of sister churches.

Baptist churches are commonly grouped into associations—local and state—for purposes of fellowship. National conventions are established among many groups to carry on educational and missionary work and to make pension plans. Most state and regional conventions meet annually with delegates from all Baptist churches in a given area. These conventions receive reports, make recommendations, and help to raise national mission budgets, but they have no authority to enforce their decisions.

In Washington, D.C., there is a Baptist Joint Committee on Public Affairs, supported by the American Baptist Churches/U.S.A., sectors of the Southern Baptist Convention, and some other bodies. This committee serves mainly to spread the Baptist conviction on public morals and to safeguard the principle of separation of church and state. Finally, there is the growing Baptist World Alliance, organized in 1905, which now includes more than 40 million Baptists in 170 member bodies. (The worldwide community of Baptist members, friends, and sympathizers is reliably estimated at 100 million.) The Alliance meets every five years to discuss common themes and problems and is purely an advisory body. Its headquarters are located in McLean, Virginia.

AMERICAN BAPTIST ASSOCIATION

Sometimes called Landmarkers because of their historic belief that no universal church or ecclesiastical authority is higher than a local congregation, members of the American Baptist Association claim that those Baptists organized in conventions are not faithful to Bible missions methods. Maintaining that their own is the true New Testament form, they hold themselves separate from all other religious groups. They "strongly protest the trend of many Baptist groups to identify themselves with Protestantism," since they believe that their faith preceded the Protestant Reformation, and indeed has a continued succession from Christ and the apostles.

Organized in 1905 as the Baptist General Association, the group adopted its present name in 1924. Teaching that the Great Commission of Christ (Matt. 28:18-20) was given to a local congregation, members believe that the local church is the only unit authorized to administer the ordinances and that it is an independent and autonomous body responsible only to Christ. Thus every church is equal "with every other like church"; they have been called church-equality Baptists.

The doctrine is strictly fundamentalist. They stand for the verbal inspiration of the Bible, the Triune God, the virgin birth and deity of Christ, the suffering and death of Christ as substitutionary, and the bodily resurrection of Christ and all his saints. The second coming of Jesus, "physical and personal," is to be the crowning event of the "gospel age"; this Second Advent will be premillennial. There is eternal punishment for the wicked; salvation is solely by grace through faith, not by law or works. There must be absolute separation of church and state and absolute religious freedom. They denounce abortion on demand, homosexuality, and premarital sex as being contrary to biblical teachings.

Government of both the local congregation and the annual meeting of the association is congregational in nature. Missionary work is conducted on county, state, interstate, and foreign levels, the program originating in the local church, and the missionaries are supported by the cooperating churches. Educational work is pursued through the Sunday schools, five seminaries, three colleges, and 27 Bible institutes.

The greater strength of this group is found in the South, Southwest, West, and Southeast, but much new work has begun in recent years in the East and North. The latest statistics from 1986 show 1,705 churches with a total combined membership of 250,000 and 1,760 ordained clergy with charges. The membership continues to shift from rural to urban.

A comprehensive publishing program includes 14 monthly and semimonthly periodicals, Sunday school literature designed to cover the entire Bible in a ten-year period, and literature for young people and vacation Bible schools. National and state youth encampments are held annually as well as pastors' and missionaries' conferences on regional and national levels.

AMERICAN BAPTIST CHURCHES/U.S.A

From the founding of the First Baptist Church in Rhode Island in 1638, Baptists in America formed autonomous local congregations through which their work was carried out. Gradually these churches began to unite as voluntary associations, the first of which was the Philadelphia Association in 1707. Others followed in South Carolina, Rhode Island, Massachusetts, New Jersey, and Virginia. These associations encouraged the building of churches, colleges, and schools.

In May 1814, representatives from these associations and churches met in Philadelphia to organize the General Missionary Convention of the Baptist Denomination in the United States of America for Foreign Missions, which quickly became known as the Triennial Convention. This was the first national Baptist organization in America. The American Baptist Publication Society and the American Baptist Home Mission Society were established in 1824 and 1832 respectively. By 1841, sectional and theological differences centered around the issue of slavery began to erode the unity of the foreign board. In 1845, one year after the final meeting of the Triennial Convention, the Northern and Southern groups met and reorganized separately as two foreign mission societies. The women of the Northern churches formed their own home and foreign missionary societies in the 1870s.

Separate appeals for funds to support these competing societies created confusion and dissatisfaction, leading eventually to the formation of the Northern Baptist Convention in 1907. This convention was actually a corporation with restricted powers in conducting religious work, receiving and expending money and affiliating itself with other bodies. The Convention reorganized in 1950, changing its name to the American Baptist Convention. In 1955 the two women's missionary societies joined administratively with their counterparts, the older foreign- and home-mission societies. The two foreign societies and the two home societies then functioned under identical officers, boards of managers, and administrative staffs. Each society maintained its own corporate identity, but in 1968 the Women's American Baptist Foreign Mission Society legally merged into the American Baptist Foreign Mission Society. These societies, with the American Baptist Historical Society, the Ministers and Missionaries Benefit Board, and the American Baptist Board of Education and Publication were cooperating organizations of the convention.

State conventions and city mission societies were drawn closer by grouping them into affiliated organizations, through which they raised and distributed funds under a cooperative plan with a unified budget; the Division of World Mission Support supervised the collection of money for this budget. Numerous other councils and committees carried on the work of the convention under the supervision of the general council, which functioned between the annual gatherings. In 1950 the first general secretary was elected.

In 1972 the convention adopted its third and present name and restructured to strengthen the representational principle and to integrate more fully the national program bodies into the structure of the American Baptist Convention. A larger (200-member) general board composed of election-district representatives and at-large representatives is the policy-making body. A general council of chief executives and staff of national program boards, chief executives of regions and other American Baptist bodies serves to coordinate the corporate affairs of the denomination under the leadership of the general secretary.

The local church, however, is still the basic and independent unit of American Baptist government and administration. There are 5,827 churches with 1,537,400 members (including children) in 34 regions. The denomination is at work in 20 children's homes and special services, 77 retirement homes and communities, 27 hospitals and nursing homes, 9 theological seminaries, and 16 senior colleges and universities. The Board of National Ministries has workers in 36 states; it supports Bacone College for Native Americans in Oklahoma and carries on widespread work among blacks, Native Americans, and Asians in the U.S. The Board of International Ministries currently supports missionaries in six countries in Asia (Hong Kong, India, Japan/Okinawa, the Philippines, Singapore, and Thailand), two countries in Africa (South Africa and Zaire), and seven countries in Latin America and the Caribbean (Bolivia, Costa Rica, the Dominican Republic, El Salvador, Haiti, Mexico, and Nicaragua). In Europe, missionaries designated as fraternal representatives relate American Baptists to Baptist Unions in 14 countries outside the former Soviet Union. Currently, missionaries are being appointed to work with unions and institutions in the republics of Russia and the Ukraine. Overseas Baptists in partner conventions outnumber American Baptists, with over 1,800,000; one of the largest partner conventions is the Myanmar Baptist Convention with a reported 500,000 members.

In matters of faith, each Baptist church speaks for itself, but certain doctrines are held in common. The Bible is the foundation of their belief; with the individual conscience the interpreter of the Bible. There is the usual Baptist insistence on the inspiration and validity of Scriptures, the lordship of Christ, immortality in a future life, the unity of humankind, and the need for redemption from sin. American Baptists are a missionary- and evangelism-minded people. They believe in and practice the baptism of believers. They emphasize the importance of religious freedom. They have historically taken a stand on such controversial issues as abolition, temperance, racial and social justice, and the ordination of women. They have traditionally been a denomination of diversity of race, ethnicity, culture, class, and theology. The ordinances of baptism and the Lord's Supper are considered aids more than necessities for salvation.

Generally it may be said that Baptists represented in the American Baptist Churches/U.S.A. are less conservative in thought and theology than those in the Southern Baptist Convention. Such doctrinal differences are not the major cause of their continuing separation. Divergent views on questions of race and open Communion and especially the Protestant trend toward ecumenicity are now the major hurdles. American Baptists are represented in the National Council of Churches of Christ in the U.S.A. and the World Council of Churches; Southern Baptists are represented in neither. American Baptists have made gestures toward union with General Baptists, Southern Baptists, the National Baptist Convention, Seventh Day Baptists, Disciples of Christ, Church of the Brethren, and the Alliance of Baptists and have welcomed Free Baptists into full fellowship. Unless and until these varying attitudes are changed or reconciled, there seems to be no real possibility of reunion for these two Baptist bodies of the U.S.

BAPTIST BIBLE FELLOWSHIP, INTERNATIONAL

Baptist Bible Fellowship is one of the "evangelical independent" groups—perhaps the largest and fastest growing body of independent Baptists in the U.S.—loosely affiliated with one another in the preaching and teaching of ultraconservative Baptist doctrine. They teach that Jesus was a Baptist in his thinking and work. They are biblical literalists, denouncing all modernists and liberals. They recognize baptism by immersion only, participate in Communion only with members of their own church, and are adamantly opposed to dancing, drinking, smoking, movies, gambling, and sexual promiscuity. No formal membership statistics are kept, but membership probably stands at more than one million.

Baptist Bible College in Springfield, Missouri, and Baptist Bible College East, in Boston, Massachusetts, are owned and supported by these independent Baptists. Recently the Baptist Bible Graduate School of Theology was founded in Springfield, Missouri. The fellowship reports 3,500 churches but does not keep Fellowship-wide membership statistics because of its commitment to independence.

BAPTIST GENERAL CONFERENCE

The history of what is now known as the Baptist General Conference began at Rock Island, Illinois, in 1852. Gustaf Palmquist, a schoolteacher and lay preacher, had arrived from Sweden the previous year to become the spiritual leader of a group of Swedish immigrants who had been influenced by the Pietist movement within the (Lutheran) state church of Sweden. At Galesburg, Illinois, he came in contact with Baptists, and early in 1852 he was baptized and ordained a Baptist minister. Visiting the Swedish people at Rock Island, he won his first converts to the Baptist faith and baptized three in the Mississippi River on August 8, 1852. From this humble beginning has come a denomination of 135,000 members, 821 churches, and 14 state or district conferences. In 1879 a national conference—the Swedish Baptist General Conference of America—was organized.

For several decades the American Baptist Home Mission Society and the American Baptist Publication Society of the American (then Northern) Baptist Convention aided the new work among the Swedish immigrants, but gradually the church became self-supporting. A theological seminary was founded in Chicago in 1871, and the first denominational paper was launched the same year. From 1888 until 1944, foreign missionary activities were channeled through the American Baptist Foreign Mission Society; after a separation in 1944, caused largely by a desire to become completely independent, the Swedish Conference set up its own foreign-mission board and today has more than 135 (plus 55 short-term) missionaries in India, Japan, the Philippines, Ethiopia, Mexico, Argentina, Brazil, the Ivory Coast, Cameroon, and France.

Following World War I, with its intensified nationalist conflicts, the transition from Swedish- to English-language church services was greatly accelerated and practically completed in three decades. In 1945, *Swedish* was dropped from the name of the conference; it already had been dropped by most of the local churches. With the language barrier removed, the growth of the conference has been rapid and far-reaching. Although its greatest strength lies in the North Central and Pacific Northwest sections of the U.S., home missionaries are at work in all the Northern states and some of the Southern states.

The conference owns and controls Bethel College and Seminary in St. Paul, Minnesota (a four-year college and a three-year theological school, with 2,300 students). Affiliated are three children's homes, seven homes for the aged, and *The Standard,* the official denominational organ issued by the Board of Overseers. Harvest Publications offers Bibles, books, and Sunday school materials.

Basically, the church's doctrine is theologically conservative, "with unqualified acceptance of the Word of God," and holds the usual Baptist tenets. It is a strong fellowship of churches, insistent upon the major beliefs of conservative Christianity but with respect for individual differences on minor points.

The Conference tends to become more and more inclusive and to appeal to people of all nationalities. Less than half of the pastors are of Swedish descent, and a large number of churches contain few members of that descent. The transition has been rapid because of the lack of Swedish immigrants, and also because of the people's quick assimilation into American society and way of life.

BAPTIST MISSIONARY ASSOCIATION OF AMERICA

Organized at Little Rock, Arkansas, in May 1950 as the North American Baptist Association, this group changed its name to Baptist Missionary Association of America in 1968. It concentrates on fostering and encouraging missionary cooperation and has had startling growth, enrolling 1,312 churches and 230,127 members in 25 states. There are workers in home missions and missionary work abroad—in Mexico, Japan, Brazil, Taiwan, Portugal, Cape Verde Islands, Uruguay, Guatemala, Costa Rica, Nicaragua, Australia, Italy, France, Africa, India, Bolivia, Honduras, Korea, and the Philippines. A strong publications department issues literature for Sunday school and training classes, pamphlets, books, tracts, and magazines in both English and Spanish. The association also owns and operates a printing business in Brazil, where literature is printed in Portuguese for use in Africa and Europe. A worldwide radio ministry is also maintained.

The members are militant fundamentalists, claiming to hold the historic Baptist faith and placing strong emphasis on the verbal inspiration and accuracy of the Scriptures, direct creation, the virgin birth and deity of Jesus, his blood atonement, justification by faith, salvation by grace alone, and the imminent personal return of Christ to earth. They brand as unscriptural open Communion, alien baptism, pulpit affiliation with heretical ministers, unionism, modernism, modern tongues movements, one-church dictatorship, and "all the kindred evils arising from these practices." The Lord's Supper and baptism are accepted as ordinances; baptism is considered "alien" unless administered to believers by "divine authority as given to the Missionary Baptist churches."

This body carries on the Landmark Baptist movement, holding to the historic succession of independent Baptist churches from the time of Christ. It shares this conviction with the American Baptist Association; before 1950, these two bodies were one.

Churches are completely autonomous in the Baptist tradition and, regardless of size, have an equal voice in the cooperative missionary, publication, evangelical, and educational efforts of the association. Member churches must, however, conform to the doctrinal standards of the association and deny alien baptism and modernism in all its forms.

Three junior colleges and several orphans' homes are maintained on a state level, and a theological seminary is located in Jacksonville, Texas.

BETHEL MINISTERIAL ASSOCIATION

Founded as the Evangelistic Ministerial Alliance at Evansville, Indiana, in May 1934, this body was incorporated as the Bethel Baptist Assembly in March 1960, then as Association in 1972. There are 5,000 members in 18 churches, 57 ordained clergy, and five Christian elementary and high schools with an enrollment of 750.

The organization sponsors a summer camping program. Its overseas outreach arm, the Bethel Foreign Missionary Foundation, supports 25 missionaries in 15 countries. The Bethel Publishing House is the body's literature clearinghouse.

Bethel has historically been a fellowship of ministers only, but now reports lay members in its congregations. It is properly classified as Pentecostal.

CENTRAL BAPTIST ASSOCIATION

This association was formed in 1956 and is composed of 37 churches in Virginia, Tennessee, Kentucky, Indiana, and South Carolina. Present membership is approximately 4,000. Following usual Baptist doctrine and polity, its officers have no jurisdiction over member churches. A tabernacle, a children's home, and a youth camp are located at Jasper, Virginia.

Its heritage is in the Primitive Baptist faith. The name is meant to indicate acceptance of the Holy Scriptures in their entirety, varying neither to the right nor to the left. One distinctive doctrine specifies two resurrections of the dead—one of the just and another of the unjust.

CONSERVATIVE BAPTIST ASSOCIATION OF AMERICA

The Conservative Baptist Association is officially described as a voluntary fellowship of sovereign, autonomous, independent, and Bible-believing Baptist churches. . . . The Association is wholly separated from all other organizations. . . . The several churches are held together . . . by a common abiding love for the work and person of Jesus Christ, and the Word of God, as well as love for and confidence in one another.

The founders of this association were active in an earlier organization known as the Fundamentalist Fellowship, founded in 1920 within the American (then the Northern) Baptist Convention. This group of conservative church people opposed what they considered the infiltration of liberal and modernist tendencies and teachings into that convention. The basic disagreement was doctrinal, having to do with fundamentally different views and interpretations of the Scriptures and of theology. The dispute was aggravated by the "inclusive" policy of the American Baptist Foreign Mission Society, under which missionaries of both conservative and liberal theology were sent to home and foreign fields.

The Conservative Baptist Association was formally organized on May 17, 1947, at Atlantic City, New Jersey, as an association of local conservative Baptist churches. As an association, it is distinguished from the Conservative Baptist movement. Several conservative Baptist institutions—the Conservative Baptist Foreign Mission Society, the Conservative Baptist Home Mission Society, and a number of schools and colleges—function as part of the movement but are separate and autonomous.

The work of the association includes building a fellowship of churches; providing resources and personnel in areas of Christian education, leadership training, new church planting, financial services to pastors and staff, stewardship ministries, women's ministries, and retirement advisory services; serving in pastoral placement; printing and distributing literature, books, and Sunday school material; endorsing chaplains for the U.S. armed forces; and providing a national magazine, the *Conservative Baptist*.

Doctrinally, the church stands for the infallibility of the Scriptures; God as Father, perfect in holiness, infinite in wisdom, measureless in power; Christ as the eternal and only begotten Son of God—his sinlessness, virgin birth, atonement, resurrection, and ascension; the Holy Spirit as coming forth from God to convince the world of sin, of righteousness, and of judgment; the sinfulness of all people and the possibility of their regeneration, sanctification, and comfort through Christ and the Holy Spirit; the church as the living body, with Christ as head; the local church as free from interference from any ecclesiastical or political authority; the responsibility of every human being to God alone; and the ordinances of baptism and the Lord's Supper.

Associational and regional officers are elected at annual meetings; a board of directors is made up of the associational officials and 18 regional representatives, elected for three-year terms. The membership totals 200,000 in 1,127 churches. It supports five schools, including seminaries in Portland, Oregon, and in Denver, Colorado.

DUCK RIVER (AND KINDRED) ASSOCIATIONS OF BAPTISTS (BAPTIST CHURCH OF CHRIST)

Confined to five Southern states, the Duck River Baptists originated in 1825 from a protest movement within the old Elk River Association, which was strongly Calvinist. In 1843 the ranks of the dissenters were broken by a dispute over the legitimacy of missions and the support of a publication society and denominational school. Those who withdrew became known as Missionary Baptists, the others as Separate Baptists or Baptist Churches of Christ. The division persists; today there are two Duck River associations.

Doctrinally, the members are liberally Calvinist; they hold that "Christ tasted death for every man"; that God will save those who come to him on gospel terms; that sinners are justified by faith; and that the saints will "persevere in grace." They stand for believer's baptism by immersion and celebrate the Lord's Supper and foot washing as scriptural ordinances. They admit their close gospel ties with Regular, United, and Separate Baptists.

The churches are congregational in government, with seven separate associations and one independent church that meet annually for fellowship in a General Association. They are located in Tennessee, Alabama, Mississippi, and Georgia.

There is a "correspondence" relationship with other associations in these states. Membership is by vote of the local congregation; the ministers are ordained by a vote of two or more ministers.

There are, as of 1993, 10,508 members in 100 churches.

FREE WILL BAPTIST

The rise of Free Will Baptists can be traced to the influence of Arminian-minded Baptists who migrated to the American colonies from England. The denomination was organized on two fronts at almost the same time. The Southern line, or Palmer movement, began in 1727 when Paul Palmer established a church at Chowan, North Carolina. The Northern line, or Randall movement, began with a congregation organized by Benjamin Randall in 1780 in New Durham, New Hampshire. Both groups taught the doctrines of free grace, free salvation, and free will. There were gestures toward union of the Northern and Southern groups until the outbreak of the Civil War. The Northern body extended more rapidly into the West and Southwest. In 1910 this line of Free Will Baptists merged with the Northern Baptist denomination, taking along 857 of its 1,100 churches, all of its denominational property, and several colleges. In 1916 representatives of remnant churches from the Randall movement reorganized into the Cooperative General Association of Free Will Baptists.

By 1921 the Southern churches had organized into new associations and conferences, and finally into a General Conference. The division continued until November 5, 1935, when the two groups merged into the National Association of Free Will Baptists at Nashville, Tennessee.

Doctrinally, the church holds that Christ gave himself as a ransom for all, not just for the elect; that God calls all of us to repentance; and that whosoever will may be saved. Baptism is by immersion. This is one of the few Baptist groups that practices open Communion. It also practices foot washing. Government is strictly congregational. There are two Bible colleges, two liberal arts colleges, and 209,223 members in 40 states, with 2,500 churches. Some 160,000 of these members reside in seven Southern states.

GENERAL ASSOCIATION OF REGULAR BAPTIST CHURCHES

Twenty-two Baptist churches of the American Baptist Convention left that convention in May 1932 to found the General Association of Regular Baptist Churches. Their protest was against what they considered the modernist tendencies and teachings, the denial of the historic Baptist principle of independence and autonomy of the local congregation, the inequality of representation in the assemblies of the convention, the control of missionary work by convention assessment and budget, and the whole convention principle in general.

Any Baptist church coming into the General Association is required to "withdraw all fellowship and cooperation from any convention or group which permits modernists or modernism within its ranks." Dual fellowship or membership is not permitted. Participation in union evangelical campaigns or Thanksgiving services or membership in local ministerial associations where modernists are involved or present is considered unscriptural.

Missionary work is conducted through six approved Baptist agencies, completely independent of any convention and completely orthodox; a close watch is maintained on these agencies before annual approval is granted. Likewise, only nine schools are approved; these, too, are guarded against any defection from approved practice or doctrine.

The association subscribes to the New Hampshire Confession of Faith, with a premillennial interpretation of the final article of that confession. It holds to the infallibility of the Bible, the Trinity, the personality of Satan as the author of all evil, humankind as the creation of God, and humankind born in sin. Doctrines deal with the virgin birth, the deity of Jesus, and faith in Christ as the way of salvation through grace. The saved are in everlasting felicity; the lost are consigned to endless punishment. There is bodily resurrection; Christ rose and ascended and will return premillennially to reign. Civil government is by divine appointment. There are only two approved ordinances: baptism by immersion and the Lord's Supper.

Church government is strictly congregational. Associated churches have the privilege of sending six voting messengers to an annual convention; thus a church with 50 members has the same power as a church with 2,500 members. A Council of Eighteen is elected—nine each year—to serve for two years. It makes recommendations to the association for the furtherance of its work and puts into operation all actions and policies of the association. Its authority depends completely on the will and direction of the association.

In 1993 there were 1,532 churches in the fellowship, with 300,000 members. The nine approved schools had a total student body of more than 7,500; 2,175 missionaries were at work in the six missionary agencies. State and regional associations have been established across the country, supplied with literature published by the Regular Baptist Press, including *The Baptist Bulletin,* a monthly magazine.

GENERAL BAPTIST

The General Baptist Church claims its name and origin in John Smyth and Thomas Helwys, and the group of Baptists organized in England and Holland in 1611 (see general article on BAPTIST). Roger Williams is held to be the first minister in the American colonies.

General Baptists in the colonies along the Atlantic coast were at first overwhelmed by the influence of Calvinism (General Baptists have always been Arminian), but their work was reopened by Benoni Stinson in 1823, with the establishment of the Liberty Baptist Church in what is now Evansville, Indiana. They spread into Illinois and Kentucky, and a general association was organized in 1870. Since that time it has grown steadily; today it is strong in Kentucky, Tennessee, Indiana, Michigan, Illinois, Missouri, and Arkansas and has located churches in Oklahoma, Nebraska, Kansas, Iowa, Arizona, California, Florida, Ohio, and Mississippi.

The confession of faith is similar to that of Free Will Baptists: Christ died for all; failure to achieve salvation lies completely with the individual; humankind is depraved and fallen and unable to save itself; regeneration is necessary for salvation; salvation comes by repentance and faith in Christ; Christians who persevere to the end are saved; the wicked are punished eternally; the dead, just and unjust, will be raised at the judgment. The Lord's Supper and believer's baptism by immersion are the only authorized Christian ordinances and should be open to all believers. Some General Baptist churches practice foot washing.

Church polity is about the same as that found in all Baptist churches, being congregational in church government. Churches of a common area are organized into local associations, which in turn are organized into a general association. Both local and general associations are representative bodies and advisory in power. A peculiar feature of the General Baptist church lies in the use of a presbytery, into which the ordained members of local associations are grouped; they examine candidates for the ministry and for the diaconate. Ministers and deacons are responsible to this presbytery, which exists only on the local level.

Current statistics show 876 churches, with a total membership of 74,156. At Oakland City, Indiana, the church maintains a liberal arts college with a theological department. A publishing house, Stinson Press, is operated at Poplar Bluff, Missouri, where the monthly paper *General Baptist Messenger* is issued, together with Sunday school literature. Denominational headquarters, housing various agencies, are in the same city.

Foreign missionary work is supported in Guam, Saipan, Jamaica, Honduras, and the Philippines, and home missionary work is actively carried out in various states.

GENERAL CONFERENCE OF THE EVANGELICAL BAPTIST CHURCH, INC.

The Evangelical Baptist Church, formerly known as Church of the Full Gospel, Inc., was organized in 1935 by members of several Free Will Baptist churches.

Its doctrine is Arminian, Wesleyan, and premillennial; organization is similar to that of Free Will Baptist, with which it still is in close fellowship. It exchanges pastors regularly with the Wilmington, North Carolina, Conference of the Free Will Baptist Church. This body reports 2,200 members in 31 churches.

LANDMARK BAPTIST

"Landmarkism" is a position held by some Baptists concerning the nature of the church and certain details of church practice. The name originated with the writings of James Madison Pendleton and James Robinson Graves in Kentucky and Tennessee in the latter part of the nineteenth century, though Landmarkers insist that their concepts go back to the apostolic period.

There are four distinguishing tenets of Landmarkism:

1. The church is always vocal and visible. The expression "the church" is used only when speaking of the institution. All saved people make up "the family of God," not "the church." While members of Protestant churches may be saved, they are not members of true churches.

2. The "commission" was given to the church; consequently, all matters covered by it must be administered under church authority.

Ministers of other denominations are not accepted in Landmark Baptist pulpits.

3. Baptism, to be valid, must be administered by the authority of a New Testament (Baptist) church. Baptisms administered by any other authority are not accepted.

4. There is a direct historic succession of Baptist churches from New Testament times—that is, Baptist churches have existed in practice, though not by name, in every century.

These principles are held primarily by the churches of the American Baptist Association, though an estimated 1.5 million members of different Baptist churches hold to the Landmark position and doctrine, the largest concentration being in the South and Southwest. More than 15 Bible institutes and seminaries are supported by these churches.

NATIONAL BAPTIST CONVENTION OF AMERICA, INC.

"National Baptists" has been the name of some aspect of organized black Baptist life since 1886 at the latest. During the three decades following the Civil War, both the longtime free and the recently freed Baptists of African American descent were developing their public life, including organized church life. By 1876 all of the Southern states except Florida had a state missionary convention. But smaller bodies had existed since the 1830s in the Midwest, and organized missionary efforts date back to that same period in the North.

These institutional efforts matured in 1895 when the National Baptist Convention, U.S.A., came into being in an Atlanta gathering. For the next 20 years a single National Baptist body functioned through a variety of activities. Publishing Sunday school material being a major one. Also they sponsored foreign mission enterprises especially to African and Caribbean countries. They founded some colleges and provided support for others, several of them the result of dedication to providing education for the emancipated people on the part of Northern churches, Baptist and others.

Then in 1915 a schism occurred that produced two National conventions. The one being described here, the NBC of America, Inc., was originally known as the NBC, uninc. (it incorporated in 1988). The other took NBC, U.S.A., Inc., as its name. The occasion for the separation was conflict over legal ownership of the publishing house. The "of America" segment followed the Boyd party—that is, the leadership of the Reverend R. H. Boyd. The other sector took the side of the Reverend E. C. Morris, who had been National Baptist president since 1897. These two National Baptist groups have often collaborated in missionary and educational efforts, but they remain separate conventions. Both bodies number many urban as well as rural churches, reflecting demographic shifts, but the "of America" convention has a larger number of small rural congregations. The National Baptist Convention of America, Inc., reports a membership in excess of 3,500,000. Its greatest strength is in the Mississippi, Texas, and Louisiana area, with large numbers of members also in Florida and California. It holds an annual convention, and officers are elected each year. There is no central national headquarters, but Nashville, Tennessee, is the home of the publishing house.

NATIONAL BAPTIST CONVENTION, U.S.A., INC.

This, the largest body of black Baptists in the U.S., shares a common history with the "of America" denomination (just described) throughout the formative years. Its formal origins date from 1895, with many roots and predecessors stretching back to the period around 1840. Until the disagreement that arose over control of the publishing house of the denomination in 1915, there was a single National Baptist body. Once the "of America" convention was created, the Foreign Mission Board became the "U.S.A." body's center of operations.

Now numbering more than 7,500,000 adherents, the U.S.A. body has widespread distribution. In 1990 it opened its World Headquarters in Nashville, where a section of the publishing industry has been located since the 1890s, and where its Sunday School Board is still located. Nashville is also the home of a seminary that has been operated (jointly with the Southern Baptists) since 1924. This convention meets annually, and its officers are elected annually. Those officers and a Board of Directors with 15 members conduct the Convention's business.

If publishing control has been the most conspicuous fact in the "of America" body, presidential influence has been "the U.S.A." body's most visible feature. That was particularly true during the tenure of Joseph H. Jackson (1953–82). A powerful and effective leader, Jackson promoted the theory and practice of racial uplift in the tradition of Booker T. Washington. "From protest to production" was his motto. It followed that he led the body to steer clear of political and social involvements on any large scale. That policy placed this group mostly outside the civil rights movement of the period 1954–72, when many black Baptist pastors and lay leaders were deeply committed to working for racial justice through that medium. As a result, another National Baptist schism occurred, out of which the Progressive National Baptist Convention was formed in 1961. Since that period, however, this once less publicly involved body has shifted its practice and has been active in civil rights causes and voter registration drives.

This denomination, too, has been active in missionary, educational, and publication ministries. Recently it has established a ministerial pension plan. It has shown a particularly high degree of commitment to the support of colleges and seminaries. These educational institutions are typically supported by Baptist churches and people rather than being officially Convention affiliated.

NATIONAL MISSIONARY BAPTIST CONVENTION OF AMERICA

The recent origin of this body of black Baptists (it came into being in 1988) correctly suggests the degree of historical heritage it shares with the two older National Baptist bodies. Once again the issue of control over denominational publication ventures led to a rupture. This new fellowship opposed the Boyd family's ownership and leadership of the Convention's Sunday school congress and publishing house. It sought an organizational plan by which the Convention itself would control the congress and publishing activities.

Already the National Missionary Baptists report some 2,140,000 members. The convention meets three times a year. Its greatest strength lies in the population of the Pacific Coast states. Keen observers of black Baptist history in America are suspending judgment, in these early years of its life, over whether this will become the fourth major black Baptist denomination in America. But there can be no doubt of its auspicious beginnings.

NATIONAL PRIMITIVE BAPTIST CONVENTION OF THE U.S.A.

The black population of the South, throughout the years of slavery and civil war, worshiped with the white population in their various churches. That was true of this group, formerly the Colored Primitive Baptist Church. The members attended white Primitive Baptist churches until the time of emancipation, when their white coworshipers helped them establish their own churches, granting letters of fellowship and character, ordaining deacons and ministers, and assisting in other ways.

The doctrine and polity are similar to the white Primitive Baptist organization, though earlier the members were "opposed to all forms of church organization." There are local associations and a national convention, organized in 1907. Each congregation is independent, receiving and controlling its own membership. A membership of one million in 1,530 churches is reported. Unlike the white church, since 1900, this group has been establishing aid societies, conventions, and Sunday schools, over the opposition of some older and more orthodox members.

NORTH AMERICAN BAPTIST CONFERENCE

The churches in this conference began as German Baptist churches, established in North America by German immigrants more than a century ago. They first settled in New Jersey and Pennsylvania, where Quakers offered the perfect religious freedom they sought. The scattered churches later became the North American Baptist Conference, organizing the first local churches from 1840 through 1851.

The prosperity of these Baptist churches followed the rise and fall of German immigration. By 1851 there were eight churches and 405 members, and in that year an Eastern Conference was organized by fellowship and mutual consideration of common problems.

The local conference idea was enlarged as the number of churches increased. As membership moved across the nation, nine such conferences were established, following geographical lines. In 1865 a joint meeting of Eastern and Western conferences, called a General Conference, was held. A Triennial Conference is now the chief administrative unit.

Twenty associations meet annually to elect their own officers and committees and guide their own work. The Triennial Conference is made up of clergy and lay representatives from all the churches. It superintends the work of publication, education, international missions, and church planting. A general council acts for the conference between sessions.

German Baptists were a part of what is now Colgate-Rochester Divinity School in Rochester, New York. In 1935 they established a seminary of their own, the North American Baptist Seminary, which relocated from Rochester to Sioux Falls, South Dakota, in 1949. The North American Baptist College and Edmonton Baptist Seminary are in Edmonton, Alberta, Canada. There are ten homes for the aged and a very strong emphasis on global church planting in Japan, Brazil, Nigeria, Cameroon, West Africa, the Philippines, Mexico, Canada, and the United States.

Theologically, there is little variance from the usual Baptist position. In general, North American Baptists follow the New Hampshire Confession, stressing the authority of the Scriptures, the revelation

71

of God in Christ, regeneration, immersion, separation of church and state, and the congregational form of government. There are 61,084 members in 388 churches, scattered across the United States and Canada.

PRIMITIVE BAPTIST

Primitive Baptists have the reputation of being the most strictly orthodox and exclusive of all Baptists. Unique in that the group has never been organized as a denomination and has no administrative body of any kind (each church should "govern itself according to the laws of Christ as found in the New Testament, and no minister, association, or convention has any authority over the churches"), it represents a nineteenth-century protest against the then newly introduced "money-based" missions and benevolent societies and the assessing of churches to support missions, missionaries, and Sunday schools. Its position was that there were no missionary societies in the days of the apostles and none directed by the Scripture; therefore, there should be none now.

Apart from this, there was objection to the centralization of authority in these societies. These Baptists believed in the religious training of children, but not in Sunday schools. They stood for evangelism as a missionary effort, but by individual responsibility and individual expense, not under sponsorship of a money-based society.

Spearheading this protest against new measures, in 1827 the Kehukee Association in North Carolina condemned all money-based and authoritarian societies as being contrary to Christ's teachings. Within a decade, several other Baptist associations across the country made similar statements and withdrew from other Baptist churches.

The various associations adopted the custom of printing in their annual minutes their articles of faith, constitutions, and rules of order. These statements were examined by the other associations, and if they were approved, there was fellowship and an exchange of messengers and correspondence; any association not so approved was dropped from the fellowship.

A strong Calvinism runs through the Primitive Baptist doctrine. In general, the members believe that through Adam's fall, all humankind became sinners; human nature is completely corrupt; and humans cannot by their own efforts regain favor with God. God elected God's own people in Christ before the world began, and none of these saints will be finally lost. The two biblically authorized ordinances are the Lord's Supper and baptism of believers by immersion. All church societies are human inventions and are denied fellowship; Christ will come a second time to raise the dead, judge all people, punish the wicked forever, and reward the righteous forever; the Old and New Testaments are verbally and infallibly inspired.

Pastors must be called by God, come under the laying on of hands, and be in fellowship with the local church of which they are members in order to administer the two ordinances; they are to deny to any clergy lacking these qualifications the right to administer such ordinances. No theological training is demanded of ministers. While there is no opposition to such education, the position is that the Lord might call an educated person, but lack of education should not bar a person from the ministry. Some Primitive Baptists still practice foot washing, but not all. In spite of their opposition to money-based missionary societies, they are intensely evangelistic. Their preachers travel widely and serve without charge, except when hearers wish to contribute to their support.

Membership is granted only after careful examination and vote of the congregation. Factionalism, divisiveness, and politics prevent an accurate report on membership, which is concentrated in the South; it is estimated at 72,000 in 1,000 churches, but the figure is probably larger.

PROGRESSIVE NATIONAL BAPTIST CONVENTION, INC.

As noted, this group of Baptists came into being in 1961, after several years of tension and discussion, breaking away from the National Baptist Convention, U.S.A., Inc. Two issues loomed quite large. First, the absence of term limits for that body's elected president, and, second, the policy of disengagement from the civil rights and other social justice struggles during the revolutionary years following the 1954 Supreme Court decision concerning desegregation of public facilities.

Its leadership rolls were a virtual who's who of the civil rights community. Along with Martin Luther King, Sr., and Martin Luther King, Jr., it attracted Gardner C. Taylor, the first president; Ralph David Abernathy; and Benjamin Mays, truly famous preachers and leaders in the national black church. From its inception, the Progressive body has taken a highly active role in civil rights, social justice, and political causes. It took a strong stand against apartheid in South Africa. From the beginning the spirit of this group has been ecumenical, seeking to work harmoniously with other black Baptist, and other Christian, denominations.

REFORMED BAPTIST

This group is a fellowship of churches, rather than a denomination, and is made up of some 300 to 400 congregations in the U.S. and Canada, not all of which use the name *Reformed*. Some do not wish to be called Baptist. The bond that unites them is a strict adherence to "five-point Calvinism"—belief in the tenets of total depravity, unconditional election, limited and definite atonement, irresistible (or invincible) calling, and the perseverance of all true saints. They also agree for the most part with the doctrines of the Synod of Dordt, the "Anabaptist doctrine of a called-out church," and the Philadelphia Confession.

These Baptists differ from various other Calvinist Baptists, who may deny the necessity of preaching to all or hold to a "Baptist succession" concept of the church. The churches involved are completely autonomous, independently supporting an unlisted number of missionaries and the publishing of church literature. No membership report is available.

The first "Sovereign Grace" conference, which gave rise to this fellowship of churches, was held in Ashland, Kentucky, in 1954. Membership is concentrated mainly in the Northeastern and Southern states.

SEPARATE BAPTISTS IN CHRIST
(GENERAL ASSOCIATION OF SEPARATE BAPTISTS)

The first Separate Baptists arrived in the U.S. in 1695, as one refugee section of the Separatist movement in England. They were especially active during the days of the preaching of George Whitefield in the early eighteenth century and in the conflict between the Old Light and New Light sects. Separate Baptist churches of this period were marked by their milder Calvinism.

In 1787, Separate and Regular Baptist churches in Virginia merged into the United Baptist Churches of Christ in Virginia. Other mergers and gestures toward union arose in New England and other states, but a few Separate Baptist churches maintained their independence. In 1988 there were 101 churches and four mission churches, with 10,000 members, 161 ordained ministers, and 14 licentiate ministers.

All creeds and confessions of faith are rejected by Separate Baptists; however, there is an annual statement of articles of belief by the several associations and the general association. These include statements of faith in the infallibility of the Scriptures and in the Trinity; three ordinances—baptism of believers by immersion only, the

Lord's Supper, and foot washing; regeneration, justification, and sanctification through faith in Christ; the appearance of Christ on Judgment Day to deal with the just and the unjust. The "election, reprobation, and fatality" of Calvinism are rejected. Separate Baptists do not claim to be Protestants: "We have never protested against what we hold to be the faith once delivered to the saints."

They are congregational in government, with associations for advisory purposes only. At present there are churches in Indiana, Illinois, Virginia, North Carolina, Kentucky, Tennessee, and Ohio.

The General Association of Separate Baptists has incorporated a mission program called Separate Baptist Missions, Inc. Through this program, support is given to various mission fields and efforts, both in the U.S. and abroad. One member from each of the seven associations is elected to this mission board each year, and a monthly publication is distributed to churches and individuals each month.

SEVENTH DAY BAPTIST GENERAL CONFERENCE

Differing from other groups of Baptists in its adherence to the seventh day as the sabbath, the Seventh Day Baptist (or Sabbatarian Baptist, as it was often called in England) was first organized as a separate body in North America at Newport, Rhode Island, in 1671. Stephen Mumford had come here from England, knowing full well the perils of religious nonconformity, and had entered into a covenant relationship with those who withdrew from "Doctor John Clarke's (Baptist) Church" under the sabbath persuasion. Other churches were organized in Philadelphia and New Jersey, and from these three centers, Seventh Day Baptists went west with the frontier; they now have 5,250 members in 90 churches and fellowships.

Belief in salvation through faith in Christ; believer's baptism by immersion; insistence on intellectual and civil liberty; and the right of every person to interpret the Bible "for himself under God" have characterized these churches. They hold only baptism and the Lord's Supper as ordinances and practice open Communion.

Local churches enjoy complete independence, although all support the united benevolence of the Denominational Budget. For fellowship and service, the churches are organized into eight regional associations, and these often assist local church councils in the ordination of deacons and ministerial candidates. The highest administrative body is the General Conference, which meets annually and delegates interim responsibilities to its president, executive secretary, and general council. The conference promotes denominational giving, channeled through mission, publishing, and educational agencies. It also accredits ministers certified to it by ordaining councils and local churches.

The denomination participates in the ecumenical movement at local, regional, national, and world levels. The Seventh Day Baptist conferences include those in Australia, Brazil, England, Germany, Guyana, India, Jamaica, Malawi, Mexico, Mynmar, the Netherlands, New Zealand, Nigeria, the Philippines, Poland, and South Africa as well as in the U.S. and Canada.

SOUTHERN BAPTIST CONVENTION

In was inevitable that Northern and Southern Baptists should split over the slavery question, even before the outbreak of the Civil War. The friction between the two sections began a quarter of a century before Bull Run. The acting board of foreign missions of the Baptists had its headquarters in Boston. Being located there, it was naturally strongly influenced by the abolition movement. There was bitter debate among the board members, and in the early 1840s it became evident that this board would not accept slaveholders as missionaries. This question of missionaries and of missionary money was the immediate cause of the split. The "brethren of the North" first suggested separation; a month later, in May 1845, the Southern Baptist Convention (SBC) was organized, establishing at once its own boards for foreign and home missions.

Southern historians now recognize that in addition to the slavery issue there was a long-standing disagreement between Baptists in the North and Baptists in the South over the nature of denominational organization. Certainly the slave issue precipitated the break, but there was a significant consequence to it. Baptists in the United States under Northern leadership heretofore had no central denominational organization. Instead there were separate and independent organizations (usually designated as "societies") for various phases of cooperative effort, such as foreign and home missions and publication. Southerners had desired instead to have one organization controlling these varied activities. From the beginning the Southern Baptist Convention was such an organization. Northern Baptists, on the other hand, waited until 1907 to form a convention uniting their societies. This cohesion of centralized organization and cooperative societies has had much to do, Southern Baptists believe, with their growth.

In Maryland, Virginia, North Carolina, South Carolina, Georgia, Louisiana, Kentucky, and Alabama, 300 churches entered the new organization. Until the outbreak of the Civil War, this convention met biennially; since 1869 it usually has met annually.

A hard struggle for existence immediately lay ahead for the new convention. It suffered badly with regard to churches, membership, and finances during the war. Homes, schools, the livelihood of citizens, indeed the very pattern of Southern society were destroyed, with devastating effect on all churches. An antimissionary movement decimated Baptist ranks, and membership—not finances or leadership in that historical era—were affected when black Baptists withdrew to form their own societies and conventions. The recovery of the Southern Baptist Convention was impressive, however. In 1845 there had been 351,951 members, of whom 130,000 were black; by 1890, 1,235,908 members, all white; in 1993, 15,365,486 members in 38,458 churches, including 300,000 members in over a thousand predominantly black churches.

As previously noted, Southern Baptists generally hold to a more conservative theology than their Northern relatives, but the basic tenets of belief are quite the same. The Southern Baptist heritage is more definitely Calvinist; one of the ironies of Baptist history is that the Southern Baptist Convention adheres more firmly to the New Hampshire Confession of Faith than do American Baptist Churches. Church polity and government are comparable in the two conventions. The American Baptists do embody a 200-member general board with some policy-making authority, in line with their commitment to the principle of representation. Membership and ministry have usually been exchanged in harmony and understanding.

Twenty denominational agencies work with 36 state conventions, three fellowships, and the Caribbean area office in home and foreign missions, Sunday schools, educational institutions, and ministerial retirement. The Home Mission Board operates throughout the U.S. and its territories, with nearly 5,000 missionaries active in the field. It cooperates with black Baptists; works among migrants in the South, Native Americans in the West and Southwest, 98 language groups, and deaf persons; and provides loans for the construction of new church buildings. In 1992, SBC churches reported 367,000 baptisms.

Foreign missionaries are at work in 131 countries on five continents, relating to 32,797 churches, of which 20,774 are self-supporting. In 1992, 251,901 baptisms were reported. There are 15,740 students in seminaries and theological institutes and 11,947 in theological extension courses; a total of 230,433 students were enrolled in 1,233 schools in 1992.

The Foreign Mission Board helps to operate 23 hospitals and 242 clinics and dispensaries overseas. In 1992 there were 51 missionary physicians, 81 missionary nurses, and 115 missionary personnel engaged in other health-care ministries. Half of the Convention's Cooperative Program allocation of funds goes to overseas missions. That amount was $69 million in 1991–92.

The Sunday School Board provides the literature for and assists the work of 8,262,521 students in 36,883 Sunday schools. The SBC maintains six theological seminaries with nearly 11,000 students, 53 colleges and universities, eight academies, and four Bible schools.

The Southern Baptist Convention is a growing denomination with a net gain of four churches and 22,400 members each week. New churches are being established in Northern, Western, and Eastern states as well as in the South. The annual convention is being held increasingly in cities outside the Southern homeland, partly because so many members live in those areas and are entitled to have geographical access to national convention meetings. The denomination has become a national body, emphatically with reference to membership distribution. The name "Southern" has become something of a misnomer, therefore.

Rapid growth and expansion beyond the Southern region is only one of the major stories about the Southern Baptist Convention in recent years. Another is the factionalism within the body. Since 1978, the elected president, who has key appointive powers, has belonged to the more conservative of the two sectors of the Convention. Avoiding defamatory titles has proven difficult for both "parties," but one popular naming has used "fundamental conservative" and "moderate conservative."

At any rate, the more conservative party is now solidly in the majority and in control of the seminaries, agencies, and boards that belong to the entire Convention. It distinguishes its position as commitment to "biblical inerrancy." The other party takes its stand on what may be termed the infallibility of biblical authority. The fact that they both are conservative by historical standards is quite clear.

State-controlled units, mission boards, colleges, and newspapers, for example, live with the pressure of the conflict, but they reflect local and subregional orientations and traditions, in varying degrees. Diversity appears in another guise as well. Since 1991, the "dissident, moderate" cause has taken organizational form as the Cooperative Baptist Fellowship. It sponsors its own missionary, educational, and social causes, although many of its churches continue to contribute to Convention treasuries. Its membership is divided on whether to create a new denomination, but it already bears some marks of taking such a step. Needless to say, each sector of Southern Baptist life claims to be the authentic carrier of the tradition that has been so large and culturally significant for a century and a half.

Yet another significant story about the Southern Baptist Convention in recent years is the adoption on June 20, 1995, of a resolution to renounce its racist origins and to apologize for its founders' defense of slavery. In its apology to African Americans, the resolution declared that members of the church must "unwaveringly denounce racism, in all its forms, as deplorable sin" and repent of "racism of which we have been guilty whether consciously or unconsciously."

UNITED BAPTIST

The United Baptist denomination represents a merging of several groups of Separate and Regular Baptists, mainly in the states of Virginia, Kentucky, and the Carolinas. While both Arminian and Calvinist theologies were held by the various bodies, they maintained a perfect freedom in preaching and polity after their union. As the years passed, many members found their way into either the Northern or the Southern Baptist conventions, but United Baptist is still recognized as a separate denomination, with 63,641 members in 586 churches. The first organization was in Richmond, Virginia, in 1787; a second group organized in Kentucky in 1801, when two associations—Salem and Elkhorn (Regular Baptists) and South Kentucky (Separate Baptists)—joined.

Doctrinally, traces of Arminianism and Calvinism remain. Generally, it is held that salvation is by grace rather than works and is conditional upon gospel requirements. Humankind is in a state of general depravity and is commanded to repent; people are led either to repentance through the goodness of God or to rebellion by the devil. It is a matter of individual choice.

The 26 associations for fellowship and counsel are quite independent of one another, yet they work together closely. Closed Communion is practiced in some associations and churches, open Communion in others. There are three ordinances—baptism, the Lord's Supper, and (in most churches) foot washing. Most churches are located in Kentucky, Ohio, and West Virginia.

UNITED FREE WILL BAPTIST CHURCH

While this group traces its history back to the same original sources as the white Free Will Baptist Church, the United Free Will Baptist Church has been independent since its official organization in 1901. Members are found largely in North Carolina, Georgia, Florida, Mississippi, Louisiana, and Texas.

Although in general agreement with the congregational polity of other Baptist bodies, this church grants a rather limited autonomy to the local church. There is a system of quarterly, annual, and general conferences, with graded authority. Doctrinal disputes may be carried up to the general conferences; district conferences may exclude members from fellowship.

Doctrinally, it is in agreement with white churches of the same faith. There is one institution of higher learning—Kinston College at Kinston, North Carolina. There were 100,000 members in 836 churches in 1952.

BEREAN FUNDAMENTAL CHURCH

In the mid-1930s, Dr. Ivan E. Olsen became the first pastor of an independent church, the Berean Fundamental Church, in North Platte, Nebraska. Following the biblical principle of evangelism found in Acts 1:8, Olsen assisted in planting 16 churches in surrounding communities.

In 1947 the churches formed the Berean Fundamental Church Council, Inc., and an aggressive evangelistic ministry resulted in the establishment of many new churches. Currently, there are 51 churches in 8 states—California, Colorado, Kansas, Minnesota, South Dakota, Oregon, Wyoming, and Nebraska—and one in Manitoba, Canada. Total membership numbers close to 3,000.

The member churches possess a common constitution, stressing the basic doctrines of Christianity: the verbal, plenary inspiration of Scripture (the inerrancy of the Bible in all matters of faith and morals); the virgin birth of Christ; the deity of Christ; the blood atonement; the bodily resurrection of Christ; and the return of Christ to earth, following the rapture and preceding the millennial kingdom. The local assemblies are also strongly Bible centered and evangelistic.

Berean Fundamental churches support a variety of independent faith missions, draw their pastors from various seminaries and Bible institutes, and freely choose their own Sunday school curricula and church literature.

The Berean Fundamental Church Council, Inc., supports its own Maranatha Bible Camp and Conference Grounds, near North Platte, Nebraska.

BIBLE FELLOWSHIP CHURCH

This body, strongly evangelical in purpose and effort, was founded in 1858 and today consists of 43 congregations in Pennsylvania, New Jersey, and New York. Its doctrinal emphases include salvation through the death and resurrection of Christ, transformed life through new birth by the Holy Spirit, the authority and trustworthiness of the Bible as the Word of God, the culmination of history in the second coming of Jesus, and "a shared-life in the church of believers, with every-member responsibility for the propagation of the Gospel by evangelism and missions." Its heritage lies in the Mennonite Church in Ontario and in the United States.

The churches support missions on five continents, the Pinebrook Junior College, the Victory Valley Camp for children and youth, a home for the aging, and Pinebrook-in-the-Pines, a conference and retreat center in Pennsylvania.

BIBLE PROTESTANT CHURCH

The churches in this body represent the 1939 separation from the Methodist Protestant Church, when some 50 delegates and pastors (approximately one-third of the Eastern Conference) withdrew to protest the union of the Methodist Protestant Church with the Methodist Episcopal Church and the Methodist Episcopal Church, South, and what they considered the modernist tendencies of those churches. While this body operates under its original Eastern Conference corporate charter, its name was subsequently changed to Bible Protestant Church.

Doctrine is conservative; this church is a member of the fundamentalist American Council of Christian Churches. Cardinal points in its belief emphasize the verbal inspiration of the Bible; the Trinity; the deity, virgin birth, resurrection, and ascension of Jesus Christ; salvation by faith in Christ's blood and sacrifice, death, and resurrection. There is a strong faith in premillennialism, with eternal punishment for the wicked and eternal joy for the righteous believer. Baptism and the Lord's Supper are practiced as divine institutions.

The churches are confined to New Jersey, New York, Pennsylvania, Virginia, and Michigan. Actually, it is a fellowship of self-governing churches, organized in a conference that meets annually with lay and clerical representation. Missionary work is conducted in Japan and among migrant workers in the U.S. by Bible Protestant Missions, Inc.; Bible Protestant missionaries also serve in Mexico and Germany under the mission boards of other churches. There are 30 churches, with 2,126 members.

BIBLE WAY CHURCH, WORLDWIDE

At a ministerial conference of black Pentecostal pastors in September 1957, some 70 churches withdrew from the Church of Our Lord of the Apostolic Faith to form the Bible Way Church, Worldwide. Its doctrine and teaching remain quite the same as those of the parent body. Phenomenal growth has been reported—from 70 to 350 churches with 300,000 members in the U.S. and more abroad. A general conference is held annually in July; a publishing house at Washington, D.C., circulates periodicals, religious pamphlets, and recordings.

BRANCH DAVIDIANS

Largely unknown before 1993, the Branch Davidians became world famous through their 51-day standoff against federal authorities. The culmination on April 19, 1993, in the fiery death of 86 members was one of the most tragic and spectacular events of the year. The members who lived at Mt. Carmel Center, a group compound near Waco, Texas, followed their messianic leader, David Koresh, who commanded resistance against government officials and finally ignited the fire that took the lives of all still living there.

This group of radical sectarians is a subset of one offshoot of the Seventh Day Adventist movement. (It was never a part of the large church that goes by that name.) In fact, the group's actual name is "Davidian Seventh-day Adventist Association," or more properly, "Branch Seventh Day Adventists." They trace a lineage to 1930 when Victor T. Houteff, a SDA church member in Los Angeles, expounded his new divinely inspired message in a book, *The Shepherd's Rod*.

Houteff and his followers found themselves unwelcome in SDA congregations and in 1935 moved to their central Texas site. Here, they believed, the redeemed 144,000 mentioned in the biblical book of Revelation would gather temporarily while directing the establishment of the Davidic kingdom. Living there together under theocratic rule, they would await the second coming of Christ.

David Koresh assumed the mantle of leadership of that theocratic regime in 1986 and the community became ever more isolated and defensive. Reports of the acquisition of a large cache of weapons and of the mistreatment of children occasioned the U.S. government's interest. By the time the confrontation ended in disaster, the power of Koresh's control had become dramatically evident.

Two other Davidian Adventist groups remain, one near Exeter, Missouri, the other near Salem, South Carolina. They too stand in the heritage of Houteff and his vision of the restoration of the King David–like theocracy, in these cases in anticipation of Christ's return.

BRETHREN

American descendants of early German Protestants, the Brethren are authentic Pietists. The inner spiritual life, piety, is cultivated in prayer and study of Scripture and through association with fellow believers. The local church is central. In it members are true brothers and sisters. The church claims their primary loyalty in a world that offers many societies for association. It is understood more as a community of people who love God and one another than as part of an organization or a body that formulates doctrine. Brethren do not emphasize tight doctrinal standards; rather, the spirit of God within each one, binding one another in love, takes precedence for them. They live a simple, unadorned life. In their early decades in Europe and America, Brethren were separatists from the state and conventional churches. While not manifesting a judgmental attitude, they devote themselves to a purity that may set them apart from other Christians, as well as from general society.

From those German Pietists came Church of the Brethren (Conservative Dunkers), Brethren Church (Progressive Dunkers), Old German Baptist Brethren (Old Order Dunkers), Church of God (New Dunkers, disbanded in August 1962), and Fellowship of Grace Brethren Churches.

One group historically unrelated to these, known as River Brethren, also took its ideology from the German Pietists. That group includes Brethren in Christ, Old Order (or Yorker) Brethren, and United Zion Church (formerly United Zion's Children). Another—the Plymouth Brethren—is totally unrelated to any of these, being British rather than German in origin (see PLYMOUTH BRETHREN).

The Brethren bodies that began in Germany were known for years simply as German Baptist Brethren. That title has largely disappeared, except in the case of the Old German Baptist Brethren.

The terms *Brethren* and *Dunker* have been the cause of much confusion; they call for careful definition. *Dunker* is a direct derivation of the German *tunken*, "to dip or immerse," and is identified with the peculiar method of immersion employed by this group of churches—triple immersion—in which the believer is immersed not once but three times, in the name of the Father, Son, and Holy Ghost. Through their long history, Dunkers have been variously called Tunkers, Täufers, and Dompelaars. They were first called Brethren when their organization was established at Schwarzenau, Germany, in 1708.

It might be said generally that these Dunkers, or Brethren, are former German Reformed bodies that took their theology and much of their practice from the Pietists of the seventeenth and eighteenth centuries. Most Pietists were Lutherans who had become unhappy with the formal worship and ritual in their state church and the general "barrenness" of German Protestantism. They took the New Testament literally and endeavored to put its teachings into practice, even in the last detail of their living. They spurned the idea of apostolic succession, and at the heart of their practice was a love feast, or *agape*, the serving of the Lord's Supper, preceded by a ceremony of foot washing. They saluted one another with a "kiss of peace," dressed in the plainest of clothing, covered women's heads at services, anointed their sick with oil for healing and consecration, refrained from worldly amusements, and refused to take oaths, go to war, or engage in lawsuits. These doctrines and practices, with certain modifications, are held today by many Brethren.

Along with the churches described under this family grouping, several other major branches of Brethren consider themselves direct descendants of the group organized at Schwarzenau: Old German Baptist Brethren, organized in 1881, with 5,475 members in 1991; Brethren Church, 1883, 13,322 members in 1991; Fellowship of Grace Brethren Churches, 1939, 39,327 members in 1991; and the Dunkard Brethren, 1926, about 1,035 members in 1980.

BRETHREN CHURCH (ASHLAND)

In 1882, a sharp division within the Church of the Brethren resulted in the organization of the Brethren Church. It is referred to as Progressive, sometimes Progressive Dunker (because of its baptism by immersion), and sometimes Progressive Brethren, referring to its opposition to some outmoded practices of Church of the Brethren, especially in education and dress.

The Ashland, Ohio, body is the Arminian wing of the Progressive Dunker movement. That description is historically significant, but this church's teachings seek a balance between the Calvinist and Arminian perspectives. It has 13,132 members in 124 churches. It supports a college and a seminary in the headquarters city, and it belongs to the National Association of Evangelicals.

BRETHREN IN CHRIST CHURCH

The church began as a group called River Brethren in about 1778, centered in Pennsylvania. There was migration to Canada by 1788.

With the outbreak of the Civil War, the draft reached into the ranks of the Brethren, and it became necessary to obtain legal recognition as an established religious organization in order to protect the objectors. The denomination opposes war, and most of its members will not participate. A council meeting in Lancaster County, Pennsylvania, in 1863 adopted the name Brethren in Christ Church; it was not incorporated until 1904.

Brethren in Christ Church pledges loyalty to the following doctrines: the inspiration of the Holy Scriptures; the self-existent, Triune God—Father, Son, and Holy Spirit; the deity and virgin birth of Christ; Christ's death as atonement for our sins and his resurrection from the dead; the Holy Spirit who convicts the sinner, regenerates the penitent, and empowers the believer; justification as forgiveness for committed sins and sanctification as heart cleansing and empowerment by the Holy Spirit; observance of the ordinances of God's house; temperance and modesty of apparel as taught in the Scriptures; the personal, visible, and imminent return of Christ; the resurrection of the dead, with punishment for the unbeliever and reward for the believer; and worldwide evangelism as the supreme duty of the church.

While the government of this church is largely in the hands of the local churches, there are eight regional conferences and a general conference, which is the ultimate authority. A board of administration has oversight of the general conference and of general church property and financial transactions.

The church has two institutions of learning: Messiah College at Grantham, Pennsylvania, and Niagara Christian College at Fort Erie, Ontario, Canada. Missionaries are at work in Africa, India, Japan, London, Colombia, Nicaragua, Venezuela, and Cuba and are engaged in Mennonite Central Committee work around the world. There were 10,819 members in 230 churches in the United States and Canada at the end of 1992.

CHURCH OF THE BRETHREN

The Church of the Brethren was formed in 1708 in Schwarzenau, Germany. Its founders were five men and three women, most under thirty years of age, who gathered in homes for Bible study and prayer. Out of their own Reformed Church background and the influence of Pietist and Anabaptist reformers, the early Brethren covenanted to be a people shaped by personal faith in Christ, prayer, and study of Scripture. They stressed daily discipleship and service to neighbor.

Severe persecution and economic conditions prompted virtually the entire movement to migrate to North America between 1719 and 1729. Included was their leader and first minister, Alexander Mack, Sr.

Commonly known as German Baptist Brethren, or even Dunkers or Dunkards, in its bicentennial year, 1908, the group adopted Church of the Brethren as its official name. *Brethren* was seen as a

New Testament term that conveyed the kinship and warmth of Jesus' early followers.

Although noncreedal from its inception, Church of the Brethren has held firmly to basic tenets of the Free Church, or Believers Church, tradition. Among the most distinctive Brethren practices are the baptism of confessing believers by threefold immersion and anointing of the ill for spiritual and bodily health. The Last Supper is observed by a service of foot washing, which symbolizes servanthood; a fellowship meal, which symbolizes family; and the commemorative Eucharist, which symbolizes Saviorhood.

As one of the three historic "peace" churches, together with Friends and Mennonites, Brethren have long held an official peace witness, often expressed in conscientious objection to military service. During World War II, Civilian Public Health camps were maintained for religious objectors who performed work in the national interest. During and after the war, many of the programs were continued under the alternative service provisions of Selective Service, and voluntary service abroad, a forerunner of the Peace Corps, was introduced.

Also growing out of the peace concern was a worldwide program of relief, reconstruction, and welfare, conducted by the Brethren Service Commission and later by the World Ministries Commission, as a service of love to those suffering from war, natural catastrophe, or social disadvantage.

Since 1948, Brethren Volunteer Service has enlisted nearly 5,000 men and women in one or two years of social service at home and abroad. Work with migrant laborers, inner-city dwellers, prison inmates, refugees, and victims of abuse exemplifies the types of activity undertaken. Increasingly, older volunteers have enrolled in the program, quite often after they have reached retirement age.

Numerous projects initiated by the group have become full-scale ecumenical enterprises. Among them are the Heifer Project International, Christian Youth Exchange, Christian Rural Overseas Program (CROP), SERRV (handcraft sales for Third World producers), and International Voluntary Service. Other pioneering ventures were agricultural exchanges begun with Poland in the 1950s and with China in the 1980s and ecumenical exchanges with the Russian Orthodox Church in the 1960s.

In polity, the Brethren combine both congregational and presbyterian practices, with final authority vested in an Annual Conference of elected delegates. The General Board of elected and *ex officio* members is the administrative arm of the church. Congregations are organized into 23 districts in 36 states at present, usually with one or more full-time executives in each district, heaviest concentration being in Pennsylvania, Virginia, Maryland, Ohio, Indiana, and Illinois. Membership in 1992 stood at 150,000 in 1,085 congregations. These figures do not include churches in Nigeria, India, and Ecuador that were once affiliated with the church and are now independent.

The Brethren are related to six accredited liberal arts colleges: Bridgewater College in Virginia; Elizabethtown and Juniata colleges in Pennsylvania; University of LaVerne in California; Manchester College in Indiana; and McPherson College in Kansas. The church sponsors one graduate school, Bethany Theological Seminary, which moved to Indiana in 1994.

General offices are in Elgin, Illinois, also the home of Brethren Press, which produces the monthly publication *Messenger* and an independent scholarly journal, *Brethren Life and Thought.*

Church of the Brethren is active in ecumenical programs in local, state, regional, national, and international arenas. It is a charter member of both the National and the World Council of Churches.

CHURCH OF THE UNITED BRETHREN IN CHRIST

This group, in existence since 1767, opposed the constitutional changes in 1889. United Brethren believe in the Trinity and in the deity, humanity, and atonement of Christ. Observance of scriptural living is required of all members, who are forbidden the use of alcoholic beverages and membership in secret societies. Baptism and the Lord's Supper are observed as ordinances.

Local, annual, and general conferences are held. The general conference meets quadrennially and is composed of ministers, district superintendents (presiding elders), general church officials, bishops, and lay delegates. Both men and women are eligible for the ministry and are ordained only once as elders. Missionary societies administer evangelism and church aid in the U.S. and in Sierra Leone, West Africa, Jamaica, India, Macao, Honduras, Hong Kong, and Nicaragua. Still insisting on loyalty to the old constitution, the church belongs to the National Association of Evangelicals and works in harmony with evangelical groups in other denominations.

A college and Graduate School of Christian Ministries are located at Huntington, Indiana, with secondary schools in Sierra Leone. There are 36,322 members in 390 churches, including the overseas ministry.

FELLOWSHIP OF GRACE BRETHREN CHURCHES

Born in the 1881–83 split in the original Brethren body in the U.S., in 1921 the Brethren Church drew up a statement of faith, the Message of the Brethren Ministry. In 1939 a crisis divided the church into bodies that came to be known as the Ashland group and the Grace group. In 1969, the Grace group adopted its own statement of faith: the primacy of the Bible; the trinitarian God; the incarnation of the divine Son of God, the Lord Jesus Christ; the work of the Holy Spirit; the sinfulness of humans; salvation through Christ; the church as made up of believers; the Christian life as a way of righteousness; the ordinances of baptism and the threefold Communion service; the reality of Satan; the Second Coming; and the future life.

The Grace group was separately incorporated in 1987 as the Fellowship of Grace Brethren Churches. It usually has its annual conference at Winona Lake, Indiana. It operates its own educational institutions and mission boards and is led by its own executives. The Grace group represents more nearly the Calvinist viewpoint in theology; the Ashland group, the Arminian position.

Churches are grouped geographically into districts, which hold annual conferences. The Grace group numbers 39,237 in 322 churches; the Ashland group has 13,322 in 124 churches.

OLD GERMAN BAPTIST BRETHREN
(OLD ORDER DUNKERS)

While the Brethren Church (Progressive Dunkers) left the Church of the Brethren (Conservative Dunkers) because the latter body seemed too conservative, the Old German Baptist Brethren (Old Order Dunkers) left because they considered the Church of the Brethren not conservative enough. The dissenters stood literally for the old order and traditions. The salient point in their opposition lay in their suspicion of Sunday schools, salaried ministers, missions, higher education, and church societies. They withdrew in 1881.

The basic objections still hold, but with certain modifications. Children are not enrolled in Sunday schools, but are encouraged to attend the regular services of the church and to join the church at an early age—anywhere from 15 to 20, the decision being left entirely to the individual. Many congregations list a majority of members between 15 and 40 years of age. The church today is not completely opposed even to higher education; a few of the youths enter high school and take training in college or professional schools for various professions.

The church stands for a literal interpretation of the Scriptures in regard to the Lord's Supper and practices closed Communion, which excludes all but its own members. While it advocates compliance with the ordinary demands of government, it opposes cooperation in war: "Any member who enters into military service will fall into the judgment of the Church." Noncooperation in political and secret societies is required; the dress is severely plain, and all worldly amusements are frowned upon. The group follows other Brethren bodies in that the church has no salaried ministers, enforces complete abstinence from alcoholic beverages, the members refuse to take oaths or engage in lawsuits, the sick are anointed with oil, the heads of the women are veiled at worship, and wedding ceremonies are not performed for previously divorced persons.

There are no missions or educational work. An annual conference that rules on matters "on which the Scriptures are silent" is held each year at Pentecost. There are 5,475 members in 55 churches, with strength in Ohio, Indiana, and Pennsylvania.

UNITED ZION CHURCH

Bishop Matthias Brinser was expelled from Brethren in Christ Church in 1855, together with about 50 other members, for building and holding services in a meetinghouse. These people organized their own group, United Zion's Children; in 1954 the body incorporated under the name United Zion Church.

This church is essentially the same in doctrine as the Brethren in Christ Church. It baptizes by trine immersion and observes foot washing as an ordinance, along with the Lord's Supper. It encourages the veiling of women and is opposed to divorce and immodest attire.

Located almost exclusively in Dauphin, Lebanon, and Lancaster counties in Pennsylvania, it lists 850 members and 13 churches. Church officers are bishops, ministers, and deacons; the top administrative body is a general conference composed of representatives from the various district conferences, the basic units of governments.

Foreign missionary work began in Chile in 1986, and the church supports two missionaries working under the Brethren in Christ Church. One home for the aged is maintained, and the church publishes a monthly magazine, *Zion's Herald.*

BUDDHIST COMMUNITIES

Buddhism has to an unusual degree resisted identification of its central teaching with particular cultural, historical, or institutional forms. Thus it has been open to adoption of features of the religious environment of the countries to which it has spread, but in the United States the assumption of forms of religious life characteristic of denominations has not been widespread.

The faith is built on the teaching of its founder, Buddha, Siddartha Gautama, the Enlightened One (c. 563–483 B.C.E.), who rejected the religious alternatives in India and initiated a new path, which spread throughout Asia. Within the last century immigrants from Eastern and Southeastern Asia have provided one of the major sources of Buddhist communities in the United States.

The Buddha diagnosed the human plight as being due to insatiable cravings that bring misery; he departed from the ascetic traditions of his time by proclaiming that one may overcome the suffering endemic in human experience by ceasing either to crave its goods or to avoid its ills without renouncing all worldly life. This analysis of the human predicament had no room for or need of theological affirmations, rejecting attention to the role of external forces in favor of one's own ability by disciplined reflection and behavior to achieve extinction of or freedom from the causes of our bondage—this is nirvana, ending the experience of rebirth in the cycle of suffering.

The group most recognizable as a denomination, the Buddhist Churches of America, traces its origin to the first U.S. Buddhist temple, consecrated in San Francisco in 1898 by the Buddhist Mission of North America. Expressing the tradition of Jodo Shinsu ("Pre Land") Buddhism, its focus is on the grace of Amida Buddha rather than on the meditation associated with Zen. Its principal constituency is Japanese American Buddhists, and it has spread to 60 churches or temples and 40 branches on the mainland and in Hawaii. One of its educational centers, the Institute of Buddhist Studies, is an affiliate of the Graduate Theological Union in Berkeley, California. Since 1987 the Armed Forces Chaplains Board has recognized the Buddhist Churches of America as an endorsing agency to certify clergy for chaplaincies.

A newer movement from Japan is Nichiren Shoshu of America, a branch of the Soka Gakkai, a lay movement that has experienced phenomenal growth in Japan. Lotus-sutra chanting, which is the focus of Nichiren Buddhist worship, is accompanied by an active life in the world. Nichiren Shoshu Soka Gakkai (the lay movement) and Nichiren Shoshu Temple are headquartered in Santa Monica, California. Although independently organized, they have links to Soka Gakkai International.

Immigrants from other Asian countries who have established Buddhist institutions in their communities include Chinese, Koreans, Cambodians, Vietnamese, and Tibetans; these groups express the Mahayana ("Great Vehicle") branch that has predominated in East Asia. There are also groups from Theravada ("Way of the Elders") countries, such as Sri Lanka and Thailand. A Tibetan Center of vigorous activity is the Nyingma Institute, centered since 1973 in Berkeley Hills, California. Of a different monastic lineage and at one time of larger scope is Vajradhatu, created by Chogyam Trungpa, Rinpoche in 1973. Located in Boulder, Colorado, Vajradhatu, in association with the Nalanda Foundation, has issued publications, held conferences and retreats, and developed other centers and educational endeavors, such as the Naropa Institute. Following the founder's death in 1987, the movement was embroiled in a great deal of controversy during the period of its second leader, Ösel Tendzin (née Thomas Rich), and many left the movement. After his death, Sawanj Ösel Mukto, son of Trungpa, became the leader in 1990, ending the earlier turmoil.

Zen traditions have been another Japanese Buddhist stream in American life since the participation of a Zen teacher at the World Parliament of Religions in Chicago in 1893. In this form, rather than groups of immigrants, we note more characteristically the interaction of Japanese teachers and American pupils. With the common attention to awareness and to meditative practice, and with representation of both Rinzai and Soto teaching, there has been a great deal of variety in the Zen Centers. Prominent have been New York's First Zen Institute of America (1930) and centers in Rochester, New York; Los Angeles; San Francisco; Cambridge, Massachusetts; and Honolulu. There are also many others in communities of smaller size and some groups that are not of Japanese inspiration, such as the Chinese Zen Ch'an Meditation Center in Elmhurst, New York, and the Buddhist Vihara Society of Washington, D.C., which traces its origins to Sri Lanka.

CHRISTADELPHIAN

John Thomas came to the United States from England in 1844. He joined the Disciples of Christ, but later became convinced that its doctrine made it the apostate church predicted by Scripture and that many more important Bible doctrines were being neglected. He left the Disciples to organize a number of societies, which under his leadership began to preach the need for a return to primitive Christianity. Loosely organized, those societies bore no name until the outbreak of the Civil War, when their members' doctrine of nonresistance forced them to adopt a name. They chose Christadelphian, or Brethren of Christ.

Christadelphians are both Unitarian and Adventist in theology. They reject belief in the devil, maintaining that the Scriptures teach that Christ is not God the Son, but the Son of God—not preexistent, but born of Mary by the Holy Spirit. Humankind is mortal by nature, and Christ is the only means of salvation. Eternal life comes only to the righteous. Strong millenarians, they believe that Christ will come shortly to reward with immortality those who are worthy and destroy the wicked; that he will take David's throne in Jerusalem; and that the faithful will be gathered and the world will be ruled from Jerusalem for a thousand years. They hold the Bible to be the inspired Word of God, inerrant in its original text.

The church is congregational in policy; local organizations are known not as churches but as ecclesias. Membership is by profession of faith and immersion. There are no paid or ordained ministers in the usual sense; each ecclesia elects serving brethren, among whom are managing brethren, presiding brethren, and lecturing brethren. Women take no part in public speech or prayer, though all vote equally in the affairs of the ecclesia. Christadelphians do not vote in civil elections or participate in war, and they refuse to accept public office. There are no associations or conventions, but there are fraternal gatherings for spiritual inspiration. Many meetings are held in rented halls, schools, or private homes, though a number of ecclesias have their own buildings.

Home-missions work is local, usually in the form of lectures and instruction in Christadelphian doctrine and righteous living. The organization maintains an Action Society and is active in publishing and in supporting eleemosynary institutions. Foreign missions and ecclesias are found in 60 countries. Summer Bible schools are held in several states. Found in 42 states from coast to coast, this "loosely organized" movement has reported 15,800 members in about 850 ecclesias. Larger numbers are located in Great Britain, New Zealand, Australia, Canada, and Germany.

CHRISTIAN AND MISSIONARY ALLIANCE, THE

This body originated in 1882 under the leadership of A. B. Simpson, a Presbyterian minister in New York City, who left that church to carry on independent evangelistic work. Organized in 1887, the group was originally two societies—the Christian Alliance for home missions work and the Evangelical Missionary Alliance for work abroad. The two bodies merged in 1897, forming the present Christian and Missionary Alliance. At the time of the founding of the Assemblies of God, about one-tenth of that constituency resulted from the departure of about one-tenth of the membership of the

Christian and Missionary Alliance. The two groups have a closely interwoven history, are doctrinally similar, and maintain ties of fellowship. Strongly evangelical, the Alliance believes in the inspiration and inerrancy of the Bible, the atoning work of Christ, the reality of supernatural religious experience, sanctification, and the premillennial return of Jesus Christ. It stresses the centrality of Christ as Savior, Sanctifier, Healer, and coming King; it also has a statement of faith (1965, 1966, 1974).

The Alliance has ministries in 54 nations. In the U.S. and Puerto Rico, work is carried on in 21 geographic and 10 intercultural districts. Ethnic groups include Cambodian, Dega, Haitian, Hmong, Jewish, Korean, Laotian, Native American, Spanish, and Vietnamese. In all districts, there are 1,923 churches fully or partially organized, with an inclusive membership of 289,391. Each church or group is engaged in missionary and evangelical activities. An overall conference of delegates, the General Council, meets annually in various cities in the U.S.

The Christian and Missionary Alliance in Canada became autonomous in 1980 but continues to send and support overseas missionaries jointly with the U.S. Alliance.

Foreign missions work is carried on in Latin America, Africa, Asia, the Pacific Islands, the Middle East, Europe, Australia, and New Zealand. There are 1,190 Alliance missionaries and 14,839 national pastors and workers ministering in 13,961 churches in those countries. Overseas Alliance membership is over 1.9 million, giving the denomination a larger constituency abroad than at home.

CHRISTIAN CATHOLIC CHURCH

The Christian Catholic Church (*catholic* in the sense of "universal," a church home for all true Christians) was formally organized before 1896 by John Alexander Dowie, a Congregational preacher educated in Scotland and ordained in Australia. Dowie also founded Zion City, Illinois, and when the city was settled in 1901, it became headquarters for the new church. Businesses and industries were developed, all controlled and governed by a theocracy of which Dowie was general overseer. He had extensive plans for educational and cultural projects; he criticized the injustices of capitalism and the excesses of labor leaders, alcoholic beverages, tobacco, medicine, the medical profession, secret lodges, and the press. He was also a tireless advocate of racial equality and integration.

Theologically, the Christian Catholic Church (CCC) is rooted in evangelical orthodoxy; it describes itself as an evangelical Protestant church. The Scriptures are accepted as the rule of faith and practice. Other doctrines call for the necessity of repentance from sin and personal trust in Christ for salvation, baptism by triune immersion, the second coming of Christ, and tithing as a practical method of Christian stewardship. Dowie emphasized the healing of disease through prayer, and his success in healing led to the establishment of a tabernacle and "divine healing rooms," first in Chicago and later in Zion City.

Several years after the church was located at Zion, Dowie claimed to be Elijah the Restorer. He maintained leadership of the group until 1906, when he was deposed and followed successively by Wilbur Glen Voliva, Michael J. Mintern, Carl W. Lee, and, currently, Roger W. Ottersen.

At first an exclusively religious community, Zion City still contains a strong Christian Catholic Church, but independent businesses have been welcomed, and many other churches are at work there. Since 1900 the church has sponsored a Zion Conservatory of Music, which today has an enrollment of 240. Begun in 1935, its annual passion play, with a cast of more than 200, has attracted thousands of visitors.

Branches of the church have been established in Michigan City, Indiana; Phoenix, Arizona; Lindenhurst, Illinois; Tonelea, Arizona; and Toronto, Canada. Missionary work is conducted in Japan, Australia, Israel, the Philippines, Guyana, Malawi, and South Africa. In addition, the church supports missionaries under InterVarsity, Campus Crusade, the Navigators, T.E.A.M., the Africa Evangelical Fellowship, and Wycliffe. In Jamaica it cooperates with the Missionary Church. It is a denominational member of the National Association of Evangelicals.

A quarterly publication, *Leaves of Healing,* is published for worldwide circulation. With five places of worship in the U.S., the church has membership of 2,500.

CHRISTIAN CHURCH, THE
(THE STONE-CAMPBELL MOVEMENT)

The Restoration impulse, to recover the message or the organization or the mission (any or all), is at least as old as the Protestant Reformation. In nineteenth-century America, however, this impulse became the sole defining mark of several Protestant movements. Those associated with Barton W. Stone and the Campbells, Thomas the father and Alexander the son, epitomized this determination. This indigenous movement traced some of its heritage to Baptists and

Presbyterians. But these leaders and their followers glimpsed this vision independently. By 1832 the "Stoneites" and the "Campbellites" had come together. Very soon thereafter, however, differences arose and, over time, three distinct fellowships emerged. Devoted in varying ways to the Restoration ideal, these continue to be influential.

CHRISTIAN CHURCH (DISCIPLES OF CHRIST)

Among the dozen largest religious groups in the United States, the Christian Church (Disciples of Christ) might be called the most American; it was born on the nineteenth-century American frontier out of a deep concern for Christian unity. All four pioneers—Barton Stone, Thomas and Alexander Campbell, and Walter Scott—were from Presbyterian backgrounds.

Barton Stone believed that Christians could and should unite on the basis of simple faith in Christ and that the divisive doctrines and practices of denominationalism should be abolished. His church at Cane Ridge, Kentucky, became the center of the famous Kentucky Revival; but Stone came out of that movement convinced that salvation has little to do with church affiliation and that "deeds are more important than creeds." Disciplinary action was brought against him and against his followers in the established churches; they withdrew from these churches, reorganized under the name Christian, and spread across Kentucky, Ohio, and the central states.

Thomas Campbell served as a clergyman in the Seceder branch of the Presbyterian Church in northern Ireland; in 1807 he settled in a church in western Pennsylvania, where he advocated closer relations with all Christians, appealed to the Bible as the basis of faith, and practiced open Communion. Censured, he led the formation of the Christian Association of Washington County, Pennsylvania, and published a Declaration and Address, which was to become the Magna Charta of the Christian Church (Disciples of Christ). In that declaration, he argued that "schism, or uncharitable divisions" in the church were "anti-Christian, anti-Scriptural, and anti-natural," and "productive of confusion and every evil work." The church and church membership should be based solely upon the belief and practices of New Testament Christianity; the articles of faith and holiness "expressly revealed in the Word of God" were quite enough, without adding human opinions or creedal inventions.

Thomas Campbell's son, Alexander Campbell, left a Seceder church in Scotland to join his father in Pennsylvania in 1810. He enlarged upon the concept that every church should be autonomous and completely independent—that creeds, clerical titles, authority, and privilege had no justification in Scripture; that the Lord's Supper should be served at every Sunday service; and that baptism should be by immersion for adult believers (persons old enough to understand the meaning of the ordinance). He argued eloquently for Christian union and freedom of individual faith, and he welcomed to his independent church at Brush Run, Pennsylvania, all who came with simple faith in Christ as the Son of God and the Messiah. He met the same opposition his father had met and, with his congregation, joined an association of Particular Baptists, only to separate from that body in 1830.

Barton Stone used the word *Christian* to designate his group, feeling that all of God's children should be known so. Campbell used the word *Disciples*. In 1832, the Christians and the Disciples merged; both names are still used, but usually and officially, the body is known today as the Christian Church (Disciples of Christ).

Early in the movement, Walter Scott popularized the term *restoration,* meaning the restoration of New Testament pattern and practice. Like Stone, Scott was suspicious of the values of the current revivalistic frenzies; he related faith more to the mind than to emotions—it was not a matter of emotional experience, but the intellectual acceptance of the truth of Christ's Messiahship. He stressed the importance of that faith, together with repentance of sin and baptism by immersion.

The first national convention of the Disciples and the first missionary society (American Christian Missionary Society) were organized in 1849; state conventions and societies had begun to meet in 1839. The group grew rapidly during and following the Civil War period, especially in Ohio, Indiana, Illinois, Tennessee, and Missouri, in spite of conflict over any emphasis on denominationalism or ecclesiastical organization. The differences between conservatives and progressives became acute in such matters as the organization of missionary societies and instrumental music in the churches; the Churches of Christ separated from the Disciples during that debate.

In matters of belief, conservative and progressive attitudes were and still are important, and the church allows for variance of opinion and complete freedom in interpretation, stemming from the conviction that there is no creed but Christ and no saving doctrines save those of the New Testament. It could be said that the Disciples are God-centered, Christ-centered, and Bible-centered; beyond that, faith is a matter of individual conviction, but there are areas of general agreement and acceptance. The Disciples are firm in their belief in immortality but do not accept the doctrine of original sin; they hold that all people are of a sinful nature until redeemed by the sacrifice of Christ; they are not concerned with speculation about the Trinity and the nature of a triune God. They have no catechism and no set orders of worship. Faith in Christ as Lord is the only requirement. For more than a century Disciples were strictly congregational in polity—a loosely bound association of local churches. But increasingly it was felt that such an arrangement, with overlapping boards and agencies and no representative voice, needed restructuring in the interests of efficiency and economy. Following a seven-year study and discussion led by a 130-member commission, a whole new design of organization was adopted at Kansas City in 1968. Under the new plan, the whole church works under a "representative government" referred to as "three manifestations"—local, regional, and general.

The local church is still the basic unit. All congregations listed in the latest yearbook are accepted as congregations. Each congregation manages its own affairs, has its own charter and bylaws, owns and controls its property, calls its ministers, establishes its own budgets and financial policies, and has voting representatives in regional and national assemblies.

The congregations are grouped in 36 regions, organized to provide help, counsel, and pastoral care to members, ministers, and congregations. Each region organizes its own boards, departments, and committees. Within policies developed by the general assembly, the regions certify the standing of ministers and provide counsel in such matters as ordination, licensing, location and installation of ministers, and the establishment or dissolution of pastoral relationships. Regions have regional ministers as their administrative leaders.

The general assembly is made up of voting and nonvoting representatives from the local churches and regions, plus ministers and a few ex officio members, the chief officers of institutions and unit boards, and members of the general board. The assembly acts upon proposed programs, policies, reports and resolutions sent up through the general board and elects officers of the church and half the members of the general board. The regions elect the other half.

The general board meets annually, processes business going to the assembly, recommends policies, reviews the total program of the church, elects or confirms the governing bodies of the various administrative units, and elects the committees of the general assembly and the members of an administrative committee. One-third of general board members are ministers; the remainder are laypersons.

The administrative committee of the general board is made up of 40 members elected by the board; officers of the church are ex officio members. Meeting at least twice a year, it provides long-range planning, implements policies, and promotes the causes and units of the church.

Officers of the church are of two classes—voluntary (nonsalaried) and salaried. There is a volunteer moderator, two vice-moderators, and a salaried general minister and president.

Membership continues to be largest along a crescent from Pittsburgh to San Antonio. There are now 1,022,926 members in 4,031 churches in the U.S.; 37 congregations with 4,209 members in Canada. There are 35 colleges, seminaries, undergraduate schools of religion, and foundations; 13 specialized services for children, youth, and the developmentally disabled; 54 health and housing centers for older adults; and a facility for family housing.

The Disciples are represented in the National Council of Churches, the World Council of Churches, and the Consultation on Church Union. The headquarters of a World Convention of Churches of Christ is in Nashville, Tennessee.

CHRISTIAN CHURCHES AND CHURCHES OF CHRIST

These independent churches do not consider themselves a denomination, having no formal organization other than that of each local congregation and parachurch agencies formed to meet specific needs, such as homes for the aged, for needy children, or particular missions.

These churches arose in a nineteenth-century reformation led by Alexander Campbell and others who endeavored to recapture the unity and simplicity of the first-century church. The Christian Church (Disciples of Christ) and the noninstrumental Churches of Christ also came from this "Restoration Movement."

Near the turn of the century, the Churches of Christ left over the music issue. In the 1920s many Christian Churches/Churches of Christ separated from the Disciples over what they felt was the Disciples' liberalism.

Christian Churches/Churches of Christ stress the divinity of Christ, the authority of the Bible, the indwelling of the Holy Spirit for the believer, future reward or punishment, and God as a loving, prayer-answering deity. They baptize by immersion and observe the Lord's Supper in open Communion every Sunday.

The total U.S. membership of Christian Churches/Churches of Christ is estimated to be 1,200,000. More than 15 congregations in this fellowship average a Sunday morning attendance exceeding 1,000. The largest of these is Southeast Christian Church, Louisville, Kentucky, with an attendance in excess of 7,500 each Sunday.

The group supports 30 liberal arts colleges, mostly preacher-training schools. Standard Publishing, in Cincinnati, Ohio, is identified with this group as well.

The North American Christian Convention, an annual preaching and teaching assembly, draws as many as 20,000 attendees to an annual nondelegate gathering each July. Very active in foreign missions, these churches sponsor a National Missionary Convention that meets each fall, with an attendance of between 3,000 and 5,000.

CHURCHES OF CHRIST

The largest of the three principal bodies in the American restoration movement, Churches of Christ are located throughout the nation but are concentrated in the South and Southwest. Because this is not a denomination but a fellowship with no central headquarters, record keeping is very difficult. Recent efforts show the membership to be about 1,400,000 in nearly 13,000 churches.

A distinctive plea for unity—a unity that is Bible-based—lies at the heart of the Churches of Christ. It is believed that the Bible is "the beginning place," in and through which God-fearing people can achieve spiritual oneness—to "speak where the Bible speaks and to be silent where the Bible is silent" in all matters pertaining to faith and morals. Consequently, members recognize no other written creed or confession of faith. In all religious matters, there must be a "thus said the Lord."

The churches are related to the restoration movement—the work and thinking of James O'Kelly in Virginia, Abner Jones and Elias Smith in New England, Barton Stone in Kentucky, and Thomas and Alexander Campbell in West Virginia (see CHRISTIAN CHURCH [DISCIPLES OF CHRIST]). These four movements, all once completely independent, eventually became one strong religious stream because of their common purpose and plea.

The leaders among the Churches of Christ in the nineteenth century were more conservative than their counterparts among the Disciples of Christ. Stressing a strict adherence to the New Testament pattern of worship and church organization, they refused to join any intercongregational organization such as a missionary society. Worship was simple, and they opposed the addition of instrumental music on the grounds that the New Testament did not authorize it and that the early church did not use it.

Around the beginning of the twentieth century, a recognition of differences between the conservative and more liberal wings of the restoration movements became evident, and in the 1906 census of religious bodies, Churches of Christ were listed separately for the first time. The groups claim to be nondenominational, with no headquarters, no governing bodies, and no clergy. They cooperate voluntarily in international radio programs sponsored by any congregation.

Today one of the outstanding features of Churches of Christ is their acceptance of the Bible as a true and completely adequate revelation. This basic concept has resulted in such practices as weekly observance of the Lord's Supper, baptism by immersion, *a cappella* singing, a vigorous prayer life, support of church needs through voluntary giving, and a program of preaching and teaching the Bible. This concept also explains the autonomy of local churches, governed by elders and deacons appointed under New Testament qualifications; dignified worship services; enthusiastic mission campaigns; and far-flung benevolence, all financed by local churches.

The scriptural doctrines usually classified as conservative are found in Churches of Christ: belief in the Father, the Son, and the Holy Ghost as members of one Godhead; the incarnation, virgin birth, and bodily resurrection of Christ; the universality of sin after the age of accountability, its only remedy the vicarious atonement of the Lord Jesus Christ. Strong emphasis is also laid on the church as the body and bride of Christ. A figurative, rather than literal, view is prevalent with reference to the book of Revelation. Membership is contingent upon an individual's faith in Jesus Christ as the only begotten Son of God, repentance, confession of faith, and baptism by immersion for the remission of sins. Church attendance is stressed.

Churches of Christ maintain that the final judgment of all religious groups is reserved unto the Lord. This view, however, still allows for a vigorous evangelism that finds unacceptable the doctrines, practices, names, titles, and creeds that have been grafted onto the original practice of Christianity.

Ministers are ordained rather than licensed, and they hold tenure in their pulpits under mutual agreement with the elders of the churches in which they preach. Their authority is moral rather than arbitrary, the actual government of the church being vested in its elders.

A vigorous missionary program is carried on in 75 nations outside the U.S., and in recent years a strong movement to extend the influence of the church in the Northeastern states has developed. Counting native workers on the foreign field and mission activities within the U.S., more than 1,000 missionaries or evangelists are supported by groups other than those to which they preach. Membership outside the U.S. approaches 1,600,000. A quota of chaplains is maintained in the U.S. Air Force and Army. Properties owned by the group exceed $2.5 billion in value. There are 21 colleges, including one in Japan and several in Europe; 70 secondary and elementary schools; 83 child-care facilities; and 46 senior citizen's facilities. The church publishes 117 periodicals, newspapers, and magazines. The oldest publication, *The Gospel Advocate*, has been published continually since the 1850s, except when it ceased during the Civil War due to lack of mail delivery. Since the status of these institutions is unofficial, and none is authorized to speak for the entire church, their conformity in ideas and teachings is all the more remarkable.

Many churches have published evangelical articles in a number of national magazines; some offer correspondence courses. The "Herald of Truth" radio and television program, sponsored by the Highland Church of Christ in Abilene, Texas and supported by hundreds of other churches and individuals throughout the country, has nationwide coverage. The "Amazing Grace Bible Class," conducted by Dr. Ira North until his death and now by Steve Flatt, is sponsored by the Madison, Tennessee, Church of Christ, the largest of the churches. The program is seen and heard over more than 100 television and radio stations and the Armed Forces Network. It is broadcast to Russia and China by World Christian Broadcasting by way of a 100,000-watt short-wave station in Anchor Point, Alaska.

CHRISTIAN CHURCH OF NORTH AMERICA, GENERAL COUNCIL

Originally known as the Italian Christian Church, this body's first General Council was held in 1927 at Niagara Falls, New York. It was incorporated in 1948 at Pittsburgh, Pennsylvania, and is described as pentecostal but does not engage in "the excesses tolerated or practiced among some churches using the same name."

The movement recognizes two ordinances—baptism and the Lord's Supper. Its moral code is conservative, and its teaching is orthodox. Members are exhorted to pursue a dedicated life of personal holiness, setting an example for others. This body affirms the experiences of salvation and spirit baptism, but does not teach the doctrine of entire sanctification, positions that make it similar, but not identical, to those of the Assemblies of God. A conversative position is held in regard to marriage and divorce. The governmental form, by and large, is congregational in nature, but district and national agencies are referred to as presbyteries, led by overseers. Affiliated and associated foreign mission work is conducted in Peru, Chile, India, Italy, Brazil, France, Bolivia, Belgium, Malaysia, England, Germany, Uruguay, Ecuador, Barbados, Colombia, Paraguay, Argentina, Australia, Venezuela, Luxembourg, Switzerland, the Philippines, Guam, China, Haiti, Japan, Nepal, Spain, Africa, Canada, Austria, Jamaica, Okinawa, Zimbabwe, Guatemala, El Salvador, and the Ivory Coast. The group functions in cooperative fellowship with the Italian Pentecostal Church of Canada and the Evangelical Christian Churches (Assemblies of God in Italy); it is an affiliate member of the Pentecostal Fellowship of North America and the National Association of Evangelicals. Its membership stands at 13,500.

CHRISTIAN CONGREGATION, INC.

The philosophy and work of the Christian Congregation, formed in Indiana in 1887, revolve around the "new commandment" of John 13:34-35. The group is a fellowship of ministers and laypeople who seek a noncreedal, nonsectarian basis for union. It is pacifistic and opposes all sectarian strife, insisting that "the household of faith is not founded upon doctrinal agreement, creeds, church claims, names, or rites," but solely upon the relationship of the individual to God. The basis of Christian fellowship is love; the actual relation of Christians toward one another transcends all individual belief or personal opinion. Because of its teachings concerning the sanctity of life, the church condemns abortion, capital punishment, and all warfare. Independent Bible study is encouraged.

Churches and pastorates are now located in every state in the union; the church still remains strongest, however, in the areas where Barton Stone preached and the original Christian Congregation groups were located—Kentucky, the Carolinas, Virginia, Pennsylvania, Ohio, Indiana, and Texas. The greater part of the group's work is carried on in rural and mountain areas; in many respects it is identical with that of the Stone movement and his original Christian Church, although these congregations were established and already at work when that church was organized.

Polity is congregational. A general superintendent presides over a board of trustees; relations among the superintendent, the board, and the people are purely advisory. There are 110,716 members in 1,447 churches or local congregations.

CHRISTIAN UNION

Christian Union began as an attempt to draw all Christians into a consciousness of unity on a scriptural basis and to offer a larger unity in thought and worship. Rebuffed in attaining that goal, it has settled for being another organization among many; yet, it still emphasizes the spiritual unity of believers. Organized in 1864 at Columbus, Ohio, its announced purpose is "to promote fellowship among God's people, to put forth every effort to proclaim God's saving grace to the lost . . . and to declare the whole counsel of God for the edification of believers.

There is no one creed that binds members of the Union, but seven principles are stressed: the oneness of the church of Christ, Christ as the only head of the church, the Bible as the only rule of faith and practice, good fruits as the one condition of fellowship, Christian union without controversy, self-government by local churches and a cooperative spirit among churches, and avoidance of all partisan political preaching. Both men and women are ordained as ministers, and the ordinances include baptism—preferably by immersion— and the Lord's Supper.

While church government is congregational, a series of councils meet for fellowship and to conduct business that concerns the entire church. Local missionary work, conducted by state boards, is largely evangelistic; a general mission board oversees home and foreign missions. Missionaries are located in Africa, Mexico, Alaska, Liberia, and Colombia. In June 1977, 20 churches with 3,500 members now called the Christian Union of Nigeria were received as an associate council of the church.

A college, Christian Union School of the Bible, is located at Greenfield, Ohio; an extension school is administered through its staff. One periodical, *The Christian Union Witness,* is published monthly at Excelsior Springs, Missouri. There are 114 churches, the majority in Ohio, with 6,000 members.

CHURCH OF CHRIST (HOLINESS) U.S.A.

A Baptist preacher in Alabama and Mississippi, C. P. Jones, seeking a new church and faith that would make him "one of wisdom's true sons . . . like Abraham, a friend of God," founded this church in 1894. Today it reports over 10,000 members in 170 churches. This body retained its Holiness emphasis when other early black churches moved into Pentecostalism.

Doctrinally, Church of Christ (Holiness) U.S.A. emphasizes original sin, the Holy Ghost as an indispensable gift for every believer, and Christ's atonement and second coming. There are two sacraments: baptism and the Lord's Supper. Foot washing and divine healing are employed as aids to the growth of spiritual life. The church is episcopal in government, with final authority vested in a biennial convention. There are seven dioceses, each under a bishop's charge; a district convention made up of elders, ministers, and local lay representatives meets semiannually.

Missionary work is conducted in the U.S. and in Liberia and Nigeria. The church supports the Christ Missionary and Industrial College at Jackson, Mississippi, and a national publishing house in Chicago.

CHURCH OF CHRIST, SCIENTIST

At Lynn, Massachusetts, in 1866, after reading the account of Christ's healing of a man with a form of palsy (Matt. 9:1-8), Mary Baker Eddy recovered almost instantly from a severe injury. Profoundly religious and a lifelong student of mental and spiritual causation, she came to attribute the cause to God and to regard God as the divine Mind as well as infinite Love. From these roots came Christian Science and the Church of Christ, Scientist.

Generally described as "a religious teaching and practice based on the words and works of Christ Jesus," Christian Science was regarded by Eddy as "the scientific system of divine healing," the "law of God, the law of good, interpreting and demonstrating the divine Principle and rule of universal harmony"; she believed "the Principle of all harmonious Mind-action to be God." Eddy included most of these definitions and descriptions in *Science and Health with Key to the Scriptures*. This volume and the Bible have become the twofold textbook of Christian Science.

Like many other religious leaders and pioneers, Eddy hoped to work through existing churches. She did not plan to create another denomination, but organization became necessary as interest in the movement spread. Under her direction, the Church of Christ, Scientist, was established at Boston in 1879. In 1892 she formed the present worldwide organization, the First Church of Christ, Scientist, and its branch churches and societies. That church in Boston is frequently referred to as the mother church.

Applied not only to the healing of sickness but also to the problems of life generally, the tenets and doctrines of Christian Science are often confusing to others and call for careful explanation. They begin with the conviction that God is the only might, or Mind; God is "All-in-all," the "divine Principle of all that really is," "the all-knowing, all-seeing, all-acting, all-wise, all-loving, and eternal; Principle; Mind; Soul; Spirit; Life; Truth; Love; all substance; intelligence." The inspired Word of the Bible is accepted as "sufficient guide to eternal Life." Another tenet states: "We acknowledge and adore one supreme and infinite God. We acknowledge His Son, one Christ; the Holy Ghost or divine Comforter; and man in God's image and likeness." Jesus is known to Christian Scientists as Master, or Way-shower. They accept his virgin birth and his atoning mission "as the evidence of divine, efficacious Love, unfolding man's unity with God through Christ Jesus the Way-shower." He was "endowed with . . . the divine Spirit, without measure." Humankind "is saved through Christ, through Truth, Life, and Love as demonstrated by the Galilean Prophet in healing the sick and overcoming sin and death." The crucifixion and resurrection of Jesus are held as serving "to uplift faith to understand eternal Life, even the allness of Soul, Spirit, and the nothingness of matter."

This "allness" of Spirit and "nothingness of matter" involves the basic teaching of Christian Science concerning reality. As *Science and Health* explains:

> All reality is in God and His creation, harmonious and eternal. That which He creates is good, and He makes all that is made. Therefore the only reality of sin, sickness, or death is the awful fact that unrealities seem real to human, erring belief, until God strips off their disguise. They are not true, because they are not of God.

God forgives sin through destroying it with "the spiritual understanding that casts out evil as unreal." The punishment for sin, however, lasts as long as one's belief in sin endures.

It is a mistake to believe that followers of Christian Science *ignore* what they consider "unreal"; rather, they seek to forsake and overcome error and evil through Christian discipleship, prayer, and progressive spiritual understanding of God's allness and goodness, and strive to see the spiritual "body," created in God's likeness, as the only real body. Error is "a supposition that pleasure and pain, that intelligence, substance, life, are existent in matter. . . . It is that which seemeth to be and is not." As Eddy stated (and this point is fundamental to Christian Science beliefs):

> If we would open their prison doors for the sick, we must first learn to bind up the brokenhearted. If we would heal by the Spirit, we must not hide the talent of spiritual healing under the napkin of its form, nor bury the *morale* of Christian Science in the grave-clothes of its letter. The tender word and Christian encouragement of an invalid, pitiful patience with his fears and the removal of them are better than hecatombs of gushing theories, stereotypes, borrowed

speeches and the doling of arguments, which are but so many parodies on legitimate Christian Science, aflame with divine Love.

She further wrote, "Nothing aside from the spiritualization—yea, the highest Christianization—of thought and desire, can give the true perception of God and Christian Science, that results in health, happiness, and holiness." Christian Scientists normally rely wholly on the power of God for healing rather than on medical treatment. There is no church pressure involved, however, nor does the church abandon those who choose a different way.

Certain terms are important in the exposition of Christian Science. *Animal magnetism* is the specific term for the hypnotic error of belief in a mind and power apart from God (typified by the dragon in the apocalypse; Jesus as the Lamb of God exemplifies the conquering of this sin in every form). Healing is not miraculous, but divinely natural; disease is understood to be basically a mental concept that can be dispelled by active Christian discipleship, spiritual regeneration, and application of the truths to which Jesus bore witness. Heaven is not a locality but "harmony; the reign of Spirit; government by divine Principle; spirituality; bliss, the atmosphere of Soul." Hell is "mortal belief; error; lust; remorse; hatred; revenge; sin; sickness; death; suffering and self-destruction; self-imposed agony; effects of sin; that which 'worketh abomination or maketh a lie.' " Mortal mind is "the flesh opposed to Spirit, the human mind and evil in contradistinction to the divine Mind." Prayer is "an absolute faith that all things are possible to God—a spiritual understanding of Him, an unselfed love." Baptism is not observed as a traditional ceremony, but is held to be a continuing individual spiritual experience, "a purification from all error."

The approximately 2,400 local Churches of Christ, Scientist, as branches of the mother church, are organized under the laws of the states or countries in which they exist. They enjoy their own forms of democratic government within the general framework of bylaws laid down by Eddy in the *Manual of the Mother Church*, which also provides for Christian Science college organizations. Reading Rooms open to the general public are maintained by all churches. The affairs of the mother church are administered by the Christian Science Board of Directors, which elects a president, First and Second Readers, a clerk, and a treasurer. The Board of Directors is a self-perpetuating body that elects all other officers of the church annually, with the exception of Readers, who are elected by the board for a term of three years.

Important in the Christian Science movement are the Readers, teachers, and practitioners. There are two readers in each branch church, usually a man and a woman elected by the church members; in all services on Sundays and Thanksgiving Day, they read alternately from the Bible and from *Science and Health.* The Lesson-Sermons of Sunday services are prepared by a committee and issued quarterly by the Christian Science Publishing Society. This system is followed by all Christian Science churches throughout the world. A midweek meeting, conducted by the first Reader alone, features testimonies of healing from sin and sickness.

Practitioners devote their full time to healing and are listed in a directory in the monthly *Christian Science Journal.* A board of education consists of three members—a president, a vice president, and a teacher of Christian Science. Under the supervision of this board, a Normal class is held once every three years. Teachers are duly authorized by certificates granted by the board to form classes. One class of not more than 30 pupils is instructed by each teacher annually.

A board of lectureship consists of about 60 members, appointed annually by the Board of Directors. At the invitation of branch churches, free public lectures are given by these members all over the world. A Committee on Publication serves as an ecumenical and informational office, representing the denomination to the press and public. The Christian Science Publishing Society carries on broadcasting activities and publishes much well-written literature, including the *Christian Science Sentinel, The Christian Science Journal, Christian Science Quarterly—Bible Lessons, the Herald of Christian Science* in twelve languages and Braille, and *The Christian Science Monitor.* The *Monitor* is acknowledged by journalists to be one of the finest newspapers in the world. A number of nursing homes for members who rely wholly on spiritual means for healing are independently maintained throughout the world.

At a time when its members were frequently citing the rapid growth of the denomination, Eddy ruled that membership statistics should not be made available for publication, believing that the number of members is no indication of true spiritual growth. Today Christian Science churches have been established in some 70 countries, with the largest concentrations in English- and German-speaking areas. Church membership appears to have declined in the last several decades, reflecting a trend among some other Protestant denominations, though there has been growth in Third World areas. Also, as is the case with probably no other church in America, the number of people studying Christian Science and attending its services, but not yet admitted to full membership, quite probably exceeds the number who have been admitted.

CHURCH OF GOD

More a widely claimed title than an actual family, Church of God is the "denominational" name of over 200 conservative Protestant groups, all of which seize upon the apostle Paul's reference to the "church of God." Some pursue it as an ambition; others exalt it as a claim. In all cases, they are emphatically devoted to the Bible.

They also affirm the nearness of God's spiritual power—the power to generate holiness and a life of righteousness, and often to equip believers with the gift of speaking in tongues. In the latter case, miracles are not exceptional but readily available, and for some groups their occurrence is requisite to spiritual authenticity. From their origins and for many decades, these people were separatists who denounced accommodation to "the world." While as dedicated and Spirit-led as ever, most have tempered their resistance to worldly fashions and have become quite modern, especially in the ways they construct their organizational life.

Several Church of God bodies trace their roots to western North Carolina and eastern Tennessee during the years just before and after 1900. In particular, the Tomlinson family and Cleveland, a town in southeast Tennessee, are focal points for these historically related bodies. Some of those treated here are the Church of God (Cleveland, Tennessee); the Church of God of Prophecy; The Church of God (Huntsville, Alabama); and The (Original) Church of God, Inc. For all the bodies that grew out of this southern Appalachian Holiness revival, restoration of the "church of God" mentioned in the New Testament is the key concern. All of these are pentecostal—that is, they practice speaking in tongues—and that same practice characterizes the black bodies: Church of God in Christ and Church of God in Christ (International).

But the Church of God (Anderson, Indiana) subscribes to Holiness teaching without being pentecostal. Moreover, its history is totally unrelated to the southern Appalachian developments; it is a predominantly Midwestern denomination. These illustrations reveal that the diversity is great and that careful attention must be paid to specific titles by anyone seeking information.

CHURCH OF GOD, THE (HUNTSVILLE, ALABAMA)

This body is rooted in the early Holiness revival of the Appalachian South. It calls itself simply the Church of God, although the headquarters location of Huntsville, Alabama, is sometimes added.

CHURCH OF GOD, INC., THE (ORIGINAL)

When A. J. Tomlinson died in 1943, his Cleveland, Tennessee, group was divided between his two sons, Milton A. Tomlinson, who remained in Cleveland as head of the Tomlinson Church of God, and Homer A. Tomlinson, who organized his followers under the name "Church of God" and established his headquarters in Queens Village, New York. Bishop Voy M. Bullen was appointed as his successor as General Overseer with Witnesses in 1956. Upon Bishop Homer's death in 1968, the headquarters was moved to Huntsville, a location much closer to the majority of the congregations. Its membership was reported at 75,890 in 1978.

The Huntsville group shares much of the doctrine and history of the Tomlinson-Cleveland movement. It does play heavy emphasis on the fulfillment of Scripture "for the last days" and on preparation for the return of Christ. It continues to make much of A. J. Tomlinson's commission to his son, Bishop Homer, to plant the church's flag in all the nations of the world. This conviction has led to the establishment of a world headquarters in Jerusalem; Israel is to be the center of the reestablished kingdom of God. Central to the body's mission is the belief that it holds the keys to bring that kingdom on earth. Saints are to be elected and placed in the governments of nations to bring in the kingdom. Its this-worldly theocratic program distinguishes it from other groups in the movement, all of which are premillennial—that is, they view the kingdom as coming upon the return of Christ. The Huntsville church believes the kingdom of God is here now.

CHURCH OF GOD, INC., THE (ORIGINAL)

This church was organized in Tennessee in 1886 under the name Church of God after a difference of opinion in regard to doctrine and teaching brought about a split among the followers of Richard G. Spurling. The faction that adhered to the original doctrines added the word *Original* and incorporated in 1922.

The church believes in the "whole Bible, rightly divided"; repentance, justification, and regeneration as defined by Martin Luther; sanctification as defined by John Wesley; divine healing; the second coming of Christ; and eternal life for the righteous and eternal punishment for the wicked. Christian fruits alone stand as evidence of faithful Christian living; creeds that bind the conscience are considered unscriptural. It believes in "filling with the Holy Spirit, with the Bible evidence of speaking with tongues as the Spirit gives utterance." Ordinances include baptism by immersion, the Lord's tithing, free-will offerings, the Lord's Supper, and foot washing.

Local churches, following the apostolic pattern, take local names, such as "Church of God at Corinth." Each local church is self-governing. The church recognizes the New Testament orders of ministers, apostles, deacons, exhorters, evangelists, bishops, and teachers, as given in Ephesians 4:11-14. A general convention meets annually; a general office, convention center building, publishing house, and denominational headquarters are at Chattanooga, Tennessee. There are 70 churches, with about 20,000 members.

CHURCH OF GOD (ANDERSON, INDIANA)

The Church of God headquartered at Anderson, Indiana, began in 1880 as a movement within existing churches. It prefers that its name be accepted in an inclusive, rather than a denominational, sense and is actually a movement in the direction of Christian unity and reestablishment of the New Testament standard of faith and life. The founders believed that the church at large was too restricted and overburdened with organization and ecclesiasticism; it should be "more directly under the rule of God."

Doctrine in this church includes belief in the divine inspiration of the Scriptures; forgiveness of sin through the atonement of Christ and repentance of the believer; the experience of holiness; the personal return of Christ, unconnected with any millennial reign; the kingdom of God as established here and now; final judgment; resurrection of the dead; reward of the righteous; and punishment of the wicked.

Baptism is by immersion. Members of this church also practice foot washing and observe the Lord's Supper, but not as conditions of fellowship. They believe the church to be the Body of Christ, made up of all Christians, and that all Christians are one in Christ. The confusion of sects and denominations, however, is an obstacle to this unity. God desires restoration of the New Testament ideal in the church—a restoration based on spiritual experience, not on creedal agreement.

There are 214,743 reported members, with 324,243 additional adherents in other nations. They are governed by a congregational system. While they preach the idea that God governs the church, they agree that human instrumentality is quite necessary. Membership is not on the basis of "joining," hence no formal records are kept. Ministers meet in voluntary state and regional conventions, which are chiefly advisory. The general assembly meets in connection with the annual international convention held at Anderson.

The Church of God (Anderson, Indiana) is not related historically to the several Church of God bodies rooted in the Holiness revival of Tennessee and the Carolinas in the late nineteenth century; although it shares their Holiness commitment, it is not pentecostal. Its largest membership concentrations are in the Midwest states, the Pacific Coast states, and western Pennsylvania. It supports Anderson University and School of Theology, two other liberal arts colleges, and one Bible college. Its growth overseas is rapid; in 1993, the church had grown to include believers in 83 countries, considerably more than in the U.S.

CHURCH OF GOD (CLEVELAND, TENNESSEE)

On August 19, 1886, in Monroe County, Tennessee, a new Christian fellowship came into being. First known as the Christian Union, it numbered eight members and was headed by Richard G. Spurling, a Baptist minister. Spurling had been led to the Bible to stem the tide of the church's spiritual indifference, formality, and accommodation to modern culture. With the formation of the group, a major Holiness revival was born. In fact, the name the Holiness Church was adopted in 1902.

The next year, A. J. Tomlinson, an American Bible Society colporteur from Indiana who had attended Bible college in Cincinnati, joined the church and in 1909 was elected general overseer. The body grew and matured in the succeeding years, despite some objections to its noisy services, since the members spoke in tongues. A critical juncture in 1923 resulted from the concern over the personal role of A. J. Tomlinson and, more important, the nature of the church's government and the leader's authority. Tomlinson's alleged misapportion of funds created a stir, but the disruption centered on the issue of theocratic government. What was the relative authority of the overseer and other leaders of the church?

The majority—those with whom the Church of God (Cleveland, Tennessee) is continuous—rejected Tomlinson's leadership and went on its way under F. J. Lee as overseer. The others continued to regard Tomlinson as general overseer and formed the body known today as Church of God of Prophecy. The Church of God (Cleveland, Tennessee) remains larger, with 1992 membership in the U.S. reported as 671,479 and a worldwide constituency of 2,720,000, especially in Central America, the Caribbean islands, South Africa, and Indonesia.

Its major doctrines blend many orthodox Protestant themes with those that are specifically pentecostal: justification by faith, sanctification, baptism of the Holy Spirit, tongue speaking, the need to be born again, fruitfulness in Christian living, and a strong interest in the premillennial second coming of Christ. It professes belief in reliance on the Bible "as a whole rightly divided rather than upon any

111

written creed." At the same time, it is thoroughly Arminian (believing in human free will). It stresses pentecostal and Holiness tenets; practices divine healing; condemns the use of alcohol and tobacco; opposes membership in secret societies; and accepts baptism, the Lord's Supper, and foot washing as ordinances.

The Church of God elects its own officers and holds state conventions and a biennial general assembly. It operates Lee College, the Church of God School of Theology, three Bible schools, and a preparatory school. Its foreign missions enterprise is extensive.

CHURCH OF GOD (SEVENTH DAY)

The Church of God (Seventh Day) grew out of the Adventist movement that developed in the first half of the nineteenth century. The church separated from other sabbath-keeping Adventists over the issue of the inspiration of E. G. White's visions, taking exception to endorsement of those visions. The church began simultaneously and independently in Iowa and in Michigan in 1860. Several denominational designations were used in its early history, including Church of Christ, Church of Jesus Christ, and Church of God. The present name was chosen in 1884.

In 1888, the united body of the Church of God established a central office in Stanberry, Missouri. In 1933, owing in part to disparate views on polity and administration, the church divided into two groups. One continued to be headquartered in Stanberry; the other established headquarters in Salem, West Virginia. A merger attempt in 1949 saw some realignment of membership and the relocation of the Stanberry headquarters to Denver, Colorado. The Salem organization retained its administrative offices and uses "7th Day" rather than "Seventh Day" in its name. It regards as inappropriate the action of the Stanberry-Denver group in forming a new body.

Beliefs of the two bodies vary slightly. The Salem body embraces apostolic succession and places emphasis on "Biblical organization" in the context of the designation of "7, 12, and 70" as appropriate numbers in church organization. That position also presupposes identity of the physical Church of God (Seventh Day) as the "true church." The Denver body does not subscribe to that position.

Membership requirements in the Church of God (Seventh Day) are based on baptism by immersion, profession of faith, and consent to fellowship within the general membership. Doctrine in the Denver body is discussed and established by ministerial councils; policy, by the general membership in session. In 1987, an attempted merger with the General Council of Churches of God (Seventh Day) in Meridian, Idaho, failed.

The Salem body claims a membership in excess of 1,000 in seven churches. The Denver body claims a membership in a wide area between Michigan and Texas and on the Pacific Coast; U.S./Canadian membership is 6,178 in 135 churches; worldwide membership is more than 60,000. The national Denver organization supports Spring Vale Academy, a boarding high school in Michigan, and the Summit School of Theology in Denver.

CHURCH OF GOD AND SAINTS OF CHRIST

In 1896, William S. Crowdy, a black Baptist deacon in Lawrence, Kansas, who claimed visions from God, a divine commission to bring the truth of God to the world, and a prophetic endowment, founded the Church of God and Saints of Christ and became its first bishop. Today the church has a membership of 38,127 in 217 churches in the U.S., with additional churches in Africa and the West Indies.

Sometimes called Black Jews, members of this church celebrate such Jewish holy and feast days as they feel have biblical authority and support; they observe the sabbath on the seventh day, the Day of Atonement, and the Jewish New Year. They believe their church is built on the patriarchs and prophets of the Jewish tradition, and "Jesus the Anointed" is their chief cornerstone. They differentiate between prophetic Judaism, "which seeks to follow the living insight into the spiritual idea to its fullest implication," as opposed to legalistic Judaism. They accept the Decalogue as the standard of conduct for all humankind. Some traits of black nationalism are blended with Christian and Jewish teachings to make this body's teachings quite distinctive.

An executive bishop stands at the head of the church and of the Bishops' Council; there is a 12-member presbytery, the law-making body, and an ecclesiastical council made of evangelists and ministers; general and district officers, deacons, teachers, and missionaries work under these officials. Local churches are headed by overseers and divided into districts; each district has an appointed evangelist who assists the bishop of that district, who calls and presides over annual district conferences. A national business assembly and religious convocation called Passover are held annually, both under the guidance of the executive bishop. The church maintains a home for older adults, an orphans' home, and a school for primary grades.

CHURCH OF GOD BY FAITH, INC.

Organized in 1914 and chartered in 1923 at Alachua, Florida, this group consists of 167 churches scattered throughout Florida, Georgia, Alabama, Ohio, Texas, South Carolina, Maryland, New Jersey, and New York. Its doctrine contains items of belief in regeneration and sanctification; baptism of the Holy Ghost; speaking in tongues; the Word of God as the Communion of the blood and body of Christ; one Lord, faith, and baptism; and the isolation of willful sinners from God and the church. Officers consist of a bishop and a board of five leading elders. A general assembly meets twice a year. A school that was maintained in Ocala, Florida, for several years is now used as a training institution for farmers. Membership is reported at 9,800.

CHURCH OF GOD IN CHRIST

Ministers C. H. Mason and C. P. Jones, rejected by Baptist groups in Arkansas for what was considered an overemphasis on Holiness, founded the Church of God in Christ (Memphis) in 1897. The name was divinely revealed to Mason, who stressed entire sanctification and had received in a revival the baptism of the Holy Spirit, together with "signs of speaking with tongues." His ardent preaching on these gifts and subjects aroused resentment among his followers, leading later to the founding of the Church of God in Christ (International).

The doctrine is trinitarian, stressing repentance, regeneration, justification, sanctification, speaking in tongues, and the gift of healing as evidence of the baptism of the Spirit. Holiness is considered a prerequisite to salvation; ordinances include baptism by immersion, the Lord's Supper, and foot washing.

Church organization is held to have its authority in Scripture; there are presiding, assistant presiding, and state bishops; district superintendents; pastors; evangelists; deacons; and departmental presidents. Missionaries are found in South Africa, Thailand, Jamaica, Haiti, Liberia, and on the west coast of Africa. A Saints Junior College is maintained at Lexington, Mississippi; there is a department of publications and a Sunday school publishing house to supply the denomination with literature. The C. H. Mason Theological Seminary is one unit in the Interdenominational Theological Center in Atlanta. There are 6,500,000 members in 12,186 churches worldwide. It is the largest Pentecostal denomination in the world today. The large increase in membership is attributed to rapid growth and the return of members from the Church of God in Christ (International).

CHURCH OF GOD IN CHRIST (INTERNATIONAL)

Fourteen bishops of the Church of God in Christ (Memphis) withdrew from that church to organize the Church of God in Christ (International) in Kansas City, Missouri, in 1969. Their disagreement with the parent body was not doctrinal but one concerned with polity and authority of government. The theological background here is Wesleyan, but emphasizes two works of grace—full baptism by the Holy Ghost and speaking with other tongues "as the Spirit gives utterance." Membership was reported at 200,000 in 300 churches in 1982.

CHURCH OF GOD OF PROPHECY

Church of God of Prophecy (the name it has borne since 1952) historically shares some of the early years of the Holiness, classical pentecostal Church of God (Cleveland, Tennessee). A dynamic pentecostal pioneer, A. J. Tomlinson was the church's most prominent figure in the first half of this century. He observed firsthand many prominent ministers of that time and eventually came under the influence of Holiness teaching and, finally, classical pentecostal theology. Under his leadership the Church of God became a national, then an international, body, and various educational, social, and ecclesiastical programs were developed.

At the death of A. J. Tomlinson in 1943, Milton A. Tomlinson was duly designated leader of the organization. His tenure as general overseer was noted for its call to unlimited social, racial, and national church unity and fellowship. The present general overseer, Billy D. Murray, Sr., began his service in 1990. His objectives are to promote Christian unity and move forward with worldwide evangelism. The following ministries have been developed: radio and television, youth camping, outreach to military personnel, world mission corps, youth mission teams, international orphanages, and the Center for Biblical Leadership, located in Cleveland, Tennessee.

The official teachings include special emphasis on sanctification and culminate with a doctrine of Spirit baptism, which involves speaking in tongues as the initial evidence of baptism in the Spirit. Other prominent doctrinal commitments include an imminence-oriented eschatology, which involves the premillennial return of the risen Jesus, preceded by a series of events; the sanctity of the home, including denial of multiple marriages; water baptism by immersion; the Lord's Supper; foot washing; total abstinence from alcoholic beverages and tobacco; modesty in all dimensions of life; and an appreciation of various gifts of the Holy Spirit.

The annual general assembly, held at the world headquarters in Cleveland, Tennessee, is a time of celebration and fellowship with church members from around the world. Doctrinal and business concerns are addressed each year; every resolution adopted must receive unanimous agreement from the male members in atten-

115

dance. Membership stands at 74,265 in 2,072 churches in the U.S. and at 286,848 in 5,6476 churches worldwide.

CHURCH OF GOD, HOLINESS

Church of God, Holiness, originated in Atlanta, Georgia, in 1914 with a group of eight people under the leadership of K. H. Burruss. Churches were established in Atlanta and in Norfolk, Virginia, in 1916; by 1922 there were 22 churches in 11 states, Cuba, the Canal Zone, and the British West Indies. At that time the churches were incorporated into what is currently known as the National Convention of the Churches of God, Holiness.

All doctrine within this group is tested strictly by New Testament standards; the Scriptures are accepted as inspired, and the New Testament "gives safe and clearly applied instructions on all methods of labor, sacred and secular," and for the conduct of the whole of life. The churches believe in the Trinity; in justification, entire sanctification, and regeneration; and that the gift of the Holy Spirit is an act subsequent to conversion. Perfection is both *present* and *ultimate*. One must believe in divine healing to be accepted as a member, but medicines and doctors, not being expressly denounced by Scripture, are approved for those who desire them. Two ordinances, baptism and the Lord's Supper, are observed. The washing of feet is approved but not regularly practiced.

Pastors are assigned by the one bishop, or president, and are assisted in local congregations by deacons. In direct supervision over the pastors is a state overseer, also appointed by the bishop. State conventions are held annually. The highest administrative body is the national convention, where the delegates elect the national bishop. The church reports 25,600 members in 32 churches.

CHURCH OF JESUS CHRIST

At least 20 independent religious bodies in the U.S. bear the name *Church of Jesus Christ.* The largest of these, headquartered in Cleveland, Tennessee, became a chartered group in 1927 under the leadership of Bishop M. K. Lawson. Several splits or divisions took place from 1934 through the 1960s; the parent church today claims a membership of 100,000.

In spite of their divisions, these several groups hold in common doctrines of justification by faith; freedom of the individual to accept or reject the plan of salvation; baptism by immersion (in the name of Christ only); baptism of the Holy Ghost, being born again of water and the Spirit; and the premillennial second coming of Christ. They have two ordinances, baptism and the Lord's Supper (with foot-washing fellowship). Each church is self-governing.

Members practice divine healing and condemn the use of alcohol and tobacco. They oppose the taking of oaths before magistrates but call for obedience to and respect for civil government, except in the use of armed force. Exclusion from church membership is imposed on persons who sin willfully. They use only the scriptural titles for church leaders: bishop, elder, evangelist, deacon, and pastor. Members do not regard this body as an organization, but as an organism, with Christ as founder and head.

Foreign missions are found in Africa, India, Haiti, Australia, Jamaica, Israel, Mexico, Panama, the Dominican Republic, and England. Home missions work stresses evangelism. The church sponsors one Bible institute and several academies, the largest located in Cleveland, Tennessee.

CHURCH OF OUR LORD JESUS CHRIST OF THE APOSTOLIC FAITH, INC.

Confident that it is "a continuation of the great revival begun at Jerusalem on the day of Pentecost in 33 C.E.," this church was organized in 1919 at Columbus, Ohio, by R. C. Lawson. Doctrine is that of the apostles and prophets, with Christ as the cornerstone. Perhaps the basic emphases are Christ's resurrection and premillennial second coming, the resurrection and translation of the saints, the priesthood of all believers, and the final judgment of humankind. Baptism is by immersion, and baptism of the Holy Spirit is necessary for second birth. Foot washing is practiced, but not as an ordinance.

Found in 32 states, the British West Indies, Africa, the Philippines, Haiti, the Dominican Republic, and London, England, the church reports a membership of 30,000 in 450 churches. A Bible college, 22 elementary schools, 18 extension schools, a clinic, and an orphanage are maintained. A national convocation meets every other year at the headquarters church, Refuge Temple, in New York City. Officers include 5 apostles, 32 bishops, 27 district elders, 3 secretaries, a treasurer, and a public information officer.

CHURCH OF THE NAZARENE

The theological and doctrinal foundations of the Church of the Nazarene lie in the doctrines of holiness and sanctification taught by John Wesley in the eighteenth-century English revival. The church resulted from the merger of three independent Holiness groups

117

already in existence in the U.S. In 1907, an eastern Holiness body, the Association of Pentecostal Churches of America, located principally in New York and New England, joined with a California body, the Church of the Nazarene. The two churches agreed on the name Pentecostal Church of the Nazarene. Then in 1908, a Southern group known as the Holiness Church of Christ merged with the Pentecostal Church of the Nazarene. By 1919, *Pentecostal* had acquired a different meaning and was dropped from the name, leaving it what it is today: the Church of the Nazarene.

The church's theological background is Methodist; it adheres closely to the original Wesleyan ideology, although modified somewhat by the American experience and the nineteenth-century Holiness revival. Most of the early Holiness groups in this country originated in the Methodist Episcopal Church; four of the five general superintendents of the Church of the Nazarene were former Methodist ministers, and the Nazarene *Manual* has been called a "rewritten and modified Methodist *Discipline.*"

The doctrine of the church is built around justification by faith and the sanctification of believers, also by faith, including their entire sanctification as a second definite work of grace, subsequent to regeneration. All ministers and local church officials must profess this experience. Other doctrines include belief in the plenary inspiration of the Scriptures as containing all truths necessary to Christian faith and living; the atonement of Christ for the whole human race; the justification, regeneration, and adoption of all penitent believers in Christ; the second coming of Christ; the resurrection of the dead; and the final judgment. Members of this church believe in divine healing, but never to the exclusion of medical agencies. The use of tobacco and alcoholic beverages is denounced. Two sacraments—baptism by sprinkling, pouring, or (most often) immersion, and Communion—are accepted as "instituted by Christ." Baptism of young children is allowed, but believer's baptism predominates. It is a middle-of-the-road church, neither extremely ritualistic nor extremely informal; one church historian calls it the "right wing of the holiness movement."

There are 5,326 local congregations grouped into 85 districts in the U.S. and Canada, and an additional 238 districts throughout the world. Pastors are elected by local churches; each district is supervised by a district superintendent, who may be elected for a four-year term by the members of the district assembly.

The General Assembly is the highest body of the church. It elects the general superintendents (currently six in number) whose terms last until the next General Assembly, and the General Board, consisting of an equal number of lay and clergy members. The General Board meets annually and oversees the five administrative divisions: World Mission, Church Growth, Sunday School Ministries, Communications, and Finance. The church is organized in 109 world areas and supports 590 missionaries. There is strong emphasis on evangelism. Eight liberal arts colleges and universities, a graduate theological seminary, and a Bible college are maintained in the U.S. In other world areas, the church maintains 26 graduate and undergraduate colleges and seminaries.

The books and periodicals of the church are produced at the Nazarene Publishing House in Kansas City, Missouri. The annual volume of business exceeds $21 million.

Church membership in the U.S. is reported at 591,134. In other world regions, membership is reported at 513,560—a total membership of 1,104,694 in 10,882 churches worldwide.

CHURCHES OF CHRIST IN CHRISTIAN UNION

This church defected from Christian Union churches (see CHRISTIAN UNION) at the 1909 meeting of that group at Marshall, Ohio. It was organized "to allow a complete freedom in the preaching of full salvation as stated doctrinally by John Wesley"—a freedom the dissenters felt was being neglected in the parent body. Their first council was held that year at Jeffersonville, Ohio, and district councils have been held since that date. In 1945, legislation was enacted to provide for the organization of additional councils, and it now reaches into 17 states and several countries abroad.

Churches of Christ in Christian Union are generally evangelistic in faith and work; camp meetings, revivals, and soul-winning campaigns are held regularly throughout the denomination. Worship follows simple forms, with little ritual. Emphasis is placed "on the blessing of God rather than on the ingenuity of man." A general council meets every two years at Circleville, Ohio, the body's headquarters. There is one college, Circleville Bible College, established to train ministers and lay workers.

The Reformed Methodist Church merged with this body in September 1952 and is now known as the Northeastern district of the Churches of Christ in Christian Union. There is a total of 10,350 members in 240 churches.

CHURCHES OF GOD, GENERAL CONFERENCE

John Winebrenner (1797–1860), a member of the Reformed Church in Maryland, was active in the religious revival that swept the

U.S. in the early years of the nineteenth century. His ardent evangelism proved unpopular in the Reformed Church, and he severed relations with it in 1825 to form an independent Church of God in Harrisburg, Pennsylvania. In 1830 Winebrenner and six other preachers organized the first eldership (the terms *eldership* and *conference* are used interchangeably). A general eldership was organized in 1845, distinguishing the national body from local or area elderships organized since 1830. The words *in North America* were added in that year; *Church* became *Churches* in 1903. In 1975 the national name was changed to Churches of God, General Conference. Each local church is a Church of God.

Arminian in theology, these churches consider the Bible the sole rule of faith and practice. They believe in justification by faith; repentance and regeneration; the Triune God; the office and work of the Holy Spirit; practical piety; observance of the Lord's Day; and the resurrection of the just and unjust at the final judgment.

The churches, according to Winebrenner, were to be "spiritual, free, and independent . . . consisting of believers only, without any human name or creed or ordinance or law." Sectarianism is held to be antiscriptural. The two obligatory ordinances are baptism by immersion (the church does, however, accept on transfer the baptismal forms of other churches) and the Lord's Supper, called Communion in many of the churches. It may be observed at any time, "as the time of observance is not of major importance nor is the posture of the communicant." The ordinance of foot washing is not obligatory.

Organization consists of 16 elderships, or conferences, which meet annually in their respective states. There is missionary work in India, Bangladesh, and Haiti, and among the Navajo in New Mexico and Arizona. The General Conference is composed of ministerial and lay delegates in equal numbers, with a proportionate number of youth from the annual conferences; it meets triennially to plan its work. Local churches are presbyterian in government, but ministerial appointments follow a modified call system. The University of Findlay and Winebrenner Theological Seminary are at Findlay, Ohio. There are 350 churches with 34,000 members; primary strength is in Pennsylvania and the Midwest.

CHURCHES OF ILLUMINATION

Described as a "church at large rather than a church of congregations," this body was organized in 1908 under the inspiration of Swinburne Clymer. His son, Emerson M. Clymer, continued the work until his death in 1983, when the church came under the direction of Gerald E. Poesnecker. Its stated purpose is to harmonize the teachings of philosophy with the truths of religion, thus offering spiritual, esoteric, and philosophical interpretations of basic Bible teachings to those in search of spiritual truth. Membership is by written request and does not require severance of membership in any other church.

The "priesthood of Melchizedek" dates from "beyond the year 4255 B.C.E. and includes all that small body of chosen seekers initiated into the mysteries of the divine law." This priesthood, which began in the days of Genesis and came down through Jesus, the Gnostics, the early Egyptians, Greeks, Indians, and Persians to the present time, is found in the Church of Illumination.

The essence of this religion is found in the biblical statement that "whatsoever a man soweth, that shall he also reap." This is interpreted as being a matter of inevitable compensation, rather than reward and punishment at the hands of God. Furthermore:

> Religion teaches the Law—the way of Life—a way which makes man aware of the all-important truth that he is, in fact, a child of God, and that within him, buried by much debris, is a spark of the Divine. This Divine Spark is the *Christos*—the unconscious Soul—which may be awakened and brought into consciousness—a second or Rebirth. This is the "talent" entrusted to man and for which he is responsible to his Creator. Neglected, it remains just as it is—a tiny spark. Recognized, aroused, awakened and brought into consciousness, it becomes an inexhaustible source of wisdom and power, lifting man to the heights of Illumination and achievement. The process that makes all this possible is, in reality, the Second Birth. It is the process of Regeneration—mortality taking on immortality—the means whereby the son of man actually and literally becomes the Son of God.

Enlarging upon this, four fundamentals are taught as the means to the fulfillment of human destiny: (1) the law of action and reaction (sowing and reaping); (2) humankind's indebtedness to God for its talents and the obligation to use them well; (3) practice of the Golden Rule; and (4) practice of the law of honesty. It is also taught that we are now in a "manistic" age (*manisis*, "the recognition of the equality of man and woman"), which will last 2,000 years, during which Revelation will become the "unsealed book of the Bible"; that the world at present is the scene of the final battle of Armageddon. There is also some emphasis on reincarnation, although belief in this is not required of adherents.

Yearly conferences of ministers and leaders are held in various parts of the country. Officially, there are 14 established churches with 9,000 members, most of whom are members only in correspondence.

CHURCHES OF THE LIVING GOD

Two churches of common origin, similar in type but differing in detail, bear the title Church of the Living God. Both came out of an organization formed in 1889 at Wrightsville, Arkansas, by William Christian, who "by virtue of a divine call, created the office of chief." Christian held that "Freemason religion" is the true expression of religion and insisted that his "organism" be known as "operative Masonry, and its first three corporal degrees shall be baptism, Holy Supper, and foot washing." Both groups are organized along fraternal lines; members tithe their incomes to support their churches, which they call temples. The body formed in 1989 claimed to be the first black church in America without Anglo-Saxon roots and that was not begun by white missionaries.

The larger body is known as Church of the Living God (motto: Christian Workers for Fellowship) and claims 42,000 members in 170 churches. It stresses believer's baptism by immersion, foot washing, and the use of water and unleavened bread in the celebration of the Lord's Supper. A chief bishop is the presiding officer. There is an annual assembly, and a general assembly meets every four years to elect other officers and determine laws for the church. Membership is biracial.

The second body—The House of God, Which Is the Church of the Living God, the Pillar and Ground of the Truth, Inc.—also is episcopal in polity and generally follows the form and thought of the other group. It has 2,350 members in 107 churches.

COMMUNITY CHURCHES, INTERNATIONAL COUNCIL OF

Community Churches in the U.S. date from the mid-1800s, but were first organized nationally in 1923. According to the most recently published history of the Community Church movement (Shotwell, *Unity Without Uniformity* [Community Church Press, 1984]), these churches are a result of the desire to eliminate overchurching in some communities and solve attendant economic and staffing problems; to replace the restrictiveness and divisiveness of denominationalism with self-determination and Christian unity; to refocus primary loyalty from organizations outside a community to the community itself and, by addressing specific needs there, to effect a more relevant religion.

Since each church is adjusted to the needs of a different community, there is much variety among Community Churches in worship, work and witness styles, and methods. Several general categories exist. Federated and United Churches have resulted from mergers of congregations previously affiliated with certain denominations—some have continued alignments with two or more denominations; others have become entirely independent. Some individual congregations also have severed denominational ties; others have affiliated with the Community Church movement while continuing relationships with one or more denominations. But the majority of Community Churches never have had denominational alignments.

The current organization, International Council of Community Churches, resulted from a 1950 merger of two other councils—one composed of predominantly black congregations, the other of churches with predominantly white memberships. It is headquartered in Homewood, Illinois.

The International Council now provides services to more than 1,500 Community Churches in all 50 states and several nations. These services include ecclesiastical endorsement; personnel placement; insurance; continuing education; direct and brokered consultation for help in various areas; and supportive networks for clergy and their spouses and children. Publications include *The Christian Community*, a monthly newspaper, and *The Pastor's Journal*, a quarterly for professionals.

The parent organization brings Community Churches into mutually beneficial relationships at national, regional, and area conferences. It endorses nonsectarian educational institutions and mission agencies that have demonstrated their ability to meet human needs and further Christian unity. It is a member of Consultation on Church Union, the National Council of Churches of Christ, and the World Council of Churches. Financial support for the International Council's activities, as well as for all institutions and agencies, is provided voluntarily by churches and individuals. Membership stands at 250,000 in 398 churches.

Understanding of the Community Church movement is complicated by two facts: Many of the movement's churches do not use *Community* in their names, and many that do include this word are purely denominational, are members of a national organization outside the historic movement, or are completely independent.

CONGREGATIONAL BIBLE CHURCHES, INC.

A pentecostal movement, this body dates back to 1922. It was founded under its present name and organization in 1977, when Light of the Way Open Door Church merged with the Independent Holiness Church.

It describes itself by such terms as *trinitarian, international, pentecostal, charismatic, evangelical,* and *missionary.* It cooperates with a number of other conservative bodies—Baptist, Assemblies of God, and Holiness and Pentecostal churches. Its Articles of Faith are the same as those of the Assemblies of God.

Reporting 100,000 members in 500 churches worldwide, this body also carries out missionary work in Guyana, India, Canada, Singapore, Nigeria, and elsewhere. In the U.S., it sponsors three Bible colleges. Its membership is strongest in Ohio, West Virginia, and Florida, with headquarters presently in Abilene, Kansas.

CONGREGATIONAL CHRISTIAN CHURCHES (NATIONAL ASSOCIATION)

This association was organized in 1955 by a group of churches desiring to "preserve historical Congregational forms of freedom and fellowship (the Congregational Way)." With 410 churches and an estimated 75,000 members, it is the largest of several Congregational bodies that did not participate when the General Council of Congregational Churches and the Evangelical and Reformed Church merged with the United Church of Christ in 1957.

The National Association brings local churches together for counsel, inspiration, and fellowship, but still preserves the independence and autonomy of the local churches. It describes its mission as encouraging and assisting local churches "in their development of vibrant and effective witnesses to Christ in congregational ways."

A moderator presides over an annual meeting of all the churches; an executive committee of 12, elected for four years, acts for the association between meetings. Six commissions—Christian education, Communication Commission, women's work, youth, world Christian relations, and spiritual resources—work under the direction of the executive committee. Five divisions of the National Association provide a Missionary Society, Building and Loan Fund, Congregational Foundation for Theological Studies, Division for Ministry, and Congregational Church Development. A unique feature of the organization is its Referendum Council, which, upon call of 10 percent of the churches and by a two-thirds vote, may modify any action or proposal of any of the national bodies or officers of the association.

There is no binding ecclesiastical authority and no required creed or program. "We are bound together not by uniformity of belief but by the acceptance of a covenant purpose to be 'the people of God.' " The association leaves to each church any decision to participate in social and political questions and action. There is widespread missionary work in the U.S. and in the Philippines, Mexico, Hong Kong, Formosa, Greece, Italy, Germany, Brazil, Central America, and South India. *The Congregationalist,* a denominational periodical founded in 1849, was revived in 1958 as the journal of the association. Two colleges—Olivet in Michigan and Piedmont in Demorest, Georgia—are supported. National offices are in Oak Creek, Wisconsin.

CONGREGATIONAL HOLINESS CHURCH

Founded January 29, 1921, the church was organized desiring to set forth the doctrinal faith that was taught by Jesus Christ and the apostles. The church is trinitarian in belief and pentecostal in experience, emphasizing the baptism of the Holy Ghost with speaking in tongues as the Spirit gives utterance to be the initiatory evidence of that experience, and the inspiration and infallibility of the Holy Scriptures. The merits of the atonement, salvation of the entire spiritual church, justification, sanctification, divine healing (without objection to medicine), the imminent personal premillennial second coming of Jesus Christ, eternal redemption for all saints who are faithful to the end, and eternal punishment for those who die outside of Christ are the tenets of the faith.

The Bible is held as the sole rule of conduct; slang language, the use of tobacco, membership in oathbound secret societies, and other forms of worldliness are condemned. Ordinances include baptism by immersion, the Lord's Supper, and foot washing.

Church government is congregational. The local churches are grouped into nine geographical districts. Each district has a Presbyter of five members. The District Presbyter Members, the General Executive Board, and General Department heads comprise the General Committee, which governs the church between the General Biennial Conferences. The General Conference is the highest ruling body of the church.

Local church officers, elected biennially, consist of deacons, trustees, a secretary, and a treasurer. Pastors are elected by a majority vote of the congregation for four-year or indefinite terms. Women are ordained. There are 174 churches with 8,347 members in the U.S. concentrated in the Southeast and Texas. There are 577 churches and missions outside the U.S. in Mexico, Guatemala, El Salvador, Honduras, Nicaragua, Costa Rica, Cuba, Brazil, and India.

CONSERVATIVE CONGREGATIONAL CHRISTIAN CONFERENCE

The origins of this group go back to 1935 and the work of H. B. Sandine, a pastor in Hancock, Minnesota, who was convinced that the Congregational Christian Churches had departed from the beliefs, policy, and practices of historic Congregationalism. He carried on a mimeographed educational effort until 1939, when his efforts were consummated in a monthly publication, *The Congregational Beacon*. This later became *The Congregational Christian* and, finally, the bimonthly *Foresee*. A Conservative Congregational Christian Fellowship was organized at Chicago in 1945. The prospect of a merger involving Congregational Christian and Evangelical and Reformed churches precipitated reorganization into the Conservative Congregational Christian Conference in 1948.

Today there are 194 member churches in the conference, with a total of 31,178 members. There are also 20 regional fellowships and associations made up of some 250 Congregational Christian churches in sympathy with the statement of faith and general polity of the conference, though not all are directly involved in its official work and actions.

The statement of faith is conservatively evangelical; it includes belief in the infallibility and authority of the Scriptures; the Trinity; the deity, virgin birth, sinlessness, atoning death, resurrection, ascension, and promised return of Christ; regeneration by the Holy Spirit; the resurrection of both the saved and the lost; and the spiritual unity of all believers in Christ.

Local churches are completely autonomous; national officers include a president, a vice president, a recording secretary, an executive director (conference minister), a treasurer, a controller, an editor, and a historian, all elected for three-year terms. A board of directors manages the property and directs the general business of the conference; an executive committee is composed of the officers, with the president as chair. Fifteen subordinate committees guide the various efforts of the conference.

Work is largely in the areas of missions, church planting, and Christian education, carried on through recognized evangelical home and foreign mission agencies, Bible institutions, colleges, seminaries, and Sunday school publishing houses. An annual meeting is held, usually in July or August. It is especially active in the fields of church extension, pastoral placement, and regional activities.

The conference is a member of the National Association of Evangelicals and the World Evangelical Fellowship, whose similarly minded groups are at work in Brazil, England, Australia, New Zealand, South Africa, Portugal, Iceland, Canada, Taiwan, Fiji, Macedonia, and the Philippines. Headquarters are in St. Paul, Minnesota.

DIVINE SCIENCE

In the late years of the last century, three sisters—Aletha Brooks Small, Fannie Brooks James, and Nona Lovell Brooks of Denver—and Malinda E. Cramer of San Francisco, independent of one another, worked out the principles and practice of Divine Science. When they met and joined forces in 1898, they incorporated the Divine Science College and their church—the First Divine Science Church of Denver—was organized. The core of its teaching is the principle of the all-inclusive God-mind:

God [is] the Omnipresence, the Universal Presence, Life, Love, Intelligence and Substance; man, a child of God, is of God, is like God; knowledge of this truth frees man into a larger concept of God and the understanding of man's higher nature; the practice of the Presence of God in daily life results in man's right attitude toward negative thinking; evolution is God's method of accomplishing, and love, conscious unity, is the fulfilling of the law.

All of the founders had the experience of divine healing, and the emphasis on healing naturally persists. Healing comes through an understanding of the nature of God, and the Universal Law and is "the cleansing of the inner man from all that is unlike God." Divine Science does not deny the existence of visible matter but interprets form and substance as manifestations of God.

Divine Science further stands for (1) God as Omnipresent Life, Love, Intelligence, and Wisdom; (2) the "brotherhood" of humankind; (3) the unity of all life; (4) higher thought in science, philosophy, and religion; (5) awareness of humanity's relation to God released into expression, in each individual life, of our divine inheritance—health, abundance, peace, and power; (6) and the transcendence and immanence of God manifested in all created things.

For many years local churches and colleges of Divine Science were independent of one another. In 1957 some of the ministers and key workers met and organized the Divine Science Federation International. This organization serves its member churches and centers and cooperates with Brooks Divinity School, which trains ministers, teachers, and practitioners. Churches, centers, and study groups are found in major U.S. cities and abroad; headquarters are in Denver, Colorado.

EPISCOPAL/ANGLICAN

This is the American branch of the worldwide Anglican (Church of England) communion, which had its initial impetus in 1534 when the English monarch, rather than the Bishop of Rome (the pope), was recognized as the head of the church on earth. It took its true form as a church during the era of Richard Hooker late in that century. This church relies totally on the traditional liturgy in its worship, but is distinctive in leaving undefined the exact nature of the Communion bread and wine, regarded as a spiritual mystery. It acknowledges no central authority, although bishops are an important symbol of unity. Its sources of belief and practice are the Bible, the tradition of the church, and reason. Aesthetic in orientation, it incorporates theology into liturgy and makes use of the senses of sight and taste as well as those of hearing and speaking. Its clergy are called priests and have the authority of the apostolate.

AFRICAN ORTHODOX CHURCH, THE

Believing that black Episcopalians should have churches of their own, a Protestant Episcopal rector, George Alexander McGuire, withdrew from that church in 1919 to establish independent black churches in the U.S., Cuba, and Canada. He called the churches Independent Episcopal, but in 1921 the first general synod of the new body changed the name to the African Orthodox Church and elected McGuire as its first bishop. He was consecrated by Archbishop Vilatte, who took his episcopal orders from the West Syrian Church of Antioch. This placed McGuire in the traditional apostolic succession, which he valued highly.

The church lays strong emphasis on the apostolic succession and historic sacraments and rituals; it celebrates the original seven sacraments of the Roman Catholic Church. Its worship is a blend of Western and Eastern liturgy, creeds, and symbols, though the liturgy is usually Western—a mingling of Anglican, Greek, and Roman patterns. Three creeds—Athanasian, Nicene, and Apostles'—are used.

The denomination maintains the position that no priest may marry the guilty party in a divorce, and innocent parties are remarried only with special permission from a bishop. The government is, of course, episcopal; bishops are in charge of dioceses, or jurisdictions; and groups of dioceses form a province, each led by an archbishop and a primate. The primate, in turn, presides over the provincial synod. At the head stands a primate archbishop metropolitan, general overseer of all the work of the church, which now extends over the U.S. into

Canada, to Latin America, and to South Africa. Membership, as in the Roman Catholic Church, is counted not by communicants but by the number of persons baptized; in the U.S. there were 17 churches and 5,100 members in 1983.

ANGLICAN ORTHODOX CHURCH

The Reverend James Parker Dees resigned from the priesthood of the Protestant Episcopal Church in 1963 to protest what he believed to be "its failure to proclaim firmly the biblical doctrine, and . . . its emphasis on the social gospel and pro-communist program." With a group of other former members, he organized the Anglican Orthodox Church to preserve the traditional tenets of Anglicanism— belief in the fundamental (King James) Bible truths and morality, the (1928) *Book of Common Prayer,* the 39 Articles of Religion, the homilies, the doctrines of the Anglican Reformers, and the basic Anglican traditions and church government. Dr. Dees was consecrated bishop by Bishop Wasyl Sawyna of the Holy Ukrainian Autocephalic Orthodox Church and Bishop Orlando J. Woodward of the Old Catholic succession.

The fundamental doctrines of the virgin birth, the atoning sacrifice of the cross, the Trinity, the resurrection, the second coming, salvation by faith alone, and the divinity of Christ are emphasized. Biblical morality is upheld. Branches of the worldwide Orthodox Anglican Communion are located in South India, Madagascar, Pakistan, Liberia, Nigeria, the Philippines, the Fiji Islands, South Africa, Kenya, Colombia, and England. The entire membership totals more than 300,000, with 6,000 of these in the U.S. An active program of Christian education is promoted both in the U.S. and on a worldwide basis. This includes, but is not limited to, weekly Sunday school Bible study classes and weekday youth clubs. The ministers of the church are trained at Cranmer Seminary in Statesville, North Carolina.

EPISCOPAL CHURCH, THE

It is stated in the preface of *The Book of Common Prayer* of the Protestant Episcopal Church—since 1967 known as the Episcopal Church—that "this Church is far from intending to depart from the Church of England in any essential point of doctrine, discipline, or worship." For a century and a half in the U.S., it bore the name Church of England.

Its history dates back to the first missionaries who went to the British Isles from Gaul, prior to the Council of Arles in 314 C.E. It can be traced from the time Henry VIII threw off the supremacy of the pope (Henry, according to Anglican scholars, did not found the Church of England; the church had always been more British than Roman); through the reign of Edward VI, when *The Book of Common Prayer* and the 42 Articles of Religion were written; through the period of Catholic restoration under Queen Mary; and through her successor, Elizabeth I, who united church and state under the Protestant banner and sent Sir Francis Drake sailing to build an empire. Drake came ashore in 1578 in what is now California. His Church of England chaplain, Francis Fletcher, planted a cross and read a prayer as Drake claimed the new land for the Virgin Queen. Martin Frobisher had reached Labrador in 1576, also with a chaplain, and later colonists came to Virginia under Sir Humphrey Gilbert and Sir Walter Raleigh. Raleigh's chaplain baptized a native named Manteo and a white baby named Virginia Dare before the settlers of Roanoke vanished. With Captain John Smith came Chaplain Robert Hunt, who stretched a sail between two trees for a shelter and read the service from *The Book of Common Prayer.*

In the South, the transplanted Church of England quickly became the established church. It was at heart a tolerant and catholic church, but the control of the crown brought an almost ruthless authority that made the church suspect in the eyes of colonists who had come here seeking freedom from all such authority. The Virginia House of Burgesses set the salary of the Virginia clergymen at "1,500 pounds of tobacco and 16 barrels of corn." It was a British clergy, supported by public taxes and assessment and contributions from the church in England through the Society for the Propagation of the Gospel. It was technically under the jurisdiction of the Bishop of London. In that fact lay one of its almost fatal weaknesses; it was necessary for colonial ministers to make the long journey to England for ordination, and few could afford it. This, coupled with the rising tide of revolutionary fervor, placed the colonial Church of England in an unenviable position.

Yet, the church did well, and membership grew rapidly. William and Mary College was established in 1693; King's Chapel in Boston was opened in 1689; in 1698 a church was established at Newport, Rhode Island, and another, Trinity Church, in New York City. When a delegation from the Society for the Propogation of the Gospel arrived from England in 1702, it found about fifty clergymen at work, from the Carolinas to Maine. The visitors sensed the need for American bishops to ordain American clergymen; they also sensed the increasing opposition of American patriots to a British-governed church.

The American Revolution almost destroyed the colonial Church of England. Under special oath of allegiance to the king, the clergy either fled to England or Canada or remained as Loyalists in the colonies, in the face of overwhelming persecution. The fact that many were loyal to the American cause meant little; the Reverend William White was chaplain of the Continental Congress, the Reverend Charles Thurston was a continental colonel, and in the pews of the church sat George Washington, Thomas Jefferson, Patrick Henry, John Jay, Robert Morris, John Marshall, John Randolph, and Charles Lee, and "Light-Horse" Harry Lee. But their presence could not stem the tide. The Anglican house was divided, and it fell. At war's end there was no episcopacy, no association of the churches, not even the semblance of an establishment. Few thought there was any future for this church, which suffered more than any other in the colonies.

However, there was a future—and a great one. In 1782, William White's pamphlet titled *The Case of the Episcopal Churches in the United States Considered* appeared. White's plea for unity and reorganization proposed that the ministry be continued temporarily without the episcopal succession, since the latter "cannot at present be obtained." In 1783 a conference of the churches met at Annapolis, Maryland, and formally adopted the name Protestant Episcopal Church—Protestant, to distinguish it from Roman Catholic; Episcopal, to distinguish it from Presbyterian and Congregational.

Also in 1783, the clergy in Connecticut elected Samuel Seabury as their prospective bishop; he went to England and waited a year for consecration at the hands of English bishops. When he was denied, he went to Scotland and obtained consecration there in 1784. Ultimately, Parliament and the Church of England cleared the way, and two other bishops-elect—from New York and Pennsylvania—were consecrated by the Archbishop of Canterbury in 1787. In 1789, during the first meeting of the House of Bishops, the church constitution was adopted in Philadelphia, *The Book of Common Prayer* was revised for American use, and the Protestant Episcopal Church became an independent, self-governing body.

Complete harmony existed for the next half century. New churches and institutions were established: Sunday schools; Bible, prayer books, and tract societies; theological seminaries; colleges; boarding schools; guilds for men and women; and a domestic and foreign missionary society. Diocesan organizations replaced state organizations, and new bishops moved into the new West. Bishops J. H. Hobart in New York, A. V. Giswold in New England, Richard Channing Moore in Virginia, and Philander Chase in Ohio worked miracles in overcoming prejudice against the church. One great

Episcopal builder, W. A. Muhlenberg, "organized the first free church of any importance in New York, introduced the male choir, sisterhoods, and the fresh-air movement, while his church infirmary suggested to his mind the organization of St. Luke's Hospital [New York], the first church hospital of any Christian communion in the country."

Muhlenberg was a man of wide vision; he inspired a "memorial" calling for a wider catholicity in the Protestant Episcopal Church, which resulted in the famous Chicago Lambeth Quadrilateral on Church Unity in 1888 and the movement that produced the further revision of the American *Book of Common Prayer* in 1892.

With the outbreak of the Civil War, the church was again threatened, but among the major Protestant churches, it alone suffered no division. New England churchmen may have been abolitionists, and a Louisiana bishop, Leonidas Polk, was a general under Lee, but Polk prayed for Bishop McIlvaine of Ohio in public, and the Ohioan prayed for Polk. They were still in one church. A temporary Protestant Episcopal Church in the Confederate States was organized to carry on the work in the South, but the names of Southern bishops were still called in the general convention in New York in 1862; once the war was over, the Episcopal house was quickly reunited.

The years following Appomattox were a time of new growth. A dispute over churchmanship, rising out of the Oxford Movement in England, resulted in the separation of a group into the Reformed Episcopal Church in 1873, but otherwise, Episcopal unity held fast. New theological seminaries were established and old ones were reorganized and strengthened. This period saw the organization of a church congress and numerous agencies. The expansion continued into the next century; two world wars failed to halt it. In 1830 the Protestant Episcopal Church had 12 bishops, 20 dioceses, 6,000 clergymen, and 1,250,000 communicants. Today the Episcopal Church stands as one of the largest denominations, with 2,471,880 members in 7,367 churches in the U.S.

The episcopal form of government closely parallels that of the U.S. federal government. It is a federal union, each diocese autonomous in its own sphere, originally associated with others for the maintenance of a common doctrine, discipline, and worship. To those objectives have been added the unification, development, and prosecution of missionary, educational, and social programs.

Most of the overseas jurisdictions will become either independent or parts of existing Anglican churches in their areas. The dioceses of the Philippine Episcopal Church was the first to become autonomous in the 1990s. Those in Mexico, the Caribbean, and Central and South America have begun trial periods leading toward eventual autonomy.

Each diocese functions through a bishop (elected locally, with the approval of the episcopate and representatives of clergy and laity from the whole church), who is the spiritual and administrative head. There is a diocesan legislative body made up of the clergy of the diocese and representatives of the local congregations, which meets annually; a standing committee of clergy and laity, advisers and assessors to the bishop; and, usually, a program board.

The normal pattern for the local congregation is the parish, which elects its own minister (rector or priest), who is vested with pastoral oversight of the congregation and, with the wardens and vestry representatives, administers the temporal affairs and the property of the parish.

Each parish and parochial district (mission or chapel) is represented in the annual diocesan convention by its clergy and elected lay delegates (usually in proportion to the congregation's constituency); each diocese is represented in the triennial General Convention of the church by its bishop (or bishops) and clergy and lay deputies elected in equal numbers (at present, four of each). The General Convention is bicameral, and the two houses of the legislature, bishops and deputies, meet and delegate separately. Either house may initiate, but concurrence of both is required to enact legislation.

Between sessions of the General Convention, the work of the church is carried on by the presiding bishop (elected for a 12-year term by the House of Bishops, with the concurrence of the House of Deputies) and an Executive Council of 43 members—20 elected by the general convention, 18 elected by the provinces (regional groups of dioceses and missionary districts) two *ex officio* (the presiding bishop and the president of the House of Deputies), and the vice-president, secretary, and treasurer.

Established in 1919 to unify the work of three previously independent boards, in 1968 the council took the further step of abolishing a somewhat rigid departmental structure in favor of a collaborative working relationship among the program areas: national mission, world mission, education, communication, administration, finance, and stewardship. As a result of reorganization of national staff in the fall of 1991, the mission of the church has been clustered around planning, operations, and support.

The members accept two creeds: the Apostles' and the Nicene. The articles of the Church of England, with the exception of the 21st and modification of the 8th, 35th, and 36th, are accepted as a general statement of doctrine, but adherence to them as a creed is not required. The clergy make the following declaration:

> I do believe the Holy Scriptures of the Old and New Testaments to be the Word of God, and to contain all things necessary to salvation; and I do solemnly engage to conform to the doctrine, discipline, and worship of the Episcopal Church.

The church expects its members to be loyal to the "doctrine, discipline and worship of the one Holy Catholic and Apostolic Church" in all the essentials, but permits great liberty in nonessentials. It allows for variation, individuality, independent thinking, and religious liberty. Liberals and conservatives, modernists and fundamentalists, find cordial and common ground for worship in the Prayer Book, which, second only to the Bible, has probably influenced more people than any other book in the English language.

Two sacraments, baptism and the Eucharist, are recognized as "certain sure witnesses and effectual agencies of God's love and grace." Baptism by pouring, sprinkling, or immersion is necessary for both children and adults; baptism by any church in the name of the Trinity is recognized as valid; baptized persons are confirmed as members of the church by the bishop. Adults who receive laying on of hands by a bishop at baptism are considered confirmed. Without stating or defining the holy mystery, the Episcopal Church believes in the real presence of Christ in the elements of the Eucharist. The church also recognizes a sacramental character in confirmation, penance, orders, matrimony, and unction.

Some Episcopal churches are "high," with elaborate ritual and ceremony; others are described as low, with less involved ceremony and more of an evangelistic emphasis. All members, high or low, have a loyalty to their church that is deep and lasting. This has been called the church of beauty, and it is an apt description. Its prayer book is eloquent in the literature of religious worship, containing the heart of both New Testament and Old Testament devotions. Members have built stately cathedrals in the U.S.: the Cathedral of St. John the Divine in New York City, the third largest in the world; and the Cathedral of Saints Peter and Paul, the national cathedral in Washington, D.C., sometimes called the American Westminster Abbey. Stained-glass windows, gleaming altars, vested choirs, and a glorious ritual are not only beautiful, but also give the worshiper a deep sense of the continuity of the Christian spirit and tradition. Next to the stress on episcopacy, its liturgical worship is a distinguishing feature, varying in degree according to high- or low-church inclinations. Its roots are in the Church of England and include the reading, recita-

tion, and intonation by priest, people, and choir of the historic general confession, general thanksgiving, collects, psalms, and prayers.
Financial support is given to funded U.S. dioceses, the Navajoland Episcopal Church (an area mission in the Southwest), and several small primarily rural Western dioceses. Special emphasis is placed on urban ministries, ministry in college communities, and ministry to black, Hispanic, Native American, and Asian congregations. Overseas missions are located in all American territories and in the Dominican Republic, Haiti, India, Japan, the Near East, Liberia, Mexico, Okinawa, Taiwan, and Central America.
The church sponsors 10 accredited seminaries in the U.S., plus three overseas; nine colleges, a university, and about 6,745 nursery through high schools for boys and girls; 81 homes for the aged; 91 institutions and agencies for child and youth care; 43 hospitals, homes, and convalescent clinics; and works for seamen in 22 U.S. dioceses. It has religious orders of monks and nuns, sisters and friars; 9 communities for men, 11 for women, and two for both men and women; both men and women are employed in schools, hospitals, and various forms of missionary work.
Two major developments in the past few years have been subjects of debate in the Episcopal Church: prayer book revision and the ordination of women to the priesthood. The General Convention of 1976 gave first approval to *The Proposed Book of Common Prayer*, the first revision of the American prayer book since 1928 and the first to use contemporary language. Much of the Tudor idiom, however, has been retained. The Holy Eucharist, Morning and Evening Prayer, the service for burial of the dead, and all the collects for the church year appear in both contemporary and traditional language; Archbishop Cranmer's Great Litany has been somewhat revised, but appears in its traditional form. All other services—such as those for baptism, matrimony, confirmation, and ordination—have been revised or rewritten in contemporary idiom. The new book is also more comprehensive, with forms for private confession, complete rites for Ash Wednesday and Holy Week, two daily offices in addition to Morning and Evening Prayer, and a special form for evening worship. The eucharistic lectionary has also been revised to include regular readings from the Old Testament. The Proposed Book was passed by an overwhelming majority at the 1979 convention, and the fully approved version is now in use. A new hymnal, the first since 1940, was approved in 1982.
The issue of women's ordination is extremely complex. Actually, it has to do with the historical doctrine of the uninterrupted line of

succession in the historical episcopate—the apostolic succession—in which men only had been ordained in the threefold ministries of deacon, priest, and bishop. The opposition to ordination of women came from two groups: (1) those who believed it impossible for women to be priests and (2) those who believed that the General Convention, though it is the supreme legislative authority of the Episcopal Church, had no right to decide this question; that such a decision should have been made only by catholic consensus or in some kind of ecumenical council.

The general convention of 1970 authorized the ordination of women to the diaconate, but "priesting," rejected at that convention and again in 1973, finally passed in 1976. In 1988, the Reverend Barbara C. Harris was elected Suffragan Bishop of Massachusetts, and in February 1989 she was ordained the first woman bishop in the historic succession.

In the wake of such changes, a minority of clergy (including bishops) and laypersons protested. Arguing that respect for tradition in a tradition-minded communion had been subverted, several thousand went so far as to form new Anglican bodies. These regard themselves as old, of course, hardly as "new." (For a brief treatment of these "new" Anglican bodies, see OTHER ANGLICAN BODIES IN THE UNITED STATES, where it is noted that some of these churches date back to the 1920s.)

REFORMED EPISCOPAL CHURCH

In 1873, the Reformed Episcopal Church was organized in New York City by eight clergy and 20 laypersons who had been members of the Protestant Episcopal Church. A long debate over the ritualism and ecclesiasticism of their former church lay behind the separation; the immediate cause of the division lay in the participation of Bishop George David Cummins of Kentucky in a Communion service held in Fifth Avenue Presbyterian Church in New York. In the face of criticism, and in the conviction that the catholic nature and mission of the Protestant Episcopal Church were being lost, Bishop Cummins withdrew to found the new denomination.

Doctrine and organization are similar to those of the parent church, with several important exceptions. The Reformed Episcopal Church rejects the doctrines that the Lord's Table is an altar on which the body and blood of Christ are offered anew to the Father; that the presence of Christ in the Lord's Supper resides in the elements of bread and wine; and that regeneration is inseparably connected with baptism. It also denies that Christian ministers are priests, in any sense other than that in which all believers are a "royal priesthood."

Clergy ordained in other churches are not reordained upon entering the ministry of the Reformed Episcopal Church, and members are admitted on letters of dismissal from other Protestant denominations. Worship is liturgical; at morning services on Sunday, the use of *The Book of Common Prayer,* revised to remove certain objectionable sacerdotal elements, is required. At other services its use is optional, while the minister may pray extemporaneously at any service.

Parish and synodical units prevail in the administration of the church. The triennial general council is like the general convention of the Episcopal Church; however, its bishops do not constitute a separate house.

The Reformed Episcopal Church in the U.S. has fellowship with its counterpart bodies in Canada, England, Spain, and Portugal. It is a member denomination of the National Association of Evangelicals.

Foreign missions are maintained in India, France, Brazil, Uganda, and Germany. In India and Africa there are 20 primary schools, two hospitals, and an orphanage. There are two seminaries in the United States—one in Philadelphia, the other in Summerville, South Carolina. There are 5,882 members in 83 local churches.

OTHER ANGLICAN BODIES IN THE UNITED STATES

Honoring the tradition of "the one, holy, catholic, and apostolic Church" is important to the worldwide Anglican communion. That spirit and practice has been critically important to some American Episcopalians who have feared the weakening of the tradition and the loss of the Church's authority and the abandonment of its mission.

Even before the Episcopal Church made major changes in the 1970s and 1980s, some members had withdrawn to form true and faithful bodies. They consider themselves more "old" than "new"— that is, they are not the ones departing or splintering. They include the Southern Episcopal Church, founded in 1962, and the Anglican Orthodox Church (1963; see separate article). From the latter body, two others broke away: the American Episcopal Church (1968) and the Anglican Episcopal Church of North America (1972).

Quite a number of Anglican separatist groups came into being after 1977 in response to two actions of the Episcopal Church: the admission of women to the Church's priesthood in 1976; and the adoption of a new—revised—prayer book in 1977. At first the dissenters sought to be a fellowship that would scrupulously continue the Anglican tradition and be part of the Anglican Church of North America.

Soon, however, this body changed its name to the Anglican Catholic Church. In turn, the newly named church has splintered into several others. The Province of Christ the King has maintained a separate existence since 1979. The United Episcopal Church was formed in 1980, the Anglican Rite Jurisdiction of the Americas in 1991. Allen C. Guelzo describes the last as the largest (perhaps 15,000 members) of the "continuing" Anglican denominations; it reflects a merger of the American Episcopal Church and a sizable portion of the Anglican Catholic Church.

Guelzo summarizes this general development with these words: "All of the 'Continuing Churches' are characterized by 'catholic' ritual and practice, except the United Episcopal Church, which is a low-church body. All are agreed in their use of the 1928 version of *The Book of Common Prayer* and their opposition to the admission of women to ordained ministry."

In 1922, members of the Episcopal Synod of America, a conservative organization within the Episcopal Church founded in 1989, formed the Episcopal Missionary Church and became the latest separatist body. It, too, reflects catholic ritual and theology, along with some evangelical and low-church elements.

EVANGELICAL CHURCH, THE

When The Methodist Church merged with the Evangelical United Brethren to form The United Methodist Church in 1968, a number of churches in the Brethren body withdrew to form a denomination of their own: Evangelical Church of North America. The new church was organized at Portland, Oregon, in June of that year and eventually came to include congregations across the country, including those of the former Holiness Methodist Church. In 1982, union occurred between that body and the Northwest Canada Conference.

The doctrinal position is Wesleyan-Arminian. In organization, conference superintendents oversee each district and annual conference; the general administration is carried on by annual conference sessions, the conference Council of Administration, and program agencies, such as evangelism, missions, Christian education, and stewardship. A general superintendent is the overseer of the work of the denomination. There is an inclusive membership of 16,398 in 185 churches in the U.S. and Canada, with particular strength in the Northwest.

EVANGELICAL CONGREGATIONAL CHURCH

Objecting to bishops' "usurpation of power in violation of the discipline," seven annual conferences and from 60,000 to 70,000 members of the Evangelical Association—later known as the Evangelical Church—withdrew from that body in 1894 to organize the United Evangelical Church. The two churches were reunited in 1922, but again a minority objected and remained aloof from the merger. The East Pennsylvania Conference and several churches in the Central, Pittsburgh, Ohio, Illinois, and West Virginia conferences continued their separate existence under the old name, later changed to Evangelical Congregational Church. Today the boundaries of the Eastern Conference are larger than at the time of the merger; the Midwest churches are combined with a Western Conference.

This church, like its parent Evangelical Church, is "Methodist in polity, Arminian in doctrine." Emphasis is on the inspiration and integrity of the Bible and "fellowship of all followers of Christ." There are annual conferences and a general conference (every four years), with equal lay and clergy representation. One bishop, with district conference superintendents, supervises an itinerant ministry. Pastors are appointed by the supervisory committee. Local congregations, as the name implies, have more freedom in temporal matters. The Division of Missions, with two adult auxiliaries, supervises the missionary programs. There are missionaries abroad and in the U.S., with 163 nationals at work in various lands.

Summer camping is held at three campsites strategically located in the conferences, with four ten-day camp meeting sessions. Church headquarters, the Evangelical School of Theology, and the Evangelical Congregational Church Retirement Village, are located at Myerstown, Pennsylvania. There are 25,000 members and approximately 15 churches.

EVANGELICAL COVENANT CHURCH, THE

This church traces its roots from the Protestant Reformation through the biblical instruction of the Lutheran state church of Sweden, to the great spiritual awakenings of the nineteenth century.

The Covenant Church adheres to the affirmations of the Reformation regarding the Holy Scriptures as the Word of God and the only perfect rule for faith, doctrine, and conduct. It has traditionally valued the historic confessions of the Christian church, particularly the Apostles' Creed, but emphasizes the sovereignty of the Word over all creedal interpretations. The Covenant's evangelical emphasis includes the necessity of the new birth, the ministry of the Holy Spirit, and the reality of freedom in Christ. It treasures the New Testament emphasis on personal faith in Jesus Christ as Savior and Lord and the church as a fellowship of believers, which recognizes but transcends theological differences. Baptism and the Lord's Supper are divinely ordained sacraments. While the denomination has traditionally practiced the baptism of infants, it has also recognized the practice of believer baptism.

The local church is administered by a board elected by the membership; its ministers, ordained by the denomination, are called, generally with the aid and guidance of the denominational Pastoral Relations Commission and the conference superintendent. Each of the nine regional conferences elects its own superintendent. The highest authority is vested in an annual meeting composed of ministers and laypeople elected by the constituent churches. An executive board, elected by the annual meeting, implements its decisions.

Foreign Mission Fields are in Zaire, Taiwan, Ecuador, Japan, Mexico, Thailand, Germany, and Russia. Educational institutions include North Park College and Theological Seminary in Chicago, Illinois; Covenant Bible College in Prince Albert, Saskatchewan, Canada; and Minnehaha Academy (K-12) in Minneapolis, Minnesota. The church has approximately 20 retirement communities and nursing homes, Swedish Covenant Hospital in Chicago, Illinois; Emanuel Medical Center in Turlock, California; two children's homes; an enabling resident for adults with developmental disabilities; transitional housing for homeless persons; and approximately 25 Bible camps and conference centers across North America and operates radio station KICY in Nome, Alaska. The church reported 91,000 adult members in 617 churches in 1992.

EVANGELICAL FREE CHURCH OF AMERICA

This church began when a group of independent congregations met with several churches of the old Swedish Ansgarii Synod and Mission Synod at Boone, Iowa, in 1884. They formed a fellowship of "free" congregations to be known as the Swedish Evangelical Free Mission (later changed to Swedish Evangelical Free Church). In 1950 the Swedish Evangelical Free Church and the Evangelical Free Church Association (formerly the Norwegian and Danish Evangelical Free Church Association) merged into the present body.

By common agreement, in 1884 this was to be a body of self-governing congregations. Churches were to elect delegates to an annual conference, which was advisory to the churches, but would legislate national and international ministries of the denomination itself. A society of ministers and missionaries was organized in 1894. Initially, the only qualification for membership in the local church was evidence of conversion and commitment to the Christian life. Polity is congregational. In 1950 the merged denominations adopted a twelve-point doctrinal statement, which is now incorporated into the constitution of most local congregations. There are approximately 1,200 churches grouped in 18 districts in the U.S., with about 150,000 members. Mission stations in Japan, the Philippines, Zaire, Singapore/Malaysia, Germany, Venezuela, Belgium, Peru, Mexico, and other places are served by 500 missionaries. The denomination sponsors three schools of higher education: Trinity Evangelical Divinity School and Trinity College, both in Bannockburn, Illinois, and Trinity Western University in Langley, British Columbia. The denomination also carries on an aggressive church-planting ministry. It is a member of the International Federation of Free Evangelical Churches and the National Association of Evangelicals.

FOURSQUARE GOSPEL, INTERNATIONAL CHURCH OF THE

Founded during the evangelistic work of Aimee Semple McPherson, this church is a tribute to the organizing genius and striking methods of its founder. Born in Ontario in 1890, McPherson was converted under the preaching of her first husband, Robert Semple, an evangelist. Semple died while they were serving as missionaries in China, and Aimee Semple returned to the U.S. in 1911, where she answered the call of God to conduct evangelistic crusades throughout North America.

In 1918, after her remarriage, Aimee Semple McPherson and her children, Roberta and Rolf, settled in Los Angeles, and with the help of those who had been blessed with her ministry, built and dedicated Angelus Temple on January 1, 1923. She also founded the Echo Park Evangelistic Association, the L.I.F.E. Bible College, and the International Church of the Foursquare Gospel religious corporations, still headquartered near Angelus Temple in Los Angeles.

With her great speaking ability and faith in prayer for the sick, McPherson attracted thousands to her meetings. Her more irreverent critics felt that the meetings were too spectacular, but others appreciated her type of presentation. There was great interest in the sick and the poor; "more than a million and a half" are said to have been fed by the Angelus Temple in her time.

The teaching of the church is set forth in a 21-paragraph Declaration of Faith written by McPherson. Strongly fundamental, it is premillennial, Holiness, and trinitarian, advocating that the Bible is as "true, immutable, steadfast, unchangeable, as its author, the Lord Jehovah." Baptism with the Holy Spirit, with the initial evidence of speaking in tongues, is subsequent to conversion, and the power to heal is given in answer to believing prayer. There are the usual doctrines on the atonement, the second coming of Christ "in clouds of glory," reward for the righteous at the judgment, and eternal punishment for the wicked. Baptism and the Lord's Supper are observed.

McPherson was president of the church during her lifetime and oversaw the denomination's expansion, together with a board of directors. Upon her death in 1944, her son, Rolf Kennedy McPherson, became president and presided in that position until May 31, 1988. Upon Dr. McPherson's retirement, the position was filled by John R. Holland.

The official business of the church is conducted by a board of directors, a missionary cabinet, and an executive council. The highest seat of authority is the convention body, which alone has the power to make or amend the bylaws of the church. District supervisors are appointed for nine districts in the United States and are ratified by pastors of the respective districts every four years. Each church is governed by a church council and contributes monthly to home and foreign missionary work. The official publication of the church is the *Foursquare World ADVANCE* magazine, published bimonthly.

While much of the membership is concentrated on the West Coast, there are Foursquare churches in all 50 states. Overseas, the Foursquare Gospel is preached in 78 countries, with 1.8 million members and adherents in nearly 27,000 churches and meeting places. Membership in the United States exceeds 200,000 in more than 1,600 churches. There are 194 foreign Bible schools and two Bible colleges in the United States—L.I.F.E. Bible College in Los Angeles, and L.I.F.E. Bible College East in Christiansburg, Virginia.

All members are required to subscribe to the Declaration of Faith. A church flag—red, gold, blue, and purple, with a red cross on the Bible background, bearing the superimposed number 4—is prominently displayed in the church. The church sponsors two radio stations: KFSG-FM in Los Angeles and KHIS-AM/FM in Bakersfield, California.

FRIENDS (QUAKER)

Dating from the 1650s in England, the Society of Friends, or Quakers, is an unconventional but much respected Protestant body. Because they affirm the "Inner Light," the spiritual nerve center that God has placed in every person, classical Friends deny the validity of clergy, liturgy, and sacraments. Worship takes the form of silent meetings, except when one is inspired to speak. The fact that every person has this inward spiritual endowment has prompted Friends to stand for the equality of all people and thus to oppose slavery and be exceptionally service minded. Their record of providing for human physical, social, and spiritual needs is truly remarkable. In North America since the mid-nineteenth century, some Friends have adapted the silent meeting to forms of church life that resemble standard evangelical practices, perhaps as much like Methodism as any other. But even there, the heritage of equality and respect for and service to all remains very strong.

With a membership in the U.S. and Canada of only 123,000 (200,000 around the world), Friends, better known as Quakers, have had a deep and lasting influence on Western society. Contributions in both religious and humanitarian spheres have won universal respect and admiration, and their amazing history and loyalty to their quiet faith offer a challenge and inspiration to all churches.

The Friends' vicissitudes and victories began when George Fox (1624–91), a British seeker after spiritual truth and peace, failed to find them in the churches of his time. He did find them, however, in a new personal relationship with Christ: "When all my hopes in [churches] were gone . . . I heard a voice which said, 'That is the Inner Voice, or Inner Light, based upon the description of John 1:9: "the true Light, which lighteth every man that cometh into the world' "—a voice available to all, having nothing to do with ceremonies, rituals, or creeds. To Friends, every person is a walking church; every heart is God's altar and shrine.

Quakerism was revolutionary, and it was treated as such by the state Church of England. To say that both state and church were wrong—that their theology and dogma meant nothing; that people need not attend "steeple houses" to find God; that it was equally wrong to pay taxes to support the state church clergy—this was rebellion.

Fox and his early followers went even further. They not only refused to go to church, but they also insisted on freedom of speech, assembly, and worship. They would not take oaths in court; they refused to go to war; they doffed their hats to no one, king or commoner; they made no distinction in sex or social class; they condemned slavery and England's treatment of prisoners and the insane. The very names they adopted—Children of Truth, Children of Light, Friends of Truth—aroused ridicule and fierce opposition. When Fox, hauled into court, advised one judge to "tremble at the Word of the Lord," he heard the judge call him "a quaker." But derision was not enough to stop the Friends. So persecution unsheathed its sword.

Quakers were whipped, jailed, tortured, mutilated, and murdered. Fox spent six years in jail; others spent decades, even dying there. From 1650 until 1689, more than 3,000 suffered for conscience's sake and 300 to 400 died in prison. But thanks to that persecution, the group grew, and the Religious Society of Friends was founded in 1652. When Fox died, Quakers numbered 50,000.

Some were already in America. Ann Austin and Mary Fisher arrived in Massachusetts from Barbados in 1656; they were promptly accused of being witches and were deported. Two days later, eight more Friends arrived from England. Hastily, laws were passed to keep them out; the whipping post worked overtime, but failed. Four were hanged in Boston. But Quakers kept coming—into New England, New York, New Jersey, Maryland, Virginia, and Pennsylvania. Rhode Island and Pennsylvania welcomed them from the beginning, and the long horror in the communities that did not welcome them ended with the passage of the Toleration Act of 1689.

With that law and Fox's death, a new phase began. Persecution waned and died; Quakers settled down to business and farming, were known for their pacifism and honesty, and became quite prosperous. During that period of quiet, the meetings and community life became well organized. It was a time of creativeness and mystical inwardness; closely knit family life was emphasized. Quaker philanthropy became widely respected, even admired; their ideas on prison reform began to take effect. Quaker schools increased; as early as 1691, there were 15 Quaker boarding schools in England.

In 1682 William Penn arrived in Philadelphia. He sat under an elm at Shackamaxon and made a treaty with the Indians—the "only treaty never sworn to and never broken." Treated like human beings, the Indians reacted in kind. If all our cities had been like Philadelphia and all our states like Pennsylvania, our national history might have been vastly different. But the holy experiment had to end. Quakers controlled the Pennsylvania legislature until 1756, when they refused to vote a tax to pay for a war against the Shawnees and Delawares, and consequently stepped down and out of power.

Quakers, looking within rather than without, began to enforce such strict discipline upon their members that they became, in fact, a "peculiar people." Members were disowned or dismissed for even minor infractions; thousands were cut off for "marrying out of Meeting." Pleasure, music, and art were taboo; sobriety, punctuality, and honesty were demanded in all directions; dress was painfully plain, and speech was biblical. They were "different" and dour; they gained few new converts and lost many old members.

Some few "fighting Quakers" went to battle in the American Revolution, but most remained pacifists, working quietly for peace, popular education, temperance, democracy—and against slavery. Their first attitude of tolerance changed slowly to one of outright opposition. In 1688 the Friends of Germantown, Pennsylvania, announced that slavery violated the Golden Rule and that it encouraged adultery; they called "traffic in the bodies of men" unlawful. It took nearly a century for Quakers to rid their own society of slavery, but they did it years in advance of any other religious body in America. Sellers or purchasers of slaves were forbidden membership in the society by the end of the eighteenth century. Persistently, across the years, they dropped their seeds of antislavery agitation into the body politic. First John Woolman and then poet John Greenleaf Whittier wielded tremendous influence. Once the Civil War was over, Friends threw their strength into such organizations as the Freedman's Aid Society; ever since, they have been active in education and legislative protection for blacks.

Divisions arose within the ranks during those years: The Hicksites separated in 1827, the Wilburites in 1845, the Primitives (a small group now extinct) in 1861. Of these separations, the one led by Elias Hicks is of primary concern. Hicks was a rural Long Island Quaker, and his liberal and rational theological views brought him into conflict with those who were more orthodox and evangelical. While the division in 1827 had personal and sociological emphases, the split was basically due to the nineteenth-century conflict between rational liberalism and orthodoxy based on Methodist ideas of evangelism and salvation. Two-thirds of the Philadelphia Yearly Meeting withdrew with the Hicksites (a name never officially adopted), and similar divisions followed in New York, Ohio, Indiana, and Baltimore. Another series of separations, a result of Wesleyan Methodist influence, was led by Joseph John Gurney and John Wilbur (see RELIGIOUS SOCIETY OF FRIENDS [CONSERVATIVE]).

The twentieth century thus far has been one of Quaker unity and outreach. A Five Years Meeting (now Friends' United Meeting) was organized in 1902, merging a large number of the pastoral yearly meetings. The two Philadelphia meetings, separated since 1827, were united in 1955; in the same year, the two New York Yearly Meetings merged, and the three Canada Yearly Meetings came together to form one body; in 1968, two Baltimore Yearly Meetings reunited; in 1972, the Southeastern Meeting, newly founded, affiliated with Friends United Meeting and Friends General Conference.

During World War I, Friends from all branches of the society were at work in the American Friends Service Committee in relief and reconstruction efforts abroad. The A.F.S.C. remains today one of the most effective of such agencies in the world. Its volunteers erected demountable houses, staffed hospitals, plowed fields, raised domestic animals, and drove ambulances. Famine relief and child-feeding programs were instituted in Serbia, Poland, Austria, Russia, and Germany; at one time, Friends were feeding more than one million German children a day; Greek refugees, Japanese earthquake victims, and miners' families in Pennsylvania, West Virginia, and Kentucky were helped as well. Thousands would have perished but for the A.F.S.C.

Friends served in the medical corps of both world wars, and some went into combat; probably more young Friends volunteered for or accepted military service than resisted on grounds of religious principle. They also worked to relieve displaced Japanese Americans during World War II, and they cooperated with Brethren and Mennonites in locating conscientious objectors in work of real importance on farms and in reformatories, hospitals, and mental institutions. They were in Spain soon after the outbreak of the Spanish Civil War; later they supplied food for children in Spain, southern France, Italy, Austria, Holland, North Africa, and Finland. In 1945 alone they sent 282 tons of clothes, shoes, bedding, and soap to Europe and still more to China and India. Counting both cash and material gifts, the income of the A.F.S.C. is apt to exceed $7.5 million annually.

Nor have Friends been satisfied to work merely in relief efforts. Peace conferences have had a prominent place, ranging from local to international and covering all age groups. Lake Mohonk in New York was founded by a Friend. Scores of youth conferences and camps in the U.S. and in foreign fields testify to devotion to the way of Christ; young volunteers in summer camps have inspired incalculable goodwill among nations and among minority groups within nations. It is little wonder that it is known as a "peace church."

Worship and business in the society are conducted in monthly, quarterly, and yearly meetings. The monthly meeting is the basic unit, made up of one or more meetings (groups) in a neighborhood. It convenes each week for worship and once a month for business. It keeps records of membership, births, deaths, and marriages; appoints committees; considers queries on spiritual welfare; and transacts all business. Monthly meetings join four times a year in a quarterly meeting to stimulate spiritual life and decide on any business that should be brought to the attention of the yearly meeting. The yearly meeting corresponds to a diocese in an episcopal system. There are 27 in the U.S. and Canada, in touch with Friends all over the world. There are standing committees on such subjects as publications, education, the social order, missions, peace, charities, and national legislation; trust fund incomes are allocated, and the work of the society is generally supervised.

Group decisions await the "sense of the meeting." Lacking unity of opinion, the meeting may have a "quiet time" until unity is found, or it may postpone consideration of the matter or refer it to a committee for study. Minority opinion is not outvoted, but convinced. Every man, woman, and child is free to speak in any meeting; delegates are appointed at quarterly and yearly meetings to ensure adequate representation, but enjoy no unusual position or prerogatives. Women and men hold positions of absolute equality.

Contrary to popular misunderstandings, church officers—elders and ministers—are chosen for recognized ability in spiritual leadership, but they too stand on equal footing with the rest of the membership. To the Friend, all members are ministers. A few full-time workers are paid a modest salary, and "recorded" ministers who serve as pastors in meetings that have programmed worship also receive salaries (about 1,000 meetings have no paid pastors).

Worship may be either programmed or unprogrammed, but the two are not always distinct. The former more nearly resembles an ordinary Protestant service, although there are no rites or outward sacraments. While Friends believe in spiritual communion, partaking of the elements is thought unnecessary. In unprogrammed meetings there is no choir, collection, singing, or pulpit; the service is devoted to quiet meditation, prayer, and Communion. Any vocal contributions are spontaneous. There is no uniform practice; most churches greatly prefer to be called meetings.

In business meetings there often is frank inquiry into members' conduct of business, treatment of others, use of narcotics or intoxicants, reading habits, and recreation. No true Friend gambles, plays the stock market, bets, owns race horses, or engages in raffles, lotteries, or the liquor business. Some follow conservative religious or theological patterns; others are liberal; all are guided by the Inner Light.

The Inner Light is highly important. Friends believe that grace, the power from God to help humankind resist evil, is universal among all people. They seek not holiness but perfection—a higher, more spiritual standard of life for both society and the individual—and they believe that the truth is unfolding and continuing. They value the Bible highly but prefer to rely on fresh individual guidance from the Spirit of God, which produced the Bible, rather than follow only what has been revealed to others. Some modern groups accept the Bible as the final authority in all religious matters. Rufus Jones says:

> They believe supremely in the nearness of God to the human soul, in direct intercourse and immediate communion, in mystical experience in a firsthand discovery of God. . . . It means and involves a sensitiveness to the wider spiritual Life above us, around us, and within us, a

dedication to duty, a passion for truth, and an appreciation of goodness, an eagerness to let love and the grace of God come freely through one's own life, a reverence for the will of God wherever it is revealed in past or present, and a high faith that Christ is a living presence and a life-giving energy always within reach of the receptive soul.

No Quaker body has ever departed from the Declaration to Charles II in 1661: "We utterly deny all outward wars and strife and fighting with outward weapons, for any end or under any pretense whatever. . . . The spirit of Christ, which leads us into all Truth, will never move us to fight and war against any man with outward weapons, neither for the Kingdom of Christ, nor for the kingdoms of this world." However, there is great tolerance for individual variations in this position. During World War II, the formal Quaker position favored applying for conscientious-objector status, either as a non-combatant within the military or in alternate service; in the case of the Vietnam war, corporate positions shifted to encouraging men to practice draft refusal and go to jail if necessary. In both cases, a wide variety of positions was accepted; the emphasis was on following individual conscience. Friends who enter military service are no longer disowned from membership, but many leave the society and join a church that does not profess pacifism. Conversely, pacifists brought up in other traditions tend to join the Friends in young adulthood.

Marriage is not necessarily a ceremony to be performed by a minister; in cases where the traditional Quaker marriage is observed, the bride and groom simply stand before a meeting and make mutual vows of love and faithfulness. In certain sections of the country, the pastor of the meeting officiates.

Friends have never been great proselytizers; they depend almost entirely on birthright membership and membership by "convince-ment." In many bodies, but not all, every child born of Quaker parents is declared a member of the society. This has resulted in a large number of nominal, or paper, members who contribute little; efforts are being made to correct this custom by establishing a junior, or associate, membership for children. This reliance on birthright membership has seriously depleted their numbers.

If Friends were ever exclusive, they no longer are; a world outreach has been evident and growing in recent years. Friends' United Meeting and Friends General Conference are members of the World Council of Churches; the Philadelphia Yearly Meeting belongs to the National Council of Churches. Friends World Committee for Consultation, organized at Swarthmore, Pennsylvania, following the Second World Conference of Friends in 1937, functions as an agent, or clearinghouse, for interchange of Quaker aspirations and experiences through regional, national, and international intervisitation, person-to-person consultations, conferences, correspondence, and a variety of publications. The committee has headquarters in Birmingham, England, and offices in Philadelphia, in Plainfield, Indiana, and in Edinburgh, Scotland. The American section has helped some 50 small U.S. Friends groups to attain monthly meeting status. The F.W.C.C. is a nongovernmental organization related to the Economic and Social Council of the United Nations, through cooperation with the A.F.S.C.; it helps operate a program at U.N. headquarters to forward world peace and human unity. Something of a world community, or "Franciscan Third Order," has been set up in the Wider Quaker Fellowship, in which non-Friends in sympathy with the spirit and program may participate in the work without coming into full membership. This is not so much an organization as "a fellowship of kindred minds—a way of life, a contagion of spirit"; it has 4,200 members, 360 of whom live abroad.

An Evangelical Friends Alliance was formed in 1965 in the interests of evangelical emphasis and denominational unity; it seeks to bring together those interested in an evangelical renewal within Christianity and a renewal of interest in the evangelical emphases of seventeenth-century Quakerism; it includes the Association of Evangelical Friends. Theology here is conservative; local pastors are elected. There are 217 churches and 24,095 members.

A further movement toward unity is found in the Religious Society of Friends (Unaffiliated Meetings), which also stresses elements and teachings of early Friends movements. This group is unique in its wide variety and experimentation in worship and polity; it is not associated with the larger bodies in the society. There are 112 churches with 6,386 members.

FRIENDS GENERAL CONFERENCE

Friends General Conference is one of three major national organizations of the Religious Society of Friends, or Quakers, in North America. The Religious Society of Friends began with George Fox and other seekers in the mid–1600s in England. Contemporary Friends, like those of Fox's time, believe that each person can and should have a direct experience of God or the Spirit that provides guidance in all aspects of one's life. A corollary of this belief is that "there is that of God in everyone," a conviction that has led Friends to refuse to participate in war and to support justice for all peoples.

Friends General Conference is an association of fourteen yearly meetings and regional associations of Friends (Quakers) in the

United States and Canada. These include some 540 monthly meetings (local congregations), most of which are unprogrammed. In unprogrammed meetings, worshipers meet in silence, expecting that one or more Friends may be moved by the Spirit to speak. No pastors are employed; the responsibilities handled by pastors in other denominations are shared among the members of the meeting.

Friends General Conference (FGC) serves the approximately 32,000 members of affiliated meetings by preparing and distributing educational and spiritual materials, by providing opportunities for Friends to share experiences and strengthen the Quaker community, and by helping monthly and yearly meetings to nurture and support the spiritual and community life of Friends in North America.

FGC was founded in 1900 by Friends from seven unprogrammed yearly meetings. It is best known for the annual "Gathering of Friends," which attracts between 1,500 and 2,000 Quakers from many parts of the United States and Canada.

FRIENDS UNITED MEETING
(FIVE YEARS MEETING)

With 55,015 members and 535 local meetings in 1992, this is the largest single Friends body in the U.S. Organized in 1902, it brought together in one cooperative relationship 18 yearly meetings at home and six abroad—in East Africa, Cuba, and Jamaica—with a somewhat different status. They work together in many departments, such as missionary service and the production of Sunday school materials; while each is autonomous, they come together for spiritual stimulation, business, and conference every three years.

The ministries are carried forward between triennial sessions by two planning commissions and the general board, which convene semiannually. Affirming the importance of personal religious experience, this group embodies a creative balance of central Quaker accents, evangelism and social concern, mission and service, worship, and ministry. Friends of various persuasions work together within the FUM spectrum. It seeks to implement its commitment as a classic "peace church." Membership is concentrated in North Carolina, Indiana, Ohio, and Iowa. Its support of higher education, with seven colleges spread from North Carolina to the Midwest to California, is remarkable in view of the size of its membership.

RELIGIOUS SOCIETY OF FRIENDS (CONSERVATIVE)

Known also as Wilburites, this group resulted from a second division. Joseph John Gurney, a British evangelical Quaker, came to

America in 1837 and began to preach and teach the final authority of the Bible and acceptance of the doctrines of atonement, justification, and sanctification. John Wilbur, a Rhode Island conservative, while not denouncing the authority of the Bible and its teachings, felt that Gurney's preaching substituted a creed for the immediate revelation of the Divine Spirit available to human beings. Both men had large followings; the outcome, from 1845 through 1904, was separation in Kansas, Iowa, Indiana, Ohio, New England, North Carolina, and Canada.

The conservative pattern generally was one "set forth by the Society in the beginning." It called for silent waiting before God, in expectation that the Spirit would instruct and move a person to speak or pray without program or ritual.

In New England in 1945 and in Canada in 1955, differences were resolved between these two groups, and they were reunited. There are still conservative yearly meetings in Iowa, Ohio, and North Carolina; they cooperate with other Friends groups in various areas of service and in intervisitation. There are 27 monthly meetings and nearly 2,000 members.

GRACE GOSPEL FELLOWSHIP

Dispensational and premillennial, this fellowship had its beginnings as a pastors' fellowship at a conference of pastors and missionaries at the Berean Bible Church in Indianapolis, Indiana, in 1943. A year later, at Evansville, Indiana, its purpose was defined in a constitution: "The purpose of this organization shall be to promote a fellowship among those who believe the truths contained in [our] doctrinal statement and to proclaim the Gospel of the Grace of God in this land, and throughout the world." That doctrinal statement includes belief in the Bible as infallibly inspired by God; the total depravity of the human race; redemption by God's grace through the blood of Christ by means of faith; eternal security for the saved; the gifts of the Spirit (as enumerated in Eph. 4:7-16); that the human nature of sin is never eradicated during this life. Its members believe in baptism by the Holy Spirit but hold that, while water baptism is biblical, it is not relevant to the present dispensation. Their method of biblical interpretation is dispensational, with emphasis on the distinctive revelation to the apostle Paul and on his ministry. Any church may vote to become affiliated with Grace Gospel Fellowship, provided it meets the doctrinal standards.

The Fellowship consists of 124 churches and 4,500 members in the U.S.; more than 1,000 churches are also found in Zaire, Puerto Rico, India, the Philippines, Australia, South Africa, Tanzania, and

South America. Grace Bible College and the headquarters of the Fellowship are located in Grand Rapids, Michigan. There are three missionary organizations—two abroad and one in the U.S.

HINDU COMMUNITIES

While groups of Hindu origin in the past have not taken on forms directly comparable to denominations, there has been an increasing presence of the Hindu tradition in the United States since the beginning of the Vedanta Society of New York in 1894. Founded by Swami Vivekananda after the 1893 World's Parliament of Religions in Chicago, this movement is characterized by an insistence on the oneness of all religions, as expressed in the monistic texts of Hindu philosophy. Returning to India, Vivekananda founded the Ramakrishna Math and Mission, named for his teacher, Sri Ramakrishna, the mystic saint of nineteenth-century Bengal. From its location at Belur Math, near Calcutta, some supervision of the American centers of the Vedanta Society is provided. The Los Angeles Vedanta Society serves in an informal administrative role for approximately a dozen other societies and retreat centers.

The Self-Realization Fellowship is the outgrowth of the work of Swami Yogananda, who settled in Boston in 1925, teaching meditation techniques known as *kriya-yoga* and initiating the Church of All Religions, which combines Hindu and Christian elements. The group in Los Angeles serves as headquarters for congregations that sometimes have individual names, such as the Temple of Kriya Yoga in Chicago and the Self-Realization Church of Absolute Monism in Washington, D.C.

Most visible in recent years has been the International Society for Krishna Consciousness (ISKCON). The Hare Krishna movement was initiated by A. C. Bhaktivedanta Swami Prabhupada, who began teaching in New York in 1965 a tradition of ecstatic devotion developed in Bengal in the sixteenth century. He subsequently settled in Los Angeles and began publishing commentaries and translations of the scriptures of the movement and other theological works. Distribution of these and other printed materials, such as the periodical *Back to Godhead,* has been continued by the Bhaktivedanta Book Trust as an important ISKCON activity. Primary for devotees is the pattern of worship, daily as well as on commemoration days. An ascetic lifestyle is espoused, viewed as the antidote to modern materialism and as the counterpart of one's spiritual awareness. After the founder's death in 1977, a governing body of commissioners assumed responsibility for the worldwide affairs of the movement. The U.S. headquarters is in Los Angeles, overseeing more than 60 temples or centers in the U.S. and abroad. A monastic community called New Vrindavan was founded in West Virginia at Moundsville, near Wheeling, in 1969, where "Prabhupada's Palace of Gold" has become a tourist attraction. Violence, including allegations of murder, and other legal problems beginning in 1985 have beset this community. In 1987, the leader, Kirtananda Swami Bhaktipada (née Keith Harn), who had pressed for various reforms was excommunicated; his followers have since been known as the International Society for Krishna Consciousness of West Virginia, which developed its own publications and changed its dress from Hindu garb to a Franciscan habit.

Other groups such as Transcendental Meditation (TM, which professes not to be a religion), founded by Maharishi Mahesh Yoga, and the Divine Light Mission of Guru Maharaj Ji continue but not on the scale of previous activity. A number of communities focus on the legacies of particular teachers; more than a hundred such groups, primarily local in scope, can be identified.

Most of these groups have not, except for leaders, involved major participation by Americans of Hindu ancestry. With increasing immigration, temples and supporting associations that have attracted Hindus have been established in approximately 80 communities in 23 states. Some have links to temples and to associated religious groupings in India, while others have sought to be inclusive of all components of the Hindu tradition. Various degrees of combination of ritual and cultural concerns of the Indian community are manifest, as are various degrees of participation of Jains and Sikhs. The ritual practices, including the designation of priests to officiate, and program patterns (e.g., educational materials, tapes for guiding worship, the nature of festival observances) are locally determined, and nothing resembling a denomination has appeared.

The United States have also seen the appearance of groups that draw on other aspects of the Indian religious heritage, such as the Jains and the Sikhs. A Sikh organization active in the United States and Canada is Sikh Dharma and its educational arm, the Health, Happy Holy Organization (3HO). Sikh origins and strengths are in northern India, in the Punjab, where Guru Nanak (1439–1538) brought together strands of Hindu and Muslim devotion. His attempted reconciliation largely alienated Muslims, and today Sikhs increasingly reject definition as a branch of Hinduism. Yogi Bhajan, founder of Sikh Dharma and a proponent of orthodox observance, precipitated a division by attacking the laxity in the practice of some Punjabi Americans. Today the Sikh Council of North America (in Richmond Hill, New York) brings together Sikh centers whose members are primarily Punjabi Americans. Jains, smaller in number in the United States, as in India, have been prone to remain closer to Hindu institutions.

INDEPENDENT FUNDAMENTAL CHURCHES OF AMERICA

Organized in 1930 at Cicero, Illinois, by representatives of various independent churches anxious to safeguard fundamental doctrine, this body has two types of membership—one for churches and organizations, the other for ministers, missionaries, evangelists, and Christian workers. As organization members, 700 churches are directly affiliated, and the pastors of 345 independent churches are affiliated. More than 1,366 ministers, missionaries, evangelists, and Christian workers are members; total membership is 78,174, with strength in California, Pennsylvania, Michigan, and Illinois. There are five Bible camps; seven Bible institutes, 23 church extension organizations; two children's homes; and 16 home and four foreign mission agencies.

The president of the body presides over an annual conference in which the members have voting power; an executive committee of 12 serves for three years. The constituent churches are completely independent but are required to subscribe to the statement of faith of the organization. A home office is maintained in Grandville, Michigan.

Directly and indirectly, the group supports a number of Bible schools. The official organ is the *Voice*, published bimonthly.

JEHOVAH'S WITNESSES

The people called Jehovah's Witnesses believe that their movement is the true realization of the one faith mentioned by the apostle Paul in Ephesians 4:5. Their certainty of this and their zeal in proclaiming it have made them, at least in point of public interest, an outstanding religious phenomenon in modern America.

Charles Taze Russell had brought about their first incorporation in 1884, and until 1931 they were known as Russellites, Millennial Dawn People, and International Bible Students. Pastor Russell, the first president, is acknowledged not as founder (there is no "human" founder), but as general organizer; passages are cited to prove the claim that Witnesses have been on earth as an organization for more than 5,000 years (Isa. 43:10-12; Heb. 11; John 18:37).

Russell was deeply influenced by a belief in Christ's second coming; he studied the Bible avidly and attracted huge crowds to hear his lectures. The first formal group was organized in Pittsburgh in 1870; Russell's books, of which 13,000,000 are said to have been circulated, had great influence on the movement. To assist Russell, a board of directors was elected by vote of all members who subscribed ten dollars or more to support the work (a practice discontinued in 1944). Under Russell's direction, the headquarters was moved to Brooklyn in 1909, and another corporation was formed under the laws of the state of New York. In 1939 the name of this corporation was changed to Watchtower Bible and Tract Society of New York, Inc.

When Russell died in 1916, Joseph F. Rutherford, known widely as Judge Rutherford, became president; he had been a lawyer and occasionally sat as a circuit court judge in Missouri. He wrote tirelessly; his books, pamphlets, and tracts supplanted those of Russell, and his neglect of some aspects of Russell's teaching brought dissension.

Administration of the group underwent change during Rutherford's presidency. The governing body today is in the hands of those older and more "spiritually qualified," who base their judgments on the authority of the Scriptures; this is not considered a governing hierarchy, but a true imitation of early apostolic Christian organization. Under that system, three corporations eventually came to serve under the direction of the governing body: Watchtower Bible and Tract Society of New York, Inc.; Watch Tower Bible and Tract Society of Pennsylvania; and International Bible Students Association of England. Judge Rutherford, as president, was a moving power in all three.

Under direction of the leaders at headquarters, local congregations of Witnesses (always called congregations, never churches) are arranged in circuits, with a traveling minister who spends a week with each congregation. Approximately 20 congregations are included in each circuit, and circuits are grouped into districts, with 38 in the U.S. district; circuit organizations are now found in 211 countries and islands around the world.

Meeting in Kingdom halls (not in churches), members witness and publish their faith in testimony and in a remarkably comprehensive missionary effort. They do not believe in separation into clergy and laity, since "Christ Jesus did not make such a separation." They never use titles such as *Reverend;* this, they feel, is not in accordance with the words of Jesus in Matthew 23:6-10.

All members give generously of their time in proclaiming their faith and teaching in private homes. Called publishers of the Kingdom, they preach only from the Bible. Pioneers, or full-time preachers, are required to give at least 90 hours per month; special pioneers and missionaries donate a minimum of 140 hours per month and are sent to isolated areas and foreign lands where new congregations can be formed. All pioneers provide their own support, but the society gives a small allowance to special pioneers, in view of their special needs.

The headquarters staff, including the president of the society, are housed at Bethel Home in Brooklyn, New York. They engage primarily in editorial and printing work and receive an allowance of $45 a month, in addition to room and board. They write, print, and distribute literature in almost astronomical proportions. The official journal, *The Watchtower,* has a circulation of 16,400,000; more than one billion Bibles, books, and leaflets have been distributed since 1920, and these are available in at least 200 languages.

Contained in the literature (all circulated without bylines or signatures) is the teaching of the Witnesses, which rests firmly on the idea of theocracy, or rule of God. In the beginning, according to Witnesses, the world was under the theocratic rule of the Almighty; all then was "happiness, peace, and blessedness." But Satan rebelled and became the ruler of the world, and from that moment, humankind has followed his evil leading. Then came Jesus, "the beginning of the creation by God" (Rev. 3:14), as the prophets had predicted, to end Satan's rule.

Jesus' heavenly rule, after he paid the ransom sacrifice of his death on earth, began in 1914. In 1918, Christ "came to the temple of Jehovah," and in 1919 when Rutherford reorganized the movement shattered by World War I, Jesus, enthroned in the temple, began to send out his followers to preach.

God, according to Witness belief, will take vengeance on wicked human beings in our time; God is now showing great love by "gathering out" multitudes of people of goodwill, to whom God will give life in the new world that is to come after the imminent battle of Armageddon. This is to be a universal battle; Christ will lead the army of the righteous, composed of the "host of heaven, the holy angels," and will completely annihilate the army of Satan. The righteous of the earth will watch the battle but will not participate.

After the battle, a great crowd of people will remain on the earth; these will be believers in God and will be God's servants. Those who have proved their integrity under test in the old world will multiply and populate the new earth with righteous people. A resurrection will also take place, as an additional means of filling the cleansed earth with better inhabitants. After the holocaust, "righteous princes" will rule the earth under Christ, King of the Great Theocracy. One special group—the 144,000 Christians mentioned in Revelation 7 and 14—will become the "bride of Christ" and rule with him in heaven. Rutherford died in 1942, leaving guidance of the movement in the hands of Nathan H. Knorr. When Knorr died in 1977, Armageddon had not yet been fought, but the certainty of its imminence persists. Frederick W. Franz replaced Knorr and served as president until his death in 1993. Milton G. Henschel is now president.

All these beliefs are based on the Bible; hence Witnesses quote elaborately from Scripture. All other teachings and interpretations are, to them, suspect and unreliable. They have been especially active in opposing what they consider the three allies of Satan: false teachings of the churches, tyranny of human governments, and oppression by big business. This "triple alliance" of ecclesiastical, political, and commercial powers has misled humankind, the Witnesses claim, and must be destroyed at Armageddon before the new world can be born. They refuse to salute the flag, bear arms in war, or participate in the political affairs of government—not because of pacifist convictions, but because they desire to remain apart from what they consider expressions of Satan's power over humankind.

This attitude has brought them into conflict with law enforcement agencies; they have also endured whippings, assaults by mobs, stonings, being covered with tar and feathers, the burning of their homes, imprisonment, and detention in concentration camps. All of this they have accepted in a submissive spirit. Their position is that they will obey the laws of the earth when those laws are not in conflict with the laws of God; their guide is Acts 5:29.

The ranks of active "publishers" across the world have grown to 4,278,820, of whom approximately 892,551 are in the U.S. In 1993 there were 9,524 congregations in the U.S.; 66,207 throughout the world. Branch offices are maintained in 97 countries, and work is reported in 211 lands; more than 6,500 people have been trained as foreign missionaries. The Bible School of Gilead was established in 1943 for this training; since 1961 it has operated out of the international headquarters in Brooklyn, New York. Kingdom Ministry Schools, designed to provide a brief training course for congregation elders, have operated in all major countries of the world since 1959.

Judaism

Judaism, the religion of the Jewish people, is as old as that historical-ethnic people. It began to take shape in the time of Abraham (perhaps 1800 B.C.E.) and was well formulated by the era of Moses (perhaps 1300 B.C.E.) and David (perhaps 950 B.C.E.). After the Diaspora (the dispersion of the people from Israel, their homeland),

Judaism came to center more on ethics, observance, and worship than on sacrifice associated with the Temple.

Over the centuries in Europe, Jewish identity strengthened in response to ostracism and persecution by Christian societies. However, the people's confrontation with modernity around 1800 threatened to erode the strength of their tradition. Many have become quite secular, and intermarriage, a genuine peril to a community defined by ethnic integrity, has become common. This encounter with modern culture has led to the formation of Reform, Conservative, and Reconstructionist schools of thought, or "denominations," alongside Orthodox.

Being biblical, Judaism is a religion of salvation—from personal insignificance and a lifestyle unworthy of God's human creation. It is the faith and practice of the Jewish people, not a message to be taken to others. Centering more in the home than in the synagogue, it makes the family the primary unit, teaching observances of the weekly sabbath and special seasons in the Jewish year.

Jews arrived early in the American colonies; some were here before 1650. A small group of Portuguese Jews found safety, if not complete understanding, in Peter Stuyvesant's New Amsterdam, where they established the first official congregation in North America, Shearith Israel or "Remnant of Israel," in 1654. Three years later, a small group had settled at Newport, Rhode Island. Jews settled in Georgia a few months later than Oglethorpe, and in that same year, 1733, organized a synagogue in Savannah. By 1850, there were 77 Jewish congregations in 21 states; at the end of the century, there were more than 600 congregations with 1,000,000 members.

Today, 5,500,000 American "Core Jews" have a widely varying synagogue membership (approx. 65 percent of these belong) as well as those "born Jews" without a current religion. (*Note:* figures in this section refer to "core Jewish population"—that is, persons who claim adherence to Judaism, both "born Jews" and "Jews by choice.") The total "Jewishly Identified Population" numbers 6,840,000. Categories making up this total that are not included in the Core Jews aggregate are adults of Jewish parentage who practice another religion; those born and raised Jewish who have converted to another religion; and children under 18 who have been raised in another religion.

Judaism rests on two pillars. One is the Hebrew Bible, particularly the Pentateuch, or the five books of Moses, known as the Torah. It is the revelation of God, divine in origin and containing the earliest written laws and traditions of the Jewish people. The other pillar is the Talmud, a rabbinic commentary and enlargement of the Torah.

JUDAISM

It is an elaborate, discursive compendium that contains the written and oral laws of the faith.

In Torah and Talmud are found the Jewish foundation principles of justice, purity, hope, thanksgiving, righteousness, love, freedom of will, divine providence and human responsibility, repentance, prayer, and messianic hope. At their heart lies the Hebrew concept of the oneness of God. Every day the practicing Jew repeats the ancient biblical verse, "Hear, O Israel, the Lord our God is one Lord." There is but one Creator, who holds the destiny of humankind and the world in his almighty hands.

Humankind, created by this one God, is inherently good. There is no original sin, no instinctive evil or fundamental impurity; human beings are made in God's image and are endowed with an intelligence that enables them to choose between good and evil. They need no mediator, such as Christians have in Christ, but approach God directly. All people—Jews and Gentiles alike—attain immortality as the reward for righteous living, although concern for life after death is an issue of minor significance for Jews.

Judaism looks forward to the perfection of humankind and to the establishment of a divine kingdom of truth and righteousness on the earth. Orthodox Jews believe the time will come when God will send the Messiah; Conservative and Reconstructionist doctrines teach variations of this idea, and Reform Judaism speaks of a messianic age. To work toward the divine kingdom, Jews have been established by God as a deathless, unique people, "a kingdom of priests and a holy nation," the "servant of the Lord."

Some of their laws provide for the great festivals of the Jewish year: Pesach or Passover, in late March or early April, a memorial of the liberation of Jews from Egypt; Shabuoth, Feast of Weeks or Pentecost, in late May or early June, commemorating Moses' receiving of the Ten Commandments; Sukkoth, Feast of Tabernacles or Booths, in October, marking the years of Jewish wandering in the wilderness; Hanukkah, Feast of Lights, in December, celebrating the purification of the Temple by the Maccabees after its defilement by Antiochus Epiphanes; Purim, Feast of Lots, in February or March, honoring the heroine Esther. Principal fasts are also observed: the Fast of Ab, memorializing the fall of Jerusalem and the destruction of the Temple; and Yom Kippur, the Day of Atonement. Particularly important to American Jews are Rosh Hashanah, or New Year's day, and Yom Kippur, which closes the Ten Days of Penitence that begin with Rosh Hashanah.

Other laws are kept as reminders of God's covenant with Israel; these include the laws of circumcision and sabbath observance. Still

159

others are held as marks of divine distinction and are kept to preserve the ideal of Israel as a chosen, separate people.

Local congregations have full independence. There are no synods, assemblies, or hierarchies of leaders. Jews are loosely bound by the "rope of sand" of Jewish unity, but with wide variation in custom and procedure. They have been influenced by the many peoples and cultures with which they have come in contact and have made adjustments accordingly. Because of differences in historical background over the centuries, some American congregations use a German-Polish, or Ashkenazic, version of the Hebrew prayer books; others use a Spanish, or Sephardic, version. Some use English at various points in the service, such as the sermon; but all use Hebrew in the prayers. Traditional Orthodox synagogues have no instrumental music, the congregation worships with covered heads, and the men and women sit separately. In Reform, Conservative, and Reconstructionist houses of worship, sermons are in English and there is no segregation by sex.

At the head of the congregation stands the rabbi, trained in seminary and fully ordained. He officiates at marriages and grants divorce decrees in accordance with Jewish law after civil divorce has been granted by the state. He conducts funerals and generally supervises burials as Jewish law requires. Congregations usually own their own cemeteries or organize cemetery societies; also, many private cemetery or burial associations are controlled by Jewish benevolent groups. Orthodox rabbis supervise the slaughtering of animals and the distribution of kosher meat products in accordance with dietary law. Many congregations engage readers, or cantors, but the rabbi is the leader and authority on Jewish law and ritual.

There are four large divisions in American Judaism; (1) Orthodox Judaism, represented nationally by the Union of Orthodox Jewish Congregations of America, the Rabbinical Council of America, and the Union of Orthodox Rabbis of the United States and Canada; (2) Reform Judaism, affiliated with the Central Conference of American Rabbis and Union of American Hebrew Congregations—the first national organization of synagogues in the United States, established in 1973; (3) Conservative Judaism, organized in the United Synagogue of America and Rabbinical Assembly of America; and (4) Reconstructionist Judaism, a movement that broke away from Conservative Judaism. In addition, newer, smaller "denominations" are present in American Jewish life. One useful name for some of them is "spinoff sects." Reconstructionism is such a body, having spun off from Conservative Judaism. Other newer bodies are "transplanted sects," with Hasidism prominent. These began elsewhere, notably in Poland and Russia, and were transplanted in the U.S. by Jewish immigration from those countries. Hasidism, in its several forms, seeks to embody piety, closeness to God, who is an all-pervasive presence.

Synagogue membership is difficult to determine; no comprehensive comparison of numbers seems available or possible. Research conducted in 1990 disclosed that 16 percent of American Jews identified with Orthodox, 43 percent with Conservative, 35 percent with Reform, and 6 percent with either Reconstructionist or no denomination. Percentages of increase are usually high; congregations are being formed faster than the various seminaries can ordain rabbis to supply their needs. In 1990, Conservative synagogues reported 890,000 members; Reform, 760,000; Orthodox, 355,000; and Reconstructionist, some 50,000. These are, of course, Core Jews. Many households do not have a synagogue affiliation.

The multiplicity of Jewish national organizations is bewildering. The *American Jewish Year Book* lists the following categories: community relations and political, 31; overseas aid, 18; religious and educational, including colleges, 130; social and mutual benefit, 15; cultural, 54; social welfare, 43; Israel-related, 88; professional associations, 29; women's organizations, 16; youth and student organizations, 17. In more than 225 larger towns and cities, the Jewish population maintains at least one central local organization—perhaps a federation welfare fund or a community council. There are some 200 periodicals and newspapers and two news syndicates. *American Judaism* is the quarterly Reform organ; the monthly *Jewish Action* speaks for the Orthodox branch; *Conservative Judaism* is a quarterly for the Conservatives. Of general interest are *Commentary, Midstream, The Reconstructionist, Judaism, Forward, Tikkun, Moment,* and *Hadassah Magazine.*

Education on all levels is a major concern. Children are enrolled in sabbath schools, weekday schools, all-day schools, and Yiddish schools. In 1990 there were about 400,000 children in all the weekday and sabbath schools.

Jewish institutions of higher learning, affiliated with the various movements, serve the community nationwide, training rabbis, of course, but also providing general Jewish learning for all interested people. The most important are (Orthodox) Rabbi Isaac Elchanan Theological Seminary of Yeshiva University in New York City; (Reform) Hebrew Union College—Jewish Institute of Religion in New York, Cincinnati, Los Angeles, and Jerusalem; (Conservative) Jewish

Theological Seminary in New York City; and Reconstructionist Rabbinical College in Philadelphia. University of Judaism in Los Angeles is a branch of Jewish Theological Seminary. Yeshiva University in New York City and Brandeis University in Waltham, Massachusetts, are the only colleges that award a B.A. degree (Brandeis is actually nonsectarian.)

Jewish charity is amazingly efficient. Federations and welfare boards maintain programs costing more than $500 million a year. This money is divided among local agencies (health, welfare, education, and recreation), national agencies (civic defense, cultural, religious, and service), and overseas (mainly to help settle refugees in Israel and other countries).

The American Jewish Committee is organized to protect the civil and religious rights of Jews around the world. It seeks equality in economic, social, and educational opportunities and gives aid and counsel in cases of intolerance or persecution.

Among Zionist groups, Hadassah, the women's Zionist group, is the largest and the most active in philanthropic and educational programs; the Zionist Organization of America is the second-largest single body numerically. In the past decade the most influential representative on behalf of aid to Israel has been the Conference of Presidents of major American Jewish organizations, a coordinating body and a forum of 22 major American Jewish organizations on all questions affecting American-Israeli affairs.

Three trends in Jewish life are noticeable: (1) a relaxation of literal observance of the time-honored Jewish law, one expression of which is found in the Reconstructionist movement, a development of some influence in both Conservative and Reform Judaism; (2) "emphasis upon youth," in which young Orthodox Jews are organized as Young Israel for future leadership in synagogues; (3) a tendency among all groups to consider the inner spiritual strength of Judaism as its only hope for the future. Under this drive, American Jews are moving toward fewer divisions and more cooperation and unity.

CONSERVATIVE JUDAISM

Conservative Judaism holds the middle ground between Orthodox and Reform Judaism. It seems to lean to the Orthodox, but in some areas it resembles Reform thinking and procedure. Established "for the preservation in America of historical Judaism," it takes from Orthodoxy its belief in the Torah, observance of the dietary laws of traditional Judaism, use of the Hebrew language, and the historic custom of men worshiping with heads covered, wearing the *tallis* (prayer shawl) on appropriate occasions.

From Reform comes the tendency to reconcile old beliefs and practices with the cultures in which it finds itself: the use of English as well as Hebrew in the prayer service read from the *siddur* (the prayer book), family pews with men and women sitting together, optional use of instrumental music and mixed choirs, and modern methods of education in the development of schools for children and youths. Generally, to the Conservative, Judaism is not static, but the deepening, growing, widening faith of a people who absorb influences from other cultures, yet retain their own ethnic and religious aspects.

ORTHODOX JUDAISM

Orthodox Judaism has been called Torah-True Judaism; it is the branch that preserves the theology and traditions of Old World Jewry in the New World. It assigns equal authority to the written and oral law and to the ancient codes embodied in the Torah, the Talmud, and their commentaries. The Torah is all-important; it is of God, given to Moses, and the way to God is through obedience to the laws of Torah. Torah is a revelation of the primacy and supremacy of God and the unity of humankind; it explains the place of Jews as the chosen people of God. Torah governs every moment of life. Moses is believed to have begun an oral tradition that continued to the time Torah was first committed to writing. There are, however, many variant emphases: the East European, Hasidic orthodoxy, which stems from Hungary, opposes change or innovation in speech, dress, and education; hence it changes very slowly when at all. German and Western European orthodoxy is a bit less severe, attempting to preserve the more important elements of traditional Jewish life, but accepting modern changes and ideas in those three areas.

Orthodox Jews believe in the political rebirth of their nation, in the return of the Jews to Israel to rebuild the temple on Mount Zion and reestablish the ancient sacrificial ritual. They look forward to the coming of the Messiah, who is to be a descendant of David. The biblical dietary laws are strictly observed and the traditional holy days and festivals faithfully kept. Hebrew language is used in synagogue prayers, English in the sermons.

RECONSTRUCTIONISM

Within Conservative Judaism exist schools of thought that seek to reconstruct Judaism as a natural religion, to make it relevant to contemporary rational and scientific thought. Originating in 1934 under the leadership of Mordecai M. Kaplan of the Jewish Theological Seminary, Reconstructionism is a movement indigenous to America. Defining Judaism as an evolving religious civilization, it attempts to assure physical and spiritual survival by demonstrating that a maximum Jewish life can be lived within the setting of a modern democratic state. Although its program is directed specifically to American Jews, its philosophy applies to Jewish life everywhere.

REFORM JUDAISM

A more liberal body, Reform Judaism began in Germany just after the Napoleonic emancipation, when reformers within Judaism shortened the synagogue services, made use of the vernacular and music in those services, and established group rather than individual confirmation. At that time, there was an unsuccessful attempt to break completely with traditional forms.

Isaac Mayer Wise, one of Reform's outstanding leaders in the U.S., founded the Union of American Hebrew Congregations (1873), Hebrew Union College (1875), and the Central Conference of American Rabbis (1889); these important groups sum up Reform Judaism's conviction that Judaism should "alter its externals to strengthen its eternals."

Reform holds that divine authority lies only in the written law of the Old Testament; this is its main distinction from Orthodox Judaism. But revelation in Reform is not confined to the Old Testament; it is progressive. Many Reform Jews limit their religious practices to the ceremonial laws of the Pentateuch, with the exception of laws that, like that of sacrifice, they regard as having no purpose in the present day. The sacrifices of the Mosaic era are seen as reflections of the culture of the time, rather than as eternally commanded observances.

Claiming that the mission of Judaism is the spiritualization of humankind, Reform sees such practices as covering the head at worship, dietary laws, and the wearing of phylacteries as anachronisms that isolate Jews from the rest of humankind and thus make such spiritualizing impossible. Hence, those practices should be abolished. In other words, Orthodox Jews accept the entire body of oral and written law as sanctified by tradition; Reform Jews have simplified the ritual and adapted it to modern needs.

Unlike the Orthodox, they do not believe in the messianic restoration of the Jewish state and the return to Jerusalem; they are abandoning belief in a personal Messiah, but still hold to faith in the coming of a messianic age. They do support return to Israel under the Zionist movement, not so much on spiritual or Talmudic grounds as in the belief that Israel offers a place of refuge for persecuted Jews of the world. They advocate the preservation in the new state of Israel of those Jewish values, customs, and traditions that have inspirational value.

LATTER-DAY SAINTS (MORMON)

Best known as Mormons, Latter-Day Saints are neither Protestant nor Catholic. Their beliefs rest on the authority provided by the discovery in the 1820s of the Book of Mormon, which details the history of God's ancient people in the Western Hemisphere between 600 B.C.E. and 400 C.E.. That book, with its distinctive message, stands alongside the Bible ("as far as it is translated correctly") as the basis of Mormon teachings. They believe that the authentic church, having gone underground for many centuries, was restored with that new revelation.

By 1850, Mormons finally enjoyed a place of their own, Utah, where they built a civilization. Committed to expansion, they continue to grow rapidly in the U.S. and many foreign countries, most dramatically in Latin America and Asia. Few modern churches live with such clear identity and manage such a high degree of loyalty and dedication. Conservative politically and morally, the denomination gives a predominant place to family life.

Latter-Day Saints have had one of the most tempestuous histories of any church in the U.S. Attacked by mobs and once invaded by U.S. Army troops, they built a religious community in what was once a desert and have established themselves as one of the outstanding religious groups in the nation.

Essentially a laity movement, the church is rooted in the visions of Joseph Smith, who organized the movement with six charter members at Fayette, New York, in 1830. Smith claimed to have experienced a series of heavenly visitations, beginning with the appearance of God and Jesus Christ in 1820, in which Smith was informed that all existing churches were in error and that the true gospel was yet to be restored. It would be revealed to him, and he was to reestablish the true church on earth. He was led by an angel to discover, buried in a hill called Cumorah near Manchester, New York, certain metal plates left there by an ancient prophet. The plates contained the sacred records of ancient inhabitants of North America and the true Word of God. According to the Mormons, North America was originally settled by Jaredites, one of the groups dispersed during the confusion of tongues at the Tower of Babel; thus

Native Americans were direct descendants of the Hebrews who came from Jerusalem in 600 B.C.E. Mormons also believe that Jesus himself visited this continent after his resurrection.

Smith translated the hieroglyphics on the plates into the *Book of Mormon,* from which the denomination's name comes. Oliver Cowdery acted as his scribe. The *Book of Mormon* is considered by the Saints as equal with the Bible. With the two other writings of Joseph Smith, *Doctrine and Covenants* and *Pearl of Great Price,* these four books contain the foundation teachings of the church. The metal plates were said to have been returned to the angel by Joseph Smith; their authenticity has been challenged by non-Mormon scholars and as ardently defended by Mormons, who offer the names of eleven other persons besides Smith who saw them. The "priesthood of Aaron" was conferred upon Smith and Cowdery by a heavenly messenger, John the Baptist, who instructed them to baptize each other. In 1829, a year before the founding of the church, three other divine visitors, Peter, James, and John, bestowed upon them the "priesthood of Melchizedek" and gave them the keys of apostleship.

Opposition arose as the church gained strength, and in 1831 the Mormons left New York for Ohio, where headquarters were established at Kirtland. Another large Mormon center developed at Independence, Missouri, where they planned to build the ideal community, with a temple at its heart. Friction with other settlers there became so acute that they left Missouri during 1838 and 1839 and settled at Nauvoo, Illinois. But violence followed them and reached its peak when Joseph Smith and Hyrum Smith, his brother, were murdered by a mob at Carthage in 1844.

With Smith's death, the Quorum of the Twelve Apostles was accepted as the head of the church, with Brigham Young as president of the Quorum. The defeated minority, objecting that Young was not the legal successor to Smith, withdrew to form other churches. Some followed James J. Strang to Wisconsin to form the sect known as Strangite; others joined various other dissenting groups. But the largest body of "anti-Brighamites" believed that the leadership belonged to direct descendants of Joseph Smith, and in 1847 these people, led by Joseph Smith, Jr., formed the Reorganized Church of Jesus Christ of Latter-Day Saints.

But Young held his office with the vote of the majority, and he had the courage and the administrative ability to save the church from disruption and further division. He led the Saints when they were driven out of Nauvoo in February 1846 and began their epic march to what is now Utah. They arrived in Salt Lake Valley in July 1847, and there they built their famous tabernacle at the heart of what was to become worldwide Mormonism, creating a self-existent community in the desert. In 1850 the Territory of Utah was formed; it became a state in 1896.

Based on the *Book of Mormon* and the Bible, plus the revelations of Joseph Smith, the faith of Mormons is like that found in many conservative Protestant churches. However, certain aspects of the theology of Latter-Day Saints depart from the traditional orthodoxy of Catholic and Protestant churches: Three persons comprise the Godhead—the Father, the Son, and the Holy Ghost; the Father and the Son have bodies of flesh and bone, but the Holy Ghost is a personage of Spirit; persons will be punished for their own individual sins, not for Adam's transgression. All humankind may be saved through the atonement of Christ and by obedience to the laws and ordinances of the gospel; these include faith in Christ, repentance, baptism by immersion for the remission of sins, the laying on of hands for the gift of the Holy Ghost, and the observance of the Lord's Supper each Sunday. They believe in the gift of tongues and of interpretation of tongues, visions, prophecy, and healing; that Christ will return to rule the earth from his capitals in Zion and Jerusalem, following the restoration of the ten tribes of Israel. It is also believed that Latter-Day Saints should adhere to the official pronouncements of the living president (prophet) of the church.

Revelation is not to be regarded as confined to either the Bible or the *Book of Mormon*; it continues today in the living apostles and prophets of the Latter-Day Saints Church. Baptism is necessary for salvation, and obedience to the principles of the gospel of Christ is of first importance. Subjection to civil laws and rules is advocated, together with insistence on the right of the individual to worship according to the dictates of conscience.

Two practices, baptism for the dead and sealing in marriage for eternity, are exclusive to this church. Baptism and salvation for the dead are based on the conviction that persons who died without a chance to hear or accept the gospel cannot possibly be condemned by a just and merciful God. The gospel must be preached to them after death; they find authority for this practice in 1 Peter 4:6: "For this cause was the gospel preached also to them that are dead, that they might be judged according to men in the flesh, but live according to God in the spirit." Baptism is considered as essential for the dead as it is for the living, even though the rites will not finally save them; there must be faith and repentance. The ceremony is performed with a living person standing proxy for the dead.

Marriage has two forms: marriage for time and marriage for eternity (celestial marriage). Mormons who are married by only civil authority still remain in good standing in the church, but marriage for time and eternity in the church's temples is regarded as a prerequisite for the highest opportunity for salvation. In connection with this, it is said that Joseph Smith informed his associates in the 1840s that multiple marriages were sanctioned and even commanded by God. Such marriages had been contracted secretly for some time before the practice was announced publicly by Brigham Young in 1852.

Following the Civil War, the U.S. federal government mounted an increasingly intense campaign against Mormon polygamy. In 1882, the Edmunds Act provided stringent penalties, and in 1887 the church was disincorporated and its properties confiscated. In 1890 the U.S. Supreme Court ruled it constitutional to deny all privileges of citizenship to members of the church. Also in 1890, the church president issued a manifesto that officially discontinued the contracting of new polygamous marriages. Some followers of Joseph Smith, Jr., deny that polygamy was ever sanctioned by the church, but a few in other groups believe that it will never end. These contemporary polygamists are excommunicated from the church.

Organization and government differ in detail among the five Mormon denominations, but they all agree on essentials. They are based on the two priesthoods: the higher priesthood of Melchizedek, which holds power of presidency and authority over offices of the church and whose officers include apostles, patriarchs, high priests, seventies, and elders; and the lesser priesthood of Aaron, which guides the temporal affairs of the church through its bishops, priests, teachers, and deacons.

The presiding council of the church is the First Presidency, made up of three high priests—the president and two counselors. Its authority is final in both spiritual and temporal affairs. The president of the church is "the mouthpiece of God"; through him come the laws of the church by direct revelation.

Next to the presidency stands the Council of the Twelve Apostles, chosen by revelation to supervise, under the direction of the First Presidency, the whole work of the church. The church is divided into areas, regions, and stakes (geographical divisions) composed of a number of wards (local churches or parishes). Members of two quorums of seventy preside over the areas, under the direction of the Twelve. High priests, assisted by elders, are in charge of the stakes and wards. Members of the Melchizedek priesthood, under the direction of the presidency, officiate in all ordinances of the gospel. The duties of the apostles and the seventies carry them into all the stakes, wards, and missions of the entire church. The stake presidents, ward bishops, patriarchs, high priests, and elders supervise the work within the stakes and wards of the church. The Aaronic priesthood is governed by three presiding bishops known collectively as the Presiding Bishopric, who also supervise the work of the members of the priesthood in the stakes and wards. In June 1978, it was ruled that "all worthy male members of the church may be ordained to the priesthood without regard for race or color."

The church influences every phase of the life of every member; it supplies relief in illness or poverty and assists with education and employment when necessary, but does not educate or employ all members. Such a program has resulted in deep loyalty. Some 37,000 young Mormons currently serve as full-time missionaries throughout the world without compensation; they devote 18 months to two years to spreading the teaching of their church at home and abroad. Only about 100 persons in full-time leadership positions receive a salary or living allowance. Their missionary experience strengthens them and their church and offers a model of church service.

CHURCH OF CHRIST (TEMPLE LOT)

Claiming status as a remnant of the church founded by Joseph Smith in 1830, this church has 2,400 members in 32 local congregations. After the death of Smith in 1844, and following the western trek of the Mormons, a number of those who remained in the Midwest became convinced that the church leaders were advocating new teachings quite at variance with the original doctrines. By 1852 there were two protesting groups. One was known as the New Organization; the other, centered in Crow Creek, Illinois, functioned under the name Church of Christ. This latter group returned to Independence, Missouri, in the "appointed year" of 1867 and began purchasing temple lots. The revelation concerning the "return" was given in 1864 through the presiding elder at the time, Granville Hedrick.

The temple lots (the subject of controversy and court action between the Church of Christ and the Reorganized Church of Jesus Christ of Latter-Day Saints, finally resolved in favor of the Church of Christ) consist of land dedicated in 1831 by Joseph Smith and other Mormon leaders for the building of the Lord's Temple. This place is said to have been designated by the Lord for that purpose. The belief is that the Lord will designate the time of building and that while the people of the church cannot build until the appointed time, they nevertheless have a sacred obligation to "hold and keep this land free; when the time of building comes, it can be accomplished as the Lord sees fit."

This Church of Christ puts its faith in the pattern and thought of the church "as it existed at the time of Christ and His apostles." Hence the highest office is that of apostle, of which there are twelve. They are charged with the missionary work and general supervision of the church. Temporal affairs are directly administered by the General Bishopric, under the direction of the general conference and the Council of Apostles; local churches administer their own affairs but must keep their teachings and practice in harmony with those of the denomination. Most of the membership is described as Gentile, with several members among the Maya Indians of Yucatan, Mexico.

The church accepts the King James Version of the Bible and the *Book of Mormon* as its standards. It holds that all latter-day revelation, including that of Joseph Smith, must be tested by these Scriptures; it does not accept all that was given through Smith. Because changes were made in the early revelations, this church prefers *The Book of Commandments* to *The Doctrine and Covenants,* which includes these changes. For this reason, the doctrines of plural marriage, baptism for the dead, celestial marriage, and plurality of gods are not accepted.

CHURCH OF JESUS CHRIST (BICKERTONITES)

The founders of this church were at one time members of a Pennsylvania Mormon body led by Sidney Rigdon. Rigdon and his followers refused to join the western march under Brigham Young, denouncing Young's teaching of polygamy, the plurality of gods, and baptism for the dead. In 1846 they purchased a farm (later lost at a sheriff's sale) near Greencastle, Pennsylvania. A small group did not go to Greencastle, but remained at West Elizabeth and, under William Bickerton, who had been one of Rigdon's elders, in 1862 formally organized as the Church of Jesus Christ. The name "Bickertonites" is employed to distinguish this body from other Mormon groups; members prefer that it be known as the Bickerton Organization. The current president is Dominic R. Thomas, elected in 1974.

Foot washing is practiced, and members salute one another with the holy kiss. Monogamy, except in case of death, is required, together with obedience to all state and civil laws. The church has its own edition of the *Book of Mormon* (in English and Italian) and publishes a monthly periodical, *The Gospel News,* along with other denominational material. A general conference meets annually at the headquarters in Monongahela, Pennsylvania. Missionary work is conducted in Italy, Nigeria, Mexico, and among Native Americans of the United States and Canada. In 1989 there were 2,707 members in the United States and more than 6,000 worldwide, including Argentina and Ghana. There are 63 churches in North America.

CHURCH OF JESUS CHRIST OF LATTER-DAY SAINTS, THE

The organization and doctrine of the church of Jesus Christ of Latter-Day Saints has been outlined in the description that introduces this section. With headquarters in Salt Lake City, Utah, it has a U.S. membership of 4.5 million in 9,800 congregations; in 146 countries and territories, a worldwide membership of 8.4 million (at the end of 1992). The membership has increased by 63 percent in the last decade. A general conference is held twice a year at Salt Lake City. The church has no paid clergy, and programs are supported by the tithes of the members, who are encouraged to give one-tenth of their incomes.

The missionary effort of this church is constant and vigorous. There are 295 missions throughout the world, with 49,000 missionaries. The death and serious disease rate among Latter-Day Saints is lower than that of any other group of the same size anywhere in the world; this is held by some to be the direct result of abstinence from alcohol and tobacco. This church maintains, as part of a self-help welfare system, storehouses for community food and clothing. Members operate vegetable, seed, and wheat farms; orchards, dairies, and cannery processing facilities; sewing centers; soap-processing plants; and several grain elevators. Most of these products are consumed by needy members, but a churchwide relief plan sends millions of dollars in relief to drought-stricken African nations and other areas of the world hit by natural disasters. Through this system the church donates thousands of tons of surplus clothing annually to needy populations around the world and sponsors water and agricultural projects in underdeveloped countries. The welfare system also includes sheltered workshops for persons with handicapping conditions and a variety of social services, including adoption and foster-care agencies.

Education is of great importance. The church's largest institutions are Brigham Young University in Provo, Utah, with an enrollment of 28,000, and Ricks College in Idaho, with 7,500 students. Some 425,000 secondary and post-secondary students worldwide are enrolled in seminary and institute classes, which provide religious instruction.

Membership is largest in Utah (1.4 million) and contiguous states—Idaho, 309,000, and Arizona, 249,000—but there are 720,000 in California and 199,000 in the state of Washington.

Outside the U.S., the largest concentration of members is found in Mexico (670,000), Brazil (442,000), Chile (331,000), and the Philippines (293,000).

CHURCH OF JESUS CHRIST OF LATTER-DAY SAINTS (STRANGITE)

This group claims that it is "the one and original" Church of Jesus Christ of Latter-Day Saints and that its founder, James J. Strang, with written credentials from Joseph Smith, was the only legal successor to church leadership. Strang translated portions of the brass plates of Laban, and these, together with certain other revelations, are found in *The Book of the Law of the Lord*. Strang also translated what is called *The Voree Record*—found under an oak tree near Voree, Wisconsin—telling in hieroglyphic characters of "an ancient people . . . who no longer exist." He was crowned "king" of this church in 1850 but was murdered in 1856 during a wave of anti-Mormonism in the Great Lakes region.

Organized at Burlington, Wisconsin, in 1844, the church denies the virgin birth, holds that Adam fell by a law of natural consequences, rather than by breaking a divine law, and that the corruption thus caused can be removed only by the resurrection of Christ. The members deny the Trinity and the plurality of gods, celebrate Saturday as the sabbath, and believe that baptism is essential for salvation. Due to "lack of prophetic leadership at the present time" they do not practice baptism of the dead.

The chief officer of the church is a high priest in the Melchizedek priesthood, chosen by the general church conference. Membership in 1984 stood at 200 in two congregations.

REORGANIZED CHURCH OF JESUS CHRIST OF LATTER-DAY SAINTS

This church claims to be the continuation of the original church organized by Joseph Smith, Jr., in 1830. It bases its claim on the rule of lineal succession found in *The Book of Doctrine and Covenants*. Court actions on two occasions—in Ohio in 1880 and in Missouri in 1894—are cited in naming it the legal continuation of the original church. The son of Joseph Smith, Joseph Smith III, it is held, was designated by his father to succeed him.

The Reorganized Church rejected the claims of the Mormons led by Brigham Young because of their abandonment of this rule, along with other doctrinal disagreements. Those holding to the lineal succession eventually reorganized, the first collective expression of this movement coming at a conference in Beloit, Wisconsin, in 1852. Joseph Smith III was chosen president in 1860 at Amboy, Illinois. All of his successors have been descendants of the founder. Since 1920, headquarters have been located in Independence, Missouri, where a temple has recently been completed.

Although the doctrine of polygamy was endorsed by Young's group in 1852, the Reorganized Church held polygamy to be contrary to the teachings of the *Book of Mormon* and *the Book of Doctrine and Covenants* of the original organization. It also differs on the doctrine of the Godhead, celestial marriage, and baptism of the dead. Basic beliefs include faith in the universality of God the Eternal Father, Jesus Christ as the only begotten Son of the Father, the Holy Spirit, the worth and dignity of persons, repentance of sin, baptism by immersion, the efficacy of various sacramental ordinances, the resurrection of the dead, the open canon of Scriptures and the continuity of revelation, the doctrine of stewardship, and the accountability of all people to God.

The work of the church is supported by tithes and free-will offerings. This is regarded as a divine principle, and the tithe is calculated on a tenth of each member's annual increase over needs and just wants.

The church has more than 245,000 members, located in 35 countries around the world and on islands in the Caribbean and South Pacific. Its membership is 150,000 in 1,001 churches. It has four-year accredited colleges at Lamoni, Iowa (Graceland College), and at Kansas City, Missouri (Park College); a leadership and ministerial school (Temple School) is in Independence, Missouri.

Church doctrines, policies, and matters of legislation must have the approval and action of a delegate conference held biennially at the auditorium in Independence. General administration of the church is by a First Presidency of three high priests and elders, a Quorum of Twelve Apostles who represent the presidency in the field, and a pastoral arm under the high priests and elders. The work of the bishops covers church properties, the stewardship of members, and church finances.

The Reorganized Church has been active in developing ministries and enlarged understanding as it has expanded since 1960 into non-Western cultures. It sponsors several homes for the elderly, medical clinics, and educational facilities both in the U.S. and abroad. It seeks to dedicate itself to the pursuit of world peace and reconciliation. The ordination of women was approved in 1984, and now more than 3,500 women have been ordained to ecclesiastical orders.

LUTHERAN

The earliest dissenting movement among those that comprised the Protestant Reformation, Lutheranism dates from Martin Luther's theological "discoveries" between 1513 and 1530. Never intending to splinter the church by leaving it, these first Protestants meant to affirm the message of the Bible as the sole authority for church life and Christian belief and practice. To this day, Lutheranism retains much from the tradition of the ancient and medieval church, including a sense of participation in the historic People of God and the traditional liturgy, revised to accord with Protestant biblicism. It is devoted to sound doctrine, systematically developed and expressed in thoughtful preaching. The historic church of Germany and the Scandinavian countries, it has been largely ethnic in the U.S., and numerous mergers have taken place as church unity has replaced ethnic identity as a primary factor.

Lutheran at first was a nickname applied to the followers of Martin Luther in the days of the Protestant Reformation. Today it stands for something far more comprehensive. "It is clear," said Abdel R. Wentz, "that 'Lutheran' is a very inadequate name to give to a movement that is not limited to a person or an era but is as ecumenical and abiding as Christianity itself." Luther's teachings of justification by faith and of the universal priesthood of believers might be called the cornerstone of Protestantism.

The story of Luther's rebellion against the Roman Catholic Church is well known. His position, briefly, was that the church and the papacy had no divine right in things spiritual; that Scripture, not the priest or the church, has final authority over conscience. "Whatever is not against Scripture is for Scripture, and Scripture is for it," said Luther. People are forgiven and absolved of their sins, he believed, not by good works or by imposition of church rite—and especially not through the purchase of indulgences offered for sale by the Roman Catholic Church—but by their Spirit-empowered turning from sin directly to God. Justification is attained through faith, not through ceremony; and faith is not subscription to the dictates of the church, but "the heart's utter trust" in Christ. "The just shall live by faith" was the beginning and the end of Luther's thought. He held that the individual conscience is responsible to God alone; he also held that the Bible is the clear, perfect, inspired, and authoritative Word of God and guide for humankind. God, conscience, and the Book—on these was Lutheranism founded.

In 1529 Luther wrote his Longer and Shorter catechisms. A year later, a statement of faith, known as the Augsburg Confession, was authored by his scholarly associate Philip Melanchthon; 1537 brought the Smalcald Articles of Faith, written by Luther, Melanchthon, and other German Reformers; in 1577 the Formula of Concord was drawn up. These documents, in explanation of Luther's ideology and theology, form the doctrinal basis of Lutheranism.

The German Reformation resulted not in a united Protestantism, but in one with two branches: Evangelical Lutheranism, with Luther and Melanchthon as leaders; and the Reformed Church, led by John Calvin, Ulrich Zwingli, and John Knox. Evangelical Lutheranism spread to Poland, Russia, Lithuania, Czechoslovakia, Austria, Hungary, Yugoslavia, France, and Holland; it later became the state church of Denmark, Norway, Sweden, Finland, Iceland, Estonia, and Latvia.

It was mainly from Germany and Scandinavia that Lutheranism came to the United States. A Lutheran Christmas service was held at Hudson Bay in 1619; the first European Lutherans to remain permanently in this country arrived at Manhattan Island from Holland in 1623. A congregation worshiped in New Amsterdam in 1649, but Lutherans did not enjoy full freedom in their worship until the English assumed control of "New York" in 1664. The first independent colony of Lutherans, New Sweden, was established at Fort Christiana along the Delaware in 1638.

The New York Lutherans were largely German. Exiles from Salzburg also settled in Georgia, where in 1738 they built the first orphanage in America; Lutherans from Wüttemberg settled in South Carolina. The great influx, however, went to Pennsylvania, where by the middle of the eighteenth century Lutherans numbered 30,000, four-fifths of whom were German, the remainder Swedish. From Philadelphia they swept into New Jersey, Maryland, Virginia, and North Carolina.

The first churches were small, often without pastors, and poor, because only a minority of the immigrants joined. The situation was relieved with the coming of Henry Melchior Muhlenberg from the University of Halle. He brought about the first real Lutheran merger in 1748 by organizing the pastors and congregations in Pennsylvania, New Jersey, New York, and Maryland into what came to be called the Ministerium of Pennsylvania, the first of many Lutheran synods in America. Others followed slowly: New York in 1786, North Carolina in 1803, Maryland in 1820, Ohio in 1836. Each synod adjusted itself to its peculiar conditions of language, natural background, previous ecclesiastical relationship with Lutheran authorities abroad, and geographical location. The need for even further organization was evident from the ever-increasing flood of Lutherans from

Europe, resulting in the formation of the General Synod in 1820. At that, the last real bonds with Europe began to break, and American Lutheranism was increasingly on its own.

The General Synod was obliged to extend its efforts farther and farther west, and the Missouri Synod was formed in 1847. From 1850 until 1860, one million Germans arrived in the U.S., the majority of whom were Lutheran. The German Iowa Synod was organized in 1854; in the same year, the Norwegian Lutheran Church was established; the Augustana Synod was created in the new West in 1860. By 1870, Lutherans were the fourth largest Protestant group in the country, with approximately 400,000 members.

The Civil War brought the first serious break in Lutheran ranks, with the organization of the United Synod of the South in 1863; three years later a number of other synods, led by the Ministerium of Pennsylvania, withdrew from the General Synod to form the General Council. To increase the complexity, Lutheran immigrants continued to arrive in larger and larger numbers; from 1870 until 1910, approximately 1.75 million arrived from Sweden, Norway, and Denmark. Lutheran church membership leaped from less than 500,000 to nearly 2.25 million; new churches, colleges, seminaries, and publications were established from coast to coast.

Since 1910 there has been an almost constant effort to unify Lutheran churches and agencies. In 1917 three large bodies united in the Norwegian Lutheran Church of America. Some of the Midwest German synods merged in the Joint Synod of Wisconsin in 1918; in that same year, the General Synod, the General Council, and the United Synod of the South merged into the United Lutheran Church. The synods of Iowa, Ohio, and Buffalo merged into the American Lutheran Church in 1930; and no fewer than eight Lutheran churches were included in mergers 1960–62. Perhaps the most cooperative effort in the history of American Lutheranism is found in Lutheran World Action, through which more than $300 million in cash and food (including U.S. government-donated commodities) has been distributed throughout the world.

In spite of their divisions, there has been real unity among Lutherans, based more on faith than organization. All the churches represent a single type of Protestant Christianity, built on Luther's principle of justification by faith alone—faith in Jesus Christ; it centers in the gospel for fallen humanity. The Bible is the inspired Word of God and the infallible rule and standard of faith and practice. Lutherans confess their faith through the three general creeds of Christendom—Apostles', Nicene, and Athanasian—which they believe to be in accordance with the Scriptures. They also believe that the unaltered Augsburg Confession is a correct exposition of the faith and doctrine of evangelical Lutheranism. The Apology of the Augsburg Confession, the two catechisms of Luther, the Smalcald Articles, and the Formula of Concord are held to be faithful interpretations of Lutheranism and of the Bible.

The two sacraments, baptism and the Lord's Supper, are not merely signs or memorials, but channels through which God bestows forgiving and empowering grace upon humankind. The body and blood of Christ are believed to be present "in, with, and under" the bread and wine of the Lord's Supper and are received sacramentally and supernaturally. Consubstantiation, transubstantiation, and impanation are rejected. Infants are baptized, and baptized persons are believed to receive the gift of regeneration from the Holy Ghost.

The congregation is usually administered between its annual meetings by a church council consisting of the pastor and a number of elected lay officers. Pastors are called by the voting members of the congregation. As a rule, ministers, after college and seminary training, are ordained at the annual meetings of the synods.

Congregations are united in synods composed of pastors and lay representatives elected by the congregations and have authority as granted by the synod constitution. In some instances, there are territorial districts or conferences instead of synods, operating in the same manner and under the same restrictions; some may legislate, while others are for advisory or consultative purposes only.

Synods (conferences or districts) are united in a general body that may be national, or even international, and are called variously "church," "synod," or "conference." Some of these general bodies are legislative in nature, some consultative; they supervise the work in worship, education, publication, charity, and mission. Congregations have business meetings at least annually; synods, districts, and conferences hold yearly conventions; the general bodies meet annually or biennially.

Worship is liturgical, centering on the altar. "No sect in Western Christendom outside the Church of Rome," said the late Lutheran Archbishop Nathan Söderblom of Sweden, "has accentuated in its doctrine the Real Presence and the mysterious communion of the sacrament as has our Evangelic Lutheran sect, although our faith repudiates any quasi-rational magical explanation of the virtue of the sacrament."

Non-Lutherans are often critical of the divisions among Lutherans, but actually they are not as divided as they may seem. At one time there were 150 Lutheran bodies in the U.S.; consolidation, unification, and federation have now reduced that number to nine.

Three of the U.S. bodies account for about 95 percent of all Lutherans in North America. With the old barriers of speech and nationality disappearing, the tendency toward union becomes continually stronger. Most recently, in 1988 the American Lutheran Church merged with the Lutheran Church in America and the Association of Evangelical Lutheran Churches. This new Lutheran body comprises approximately 5.5 million baptized members and 11,000 congregations.

On the international front, united efforts are noticeable also. Groups of lay and ministerial delegates from major Lutheran churches in 22 countries formed a Lutheran World Federation in 1947 for the purpose of relief and rehabilitation on a global scale among Lutherans.

Historically, Lutherans have shown a tendency to remain apart from the rest of Protestantism. The U.S. churches were founded by immigrant groups deeply conscious of their national and linguistic origins, but as the older membership passed, English became the predominant language. The larger Lutheran churches have been constituent members of the National Council of Churches of Christ; some participated in the organization of the World Council of Churches. Lutheran groups that are part of interdenominational organizations have always insisted on the operation of two principles within those organizations: the evangelical principle that the churches in the association should be those confessing the deity and saviorhood of Jesus Christ, and the representative principle that the governing and operating units of the organizations should be made up of officially chosen representatives of the churches.

AMERICAN LUTHERAN CHURCH, THE

At a constituting convention held April 22–24, 1960, in Minneapolis, three major Lutheran churches were formally merged into this body, which was known as the American Lutheran Church. The three were the American Lutheran Church, of German background, which originated during the formation of the Ohio Synod in 1818; the Evangelical Lutheran Church, of Norwegian heritage, at the time of the merger the third largest Lutheran church in America; and the United Evangelical Lutheran Church, founded in 1896 by Danish immigrants. A fourth body, the Lutheran Free Church, of Norwegian background, joined those three on February 1, 1963, giving the new American Lutheran Church an inclusive membership of 2,499,373 in 5,239 churches. The Evangelical Church of Canada was founded by that group in 1906. In 1988, the American Lutheran Church, the Lutheran Church in America, and the Association of Evangelical

Lutheran Churches merged into one body, with a combined baptized membership of 5.2 million.

The 1960 merger crossed ethnic lines, and the problems involved were complex in polity and doctrine, but were successfully resolved. In government, the highest constitutional authority was vested in a general convention that met every two years and had approximately 1,000 delegates (500 lay, 500 clergy), elected from the 19 districts into which the church was geographically divided. There were three national officers—general president, vice president, and secretary. A church council was composed of the general officers, and a lay and a clergy representative from each district, together with the district presidents, two representatives from the board of trustees, and two youths elected by the Luther League, to serve in an advisory capacity. This council met as the interim body between general conventions and made recommendations on all matters directed to it by the districts, boards, and standing committees of the church.

APOSTOLIC LUTHERAN CHURCH OF AMERICA

Sometimes called the Church of Laestadius, for Lars Levi Laestadius, a minister of the state church of Sweden, this church originated with Finnish immigrants in and around Calumet, Michigan, in the middle years of the nineteenth century. They first worshiped in the Lutheran Church of Calumet, under a Norwegian minister. However, differences between the two national groups led to the formation, in 1872, of a separate Finnish congregation: the Solomon Korteneimi Lutheran Society, led by Solomon Korteneimi. The church was first incorporated in Michigan in 1879 under the name Finnish Apostolic Lutheran Church of America, which actually was a merger of independent Apostolic Lutheran congregations. Spreading over Michigan, Minnesota, the Dakotas, Massachusetts, Oregon, Washington, and California, the new church was divided into two districts—Eastern and Western—with foreign missions in Nigeria, Liberia, and Guatemala.

A scriptural Christian experience is required for voting membership in spiritual matters; supporting members may vote on temporal matters only. The church accepts the three ecumenical creeds and puts strong emphasis on the confession of sins, absolution, and regeneration. Confession may be made to another Christian, but if someone has fallen into sins unknown to others, private confession is not sufficient; the person "should confess them publicly before the congregation and receive absolution."

The 64 local congregations are quite free to govern themselves; at the annual church convention where every congregation has a vote, three members are elected to a nine-member executive board for three-year terms; the board elects a president, vice president, secretary, and treasurer. Three members are also elected to the Eastern and Western mission boards and to the Elder's Home Board. In 1993 there were about 9,000 members.

CHURCH OF THE LUTHERAN BRETHREN

This is an independent Lutheran body made up of autonomous congregations scattered across the U.S. and Canada. The synod was organized in 1900 for the purpose of serving its member congregations in the larger ministries of Christian education and in home and world missions.

The church maintains a firm commitment to the supreme authority of the Scriptures. It accepts the basic Lutheran teachings and emphasizes the need for a personal faith in the Lord Jesus Christ that demonstrates itself in daily life. Membership in the local congregation is based on an individual's personal profession of faith. Worship services are characterized by a nonliturgical style, the use of both traditional and contemporary music, lay participation, and biblical teaching and preaching that is evangelistic and personal in application.

In 1993, 117 congregations across the U.S. and central Canada supported a seminary, Bible school, and four-year secondary academy. These institutions, as well as the headquarters, are located in Fergus Falls, Minnesota.

Home mission congregations are being planted in many areas of the U.S. and Canada. Extensive mission projects are carried on in Chad, Cameroon, Japan, and Taiwan. Each country has its own seminary, and the church in Japan supports a missionary couple in Indonesia.

Membership in the U.S. and Canada in 1993 was 12,687; worldwide, it is more than 130,000.

CHURCH OF THE LUTHERAN CONFESSION

This confessional church, organized in 1960, is made up of clergy and laypeople who had withdrawn from several synods of the Synodical Conference of North America as the result of differences that had arisen in the interpretation of Scripture doctrine. The Church of the Lutheran Confession holds firmly to the doctrine of verbal inspiration and inerrancy of the Bible; it holds without reservation to all the historic confessions of the Lutheran Church and faith. Membership numbers 8,910 in 70 churches, concentrated in South Dakota, Minnesota, and Wisconsin; it also engages in mission work in India and Nigeria. A high school, college, and seminary in Eau Claire, Wisconsin, are supported by the church.

EVANGELICAL LUTHERAN CHURCH IN AMERICA

On January 1, 1988, the Evangelical Lutheran Church in America (ELCA) was formed by a union of the Lutheran Church in America, the American Lutheran Church, and the Association of Evangelical Lutheran Churches. The ELCA now includes 5.2 million members in more than 11,000 congregations, served by 17,375 clergy.

One of the merged bodies, the American Lutheran Church (ALC), was formed in 1960, itself the result of a merger of four separate Lutheran groups. The ALC headquarters was in Minneapolis, and at the time of the 1988 merger, there were 2.25 million members in 4,958 congregations.

A second body, the Association of Evangelical Lutheran Churches, had 103,000 members in 250 congregations. It was established in 1976 as a result of separation from the Lutheran Church—Missouri Synod and was based in St. Louis, Missouri.

The third group, the Lutheran Church in America (LCA), was based in New York and Philadelphia. Formed in 1962 from the union of four separate Lutheran bodies, the LCA had roots in North America dating from the mid-1660s, when Dutch Lutherans formed congregations in the New York area. Its membership stood at 2.9 million in 5,832 congregations.

Efforts to form the ELCA began in 1982 when the three uniting churches elected a 70-member commission to draft the constitution and other documents for their new church. In August 1986, the conventions of the individual bodies approved the constitution, and the following May, the ELCA Constituting Convention elected Dr. Herbert Chilstrom as bishop. In succeeding weeks, each synod held a convention to elect a bishop and other officers.

The ELCA is now the largest of the U.S.-based Lutheran bodies. Next in size is the Lutheran Church—Missouri Synod, based in St. Louis. Third is the Wisconsin Evangelical Lutheran Synod in Milwaukee, Wisconsin, with 416,000 members. The Evangelical Lutheran Synod and the Association of Free Lutheran Congregations have about 20,000 members each, and there are several other smaller Lutheran groups. (See page 184 for further information.)

The ELCA's headquarters is located in Chicago. Its 11,000 congregations are grouped into 65 synods throughout the U.S. and the Caribbean. Nine regions coordinate the work between synods, and between synods and churchwide organizations.

The biennial Churchwide Assembly, which includes about 600 lay voting members equally divided by gender and about 400 clergy voting members, is this church's highest legislative authority. A 37-member Church Council, elected by the assembly, serves as the board of directors and interim legislative authority between assemblies.

The bishop is the church's chief pastor and executive officer. The term of office is four years, eligible for reelection by Churchwide Assembly. Also elected to four-year terms are the treasurer, secretary, and executive directors.

The organization of the ELCA provides for Divisions for Congregational Life, Higher Education, Global Mission, Ministry, Outreach, and Church in Society Ministries. Its publishing house, with primary offices in Minneapolis and Philadelphia, produces and distributes printed and other media resources for the church. Among the publications is the magazine of the church, *The Lutheran,* which replaces the LCA *Lutheran,* the ALC *Lutheran Standard,* and the AELC *Perspective.*

The Department for Ecumenical Affairs coordinates ecumenical, inter-Lutheran, and interfaith activities and administers relationships with the Lutheran World Federation, the National Council of Churches, and the World Council of Churches.

Since the merger of the American Lutheran Church (ALC) and the Lutheran Church in America (LCA) is still so recent, the articles for those two bodies that appeared in the Eighth (1985) and the Ninth (1990) editions are included here.

EVANGELICAL LUTHERAN SYNOD

This synod was formed in 1918 by a minority group that declined to join the other Norwegian groups when they united in the Norwegian Lutheran Church (the former Evangelical Lutheran Church) in 1917. The name was not changed until 1958.

The jurisdiction of the synod is entirely advisory; all synod resolutions are accepted or rejected by the local congregations. The officers and boards of the synod, however, direct work of common interest insofar as they do not interfere with congregational rights or prerogatives.

For some years the synod used the facilities of the colleges and seminaries of the Missouri and Wisconsin synods, within the framework of the Synodical Conference; in 1963 the Evangelical Lutheran Synod withdrew from the conference because of doctrinal differences with the Missouri Synod, but it is in fellowship with the Wisconsin Synod. It has maintained Bethany Lutheran College at

Mankato, Minnesota, since 1927, and Bethany Lutheran Theological Seminary since 1946. It has 12 home mission stations in the U.S., foreign missions in Peru, one preparatory school, and 21,454 members in 126 churches.

FREE LUTHERAN CONGREGATIONS, THE ASSOCIATION OF

Established in 1962, this is a conservative and quite independent body. Doctrinally, it stresses the inerrancy and supreme authority of the Bible. It expresses the conviction that the congregation is the final and correct form of the kingdom of God on earth and that the spiritual union, fellowship, and cooperation of believers transcend all synodical, racial, and national boundaries. It admits no authority except that of the Word and Spirit of God. A widespread evangelistic program calls for personal experience with and devotion to Christ, in addition to a "wholesome Lutheran pietism" in the religious community. It reports almost 30,000 members in 225 churches, located in 26 states and three Canadian provinces, with missionary work in Brazil, Mexico, and India.

LUTHERAN CHURCH—MISSOURI SYNOD, THE

With 2,609,000 members and 5,369 churches, this is the second largest Lutheran church in the U.S. (The newly formed Evangelical Lutheran Church in America is the largest.) *Missouri* is included in the name because the denomination was founded in that state by German immigrants in 1847. From the beginning, members have been devoted to the maintenance of confessional Lutheranism, coupled with a strong sense of mission outreach.

Christian education for members of all ages has always been stressed. The synod operates 16 colleges and seminaries in North America, with an enrollment of more than 8,000. Its elementary and secondary system of more than 1,500 schools is the largest of any Protestant denomination in the U.S. Mission work is conducted in 30 foreign countries, while more than 100 new North American ministries were started each year during the 1980s.

The synod has long been considered a leader in the field of communications. It operates the world's oldest religious radio station, KFUO in Saint Louis; provides the 50-year-old "Lutheran Hour," heard in more than 100 countries; and produces "This Is the Life," after 30 years the longest-running syndicated dramatic series on television.

A doctrinal controversy in the 1960s concerning the authority and interpretation of Scripture resulted in the departure of about 100,000 members, but little evidence of that controversy remains. Church historians maintain that it was the first time a major denomination had turned back a liberal trend and retained its founding doctrine.

Because of differences in doctrine and practice, the Missouri Synod was not a part of the 1988 merger that united three other Lutheran denominations. However, it continues to cooperate with those churches in a variety of ministries, particularly in areas of social work, such as world hunger relief and the resettlement of refugees.

The church's headquarters are in the International Center, a new building in suburban Saint Louis. Directors for the church body are set by a triennial convention of pastors and laypeople, representing the congregations.

LUTHERAN CHURCH IN AMERICA

With about 2.9 million members, this was the largest Lutheran body in the U.S. until the 1988 merger. It represented a 1962 consolidation of four former Lutheran groups (the United Lutheran Church in America, the Augustana Evangelical Lutheran Church, the American Evangelical Lutheran Church, and the Finnish Evangelical Lutheran Church).

The United Lutheran Church was the youngest of the four bodies, formed in 1918 in the uniting of 45 synods previously found in the General Synod, the General Council, and the United Synod of the South. The United Lutheran Church brought a total of almost 2.5 million members, in 4,600 congregations, into the 1962 merger.

The Augustana Evangelical Lutheran Church originated in scattered Swedish families and congregations in Iowa and Illinois in the mid-1800s; the Augustana Synod was formed in 1860, with 5,000 communicants and 49 congregations, of which 36 were Swedish and 13 Norwegian. The name *Augustana* affirmed the group's loyalty to the doctrine of the Augsburg (in Latin, *Augustana*) Confession. Ten years later, the Norwegians withdrew to form a church of their own; at the time of the 1962 merger, the Augustana body had more than a half million communicants in 1,200 congregations.

The Finnish Evangelical Lutheran Church (better known as the Suomi Synod) was organized at Calumet, Michigan, in 1890; it was strictly a confessional church, using the three ecumenical creeds and the unaltered Augsburg Confession. Originally the Finnish language was employed in the services of this church, which had 36,000 members and 153 congregations in 1962.

WISCONSIN EVANGELICAL LUTHERAN SYNOD

The American Evangelical Lutheran Church was the smallest of the uniting bodies, with 25,000 members in 79 congregations. It was of Danish origin, founded under the direction of ministers sent from Denmark in 1872 and originally named Kirkelig Missionsforening. It was deeply concerned with the place and meaning of the Bible in Lutheran theology; yet it had a strong tradition of ecumenical interest and was represented in the National Lutheran Council, the National Council of Churches of Christ, and the World Council of Churches. The Lutheran Church in America merged with the American Lutheran Church and the Association of Evangelical Lutheran Churches in 1988. The new Lutheran body comprises approximately 5.2 million baptized members and 11,000 congregations.

PROTESTANT CONFERENCE (LUTHERAN)

A protest against the "high-handed" tactics of church officials and against the inroads of legalism into the life of the Wisconsin Evangelical Lutheran Synod led to the suspension of 47 pastors and teachers in 1927—and to the formation of this conference. Its current purpose is to "break down within our Lutheran Church, and wherever else it may flourish, the spirit of self-righteousness and self-sufficiency through a reemphasis upon the Gospel of forgiveness of sins . . . coupled with the warning of the hardening of hearts and of judgment upon those who reject this message and its implications."

A general conference meets three times a year, and a publication, *Faith-Life,* is issued in LaCrosse, Wisconsin. Membership stands at 1,004 in the seven churches and several "home" congregations.

WISCONSIN EVANGELICAL LUTHERAN SYNOD

Organized in 1850 in Milwaukee as the German Evangelical Lutheran Synod of Wisconsin, this church merged with two other synods—Minnesota and Michigan—in 1917 to become the Evangelical Lutheran Joint Synod of Wisconsin and Other States. In 1959 the present name was adopted. This synod subscribes to an orthodox confessional Lutheranism, committed without reservation to the inspired, infallible Holy Scriptures. It is opposed to fellowship with other church bodies unless there is full agreement in doctrine and practice.

Divided into 12 districts, it maintains its national headquarters in Milwaukee. There is a baptized membership of 419,750 in 1,200 congregations in all 50 states. Sister mission churches are supported in Zambia, Malawi, Brazil, Mexico, Puerto Rico, Colombia, Japan,

Taiwan, Hong Kong, Indonesia, India, Cameroon, Nigeria, Russia, Bulgaria, and among Native Americans in Arizona.

For the education of its pastors and Christian day-school teachers, the synod maintains two colleges, three academies, and a theological seminary. Congregations support 20 Lutheran high schools with an enrollment of 4,048 and 370 Christian day schools with 31,501 students. Associations of congregations operate seven homes for the aged and a social service agency.

MENNONITE

Dating from the 1520s in Central Europe, these radical Protestants take their name from Menno Simons, an early Dutch leader. "Radical" in yearning to get to "the roots" of the biblical manner of living, they rejected the "magisterial Reformation" of Luther and Calvin and were in turn treated as outsiders, even heretics. Their concerns have not been with proper theology, the sacraments, or liturgy. Rather, they are called to exemplify godly living.

Until recently, most (and still some) of those quietly dedicated Christians frowned on involvement in secular activity, refusing to take oaths, bear arms, vote, or hold public office. They are a called-out (from the state, from conventional society) fellowship of believers. Always emphasizing the local congregation, some groups insist on living in "intentional communities." In many ways akin to the Brethren family, they pursue their own course in giving primacy to lifestyle rather than to cultivated piety.

The first Mennonite congregation of historical record was organized at Zurich, Switzerland, in 1525; it consisted of Swiss Brethren, or *Täufer,* who disagreed with Ulrich Zwingli in his readiness to consent to a union of church and state. They also denied the scriptural validity of infant baptism and hence were labeled *Anabaptist,* or Rebaptizers. Anabaptist congregations were organized in Holland by Obbe Philips as early as 1534.

Philips baptized Menno Simons (ca. 1496–1561) in 1536, and Simons, a converted Roman Catholic priest, organized so many Anabaptist congregations that his name became identified with the movement. Many of his Flemish adherents—Mennonites—crossed the channel at the invitation of Henry VIII of England. But in England, as well as in Germany, Holland, and Switzerland, they met opposition, largely because of their determined distrust of any union of church and state. An impressive martyr role was created; it might have been much greater, had it not been for the sudden haven offered in the American colonies.

Thirteen families settled in Germantown near Philadelphia in 1683, and eventually a Mennonite congregation was established there, although many of the members, before they departed from Crefeld, Germany, had left the Mennonite fold to unite with Quakers. Nevertheless, Mennonite immigrants from Germany and Switzerland spread over Pennsylvania, Ohio, Virginia, Indiana, Illinois, and into the far west and Canada; these were later joined by others from Russia, Prussia, and Poland. Thanks to their historic insistence on nonresistance, their colonial settlements were comparatively peaceful and prosperous.

Mennonite beliefs are based on a confession of faith signed at Dordrecht, Holland, in 1632. In 18 articles, the following doctrines were laid down: faith in God as Creator; humanity's fall and restoration at the coming of Christ; Christ as the Son of God, who redeemed humankind on the cross; obedience to Christ's law in the gospel; the necessity of repentance and conversion for salvation; baptism as a public testimony of faith; the Lord's Supper as an expression of common union and fellowship; matrimony only among the "spiritually kindred"; obedience to and respect for civil government, except in the use of armed force; exclusion from the church and social ostracism of those who sin willfully; future reward for the faithful and punishment for the wicked.

The Lord's Supper is served twice a year in almost all Mennonite congregations; in most, baptism is by pouring. Most also observe the foot-washing ordinance in connection with the Supper, after which they salute one another with the "kiss of peace." The sexes are separated in the last two ceremonies. All Mennonites baptize only on confession of faith, refuse to take oaths before magistrates, oppose secret societies, and strictly follow the teachings of the New Testament. They have a strong intrachurch program of mutual aid and a worldwide relief and eleemosynary service through their relief organization, the Mennonite Central Committee.

The local congregation is more or less autonomous and authoritative, although in some instances appeals are taken to district or state conferences. The officers of the church are bishops (often called elders), ministers, and deacons (almoners). Many ministers are self-supporting, working in secular employment when not occupied with the work of the church. Other officers are appointed for Sunday school, young people's work, and other duties.

The Amish movement within the ranks of the Mennonites takes its name from Jacob Amman, a Swiss (Bernese) Mennonite bishop of the late seventeenth century, who insisted on strict adherence to the confession of faith, especially in the matter of shunning excommunicated members. This literalism brought about a separation in Switzerland in 1693; about 200 years later, the divided bodies, with the exception of three Amish groups, were reunited.

Early Amish immigrants to the U.S. concentrated in Pennsylvania and spread into Ohio, Indiana, Illinois, Nebraska, and other Western states and into Canada. Many Amish, distinguished by their severely plain clothing, are found in the Conservative Amish Mennonite Church and Old Order Amish Mennonite Church. They are still the literalists of the movement, clinging tenaciously to the Pennsylvania Dutch language and seventeenth-century culture of their Swiss-German forebears. They oppose the use of automobiles, telephones, and higher education and are recognized as extremely efficient farmers.

BEACHY AMISH MENNONITE CHURCHES

These churches are made up mostly of Amish Mennonites who separated from the more conservative Old Order Amish over a period of years, beginning in 1927 in Somerset County, Pennsylvania. They were led by Bishop Moses M. Beachy, who died in 1946. Today there are 99 congregations and 6,872 members, principally in Pennsylvania and Ohio.

To some degree, they resemble the Old Order Amish in garb and general attitude, but their discipline is milder and more relaxed. These Mennonites worship in church buildings, have Sunday schools, and are active in supporting missionary work. Nearly all of the churches sponsor Christian day schools. They sponsor a monthly publication, *Calvary Messenger,* and an annual 12-week Calvary Bible School.

CHURCH OF GOD IN CHRIST, MENNONITE

This church grew out of the preaching and labors of John Holeman, a member of the Mennonite church in Ohio, who became convinced that the church was in error in many of its teachings and practices. He preached ardently on the necessity of the new birth, Holy Ghost baptism, more adequate training of children in the fundamentals, disciplining of unfaithful members, avoidance of apostates, and condemnation of worldly minded churches. He separated from the Mennonite Church and in 1859 began to hold meetings with a small group of followers. They then formally organized into the Church of God in Christ, Mennonite.

The church holds that the same confession of faith must be believed and practiced by all churches, "from the time of the apostles to the end of the world," and that the Bible, as the inspired, infallible Word of God, must govern all doctrine and teaching. It accepts the Eighteen Articles of Faith drawn up at Dordrecht, Holland, in 1932.

The highest decision-making authority is the General Conference, a convention of ministers, deacons, and delegates that convenes every five years or as the need arises. The church practices the mode form of baptism and teaches nonconformity to the world in dress, bodily adornment, sports, and amusements.

Missions are operated in the U.S., Canada, Mexico, Guatemala, Haiti, the Philippines, India, Nigeria, and other countries. There are 15,277 members in more than 100 congregations worldwide. Kansas is the state of heaviest concentration.

CONSERVATIVE MENNONITE CONFERENCE

The Conservative Mennonite Conference (CMC) was formed in 1910 in a meeting of concerned Amish Mennonite church leaders at Pigeon, Michigan. A second meeting was held at Grantsville, Maryland, in 1912, followed by annual meetings since. The 1910 and 1912 meetings included church leaders from Hartville, Ohio; Belleville, Pennsylvania; Pigeon, Michigan; Grantsville, Maryland; Kalona, Iowa; Topeka, Indiana; and Centralia, Missouri. The organization was known as Conservative Amish Mennonite Conference from 1912 until the present name was adopted in 1954. The CMC subscribes to *Mennonite Confession of Faith* (1963) and to the *Conservative Mennonite Statement of Theology* (1991). These documents affirm the full humanity and full divinity of Jesus Christ; the full inspiration and autographical inerrancy of the Scriptures; believers' baptism; and nonviolence. The official organ of CMC is *Brotherhood Beacon*.

The Conservative Mennonite Conference is an autonomous affiliation of congregations within the Mennonite church. Membership in the United States numbered 8,856 in 1992. Internationally affiliated church bodies are found in Costa Rica, Nicaragua, Ecuador, Haiti, Germany, and Kenya. The missions arm of Conservative Mennonite Conference is Rosedale Mennonite Missions. Rosedale Bible Institute is an educational institution that offers college-level courses in various Christian studies.

EVANGELICAL MENNONITE CHURCH

Formerly the Defenseless Mennonite Church, this body was founded about 1865 under the leadership of Henry Egly to emphasize teachings on regeneration, separation, nonconformity to the world, and nonresistance. Its program today is largely one of missions

189

and church-extension evangelism. A children's home in Flanagan, Illinois, and a camp near Kalamazoo, Michigan are maintained. There are 4,130 members in 29 churches.

FELLOWSHIP OF EVANGELICAL BIBLE CHURCHES

Formerly known as the Evangelical Mennonite Brethren, this group emanates from the Russian immigration of Mennonites into the U.S. and Canada during 1873 and 1874. The Conference was founded in 1889, with emphasis on true repentance, conversion, baptism on confession of faith, and living lives committed to Jesus Christ.

With 4,400 members in 37 churches, its strong missions emphasis is evident in the 156 missionaries who serve with faith mission agencies in all areas of the world.

In belief, it adheres to the inerrant, inspired Word of God and to dispensational interpretation.

GENERAL CONFERENCE MENNONITE CHURCH

A group of Mennonite congregations, eager to improve and enlarge foreign missionary efforts, offer better training for prospective leaders, and establish a church periodical, organized at West Point, Iowa, in 1860 to form this denomination. The desire to unite all Mennonite churches and conferences was, and still is, strong among its members. They accept established Mennonite doctrine but place strong emphasis on the autonomy of the local congregation; in their insistence on freedom from the traditional Mennonite regulations on attire, they have been regarded as "liberal in conduct" by some other Mennonites.

Ten district conferences meet annually, and a general conference meets triennially for fellowship and the transaction of official business. Elected commissions—overseas mission, home ministries, education—a General Board, and Division of General Services direct the work of the General Conference. The conference maintains two liberal arts colleges, three Bible colleges, a Bible institute, and a theological seminary. There are 34,000 members in 229 churches in the U.S.; 26,713 members in 134 churches in Canada; and 12 additional churches in South America. Mission work is carried on in 17 overseas countries, where the membership totals about 80,000.

General Conference Mennonites are strong supporters of the relief service and developmental work of Mennonite Central Committee, an inter-Mennonite agency. Also, this body is officially exploring the possibility of merging with the Mennonite Church.

HUTTERIAN BRETHREN

This church was founded by Jacob Hutter, a sixteenth-century Tyrolean Anabaptist who advocated communal ownership of property. He was burned as a heretic in Austria in 1536. Many Hutterites left Russia for Canada and the U.S. about 1874 and have moved back and forth across the border ever since. Most are of German ancestry and use that language in their homes and churches. Aside from the idea of common property, they are quite similar to the Old Order Amish; they seek to express their Bible-centered faith in brotherly love and aim at the recovery of New Testament spirit and fellowship. They feel this requires nonconformity to the world and, accordingly, practice nonresistance, refuse to participate in local politics, dress in outdated attire, and make no contribution to community projects. They maintain their own schools, in which the Bible is paramount. Their exclusiveness has made them unwelcome in certain sections of the country, and their status is always somewhat uncertain. There are 6,700 members in 95 colonies in Minnesota, Montana, Washington, and the Dakotas.

MENNONITE BRETHREN CHURCHES, GENERAL CONFERENCE

Dutch and German in background, this church was organized in 1860 upon the withdrawal of a small group from the Mennonite church in the Ukraine. Pietistic in orientation, it adopted a Baptistic polity, seeking closer attention to prayer and Bible study. Small bodies reached Kansas in 1874, then spread to the Pacific coast and Canada.

A general conference meets biennially as the chief administrative body, gathering delegates from its two areas (Canada and the U.S.). Each area has a number of districts. The area conferences supervise work in home missions, education, and publications. Foreign missions are found in Africa, Asia, Europe, South America, and Mexico; a radio ministry broadcasts worldwide in English, German, and Russian; and a French-language Bible Institute was established in Quebec in 1976.

The Krimmer Mennonite Brethren merged with this church in 1960, bringing the total membership to 45,000 in 350 churches.

MENNONITE CHURCH

The largest group of Mennonites in the United States, with 102,000 members in 1,100 churches, was founded in Switzerland in 1525 and brought to Germantown, Pennsylvania, in 1683 by Dutch and German immigrants. The Dordrecht Confession was adopted at a conference of Pennsylvania Mennonite ministers in 1725 as a Mennonite statement of faith. In 1921, Christian Fundamentals was adopted. A confession adopted in 1963 sought, without attempting to make the body into a creedal church, to set forth the major doctrines of Scripture as understood in the Anabaptist-Mennonite tradition. It stresses faith in Christ, the saved status of children, the importance of proclaiming God's Word and "making disciples," baptism of believers, absolute love, nonresistance rather than retaliation as one's personal response to injustice and maltreatment, and the church as a nonhierarchical community.

The General Assembly meets every two years. It brings together representatives from all area conferences and from many congregations throughout North America. Discussion is open to all, with open sessions; only elected delegates (women and men, ordained and nonordained) may vote.

Churchwide program boards are in charge of mission, congregational ministries, education, publishing, and mutual aid work; all are under the supervision of the church's general board. Home missions stress evangelism, and missions are found in Asia, Africa, Europe, and Central and South America. There are three colleges and two seminaries—one of each located in Goshen, Indiana—and numerous secondary and elementary schools, church-sponsored hospitals, retirement homes, and child-welfare services. Membership is strongest in Pennsylvania and the Midwest states.

OLD ORDER AMISH CHURCH

Continuous since the Amish immigration of 1720–40, this church adheres to the older forms of worship and attire, using hooks and eyes instead of buttons; worships in private homes; and has no conferences. Members do not believe in missions or benevolent institutions or centralized schools; some, however, do contribute to the missions and charities of the Mennonite Church. There are 876 Old Order Amish Church districts, each averaging 100 to 150 members, with approximately half that number baptized.

OLD ORDER (WISLER) MENNONITE CHURCH

This church was named for Jacob Wisler, the first Mennonite bishop in Indiana, who led a separation from that church in 1872 to protest the use of English in the services and the introduction of Sunday schools. Joined in 1886, 1893, and 1901 by groups with similar ideas from Canada, Pennsylvania, and Virginia, the church is still maintained on the basis of those protests.

Each section of the church has its own district conference, and there are conferences twice each year in each community. All churches take part in relief work, especially for the needy at home and in foreign lands, and some contribute to the work of the Mennonite Church. There are 9,731 members in 38 churches, 19 bishops, 76 ministers, and one church school.

REFORMED MENNONITE CHURCH

Organized under the leadership of John Herr in Lancaster County, Pennsylvania, in 1812, Reformed Mennonites hold closely to New Testament teachings and maintain that there can be but one true church for all believers. They recognize the ordinances of baptism, the Lord's Supper, foot washing, marriage, and the kiss of peace; but these are "for edification and not a means of salvation." Baptism by pouring or sprinkling is considered an outward testimony of the baptism of the Spirit within the heart, which must precede water baptism.

The Communion service signifies unity with God and with one another and is observed only by members of the church. They observe strictly the instructions in Matthew 18 regarding laboring in love with an erring brother; they greet one another regularly with the kiss of peace and insist upon modest and uniform clothing—the women wear head coverings.

They are nonresistant, do not vote or hold any governmental office, and refuse to worship with anyone who is not united in faith and practice. All converts join the church of their own free will. The bishops, ministers, and deacons are chosen from local congregations and receive no salary. They have no Sunday schools, believing that parents must teach their own children. This church reports 310 members in 10 congregations.

UNAFFILIATED MENNONITE

A number of small groups and single congregations do not officially participate in the program and activities of Mennonite Church General Assembly. These also hold an unaffiliated status with all other Mennonite bodies. These Mennonite churches claim 17,200 members in 353 congregations. All hold to the fundamental doctrines of the Christian faith, the suffering of injustice without retaliation, believer's baptism, the New Testament view that Christians must be separate from the evils of an unregenerate society, and moral earnestness. They are widely scattered in the United States, with most located in Indiana, Pennsylvania, Ohio, and Virginia, and a few congregations in Canada.

METHODIST

Beginning as a movement within the Church of England, Methodism expanded over the years between 1738 and 1790 under the leadership of John Wesley and Charles Wesley. The direct and warm action of the Holy Spirit infused and vivified the formal and often perfunctory liturgy. And although Methodism remains history-minded and respectful of liturgy, it typically has been concerned with ministry to the poor and disadvantaged, expressing its faith in compassion for the human condition. In a variety of ways, the witness of the Spirit has been an impelling force—for worship, love of neighbor, personal piety, and evangelization.

England's famed Oxford University has been called the cradle of lost causes, but at least one cause born there has not been lost—Methodism. Known and ridiculed at Oxford in 1729, today it claims some 13 million adherents in North America, more than 18 million around the world.

The Oxford Methodists, a tiny group of methodically religious students (also dubbed Bible Bigots, Bible Moths, and the Holy Club) who gave stated time to prayer and Bible reading, numbered among their members John and Charles Wesley and George Whitefield. They talked of the necessity of being "justified" before they could be "sanctified" and of the need for holiness in human living; they read and discussed William Law's *A Serious Call to a Devout and Holy Life* and *A Treatise on Christian Perfection*. The Wesley brothers were sons of a Church of England clergyman. With the other members of the Holy Club, they stood their ground against jeering students and went out to preach and pray with the poor and desperate commoners of England—prisoners in jail, paupers in hovels, bitter and nearly hopeless "underdogs of a British society that was perilously close to moral and spiritual collapse." Methodism began on a campus and reached for the masses.

The Wesleys arrived in Georgia in 1736. Charles came as secretary to General Oglethorpe, and John was sent by the Society for the

Propagation of the Gospel to be a missionary to the Native Americans. It was an unsuccessful and unhappy two years for John, with but one bright spot: On shipboard en route to the colonies, he met a group of Moravians and was deeply impressed by their piety and humble Christian way of life. When he returned to London, he went to the meeting of a religious society in Aldersgate Street. There he heard the preacher read Luther's *Preface to the Epistle to the Romans,* and he felt his heart "strangely warmed" as the meaning of the Reformer's doctrine of "justification by faith" sank into his soul. That was the evangelistic spark that energized his life and started the flame of Wesleyan revival in England. From the pious Moravians, via Wesley, came the warmhearted emphases on conversion and holiness that still are the central themes of Methodism.

Whitefield and the Wesleys were too much afire to be boxed in by the staid Church of England. When its doors were closed to them, they took to the open air, Charles writing hymns of revival for the streets, barns, private homes, and mining pits of Cornwall; John preaching repentance, regeneration, justification, holiness, and sanctification. The upper classes laughed, but the lower classes listened to the first words of hope they had heard in many years. Converts came thick and fast; it became necessary to organize into "societies." One was attached to a Moravian congregation in Fetter Lane, London, in 1739 and later moved to its own quarters in an abandoned government building known as the Foundry, where in 1740 it became the first self-sustaining Methodist society in London.

Between 1739 and 1744 the organizational elements of Methodism were instituted: a circuit system and itinerant ministry, class meetings and class leaders, lay preachers and annual conferences. There was phenomenal growth in membership; more than 26,000 Methodists were worshiping in England, Ireland, Scotland, and Wales in 1767. Their impact on British society was startling; the crudities and barbarisms of the times were alleviated and a "French revolution" averted.

Methodism was primarily a lay movement. Wesley did his best to keep it within the Church of England; an evangelical party grew within that church, but the greater numbers recruited from among the unchurched made a separate organization imperative. In 1739 Wesley drew up a set of general rules, which are still held by modern Methodists, and an ideal delineation of Bible rules and conduct. A Deed of Declaration in 1784 gave legal status to the yearly Methodist conference. But John Wesley died in 1791, before Methodism in England became a recognized church, the Wesleyan Methodist Connection.

Meanwhile, the movement had invaded Ireland and the American colonies. Wesley had begun to send out leaders; the first in this country were Joseph Pilmoor and Richard Boardman. Philip Embury, an Irish lay leader, encouraged by his cousin Barbara Heck, preached in New York and inspired the organization, about 1766, of the first Methodist society overseas. By 1769, New York Methodists had built Wesley Chapel, now known as John Street Methodist Church. Captain Thomas Webb, a veteran of Braddock's ill-fated army, established societies in Philadelphia; Robert Strawbridge started a revival in Maryland and built a log-cabin church at Sam's Creek. Devereux Jarratt, a transplanted Anglican minister, led a revival in Virginia that won thousands.

The true center of Methodism in those days lay in the South; of 3,148 Methodists in the colonies in 1775, about 2,000 lived south of Mason and Dixon's Line. Wesley, aware of the rapid spread of the movement, sent emissaries to take charge, among them Francis Asbury and Thomas Rankin, the latter as "superintendent of the entire work of Methodism in America." Rankin presided over the first conference in America, called at Philadelphia in 1773 and attended by about 1,160 Methodists, ten of them ministers.

But when the Liberty Bell rang in 1776, there were fewer than 7,000 Methodists, and they seemed doomed to disappear as quickly as they had gathered. The majority of preachers had come from England; they were incurably British and were so roughly handled by the patriots that by 1779, nearly all had fled either to Canada or home to England. Wesley's pro-British attitude also aroused resentment, and Francis Asbury, working almost single-handedly, found it difficult to keep some of the churches alive. But a miracle happened; of all the religious groups in the colonies, Methodists alone actually seemed to prosper during the Revolution. By the end of the war, the membership had grown to 14,000, and there were nearly 80 preachers. It was now an American church, free of both England and the Church of England. Wesley accepted the inevitable; he ordained ministers for the colonies and appointed Asbury and Thomas Coke as superintendents.

Coke brought with him from England certain instructions from Wesley, a service book and a hymnal, and authority to proceed with the organization. The Christmas Conference, held at Baltimore in December 1784, organized the Methodist Episcopal Church and elected Coke and Asbury as superintendents (later called bishops). The Sunday Service (an abridgment of *The Book of Common Prayer*) and Articles of Religion were adopted as written by John Wesley, but another article was added: that as good patriots, Methodists should vow allegiance to the United States government. The first General Conference of the new church, made up solely of ministers, was held in 1792. It was not until 1872 that the laity was admitted to what had then become a quadrennial General Conference. Membership soared; from 14,000 in 37 circuits at the close of the Revolution, by the middle of the nineteenth century it had increased to 1,324,000.

Methodism not only swept through the cities, but it also developed an amazing strength in small towns and rural areas. Circuit riders, ministers on horseback who traveled the expanding frontier, went everywhere—to mountain cabins, prairie churches, schoolhouses, and camp meetings—preaching free grace and individual responsibility and the need for conversion and regeneration. Their itinerant ministry was perfectly adapted to the democratic society of the frontier. The Methodist Book Concern was established in 1789, putting into the saddlebags of the circuit riders religious literature that followed the march of the American empire south and west. The camp meeting, born among the Presbyterians, was adopted by the Methodists and exploited to the limit. Its revivalistic flavor and method were made to order for the followers of Wesley and Whitefield.

All was not peaceful among the Methodists, however; divisions came. Objecting to what they considered abuses of the episcopal system, several bodies broke away: the Republican Methodists, later the Christian Church, withdrew in Virginia; Methodist Protestants seceded in 1830. Between 1813 and 1917, large groups of African Americans formed independent churches: the African Methodist Episcopal Church; the Union Church of Africans, now the Union American Methodist Episcopal Church; the African Methodist Episcopal Zion Church. In 1844 came the most devastating split of all, the bisecting of the Methodist Episcopal Church into the Methodist Episcopal Church, the Northern body, and the Methodist Episcopal Church, South, organized in 1845.

The cause of this major split was, of course, slavery. Bishop Andrew, a Georgian, owned slaves through inheritance, and his wife also was a slaveholder. It was not possible for them to free their slaves under the laws of Georgia, but the General Conference of 1844, held in New York City, requested that the bishop desist from the exercise of his office while he remained a slaveholder. Incensed, the Southern delegates rebelled, a provisional plan of separation was formulated, and the Southerners went home to organize their own church.

Basic to the separation was the constitutional question of the power of the General Conference, which, the Southerners maintained, assumed supreme power in virtually deposing a bishop who had violated no law of the church and against whom no charges had been brought. It was a split that concerned neither doctrine nor polity; purely political and social, it was a wound that was not healed until 1939, when the Methodist Episcopal Church; the Methodist Episcopal Church, South; and the Methodist Protestant Church were reunited at Kansas City, Missouri.

The uniting conference of that year adopted a new constitution in three sections: an abridgment of the Articles of Religion drawn up by John Wesley; the General Rules, covering the conduct of church members and the duties of church officials; and the Articles of Organization and Government, outlining the organization and conduct of conferences and local churches. This constitution cannot be changed by any General Conference unless and until every annual conference has acted upon the proposed changes.

In matters of faith, there has been very little occasion for confusion or difference; doctrinal quarrels have been noticeably absent. Historically, Methodists have never built theological fences to keep anyone out; they have stressed the foundation beliefs of Protestantism and offered common theological ground. Not all of the churches repeat the Apostles' Creed in their worship, though the discipline of the church provides for its use in formal worship. The theology is Arminian, as interpreted by Wesley in his sermons, his *Notes on the New Testament,* and his Articles of Religion.

The church preaches and teaches the doctrines of the Trinity, the natural sinfulness of humankind, its fall and the need of conversion and repentance, freedom of the will, justification by faith, sanctification and holiness, future rewards and punishments, the sufficiency of the Scriptures for salvation, the enabling grace of God, and perfection. Two sacraments, baptism and the Lord's Supper, are observed; baptism is administered to both infants and adults, usually by sprinkling. Membership—full, preparatory, or affiliate (for those away from their home church who wish to affiliate where they live)—is based on confession of faith or by letter of transfer from other evangelical churches; admission of children to membership is usually limited to those 13 years of age or over, but in the South the age may be a few years younger. There is wide freedom in the interpretation and practice of all doctrines; liberals and conservatives work in close harmony.

The local churches of Methodism are called charges; ministers are appointed by the bishop at the annual conference, and each church elects its own administrative board, which initiates planning and sets goals and policies on the local level; it is composed of staff members, chairs of various committees, those representing various program interests, and members at large. Charge, annual, and general conferences prevail in most Methodist bodies; while the government is popularly called episcopal, it is largely governmental, through this series of conferences. The charge conference meets at the local church or on the circuit, with the district superintendent presiding. It fixes the salary of the pastor, elects the church officers, and sends delegates to the annual conference; it may delegate responsibility for many of these duties to the administrative board.

Some areas have a district conference between the charge and the annual conference, but it is not a universal arrangement. Annual conferences cover defined geographical areas; they ordain and admit ministers, vote on constitutional questions, supervise pensions and relief, exchange pastors with other annual conferences through acts of the bishop; and, every fourth year, elect lay and ministerial delegates to the General Conference. The General Conference is the lawmaking body of the church, meeting quadrennially; the bishops preside, and the work of the conference is done largely in committees, whose reports then may be adopted by the General Conference.

Worship and liturgy are based on the English prayer book, with widespread modifications. The language of the prayer book is much in evidence in the sacraments of Methodist churches. In many forms of worship, however, each congregation is free to use or change the accepted pattern as it sees fit. Of the 23 separate Methodist bodies in the U.S., The United Methodist Church is numerically the strongest.

AFRICAN METHODIST EPISCOPAL CHURCH

One of the three largest Methodist groups in the U.S., this church began in 1787 when a number of members of St. George's Methodist Episcopal Church in Philadelphia withdrew in protest against racial discrimination. They built Bethel Chapel with the assistance of Bishop William White of the Protestant Episcopal Church. Francis Asbury dedicated the chapel in Philadelphia and ordained Richard Allen as its minister.

The body was formally organized as the African Methodist Episcopal Church in 1816; in the same year, Allen was consecrated as its first bishop, again by Bishop Asbury. From the beginning, it provided social, educational, and journalistic services.

In the years preceding the Civil War, the church was largely confined to the Northern states; following the war its membership increased rapidly in the South, and today it is found all across the nation. Membership now stands at 3,300,000 in 7,200 churches.

There are 20 bishops, 11 general officers, and 18 connectional officers in 13 districts; a General Conference is held quadrennially.

Foreign missions are supported in South Africa; West Africa; India; London, England; the Caribbean; and South America. There are six colleges, two theological schools, and several elementary and secondary schools. Journalism has been a central part of the church's work from its early years: The AME Book Concern dates to 1816, and the weekly *Christian Reader* has been published since 1848.

AFRICAN METHODIST EPISCOPAL ZION CHURCH

This church dates from 1796, when it was organized by a group of members protesting discrimination in the John Street Church in New York City. Their first church, named Zion, was built in 1800, and that word was later made part of the denominational name. The first annual conference was held in that church in 1821, with 19 preachers from six black Methodist churches in New Haven, Connecticut; Philadelphia, Pennsylvania; and Newark, New Jersey, presided over by the Reverend William Phoebus of the white Methodist Episcopal Church. James Varick, who had led the John Street dissension, was elected the first bishop. The present name was approved in 1848. The church spread quickly over the Northern states, and by 1880 there were 15 annual conferences in the South.

Livingstone College, the largest educational institution of the church, was established in 1880. Departments of missions, education, and publications were created in 1892; later came administrative boards to direct work in church extension, evangelism, finance, ministerial relief, and so on. Home missions are supported in Louisiana, Mississippi, and several Western states, principally Oklahoma; missionaries are found also in Liberia, Ghana, Nigeria, South America, and the West Indies. There are five secondary schools and two colleges—Livingstone at Salisbury, North Carolina, and Clinton Junior College in Rock Hill, South Carolina. Membership figures list 1,200,000 in 3,000 churches.

CHRISTIAN METHODIST EPISCOPAL CHURCH

This body was established in 1870, in an amicable agreement between white and black members of the Methodist Episcopal Church, South. There were at the time at least 225,000 slave members of the Southern church, but with the Emancipation Proclamation, all but 80,000 joined the two independent black bodies. When the general conference of the Methodist Episcopal Church, South, met at New Orleans in 1866, a commission from the black membership asked to separate into a church of its own. The request was granted, and the Colored Methodist Episcopal Church was organized. That name was held until the meeting of its general conference at Memphis in May 1954, when it was changed to the present name.

The doctrine is that of the parent church; this denomination adds a quarterly conference to the district, annual, and quadrennial conferences usual in Methodism. There are ten episcopal districts, each supervised by a presiding bishop; ten departments oversee the national work, each chaired by a bishop assigned by the College of Bishops.

The general secretaries of the various departments are elected every four years by the General Conference, and the president of the Women's Missionary Council is elected every four years by the quadrennial assembly of the Missionary Council. The church issues two periodicals and supports five colleges, a seminary, a hospital, and several low-rent and senior-citizen housing complexes. There are 800,000 members and 3,000 churches.

CONGREGATIONAL METHODIST CHURCH

This church was established in Georgia in 1852 by a group that withdrew from the Methodist Episcopal Church, South, in objection to certain features of the episcopacy and itinerancy. Two-thirds of the membership of this church withdrew in turn in 1887 and 1888 to join the Congregational Church.

Local pastors are called by the local churches; annual conferences grant licenses, ordain ministers, and review local reports. Annual and general conferences are recognized as church courts, empowered to rule on violations of church law and to coordinate, plan, and promote general church activities. There is a missionary program among the Navajo in New Mexico and Mexico. Wesley College and the denominational headquarters are in Florence, Mississippi. There are 14,738 members in 187 churches.

EVANGELICAL METHODIST CHURCH

Organized at Memphis in 1946, this church is "fundamental in doctrine, evangelistic in program, and congregational in government." It represents a double protest against what was considered an autocratic and undemocratic government, on the one hand, and a tendency toward modernism, on the other, in The Methodist Church.

The church is Arminian in theology and Wesleyan in doctrine. Members seek to apply the spirit and revivalistic fervor of original Wesleyanism to the needs of society today. Fundamentalist, they oppose the "substituting of social, educational, or other varieties of cultural salvation for the gospel message."

Local churches own and control their own property and select their own pastors. There are seven districts and seven district superintendents; Mexico and Bolivia constitute mission conferences. The General Conference meets quadrennially; international headquarters are in Wichita, Kansas. There are 138 churches, with a membership of more than 9,500.

FREE METHODIST CHURCH OF NORTH AMERICA

This is one of the more conservative among the larger bodies of American Methodism in both doctrine and standards of Christian practice. Its founders were the Reverend B. T. Roberts and his associates, who objected to "new school" Methodism, which they believed compromised the Wesleyan standards of the church. They were "read out" of their churches and organized the Free Methodist Church in Pekin, New York, in 1860. The Genesee Conference, of which Roberts had been a member, restored his credentials to his son in 1910, but no reunion of the group with The United Methodist Church has yet been effected. A merger with the Holiness Movement in Canada was approved in 1960.

Doctrinally, the Free Methodists call for a return to original Wesleyan teaching and practice. They stress the virgin birth, the deity of Jesus, and his vicarious atonement and resurrection. No one may be received into membership without undergoing confession and forgiveness of sin, and the experience of entire sanctification is sought in all members. The membership covenant is based on the general rules of Methodism, and membership in secret societies is forbidden.

The Free Methodist Church has become a world fellowship, consisting of five general conferences—Egypt, Japan, North America, Rwanda (1958), and Canada (1989) and three provisional general conferences with national bishops in Burundi, India, and Zaire—with a common constitution formally ratified by each General Conference in 1964. All legislative actions are reviewed by a constitutional council elected from the General Conference. There are 84,592 members in 1,226 churches in North America and the United Kingdom, with a world membership of 345,647. The Free Methodist Church is organized in 30 countries around the world.

There are four senior colleges and a cooperative program with other denominations in another senior college; one junior college; a Bible college; and a seminary foundation maintained in cooperation with Asbury Theological Seminary and Western Evangelical Seminary. Social services include a 250-bed hospital, a home for unwed mothers, five retirement and nursing facilities for the elderly, and many day-care centers for children.

PRIMITIVE METHODIST CHURCH, U.S.A.

This church came into being as a result of the camp-meeting movement in the English midlands. Following an all-day meeting held at Mow Cop, Staffordshire, on May 31, 1807, Hugh Bourne and William Clowes, local preachers, were dismissed from the Wesleyan Church. A group of people, converted as a result of the open-air meetings, joined with Bourne and Clowes in 1810. Growth was such that by February 1812 the group took the name Society of the Primitive Methodists—referring to the conduct of early Methodism. Four missionaries were sent to the U.S. in 1829 to work with other Primitive Methodists who had settled mainly in the East and Midwest.

The denomination has an annual conference that is both administrative and legislative, the churches being divided into six districts. The president is elected every four years, and there is one salaried official, an executive director. The relationships and arrangements of ministers are reviewed annually, and vacancies are filled with student ministers or ordained deacons and elders.

Doctrinally, modified Wesleyan Articles of Religion are accepted. The main mission endeavors are located in Guatemala and Spain. There are 8,487 members in 83 churches.

REFORMED METHODIST UNION EPISCOPAL CHURCH

This church began in 1885 at Charleston, South Carolina, as the result of a withdrawal of persons from the African Methodist Episcopal Church. The immediate cause of the division was a dispute over the election of ministerial delegates to the General Conference. Intended at first as a nonepiscopal church, the body later adopted the complete polity of the Methodist Episcopal Church in its General Conferences of 1896 and 1916. Its first bishop was consecrated in 1899 by a bishop of the Reformed Episcopal Church. Class meetings and love feasts are featured in the local congregation; there are 3,800 members in 18 churches.

SOUTHERN METHODIST CHURCH

Doctrinally, the Southern Methodist Church remains the same as the body out of which it grew: the Methodist Episcopal Church,

South. Its members opposed the merger of that church with the northern Methodist Episcopal Church in 1939, on grounds of the "alarming infidelity and apostasy found therein." They regard the Southern Methodist Church not as a separatist body but as a church "brought into existence to perpetuate the faith of John Wesley."

There are no bishops, but there are the usual Methodist annual and general conferences; a president is elected every four years from the elders of the clergy. Laypeople and clergy have equal voice and voting privileges in the conferences.

Local churches own and control their own property and buildings and call their own ministers, who must be approved by their annual conferences. There are 7,800 members in 130 churches, from Virginia to Texas. There is one college and a publishing house, Foundry Press, both located at Orangeburg, South Carolina.

UNION AMERICAN METHODIST EPISCOPAL CHURCH

This was one of the first black bodies to establish an independent Methodist church. A group of members left the Asbury Methodist Church in Wilmington, Delaware, in 1805. They worshiped outdoors and in private homes until 1813, when they built a church and incorporated as the Union Church of Africans. Defections from the membership were responsible for the formation of another body, known as the African Union Church, which forced the change to the present name.

General, annual, district, and quarterly conferences are held; general conferences are called only to consider proposed changes in name, law, or polity. There are two educational institutions, and the church claims some 15,000 members in 55 congregations, primarily on the East Coast.

UNITED METHODIST CHURCH, THE

Two mergers of major importance produced The United Methodist Church, the largest Methodist body in this country, with 8,650,388 members in 36,771 local churches in the U.S. and 1,157,816 members in 5,165 congregations outside the U.S. The first merger was actually a rejoining of three existing Methodist groups. At a conference in Kansas City in 1939, the Methodist Episcopal Church, the Methodist Episcopal Church, South, and the Methodist Protestant Church were reunited under a new name, The Methodist Church. In 1968 The Methodist Church merged with the Evangelical United Brethren to form The United Methodist Church.

The history of the Methodist Episcopal Church and the break between that body and the Methodist Episcopal Church, South, has already been discussed. The Methodist Episcopal Church, South, was organized at Louisville, Kentucky, in 1845 and held its first General Conference a year later in Petersburg, Virginia, under the presidency of Bishops James O. Andrew and Joshua Soule. In 1939 it brought a membership of 2.5 million to the reunited church. The Methodist Protestant Church was founded at a conference in Baltimore in 1830, in protest of the almost total rule of clergy in the Methodist Episcopal Church and the exclusion of laypeople from its councils. There were about 200,000 members in 1939.

The Evangelical United Brethren Church grew out of a series of mergers in two groups: United Brethren in Christ and the Evangelical Church. The Evangelical Church, originally Evangelical Association, began as a result of the labors of Jacob Albright (1759–1808) among the German people of Pennsylvania; preaching first as a Lutheran and then as a Methodist exhorter, Albright was made a bishop at the first annual conference of the Evangelical Association in 1807. He used the Methodist *Discipline* until 1809, preached Methodist doctrine, and was so effective that for quite some time his followers were known as the Albrights. A split in 1891 resulted in a separate denomination, the United Evangelical Church; the two groups were reunited in 1922 under the name Evangelical Church.

Another group, Church of the United Brethren in Christ, developed in a parallel manner through the preaching of William Otterbein (1726–1813) and Martin Boehm (1725–1812) among the Germans in Pennsylvania, Maryland, and Virginia; they were elected bishops at a conference in September 1800. That conference created the Church of the United Brethren in Christ, which also was strongly Methodist in polity, doctrine, and practice. Both groups had a *Discipline* modeled on that of the Methodists. The Church of the United Brethren in Christ and the Evangelical Church had too much in common to remain separated and were merged into the Evangelical United Brethren Church (E.U.B.) at Johnstown, Pennsylvania, in 1946.

Both the Methodist and the E.U.B. churches, across the years, had been deeply conscious of their common historical and spiritual heritage. Their doctrines were similar—both were episcopal in government; both traced their origins to John Wesley; both had nearly the same *Book of Discipline*. Their preachers often exchanged pulpits and congregations, worked together, and shared the same buildings. The only major difference was that of language—German among the

205

Brethren, English among the Methodists—but in time this barrier began to mean less and less. Conversations concerning a merger began as early as 1803 and were consummated when the two churches became The United Methodist Church at Dallas, Texas, on April 23, 1968.

There was some dissent at Dallas; 51 congregations and 79 ministers of the Evangelical United Brethren withdrew from the Pacific Northwest Conference to establish the Evangelical Church of North America; 18 of the 23 E.U.B. congregations in Montana left to establish the Evangelical Church of North America in Montana; 13 other congregations in the Erie and Ohio Southeast Conferences petitioned to leave, but those petitions were denied. The split concerned theological issues and the question of church ownership. But roughly 750,000 Brethren accepted the union, and their strength gave the new United Methodist Church a membership of nearly 11 million.

In this union no significant changes were made in either doctrine or polity. The Confession of Faith of the Evangelical United Brethren Church, adopted in 1962, was placed beside the Methodist Articles of Religion; Wesleyan standards dominate both statements, and both are used as each congregation elects to use them. The same system of bishops and conferences was in use in both denominations and is still maintained. There are now 68 annual conferences in the United States, with a total of 36,771 organized churches and 38,486 ministers. Outside the U.S. are 48 annual conferences, with 5,165 congregations and 3,609 clergy.

Above the annual conferences are five jurisdictional conferences, established for geographical convenience in administrative matters. These meet quadrennially, at times determined by the Council of Bishops, to elect new bishops and to name the members of the larger boards and commissions. Outside the continental U.S., central conferences correspond to jurisdictional conferences; they meet quadrennially and, when authorized to do so, may elect their own bishops. All bishops are elected for life (except in some overseas conferences, where the term is four years) with retirement set at age 66 and 70; 66 bishops in the United States and abroad are in charge of the areas of the church—the New York Area, the Denver Area, and so on. Together, they constitute the Council of Bishops, which meets at least once a year but usually twice a year, "for the general oversight and promotion of the temporal and spiritual affairs of the entire church."

The General Conference consists of 1,000 delegates, half laity and half clergy, elected on a proportional basis by the annual conferences. A Judicial Council determines the constitutionality of any act of the

General Conference that may be appealed, and it hears and determines any appeal from a bishop's decision on a question of law, in any district or annual, central, or jurisdictional conference. The council is made up of nine members, clergy and lay, and has become so important that it is often called the Supreme Court of the church.

The General Conference of 1972 restructured the administrative bodies of the church. The Council of Bishops and a Council on Finance and Administration were made responsible to the General Conference, and a new Council on Ministries was set up as a coordinating body between the conference and various other commissions, support services, and program boards. The commissions now include those on archives and history, religion and race, and the status and role of women. The support services include the Board of Publications, United Methodist Communications, and the Board of Pensions. The program boards were rearranged to include boards on church and society, discipleship, higher education and ministry, global ministries, and Christian unity and interreligious concerns.

The 1972 General Conference also broadened the basis of doctrine in the church in the first restatement since the eighteenth century. The classic documents of the merging Methodist and Evangelical United Brethren churches were maintained, but the doctrinal door was left open to theological change and revision. A revised statement was adopted in 1988: "In theological reflection, the resources of tradition, experience, and reason are integral to our study of Scripture without displacing Scripture's primacy for faith and practice" (*Book of Discipline 1988*, p. 86).

This church has property valued at $22.1 billion, not including educational plants, hospitals, or homes for the elderly. There are 224 institutions devoted to long-term care, 78 to health care, and 60 to child care. There are 87 United Methodist colleges and universities, 13 schools of theology, 12 two-year colleges, and a medical college. The church is at work in 79 countries; 17 bishops administer the work overseas, with many hundreds of missionaries serving in a great many capacities.

The World Methodist Council, organized in 1881 and designed to draw the whole Wesleyan movement closer together in fellowship and devotion to the Wesleyan heritage, has become increasingly active in recent years. Fifteen ecumenical conferences have been held since 1881; headquarters is established at Lake Junaluska, North Carolina.

METROPOLITAN COMMUNITY CHURCHES, UNIVERSAL FELLOWSHIP OF

Founded in 1968, this Protestant body is best known for its outreach to homosexuals. It professes orthodox Christian theology on such doctrines as Scripture, the Trinity, and the sacraments. They hold the belief that theology is the basis to present the good news of God's love to a segment of society often excluded from, and sometimes ridiculed for, participation in church life.

This awareness prompted Troy D. Perry to create a denomination where such people could find genuine acceptance in a context of Christian worship and service. Perry, himself a homosexual, had been discharged from the church he served as pastor and ostracized from his denomination. He called a congregation into being in Los Angeles, and soon churches were organized in other cities. In the summer of 1970, the first general conference was held.

The church reports a membership of 32,000, with 291 churches in 17 countries. Heterosexuals may and do belong, but a large percentage of the membership is homosexual. The denomination describes its ministry as a shared one—lay and clergy, women and men, privileged and underprivileged, lesbian, gay, and heterosexual. Forty-three percent of its clergy are women.

The body applied for membership in the National Council of Churches of Christ in 1983 and was turned down, but it hopes eventually to become a part of that ecumenical organization, with which it remains in dialogue. It does participate as an official observer in World Council of Churches events.

Its membership is active in a variety of ministries, reflecting its primary orientation to such traditions as the social gospel and liberation theology. In particular, it has sought to address the needs of the hungry, the homeless, and the powerless. It supports a freeze on nuclear weapons and is committed to eradicating sexism in its theology and in society at large. The civil rights of all people are a major concern. It also addresses the AIDS epidemic as a major social issue, partly because incidences of the disease are so prevalent among its own membership.

The church faces the controversial nature of its existence by stating that its members accept homosexuality as "a gift from God," just as heterosexuality is "a gift from God." "But our sexuality is not and should not be the focal point of our lives. The MCC emphasizes that everything in our life, including our sexuality, must center on our relationship with God, through faith in Jesus Christ."

MISSIONARY CHURCH

The Missionary Church is made up of two groups that merged in March 1969: the Missionary Church Association and the United Missionary Church. The new denomination claims 309 congregations and 25,000 members in 10 districts in the U.S. The Missionary Church Association was founded at Berne, Indiana, in 1889. The United Missionary Church was formed in 1883 in Englewood, Ohio, as the Mennonite Brethren in Christ; it was renamed in 1947. Both former denominations had a Mennonite heritage and came into existence through the holiness revivals of the late 1800s.

The Missionary Church is conservative and evangelical in theology and practice. Local churches are free to manage their own affairs, but recognize and adhere to the authority of a general conference made up of ministers, missionaries, and laity, held biennially. Working under the general conference is a general board that oversees a variety of agencies and missions activities. The president, vice president, and secretary are elected for terms of four years.

The U.S. Missionary Church works jointly with the Missionary Church of Canada in overseas ministry in the joint venture named World Partners. Church planting, Bible translation, correspondence courses, Bible schools, a theological college, extension seminaries, clinics, youth camps, and other programs are carried out by 139 missionaries, in cooperation with the national churches. Countries served include Brazil, the Dominican Republic, Ecuador, France, Haiti, Jamaica, Nigeria, Sierra Leone, Spain, and others. There are also indigenous churches in India, Mexico, and Venezuela. Further outreach is achieved through other evangelical mission boards in 23 countries worldwide.

The church is affiliated with one educational institution in the U.S.: Bethel College in Mishawaka, Indiana.

MORAVIAN

The roots of the Moravian Church run back as far as the ninth century, to the work of Constantine and Methodius among the Slavic populations of Bohemia and Moravia, then struggling for political and religious freedom. Later, the people followed John Hus, who was martyred in 1415, and Jerome of Prague, martyred in 1416. The first association was formed in Bohemia in 1458; after that time, the church was called either *Jednota Bratrska* ("The Union of Brethren") or *Unitas Fratrum* ("Unity of the Brethren").

By the middle of the sixteenth century there were about 60 congregations in Bohemia, between 80 and 90 in Moravia, and, somewhat later, 40 in Poland. The numbers remained virtually unchanged until the outbreak of the Thirty Years' War (1618–48). Fierce persecution under the Hapsburgs at that time almost exterminated the church, but it survived. In 1722, two families named Neisser, led by Christian David, fled from Moravia. At the invitation of Nicholas Louis, Count of Zinzendorf, the small band found refuge on his estate in Saxony, where they built the town of Herrnhut. The count called the people Moravians because they had come from northern Moravia.

Zinzendorf was made a bishop in 1737. In America (1741–43) he was active in establishing the church in Pennsylvania, where three towns were founded—Bethlehem, Nazareth, and Lititz—following a failure to plant churches in the colony of Georgia. Churches in Hope, New Jersey, and Salem, North Carolina, also proved failures, but the current Moravian Church, concentrated in the eastern U.S., is one of the most solid religious establishments in the nation.

MORAVIAN CHURCH (*UNITAS FRATRUM*)

It is said of Moravians that "a unified system of doctrine was never developed." That may be an overstatement, but it certainly is true that no doctrine is peculiar to them; the church is broadly evangelical, insisting on the principle "in essentials unity, in nonessentials liberty, and in all things charity." The scriptural interpretations agree substantially with the Apostles' Creed, the Westminster and Augsburg confessions, and the Articles of Religion of the Church of England. The Scriptures are held to be the inspired Word of God and an adequate rule for faith and practice. The main doctrinal emphasis may be said to be the love of God manifested in the redemptive life and death of Jesus, the inner testimony of the Spirit, and Christian conduct in everyday affairs.

The sacrament of infant baptism by sprinkling, or occasionally by pouring, is practiced. Membership totals 60,000 in 180 churches, concentrated in eastern Pennsylvania, western North Carolina, and the Kuskokwim River Valley in Alaska. The Lord's Supper is celebrated at least six times a year, and the custom of the love feast is preserved; both are primarily devoted to hymn singing. A variety of liturgies is used in worship; an especially beautiful outdoor sunrise service at Easter is notable.

The Moravian Church in North America is divided into three provinces—Northern, Southern, and Alaska. The highest administrative body in each is the provincial synod. Composed of ministers and laypeople, it meets every three or four years to direct missionary, educational, and publishing work and to elect a provincial elders' conference, or executive board, which functions between synod meetings. Bishops, elected by provincial and general synods, are the spiritual, but not the administrative, leaders.

Missionary work has always been a first concern; with a comparatively small membership, the church conducted the most efficient missionary work among Native Americans of any of the early colonial churches. The worldwide Moravian Church has 19 provinces—in Europe; in North, Central, and South America; and in Africa and the Caribbean. Of the world's 610,000 Moravians, 60 percent are in Tanzania and South Africa. The church sponsors a mission to Tibetan refugees in northern India and a rehabilitation center for persons with handicaps at Ramallah, on the West Bank of the Jordan river.

Always committed to education, the church supports Moravian College and Moravian Theological Seminary in Allentown, Pennsylvania, and Salem College in Winston-Salem, North Carolina.

UNITY OF THE BRETHREN

Known until 1962 as the Evangelical Unity of the Czech-Moravian Brethren in North America, this body originated among immigrants who arrived in Texas in the late nineteenth century. The present name, translated from *Unitas Fratrum,* or *Jednota Bratrska,* dates from 1457.

A synod meets every two years. The church has no colleges or seminaries. In 1991 there were 2,615 members in 26 churches.

MUSLIM (ISLAM)

Islam claims more than 6 million adherents in the U.S. There is no central authority (indeed, no church or priesthood in all of Islam), but there are Islamic Centers in Washington, D.C., Toledo, Detroit, New York, and other cities all over the U.S. * *The center in Washington, D.C., includes a beautiful mosque, a library, classrooms for study, and administrative offices; it is open for daily prayer and offers lectures and publications about the philosophy, religion, and arts, of Islam.*

The word *Islam* signifies peace, submission to God's will and obedience to God's laws. It does not claim to be a new religion formulated by the Prophet Muhammad, but rather "the continuation of all former religious principles decreed by God through his revela-

---

* The national organization in the United States is called the Islamic Society of North America.

tions to all prophets." Those prophets include Jesus (Muslims accept him as prophet but not as divine) and many Jewish prophets and leaders of the Old Testament, from Noah to Zephaniah.

The members revere and honor Muhammad but do not worship him; their creed is that "there is no deity worthy of worship except God [Allah], and Muhammad is God's Messenger." This is "the religion of the Book," and the book is the Qur'an (Koran), said to have been revealed to Muhammad (b. 571 C.E.) via the angel Gabriel. The Quran contains the fundamental teachings of Islam and describes the way Muslims are to practice various aspects of their faith and their relation to their fellow human beings. Its teaching encompasses public and private life, war, peace treaties between nations, and such matters as marriage, divorce, inheritance, economic activity, women's rights, and the concept of worship.

Also embodied in the Quran are the ethical teachings of previous scriptures, the foundational Beliefs and the Pillars of Faith, which are the heart of Islam. These Pillars include (1) recital of the creed; (2) recital of prayer five times daily facing Mecca (the Kaaba at Mecca is held to be the first house built by Abraham for the worship of God); (3) giving of tithes for the support of the poor and the expansion of the faith; (4) observation of Ramadan, the ninth month of the Muslim calendar, with fasting during daylight in commemoration of the first revelation of the Quran; (5) a pilgrimage to Mecca, when physically and financially able. The major beliefs are (1) God is called *Allah* (Arabic, "One and Absolute"); (2) revelation has come from time immemorial and resulted in scriptural traditions such as those of Jews, Christians, and other "People of the Book"—the Quran is the final revelation that encompasses and supersedes previous scriptures; (3) God's angels are heavenly beings created to serve God, and they are opposed to evil spirits; (4) God sent prophets to earth at stated times for stated purposes (the last of these was Muhammad), and makes no distinction between those messengers; (5) the Day of Judgment will find good and evil weighed in the balance; (6) the lives and acts of people are known to God. Islam, however, still leaves humankind "the architect of [its] own destiny, free to make or mar [its] own future [lives] of honest endeavor."

Muhammad accomplished his mission, which was primarily to proclaim the unity of God. When he died at age 63, the precepts of the Quran became the great unifying force around which a billion people eventually became followers of Islam (Muslims). They are spread all over the world, but are concentrated in Africa and Asia. Muslims regard Mecca, Medina, and Jerusalem as sacred places. Some divisions and sects have appeared (Shiites, Sunnites being the two major ones) with variations in interpretation and practice, but by and large, there has been firm allegiance to the Quran and traditional Muslim practices. Islam allows polygamy in certain cases, with strict conditions. Where local custom prevails, women wear a traditional covering or veil in public.

While the pillars of the faith and the ethical practices of Islam define the ideal Muslim, the social and intellectual traditions have given rise to a cosmopolitan and diverse civilization. The artistic, architectural, and scientific heritage of Muslims has played an important role in bridging Muslim and Western history and societies.

Islam emphasizes the intellect; every Muslim is a student. There is a saying that God's first creation was the pen, and the first word God revealed to Muhammad was read. It is obligatory in Islam to read and study and seek knowledge; the ink of the scholar is considered, according to a saying of Muhammad, to be more valuable than the blood of a martyr.

AFRICAN-AMERICAN MUSLIM

It is believed that among African slaves transported to America were many whose background and heritage were Muslim. However, it was not until this century that organized Muslim groups of African American origin emerged.

The first group in the U.S. began when Timothy Drew founded a Moorish Science Temple in Newark, New Jersey. Drew took the name Noble Drew Ali and preached that American blacks were actually Moors whose forebears had lived in Morocco. His followers divided into several groups when he died in 1920.

A group in Detroit was led by Wallace D. Fard, who called himself the reincarnation of Noble Drew Ali. He taught "The Religion of the Black Men of Asia and Africa," based at first on the Bible and Qur'an. But Fard soon attacked the Bible and announced that he was a tool in the hands of Allah. Black people, he said, were gods; the white race was the serpent devil and would ultimately be destroyed. Fard disappeared mysteriously in 1933, and soon his followers claimed that he had been Allah personified—God, the Son of Man, the Savior.

He was succeeded by Elijah Poole, known as Elijah Muhammad, who traced black ancestry back to people living on the moon 66 trillion years ago. Elijah Muhammad continued to preach Fard's gospel of black revolution, which would rid blacks of white domination and give them their rightful place (as an independent Black Nation of Islam) within the U.S. Building on the desperate conditions of poverty in the black ghetto areas, the movement spread across the country and increased to a militant membership that captured national interest—religiously, politically, socially, and economically.

Among Elijah Muhammad's converts was Malcolm X (who used the symbol X to mark his unknown name and to reject the name acquired during slavery). His preaching helped build membership in the Nation of Islam. Subsequently disagreements developed between Malcolm X and Elijah Muhammad. Malcolm X was murdered in New York City in 1965. Elijah Muhammad died ten years later. Today membership claims vary from 750,000 to one million.

Elijah Muhammad was succeeded by his son Warith Deen Mohammed, who has reoriented and decentralized the movement, bringing its teachings closer to Islamic tradition. Meanwhile, another group led by Minister Louis Farrakhan, based in Chicago, has continued to emphasize the more radical aspects of the former teaching and has, through its public activities and teachings, often generated controversy.

Although subject to controversy and occasional violence, the movement has achieved some definite accomplishments. It established a chain of industries to relieve black poverty—such as barbershops, supermarkets, bakeries, restaurants, cleaning establishments, and farms. Black Muslims do not gamble, smoke, drink, overeat, or buy on credit. They arrange parole for convicts and offer postprison guidance. They claim to give blacks self-respect and a sense of identity, and they have reached many persons the mainstream church has been unable to reach; this may account for much of their popularity.

NATIVE AMERICAN CHURCH

Beginning around the turn of this century, a group of Native Americans formed the Native American Church with principal concentration of membership in the Southwest. Its beliefs and practices are syncretistic, blending elements of Christianity with traditional Native American religion. Some refer to it as one kind of "pan-Indian" religion, since it borrows aspects of many tribes and nations. It was chartered in 1918 and as late as the mid-1980s reported about 300,000 members.

One popular name for this body is the "peyote religion." Its ceremonies frequently make use of the button or crown of the peyote plant, a species of the cactus family that grows in deserts in the Southwest. The plant is a type of hallucinogen; it has been ruled nonnarcotic and not habit forming. Native American Church participants hold all-night ceremonies in which peyote is consumed. The reason for its use is not individual ecstasy but to serve as a communal ritual, to foster bonded relationships. These ceremonies also feature singing, drumming, and praying. Males perform the leadership functions; the central figure is the shaman, who is thought to be endowed with psychic abilities.

In addition to its specifically religious activities, the Native American Church seeks to deal with various social problems, including drug and alcohol abuse.

NEW APOSTOLIC CHURCH OF NORTH AMERICA

The New Apostolic Church of North America is a variant or schism of the Catholic Apostolic Church movement in England. It claims common origin with that church through the appointment of an apostle in the parent body in 1832. Debate arose in 1860 over the appointment of new apostles to fill vacancies left by death. Insisting on twelve apostles at the head of the true church and proposing the election of new ones, Bishop Schwarz of Hamburg was excommunicated from the Catholic Apostolic Church in 1862. To lead the dissenting body, a priest named Preuss was elected to the office of apostle "through the spirit of prophecy," and Bishop Schwarz served under him until his own elevation to the apostolic office.

Under Preuss and Schwarz the New Apostolic Church spread from Europe to North America, where today it is organized into districts under apostles, bishops, and elders. Each church has a rector and one or more assistants (priests, deacons, and so forth) who usually serve without remuneration. All ministers and other "office-bearers" are selected by the apostleship. The American church is a constituent of the international organization supervised by Chief Apostle Richard Fehr in Zurich, Switzerland.

Just as the true church must be governed on the scriptural pattern by twelve apostles, so also members of this church believe that only the apostles have received from Christ the commission and power to forgive sin. The New Apostolic Church of North America accepts the Apostles' Creed and stresses the authority and inspiration of the Bible, the apostolic ordinances of the laying on of hands, the necessity of gifts of the Holy Spirit, freewill offerings, and the speedy, personal, premillennial return of Christ. Three means of grace are found in three sacraments: baptism (including children), Holy Communion, and Holy Sealing (the dispensing and reception of the Holy Spirit). Work "along broader interior and missionary lines" is conducted in the U.S., Canada, Mexico, and Puerto Rico. The U.S. has 33,405 members in 375 churches and 37 missions; the International organization has more than 7.5 million members in 52,000 branches, in 184 countries.

OLD CATHOLIC

Old Catholic churches in the U.S. are an outgrowth of the Old Catholic movement of Europe. The European bodies originated in protest against the doctrine of papal infallibility, adopted by the Roman Catholic Church's Vatican Council of 1870. Roman Catholic priests in Germany who refused to accept the doctrine were excommunicated and organized the Old Catholic Church under the leadership of Ignatz von Dollinger in 1871. Similar ruptures occurred in Holland and Switzerland, where other Old Catholic churches were established.

This revolt did not break with every aspect of Roman Catholicism. Although it rejected papal infallibility, the doctrine of the Immaculate Conception, compulsory celibacy of the priesthood, and, in some instances, the filioque clause of the Nicene Creed, it kept many of the other doctrines, creeds, customs, and liturgies of the Roman Catholic Church. It also was dedicated to preserving the orders and apostolic succession of its bishops and priests, inasmuch as the succession was considered vital to a valid Christian ministry. It is independent of all three traditional apostolic sees, Rome, Constantinople, and Canterbury. Nevertheless, it insists on standing in the line that stretches back to Christ and the apostles, and it claims an unbroken linkage with them.

Much confusion has resulted, in Christian churches generally, over conflicting claims of succession and validity of orders, but that has been especially true in the Old Catholic churches in the U.S. All Old Catholic bodies here were at one time connected with European bodies, but that is no longer true. Most American groups have severed those ties. Only the Polish National Catholic Church is recognized by the Old Catholics in Europe. American developments really turn out to be a kind of new movement in that few of the leaders or members were raised in the Old Catholic tradition.

Old Catholic missionaries were in America soon after 1871, and when Joseph René Vilatte, a French priest ordained by Old Catholics in Switzerland, attempted to organize the scattered congregations, he at once became the center of the rising confusion. Vilatte himself vacillated between rival bodies; he studied at a Presbyterian college in Montreal and twice returned to submit to the Roman Catholic Church. Vigorously opposed within his own church and by Episcopalians, whose ranks he refused to join, he went to Switzerland in 1885 for ordination as an Old Catholic bishop. Finally he was consecrated as an archbishop by Alvarez of Ceylon, an archbishop who claimed orders through the Syro-Jacobite Church of Malabar. Vilatte then returned to America to found the American Catholic Church. When he died in 1929, he was living in a Cistercian Abbey in France. Although separated and competing, Old Catholics in the U.S. share a common doctrinal basis with the Orthodox and Latin churches from the centuries before those bodies separated, although the Old Catholic Church is now more Eastern than Western. It accepts the seven ecumenical councils that the church held before the division. Bible reading is encouraged, and the vernacular rather than Latin is used in all worship.

Three historic divisions of Old Catholic churches maintain strength in the U.S., with an approximate total of 500,000 members: the Mariavite Old Catholic Church, the Old Roman Catholic Church (English Rite), and the North American Old Roman Catholic Church. The African Orthodox Church is sometimes classified here, but it is actually Episcopal/Anglican in origin and connection. The Polish National Catholic Church has certain Old Catholic roots and doctrines and is listed here; it shares much with the tradition, even though its national identification is strong. The Liberal Catholic Church also bears a strong relation to the Old Catholic movement and is listed here as well.

LIBERAL CATHOLIC CHURCH, THE

This church originated in 1916 in Great Britain as a branch of the Old Catholic Church movement that began in Holland in the eighteenth century. Its founding bishops were members of the Theosophical Society. Tracing its orders to an apostolic succession that runs back to the Roman Catholic Church under the reign of Pope Urban VIII, the Liberal Catholic Church aims at a combination of efficient traditional Catholic forms of worship, with the utmost freedom of individual conscience and thought. It claims to be neither Roman nor Protestant, but still *catholic* in the broadest sense of the word.

International headquarters are in London; the U.S. headquarters is in Ojai, California. A quarterly magazine, *Ubique,* is published, and an extensive overview of church history/teachings/worship is available. Membership stands at just over 2,800.

The Nicene Creed is generally used in the services, but there is no requirement of submission to any creed, Scripture, or tradition; members seek not a common profession of belief, but service to humanity through corporate worship in a common ritual. While there is no emphasis on the precepts of the Theosophical Society, theosophia (divine wisdom) is strongly stressed and incorporates many basic tenets of Eastern mysticism, while holding up the goal of becoming a truly gnostic church. Paramount in the thinking is a central inspiration from faith in the living Christ, based on the promises of Matthew 18:20 and 28:20. These promises are regarded as "validating all Christian worship," but special channels of Christ's power are found in the seven sacraments of the church: baptism, confirmation, the Holy Eucharist, absolution, holy unction, holy matrimony, and holy orders. Priests and bishops may marry, and they exact no fee for the administration of the sacraments; most are employed also in secular occupations. Bishops are elected by a general episcopal synod, and a board of trustees administers church affairs.

MARIAVITE OLD CATHOLIC CHURCH

Mariavites derive their name from the Latin *Mariae vitae imitantur,* meaning "to imitate the life of Mary," the mother of Christ. This ideal originated in late nineteenth-century Poland, a heavily Roman Catholic country. The Mariavite Order of priests and sisters was founded August 2, 1893, by Mother Maria Franciszka, then Superior of the Order of the Poor Sisters of St. Clare, through an express revelation made to her by God. The motto of the order is "Everything for the greater glory of God and the honor of the Most Blessed Virgin Mary." From the beginning, its members endeavored to practice an aesthetic-mystical religious life, in accordance with the primitive Rule of St. Francis of Assisi. Their goal is to maintain a deep inner spiritual life among themselves and their faithful by being pastors and servants, not through cloistered or contemplative communities. Candidacy requirements are firm and sacrificial, with a tendency toward the ascetic.

Ecclesiastic and civil opposition marked the early decades of the Mariavites in Poland. In 1906 they formed a church independent of Rome, and in 1909 became part of the Old Catholic Church at Utrecht, Holland. That church had been independent of Rome since 1724 and is still active in Poland. In 1930 the Mariavite Old Catholic Church was established in the U.S.

During World War II it was impossible for the churches to maintain close contact, and by 1955 the U.S. church had become autonomous and self-reliant. Its work continues under the leadership of an archbishop, bishops, priests, religious Brothers and Sisters, and a secular Third Order, the Mariavite Society of Perpetual Suppliant Adoration.

The church's faith is based on the Old Catholic tenets of faith and morals contained in the canonical books of Holy Scripture in the Old and New Testaments, as well as on the early traditions of the universal church that were dogmatically defined at the first seven ecumenical councils. The traditional seven sacraments and three creeds—

Apostles', Nicene, and Athanasian—are acknowledged. Worship is celebrated according to the Tridentine Rite of 1570—in the vernacular in Poland; in Latin, English, and Polish in the U.S. The Roman Catholic dogmas of papal infallibility and primacy, the immaculate conception, and the assumption of the Virgin are rejected as necessary for salvation. Accepted instead regarding these are the teachings in the early centuries of Christianity, before the schism of East and West.

As revealed to Mother Franciszka by God, the principal purpose of the Mariavite Church, which came to be known as the Work of Great Mercy, is "the propagation of devotion to the Most Blessed Sacrament and the invocation of the Perpetual Help of Mary as a means of final salvation for a world perishing in its sins." In both Poland and the U.S., the church cooperates with all Christian denominations.

Each Mariavite Religious observes an hourly adoration of supplication and reparation before the Most Blessed Sacrament, which is perpetually exposed in the monstrance on all Mariavite altars. Candidates for the religious life and priesthood are educated at the Christian Academy of the Mariavites in America. The Mariavite Old Catholic Church numbers one archbishop, two bishops, 48 priests, 30 Religious Sisters, 10 Religious Brothers, and 358,176 adherents in the ecclesiastic province of North America. It directs missionary work in Austria, France, and West Germany.

NORTH AMERICAN OLD ROMAN CATHOLIC CHURCH

Two Old Catholic groups bear this name, typical of the confusion and debate among Old Catholics. One body, identical in faith, thought, and worship with the Roman Catholic Church, but differing in discipline, was "received into union" with the Eastern Orthodox Church by the Archbishop of Beirut in 1911 and again by the Orthodox Patriarch of Alexandria in 1912.

The second church, still in existence as an Old Catholic Church, claims proven succession of Catholic orders, though it is not under papal control or jurisdiction. The Knott Missal is used for all masses, but the Pontificale is used for all Order rites. Some 62,611 members are reported in 133 churches.

OLD ROMAN CATHOLIC CHURCH (ENGLISH RITE)

Arnold Harris Matthew, consecrated to the episcopacy in 1911 by Archbishop Gerard Gul of the Old Catholic Church of Utrecht,

Holland, consecrated a Hungarian, Prince de Landes Berghes de la Rache, in 1912 and sent him to America to consolidate the small, scattered Old Catholic churches. De Landes settled in Waukegan, Illinois, and in October 1916 consecrated William Henry Francis Brothers and Carmel Henry Carfora as bishops. Less than a month later, at the suggestion of Matthew and after a dispute over the question of Minor Orders, de Landes excommunicated Brothers. Carfora then organized and incorporated the North American Old Roman Catholic Church, which remained the official name until 1963, when it was changed to Old Roman Catholic Church (English Rite) following the death of Carfora.

Many immigrants from Poland and Lithuania were brought into the church, and by 1973 it had a membership of 65,128 in 186 churches. It is similar to the Roman Catholic Church in worship and discipline, but denies papal infallibility and differs slightly in doctrine. It celebrates the mass, has seven sacraments, and teaches transubstantiation, "the Veneration and Invocation of the Glorious and Immaculate Mother of God, of the Angels and of the saints." It offers prayers for the dead and advocates celibacy for priests, but permits them to marry. Worship services are in English.

In 1963, the Archbishop Metropolitan for North America, Robert Alfred Burns, led the church into union with the Old Roman Catholic Church (English Rite) in Great Britain. Upon Burns's death in 1974, Robert William Lane became Archbishop Metropolitan.

POLISH NATIONAL CATHOLIC CHURCH OF AMERICA

A strictly American church born on American soil, this body was formally organized at Scranton, Pennsylvania, on March 14, 1897, after a long period of conflict between the Roman Catholic Church and many Polish immigrants. Roman Catholic in background, these adherents objected that in the U.S. they had no Polish bishops and few priests, that they could not teach in Polish in their parish schools, and that under the ruling of the Roman Catholic Council of Baltimore in 1884, they had no right to establish parishes of their own. All of this, they felt, gave the Roman hierarchy and priesthood unwarranted power over the parishioners and permitted "an unlawful encroachment upon their right to private ownership and paved the way for the political and social exploitation of the Polish people." (Some scholars feel that the roots of the dissension lay in the demand for a Polish National Church during the Reformation era.)

Resentment smoldered into open revolt in Chicago, Detroit, Cleveland, Buffalo, and Scranton, gradually resulting in the formation, mainly in the Eastern states, of an independent Polish body with approximately 20,000 members. This was the only break of any size from the Roman Catholic Church in the U.S., but some Slovak, Lithuanian, Ruthenian, and Hungarian groups also have broken away; several Slovak and Lithuanian parishes have merged with the Polish National Catholic Church.

A constitution for the new church was adopted by the Scranton parish in 1897, claiming the right to control all churches built and maintained by the Polish and to administer such property through a committee chosen by each parish. The first synod was held in 1904, with 146 clerical and lay delegates representing parishes in Pennsylvania, Maryland, Massachusetts, and New Jersey. Francis Hodur was chosen bishop-elect; he was consecrated in 1907 at Utrecht, Holland, by three bishops of the Old Catholic Church. Following the synod, the vernacular, first Polish and then English, gradually replaced Latin as the liturgical language.

The doctrine of this church is founded in the Holy Scripture; holy traditions; and the first four ecumenical synods of the undivided church, though not excluding the three following as having lesser importance. The Apostles' and Nicene creeds are accepted. A confession of faith includes belief in the Trinity; the Holy Spirit as the ruler of the world and the source of grace; the necessity of spiritual unity of all Christians; Christ's one Body, the church, apostolic and universal, as teacher, steward of grace, and a light unto salvation; the equal right of all to life, happiness, and growth in perfection; equal responsibility to God of all people and nations; immortality; and the future justice and judgment of God. Embracing the constant teaching of Holy Scripture and the Fathers of the Church, the Church hopes and prays for the salvation of all through Jesus Christ the Lord. Faith is necessary to salvation, and from that faith flow good works. Sin is "a misunderstanding of the being and purpose of God on the part of the individual, the nation, and even all humanity."

The Church recognizes the same sacraments as the Old Catholic, Orthodox, and Roman Catholic churches. In addition to these liturgical sacraments, listening to the Word of God preached has the power of a Sacrament! Two forms of confession are in general use—a private confession for children and youths, and a general confession for adults only.

A general synod is the highest legislative authority. It meets every four years, except for such special sessions as may be necessary, and is composed of active bishops, clergy, and lay delegates from every parish.

The administration and destiny of this church, according to its constitution, rest with the Prime Bishop. A Supreme Council meets annually or on call and is composed of all active bishops, plus six clergy and 14 lay delegates approved by the general synod. In like manner, the authority of the diocese is vested in a diocesan bishop and a synod, which meets every four years.

Each parish is governed by an elected board of trustees. There are 282,411 members in 162 parishes in the U.S. and Canada, divided into five dioceses: Buffalo, Pittsburgh, Canadian, Eastern, and Western. Polish and English are used in worship and in the educational programs of parish schools taught largely by pastors. Clergy may marry, but only with the knowledge and permission of the bishops.

The Polish National Union, a fraternal and insurance organization established by Bishop Hodur in 1908, is set up as an adjunct to parish life. It consists of 12 districts divided into 224 branches and has approximately 32,000 members, not all of whom are required to be members of the church. There is a theological seminary in Scranton, Pennsylvania, and a home for the aged, Spojnia Farm in Waymart, Pennsylvania.

Missionary work was begun in Poland in 1919, and by 1939 there were more than 50 parishes, with a theological seminary in Kracow. Bishop Padewski was arrested by the communists and died in prison the same year; since that time the church in Poland has become autocephalous, but the two churches remain in theological and ideological harmony.

In 1912 the Lithuanian National Catholic Church was established under the jurisdiction of the Polish National Catholic Church. This church also does missionary work among the Polish in Brazil. As the only member of the Old Catholic Union of Utrecht, it has in recent years strengthened its ties with European Old Catholics.

Lately, the Polish National Catholic Church has entered into dialogue with the Roman Catholic Church, the Antiochian Orthodox Church, the Episcopal Church, and the Anglican Church of Canada.

OPEN BIBLE STANDARD CHURCHES, INC.

This body was originally composed of two revival movements: Bible Standard, Inc., founded in Europe, Oregon, in 1919; and Open Bible Evangelistic Association, founded in Des Moines, Iowa, in 1932. Similar in doctrine and government, the two groups joined on

July 26, 1935, taking the combined name Open Bible Standard Churches, Inc., with headquarters in Des Moines.

The Pacific Coast group, with activities centered in Oregon, spread through Washington, California, and into the Rocky Mountain areas of the West; the Iowa group expanded into Illinois, Missouri, Ohio, Florida, and Pennsylvania. There are now churches in 31 states, concentrated in the central and far west states.

The teachings are "fundamental in doctrine, evangelical in spirit, missionary in vision, and pentecostal in testimony"; they include emphasis on the blood atonement of Christ, divine healing, baptism of the Holy Spirit, personal holiness, the premillennial return of the Lord, and baptism by immersion.

Churches are grouped into five geographical regions, subdivided into 25 districts; district superintendents guide the work under the supervision of regional superintendents. Individual churches are congregationally governed, locally owned, and affiliated by charter with the national organization. Seventeen departments function under the leadership of six executive directors with the advice of committees under the supervision of the national board of directors. The highest governing body is the general convention, which meets biennially and is composed of all licensed and ordained ministers, with a lay delegate for each 100 members.

The denomination ministers in 30 countries under the direction of 32 U.S. missionaries and 22 national directors.

A board of publications is responsible for the preparation of conference literature. The denomination publishes a monthly periodical, *Message of the Open Bible,* and provides lesson material for Sunday schools through its Christian education department. The missions department publishes a monthly *World Vision* and a semiannual *Outreach* magazine.

The 360 churches—with approximately 46,000 members—hold membership in the Pentecostal Fellowship of North America and the National Association of Evangelicals.

ORTHODOX (EASTERN)

A major sector of historic Christianity, the Eastern Orthodox tradition claims direct descent from Christ and the apostles. For the first thousand years, the Eastern and the Roman were two branches of the same church. In 1054, an official division occurred with mutual excommunication. Since then, Orthodoxy has lived in a number of distinct organizational forms, usually national churches such as the Greek, Romanian, Russian, and Syrian. The focus is on worship, liturgically conducted. The church acknowledges the creeds pro-

duced by the first seven Ecumenical Councils and shares many prayers, litanies, and eucharistic forms with the Roman Catholic Church. Orthodoxy is unusually sight oriented, creating for worship a variety of icons meant to represent the reality of God, which make the setting quite elaborate in color, shape, and brightness.

When Constantine moved his capital from Rome in 330 C.E. and began to rule his vast empire from the new Constantinople (formerly Byzantium), the most important split in the history of Christianity was underway. In the East there were four patriarchs, each traditionally equal with the fifth patriarch, the pope of Rome; all accepted the Nicene Creed, and all were sacramental and apostolic. There were, however, certain basic differences that made for confusion; racially, socially, linguistically, mentally, morally, and philosophically, deep gulfs existed. The East was Greek in blood and speech; the West was Latin. The transference of the capital from West to East meant a shifting of the center of political, social, and intellectual influence. When the Goths swept down upon Rome, that city turned for help—not to Constantinople, but to the Franks; in gratitude for the aid of Charles the Great, the pope crowned him emperor on Christmas Day in 800, and the Roman Church became coterminous with the Holy Roman Empire.

Conflict deepened between the pope at Rome and the patriarch at Constantinople. In 857 Ignatius of Constantinople refused to administer the sacrament to Caesar Bardas on the ground that he was immoral. Tried and imprisoned by the emperor, Ignatius was succeeded by Photius, an intellectual giant for whom the weaker pope was no match. Their increasing friction broke into flame at the Council of St. Sophia, where Photius bitterly condemned the Latin church for adding the word *filioque* to the Nicene Creed. The Eastern church held that the Holy Spirit proceeded directly from the Father; the Western church had adopted the view that the Spirit proceeded from the Father *and* the Son—*filioque.*

Political and ecclesiastical jealousies fanned the flame until, in 1054, the pope and the patriarch excommunicated each other, the result being two churches, Eastern and Western. The pope remained head of the Western church; at that moment, in the East, four patriarchs were guiding the destiny of Eastern Orthodoxy. This is important to an understanding of the Eastern Orthodox Church. It is not a monarchy with one all-powerful ruler at the top, but "an oligarchy of patriarchs," based on the body of bishops and responsible to local, or general, church councils. No one patriarch is responsible to any other patriarch; yet all are within the jurisdiction of an ecumenical council of all the churches, in communion with the patriarch of Constantinople, who holds the title Ecumenical Patriarch.

Today Christendom remains divided into three principal sections: Roman Catholic, Eastern Orthodox (frequently referred to as the Greek church), and Protestant. The Eastern Orthodox Church consists of those churches that accept the decisions and decrees of the first general church councils—two at Nicea, three at Constantinople, one at Ephesus, one at Chalcedon—and those of other churches that originated in missionary activities and have grown to self-government but still maintain communion with their parent churches. Certain Eastern bodies refused to accept the christological definition of the Council of Chalcedon (451) and are generally referred to as Ancient Eastern churches—Syrian-Antiochian, Malabar Syrian, Armenian, Copt of Egypt, and Ethiopian.

Claiming to be "the direct heir and true conservator" of the original primitive church, Eastern Orthodoxy has tended to divide into independent national and social groups—Syrian, Russian, Serbian, Bulgarian, Romanian, Albanian, Greek, Georgian. These groups have struggled for existence, caught between Arab, Tartar, Turkish, and Western armies in endless wars. Generally, it may be said that Greek Christianity became the faith of the people of the Middle East and the Slavs in Europe, while Latin Christianity became the religion of Western Europe and the New World.

There are at present four ancient Eastern Orthodox patriarchates (Constantinople, Alexandria, Antioch, and Jerusalem), with the modern patriarchates of Russia, Serbia, Romania, Bulgaria, and Georgia. In 1970, the former Russian Orthodox Greek Catholic Church in North America was granted autocephaly, with the new name Orthodox Church in America. Mount Sinai, Cyprus, and the national Orthodox churches of Greece, Albania, Finland, Poland, Japan, and Czechoslovakia have autonomous status.

The Turkish conquest of Constantinople greatly depleted the power of the patriarchate in that city, although it has retained its primacy among the Orthodox—while World War I and the Russian Revolution of 1917, with the attendant disruption of the Russian Empire, led the Eastern Orthodox churches in Poland, Finland, Estonia, and Latvia to assert their independence. (Lithuania remained loyal to Moscow.) After World War II, Estonia and Latvia were reintegrated into the Russian Orthodox Church. Widely separated, all are still in essential agreement as to doctrine and worship, and they make up what we know as the Holy Eastern Orthodox Church. Nearly all European and Asiatic bodies of the church have established dioceses in America; some are governed by one or another of the five major patriarchates, while others have declared themselves independent and self-governing.

In the U.S. today, Albanian, Bulgarian, Greek, Romanian, Russian, Serbian, Ukrainian, Carpatho-Russian, and Syrian churches are under the supervision of bishops of their respective nationalities and usually are related to their respective mother churches in tradition and spirit, if not in administration. The patriarch of Moscow and of Alexandria each has jurisdiction over a few parishes.

The Nicene Creed in its original form (without the filioque clause) is recited in all liturgies and in various other services, the Eastern churches holding that a "creed is an adoring confession of the church engaged in worship"; its faith is expressed more fully in its liturgy than in doctrinal statement. Actually the basis lies in the decisions and statements of the seven ecumenical councils that defined the faith of the early undivided church against the heresies of the period, and in the later statements that defined the position of the Orthodox Church of the East with regard to the doctrine and practices of the Roman Catholic and Protestant churches. The dogma of the pope as the sole "vicar of Christ on earth" is rejected, together with that of papal infallibility. Members of Orthodox churches honor the Virgin Mary as *theotokos* but do not subscribe to the dogmas of the Immaculate Conception and the Assumption. They reverence the cross, the saints, and nine orders of angels but reject the teaching of the surplus merits of the saints and the doctrine of indulgences. Icons (consecrated pictures) of revered persons and events are honored, and bas-reliefs are permitted in some groups; but the use of carved images is forbidden. The Orthodox churches venerate, but do not worship, icons. Since God became incarnate in Christ, God's human nature is depictable. Refusal to venerate an icon is seen as denying the concrete reality of the Incarnation.

The mysteries, or what are called sacraments in the Western church, are central in Orthodox life. The seven that are definitive in the Roman Catholic Church are present and important in the Orthodox tradition, but there is little disposition to number them formally; one reason is that many other rites have a sacramental character. The Holy Eucharist, or Communion, is the "mystery of mysteries." It is preceded in the life cycle by baptism and followed by chrismation (or confirmation), penance, holy orders (for those so called), marriage (for most), and the anointing of the sick. Anointing is administered to the very ill, but not always as a last rite. The Eucharist is the chief service on all Sundays and holy days, and all Orthodox churches teach that the bread and wine are the body and blood of Christ. Purgatory is denied, but prayers are offered for the dead; it is believed that the dead may and do pray for those on earth. For justification, both faith and works are considered necessary.

Government is episcopal. There is usually a council of bishops, clergy, and laypeople, and a synod of bishops, over which an elected archbishop, metropolitan, or patriarch presides. In the U.S., each jurisdiction is incorporated, with a church assembly of bishops, clergy, and laity. There are three orders in the ministry: deacons (who assist in parish work and in administering the sacraments), priests, and bishops. Deacons and priests may be either secular or monastic; candidates for the deaconate and priesthood may marry before ordination but are forbidden to marry thereafter. Bishops are chosen from members of the monastic communities; all belong to the monastic rule of St. Basil the Great and are under lifelong vows of poverty, chastity, and obedience.

Church services are brilliantly and elaborately ritualistic. The liturgy is that of the Eucharist, celebrating the fact and power of Christ's crucifixion and resurrection. Lighting, clerical vestments and altar adornments, icons, music, and, centrally, consecrated bread and wine bring the kingdom of God into the present. Since *orthodox* means "true glory" (as well as "straight teaching"), "giving glory to God is the purpose of life" is the keynote of this tradition. Praising God, giving God thanks, and receiving God's presence in the sanctified gifts capture the heart of worship. Through worship, and in God-informed relationships and responsibilities, these Christians mean to move toward sanctification. The Christian goal is *theosis*, perfection or deification, living in genuine unity with God in the here and now and for eternity.

Membership statistics are confusing and often unreliable, inasmuch as membership is based on baptismal records rather than communicant status. But there are certainly 3.5 million Orthodox church members in the U.S.

After a century or so of "creeping disunity" within U.S. Orthodoxy, during the period of large-scale immigration and the formation of the Orthodox communities of faith here, several signs of drawing together have been appearing. One is the organization in 1960 of the Standing Conference of Canonical Orthodox Bishops in the Americas; it comprises nine jurisdictions that represent the majority of the Orthodox in America. Another is two pan-Orthodox seminaries of recent emergence.

It must be kept clear, however, that other so-called Orthodox churches in the U.S. are not recognized as canonically "Orthodox." These irregular Eastern churches might be called autogenic, or self-starting, but they cannot properly be called Orthodox, since the

227

churches must be in canonical relationship with the Patriarch of Constantinople and with one another.

ALBANIAN ORTHODOX ARCHDIOCESE IN AMERICA

The Albanian Orthodox Church in America is the spiritual descendant of the ancient ecclesiastical Western Illyricum (the Holy Illyria) of early Christianity and the early church. It has suffered a bewildering series of persecutions and changes in the religious and political struggles of the Balkan area. Under the peace of Constantine, at the time of the division of the Roman Empire, it was placed under the jurisdiction of the Western church; under the Byzantine (Greek) emperors it was assigned to the Patriarch of Constantinople. Christianized by both Latin and Greek missionaries, Albania, as part of Illyricum, had both Latin- and Greek-rite Christians. There were close ties with Rome and Constantinople until the Moslem Turks became the masters of Albania in 1478–79, when half of its people became Moslems and a small minority remained divided between Latin-rite Christians in the north and Greek-rite Christians, subordinated to Constantinople, in the south. Four centuries of oppression ended in political and religious revolts in the nineteenth and twentieth centuries, and when Albania became independent, its people demanded a church independent of Constantinople.

The Turkish rulers had long forbidden the Albanian people to use their native language within the context of church worship and public education, with the imposed language being Greek. This action was enforced by church authorities in Constantinople. Therefore, with this in mind the Russian Greek Orthodox Catholic Church in America set up an Albanian diocese here under an Albanian archmandrite-administrator, Father Theophan S. Noli, with a liturgy translated into Albanian in 1908 by Father Noli. With the outbreak of the Russian revolution, the ties with the Russian Church were severed, and Noli was consecrated the first bishop in 1923 at the Korche Cathedral in Albania as the Archbishop and Metropolitan of Durres. In so doing, he became bishop of a completely independent Albanian Archdiocese, a "mother church" that, strangely enough, spread its influence back into Albania. Therefore, Albanian candidates for the priesthood in America were ordained in Albania. He returned home to establish a metropolitan throne with its see in Boston. At present, 13 organized territorial parishes have joined in the Autocephalous (self-governing) Orthodox Church in America in 1971, thus moving toward the fulfillment of Metropolitan Noli's dream of an American Orthodox Patriarchate.

There are 45,250 members in two groups: the Albanian Orthodox Archdiocese of America and the Albanian Orthodox Diocese of America. The Archdiocese group is larger, with 40,000 members. The church has made outstanding contributions, the most notable of which is the production of a liturgical literature in an early Indo-European language, Pelasgo-Illyrian. Their "Albanian Rite" liturgy linguistically preceded the liturgy of the Albanian-rite church in Albania. Uniquely, this church has never depended on the church of its native land, but there has been mutual influence. Because of the official closing of all religious institutions in Albania in 1967, communication between the two churches is no longer possible, but the strong influence of the American church remains.

AMERICAN CARPATHO-RUSSIAN ORTHODOX GREEK CATHOLIC CHURCH

The Carpatho-Russian people derive their name from the Carpathian mountain region of eastern Czechoslovakia, where they have resided for centuries. They are akin to the population of Russia because of their geographical location and their common Slavic background and Orthodox religious heritage.

For many years the mother church endured strife between Orthodoxy and Roman Catholicism. Under political pressure in the seventeenth century, it became a Uniate church, with Eastern rites and customs, but recognized the supremacy of the Roman Catholic pope.

The struggle to separate from Rome and become completely Eastern was transferred to America when large numbers of members migrated to the U.S., especially to the coal-mining and industrial areas. In 1891, Alexis Toth, a Carpatho-Russian Uniate priest, led his Minneapolis parish back to the Orthodox Church, and with several other pastors and parishes was absorbed into the Russian Orthodox Greek Catholic Church in the U.S.

In 1938, a new American Carpatho-Russian Orthodox Greek Catholic diocese was established and canonized by Benjamin I, the ecumenical patriarch of Constantinople. Orsetes P. Chornock became its first bishop. In 1977 his auxiliary, John R. Martin, succeeded Chornock, and Nicholas Smisko was elected ruling prelate upon Bishop Martin's death in 1984.

Under the jurisdiction of the ecumenical patriarchate, the diocese has 72 churches in ten states and a membership of 18,000. Both the diocesan headquarters (Christ the Savior Cathedral) and Christ the

Saviour Seminary are located in Johnstown, Pennsylvania. The diocese maintains a youth camp, retreat, and conference center in Mercer, Pennsylvania, and a monastery in Tuxedo Park, New York. In September 1988, the diocese celebrated the fiftieth anniversary of its canonical establishment.

ANTIOCHIAN ORTHODOX CHRISTIAN ARCHDIOCESE OF NORTH AMERICA

This church is made up of two groups that merged in 1975: the Antiochian Orthodox Christian Archdiocese of New York and All North America (formerly Syrian Antiochian Orthodox Archdiocese of New York and North America) and the Antiochian Archdiocese of Toledo, Ohio, and Dependencies in North America. It is under the jurisdiction of the Greek Orthodox patriarch of Antioch and has a membership of 350,000 churches. These figures reflect a substantial increase in membership due to immigration from the Middle East.

The church contributes to the support of St. Vladimir's Orthodox Theological Seminary in Crestwood, New York, and to St. John of Damascus Orthodox Theological Academy near Tripoli, Lebanon. Its work is accomplished through 24 departments and commissions and four service organizations. The Archdiocese was a pioneer in the use of the English language in the Orthodox churches. Since 1940 it has operated a full-service publishing department.

BULGARIAN EASTERN ORTHODOX CHURCH

Before the outbreak of the Macedonian revolution in 1903, very few Bulgarians immigrated to the U.S.; in 1940, there were only about 60,000 residents. Coming from the Bulgarian Orthodox Church, the state church of that country, they brought with them memories of the church's long struggle for independence from Constantinople. In 1872 the church finally won its freedom.

In 1909 the church was formed in this country as the Bulgarian Orthodox Mission; it established a bishopric in 1938. Attached directly to the Holy Synod of Bulgaria, its membership is made up of descendants of immigrants from Bulgaria, Macedonia, Thrace, Dobruja, and other parts of the Balkan peninsula. Services are in the Bulgarian and English languages, and doctrine is in accord with that of other Eastern Orthodox churches.

Membership is reported at 86,000 in 13 churches, under the leadership of the Metropolitan Archbishop of North and South America and Australia. Until 1989, there were two American dioceses, in New York City and in Akron, Ohio; they merged that year under the official name, Bulgarian Eastern Orthodox Diocese of the U.S.A., Canada, and Australia.

GREEK ORTHODOX ARCHDIOCESE OF NORTH AND SOUTH AMERICA

Greeks arrived in the U.S. in increasing numbers between 1890 and 1914, and from 1918 through 1929, from the Greek mainland, the islands of the Aegean Sea, the Dodecanese, Cyprus, Constantinople, Smyrna, and other sections of Asia Minor. They asked for and secured the services of Orthodox priests sent to them by the Holy Synod of Greece or the Ecumenical Patriarchate of Constantinople. Each priest maintained relations with the synod or patriarchate from which he came, since there was at first no central organization.

A period of confusion existed from 1908 to 1922, during which the jurisdiction of American churches shifted from the Ecumenical Patriarchate of Constantinople to the Holy Synod of Greece and back again. Then an act known as the Founding Tome of 1922 established the Greek Orthodox Archdiocese of North and South America, which consisted of four bishoprics under the supervision of Archbishop Alexander and the Patriarchate of Constantinople. Alexander's successor, Archbishop Athenagoras, was elected Patriarch of Constantinople in 1948 and was succeeded in turn by Archbishop Michael and Archbishop Iakovos, the incumbent since 1959.

Doctrine, polity, and worship follow the usual Orthodox Christian patterns. There are 2.5 million members in 535 churches and 11 dioceses, 18 parochial schools, nine summer camps, a school for orphans and children from broken homes, a college, a seminary, three homes for teenage boys, and a home for the aged. The Greek Orthodox Archdiocese is the largest Orthodox jurisdiction in the U.S. It participates in dialogue with other bodies and is active in both the National and World Councils of Churches.

ROMANIAN ORTHODOX EPISCOPATE OF AMERICA

This body was organized April 25, 1929, at a church congress convened in Detroit by clergy and lay representatives of Romanian Orthodox parishes in the U.S. and Canada. It was under the canonical jurisdiction of the Romanian Orthodox Patriarchate in Bucharest until political conditions forced its separation and is now under the autocephalous Orthodox Church in America. The bishop is a member of the Holy Synod of the Orthodox Church in America, and the diocese is recognized as an administratively self-governing body.

The episcopate is headed by a bishop elected for life by a special Electoral Congress, the chief legislative body, made up of one clerical and two lay delegates from each parish. It meets annually in July. With the aid of an episcopate council composed of ten laypersons and five clergy, elected for two years by the congress, the bishop supervises all matters of administration and also presides at all council meetings, which are held as need arises.

There are six deaneries, or districts, in the U.S., with 53 churches and 60,000 members, concentrated in the Great Lakes industrial area.

RUSSIAN ORTHODOX CHURCH

Eastern Orthodoxy came to Russia with the baptism of Grand Prince Vladimir of Kiev in 988 C.E. The church at first was ruled by metropolitans appointed or approved by the Patriarch of Constantinople. About 500 years ago, a man named Job became the first patriarch of all Russia. During the reign of Peter the Great, the office of patriarch was abolished, and a Holy Synod was substituted; the other Orthodox churches recognized this synod as being patriarchal in effect. From 1721 until 1917, the Holy Synod was made up of three metropolitans and other bishops from various parts of Russia who sat in rotation at its sessions. A civil officer of the czar, known as the chief procurator, attended its sessions as the czar's representative. This pre–1917 church, like every public organization in Russia, was administratively dominated by the czarist regime.

In 1917 dramatic changes were instituted by the Great Sabor, or church assembly. Administration was changed, the office of chief procurator was abolished, and the church returned to the old patriarchal form of government. As the Great Sabor held its sessions, however, the gunfire of revolution was heard in the streets, and once the followers of Lenin had taken over the state, they immediately applied Marxist/Leninist principles: Church was separated from state and school from church, and church activity, in large measure, was restricted to worship. The patriarch and the synod resisted, but the government found some priests and bishops ready to support the new regime; they held an assembly that deposed the patriarch, endorsed communism, and declared itself the governing body of the Russian church.

Calling itself the Renovated, or Living, Church, this group changed the ancient disciplinary rules and instituted liturgical reforms. With the support of Soviet authorities, who hoped thus to divide and weaken the church, that body held control for several years but was never recognized by the great majority of clergy or people. The government considered opposition to the Living Church a civil offense and, on this basis, banished thousands of bishops, clergy, monastics, and laypersons to labor camps.

In 1927 the Soviet government prevailed upon Metropolitan Sergius, the deputy *locum tenens* of the then vacant patriarchal see, to submit the policy of the church totally to the Soviet regime. This was *sine qua non* recognition of the church's right to exist as a legal entity. Yet it was not until 1943 that Hitler's invasion of the U.S.S.R. altered the plan for the annihilation of the church, and Stalin engineered the meeting of a small group of bishops to elect Metropolitan Sergius as Patriarch of Moscow and All Russia.

Sergius called upon his people to support the government in the defense of their country, and this marked a turning point in the Soviet policy toward the church; the Living Church was discarded, and the patriarch's authority was recognized by the state. Many surviving clergy and bishops who had been banished were permitted to return, and gradually the patriarchal administration became again the sole authority in the Orthodox Church of Russia.

The main missionary efforts of Russian Orthodoxy were historically directed toward the Muslim, Buddhist, and animistic populations of central Asia and Siberia. In the mid-eighteenth century, an Orthodox mission was established in China; in the late nineteenth century, one was begun in Japan.

Eight Russian Orthodox monks entered Alaska in 1792, established headquarters at Kodiak, and built the first Eastern Orthodox Church in America; 12,000 people were baptized there within two years' time. Orthodox monks and bishops created an alphabet and printed a grammar in the Aleutian language, translated portions of the Bible, and built a cathedral at Sitka.

Early in the nineteenth century, a chapel was built at a Russian trading post near present-day San Francisco. The episcopal see was transferred to that city in 1872, but moved to New York City in 1905, as waves of immigration brought thousands of Slavs to the eastern states. For many years, immigrants from other countries with Orthodox churches—Serbia, Syria, Greece—were cared for by the Russian hierarchy in America. Many Eastern-rite Catholics from the old Austro-Hungarian empire, having been in Uniate churches, came to the U.S. to find themselves placed under the direction of Irish or German Roman Catholic bishops. Torn between conflicting demands and loyalties, many Uniate parishes transferred to the jurisdiction of the Russian Orthodox Church.

Hard days were ahead, however. The revolution of 1917 cut off the financial support that had come from the mother church, now fighting for its life. The Living Church faction in Russia, supported by the communist government, sent an emissary to secure control of Russian Orthodox Greek Catholic Church property in the U.S.; through action in the civil courts, it gained possession of the cathedral in New York City. In 1924, an assembly of the Diocese of North America, in an attempt to prevent further seizures, declared that, on a temporary basis, it was administratively, legislatively, and jurisdictionally independent of the church in Russia. But this was not recognized by the Patriarchate of Moscow or by the Russian Orthodox Church Outside Russia, headquartered at that time in the former Yugoslavia.

The Russian Orthodox Church Outside Russia now holds that the Moscow Patriarchate has forfeited its right to be considered a true Orthodox church, because it has adopted a position of submission to the Atheistic Soviet regime, not only in regard to politics and external matters, but with respect to its internal policies and affairs.

The metropolitan and synod of the Church Outside Russia administer like-minded Russian Orthodox believers all over the world—at one time, largely Russian exiles of the revolution and displaced persons during World War II. When armed resistance to the Soviet revolution finally ceased, many sought refuge abroad. A number of bishops and clergy gathered at Constantinople; they later transferred to Sremski Karlovici in Yugoslavia and set up a synod to give spiritual leadership to the refugees. During World War II, the administrative headquarters was moved to Munich, which proved fortuitous because of the displaced persons' camps set up there after the war. Relief programs of the churches brought great numbers to America, and the headquarters of the synod was moved to New York City in 1952. Its complete rejection of the Moscow Patriarchate conformed to the attitude of many of these new arrivals and kept them from uniting with the Russian church, already established in North America.

The Russian Orthodox Church Outside Russia maintains bishops and clergy wherever Russian refugees are resettled—in Canada, South America, Australia, Africa, Europe, and the Middle East. With the growth of Orthodox participation in the ecumenical movement, the constituency of the church has been augmented by a significant number of parishes and individuals of other Orthodox jurisdictions because of its steadfast opposition to the ecumenical movement and its theological implications.

The third body is the Patriarchal Parishes of the Russian Orthodox Church in the U.S.A. It accepts the full authority of the Moscow patriarchate and is its representative in America. De facto occupancy of the old Russian cathedral in New York City was established when the former emissary of the Living Church faction submitted to the patriarch's representative. It is governed by a bishop appointed by the patriarchs and an assembly elected by the parishes. There are 10,000 members in 38 churches. Officially known as the Orthodox Church in America, the largest and most widespread body of Russian Orthodoxy in the U.S.A. reports 1,030,000 members in 1,000 churches.

SERBIAN EASTERN ORTHODOX CHURCH IN THE U.S.A. AND CANADA

From the seventh century until the thirteenth, the church in Serbia was under the jurisdiction of the Greek Patriarchate of Constantinople; it became the independent National Serbian Church in 1219. The church made notable contributions to art and architecture and played an important part in the Serbian struggle for independence through the long period of Turkish invasion and domination (1389–1876), during which it suffered unbelievable persecution.

Serbian immigrants to the U.S., coming more for political than economic reasons, began to arrive in large numbers about 1890. They worshiped at first in Russian churches, accepting the ministrations of Russian priests and the supervision of Russian bishops. The Serbian Patriarchate of Yugoslavia approved the organization of the Diocese of the United States and Canada in 1921 and sent its first bishop in 1926. Today there are 68 parishes and 67,000 members. Doctrine and polity are in harmony with other branches of the Orthodox Church.

SYRIAN ORTHODOX CHURCH OF ANTIOCH (ARCHDIOCESE OF THE U.S.A. AND CANADA)

The use of the word *Antioch* in the name of this church is important, for its origin is traced back to Saint Peter, believed to have established the first patriarchate in Antioch. Today the American group is under the jurisdiction of the Syrian Orthodox Patriarch of Antioch and All the East. The church professes the faith of the first three Ecumenical Councils of Nicea, Constantinople, and Ephesus.

Syrians were few in number in the U.S. until the turn of the century. The first priest arrived in 1907. Their first patriarchal vicar, Archbishop Mar Athanasius Y. Samuel, was appointed in 1949, and the Archdiocese of the Syrian Orthodox Church in the U.S.A. and Canada was organized in 1957.

In 1993 there were 34 archdiocesan parishes in 14 states in the U.S., four in Canada. There were 30,000 members in 38 churches and a larger membership in the Middle East, India, Europe, and Australia. There is an annual archdiocesan convention.

THE UKRAINIAN ORTHODOX CHURCH OF THE U.S.A.

Tradition has it that Saint Andrew, the first called apostle, in the early years of his apostolic ministry preached the gospel in what is presently Kyyiv (Kiev), the capital of the Ukraine. The seeds of the gospel preached by Saint Andrew bore fruit. Circa 862, the first Orthodox Christian community was founded on the outskirts of Kyyiv, during the reign of two princes, Askold and Dyr. Instrumental in making Orthodox Christianity known in Rus-Ukraine was the Kyyivian Princess Olha, baptized in 975, grandmother of St. Volodymyr (Vladimir) the Great. After considerable reflection and investigation, Volodymyr (baptismal name, Basil) proclaimed Orthodox Christianity the official faith of his kingdom of Rus-Ukraine in 988. The year 988 signals the beginning of the Kyyivan Metropolia, the mother church of Orthodox Christian Ukraine. For over 600 years, the Kyyivan Metropolia enjoyed autonomy within the jurisdiction of the Ecumenical See of Constantinople. This autonomy ended in 1686 with the forced subjugation of Ukraine's mother church to the Patriarchate of Moscow. As a consequence of the 1917 revolution, the Ukrainian Orthodox Church sundered jurisdictional ties with Moscow and declared autocephaly in 1921. The autocephalous Ukrainian Orthodox Church was reestablished twice in this century, first in 1941 and in 1989 as a result of *glasnost* and *perestroijka*. The June 5, 1990, Sobor of the Ukrainian Autocephalous Orthodox Church in Ukraine established its own patriarchate and elected as its first patriarch Metropolitan Mstyslav, Primate of the Ukrainian Orthodox Church of the U.S.A. As a consequence of his death in 1993, two patriarchs were elected, Dmytrij to head the Ukrainian Autocephalous Orthodox Church jurisdiction, and Volodymyr to head the Ukrainian Orthodox Church-Kyyivan Patriarchate.

The Ukrainian Orthodox Church of the U.S.A., presently headed by His Eminence Metropolitan Constantine, was established in 1919. Its chief shepherds were Metropolitan John Theodorovich and Metropolitan Mstyslav Skrypnyk. It has a total of 95 parishes in the U.S., a central headquarters and theological seminary in South Bound Brook, New Jersey, and cares for the needs of some 20,000 persons. Primary areas of strength lie in Chicago, western and eastern Pennsylvania, New England, New York, and Maryland. The U.S.-based church has no jurisdictional ties with either church jurisdiction in the Ukraine.

The second body of Ukrainian Orthodox Christians in the U.S., under the immediate jurisdiction of the Ecumenical Patriarchate of Constantinople, is the Ukrainian Orthodox Church of America and Canada, established in 1924 and presently headed by His Grace Bishop Vsevolod. This jurisdiction, based in Jamaica, New York, records some 23 parishes in the U.S. and nine in Canada. Statistics are unavailable. This body also has no jurisdictional ties to Ukrainian Orthodox jurisdictions in the Ukraine.

PENTECOSTAL

Described by a term that refers to the first Pentecost, which took place fifty days after Christ's resurrection, when the Spirit enabled Christians to speak in unfamiliar languages, these conservative Protestants have grown rapidly since their modern beginnings in the U.S. around 1900. They believe that through the Holy Spirit, what happened during Pentecost can happen now. In fact, seeking and receiving the gift of tongues is regarded as a sign of the baptism of the Holy Spirit, itself requisite to full discipleship. Other spiritual gifts—healing, love, joy, answers to prayer—also make up Pentecostals' experience of God.

Although they differ somewhat in doctrine and practice, both black and white churches participate in the Pentecostal movement. Once largely confined to the uneducated populations of rural areas, this group has attained strength in many socioeconomic sectors. The term Neo-Pentecostalism has been used recently to describe the direct Spirit action concerned with "speaking in tongues," which is now quite common in churches whose liturgies historically were very different from those of Pentecostal churches.

Many of these revivalistic bodies have either a Methodist or a Baptist background and are primarily concerned with perfection, holiness, and the Pentecostal experience.

Their statements of faith are often long, involved, and highly repetitious, but through them run certain common strains and elements. Most believe in the Trinity, original sin, salvation through the atoning blood of Christ, the virgin birth and deity of Jesus, the divine inspiration of literal infallibility of the Scriptures, manifestations and "blessings" of the working of the Holy Spirit—the fiery Pentecostal baptism of the Spirit—premillennialism, and future rewards and punishments. Two sacraments are found in most groups: baptism, usually by immersion, and the Lord's Supper. Foot washing is frequently observed in connection with the Lord's Supper. Many practice divine healing.

Varying in size from small groups to huge mass meetings, Pentecostal churches are found in every state in the union, with greatest strength in the South, West, and Midwest. They bear a great variety of names that do not always include the word *Pentecostal*—for instance, the largest single group, Assemblies of God, with more than two million members, and most of the Church of God groups. No accurate count of total membership is possible, since some never issue statistical reports.

ASSEMBLIES OF GOD, GENERAL COUNCIL OF

The second largest of the Pentecostal bodies, with 2,257,846 members and 11,689 churches, the General Council of the Assemblies of God is actually a group of churches and assemblies that joined together at Hot Springs, Arkansas, in 1914. The founders were former pastors of evangelical persuasion who wished to unite in the interest of more effective preaching and an enlarged missionary crusade. It was a charter member of the National Association of Evangelicals (1943), in which it is the largest denomination.

Ardently fundamentalist, its theology is Arminian; there is strong belief in the infallibility and inspiration of the Bible, the fall and redemption of the human race, baptism in the Holy Spirit, a life of holiness and separation from the world, divine healing, the second advent of Jesus and his millennial reign, eternal punishment for the wicked, and eternal bliss for believers. Two ordinances, baptism and the Lord's Supper, are practiced. They are especially insistent that baptism in the Holy Spirit be evidenced by speaking in tongues. The Assemblies of God believe that all the gifts of the Spirit should be evident in the normal New Testament church.

The government of the assemblies is an unusual mixture of presbyterian and congregational systems. Local churches are independent in polity and in the conduct of local affairs. District officers have a pastoral ministry to all the churches and are responsible for the promotion of home missions. Work is divided in 56 districts in the U.S. and Puerto Rico, including 10 foreign-language districts, each with a district presbytery that examines and recommends credentialing of ministers. The General Council consists of all ordained ministers; licensed ministers are members of district councils. Local churches are represented by one lay delegate each. This biennial General Council elects general officers, sets the doctrinal standards, and provides for church expansion and development.

Missionary work is conducted under the guidance of a central missionary committee; there are 1,677 foreign missionaries at work on a missionary budget of $85,780,463—unusually high among Protestant churches. A weekly periodical, *The Pentecostal Evangel*, has a circulation of approximately 280,000; a prosperous church press produces books, tracts, and other religious literature. In the U.S. there are nine Bible colleges; an Arts and Sciences college; six institutes; a nontraditional college and a seminary in Springfield, Missouri; and 417 Bible schools abroad. An international weekly radio program, "Revivaltime," is broadcast on 550 stations.

ELIM FELLOWSHIP

Established in 1947, this body is an outgrowth of the missionary-oriented Elim Ministerial Fellowship, formed in 1932, and the work of graduates of the Elim Bible Institute in Lima, New York, founded in 1924. The organizational pattern is congregational, and doctrine is basically premillennial, holding the usual tenets of belief in an inspired and infallible Bible, the Trinity, sanctification, baptism of the Holy Spirit, divine healing, and resurrection of the saved and unsaved for eternal reward or punishment. Some 20,000 members are found in 180 churches, and missionaries are at work in Africa, Asia, Europe, and South America. Headquarters are located on the former campus of Genesee Wesleyan Seminary, purchased in 1951. The assemblies hold membership in the Pentecostal Fellowship of North America and the National Association of Evangelicals.

INDEPENDENT ASSEMBLIES OF GOD, INTERNATIONAL

A Holiness group, this is an unaffiliated incorporated association of Pentecostal churches, sometimes called Philadelphia. Members have a Swedish background and work closely with the Swedish Pentecostal movement, with which they conduct an extensive missionary program. It is claimed that their missionary church in Brazil is the largest Protestant church in that country, having "close to half a million followers." There are also 200 missionaries in the Philippines, Africa, and India.

The government follows the autonomous pattern of other Pentecostal groups. There are 800 churches, 1,800 ministers and evangelists, and 12 Bible schools.

INTERNATIONAL PENTECOSTAL CHURCH OF CHRIST

The International Pentecostal Church of Christ, with headquarters in London, Ohio, grew as a result of a 1976 consolidation of the International Pentecostal Assemblies and the Pentecostal Church of Christ. The number of total adherents is 3,561 in 76 churches in the U.S.

The International Pentecostal Assemblies was officially founded in 1921 and was based in Atlanta, Georgia. It grew out of the founding of *The Bridegroom's Messenger* in 1907, which continues to be the official organ. The Pentecostal Church of Christ was organized in 1917 by John Stroup in Flatwoods, Kentucky, with subsequent headquarters at Ashland, Kentucky, and London, Ohio.

The church is a member of the National Association of Evangelicals and the Pentecostal Fellowship of North America and subscribes to the basic doctrines of the traditional Evangelical and Pentecostal movements.

Beulah Heights Bible College of Atlanta, Georgia, is owned and operated by the International Pentecostal Church of Christ. The denomination also maintains a home for the elderly in West Virginia and a conference center in Ohio. Active missions work is conducted in Kenya, Brazil, India, Mexico, Jamaica, Hong Kong, Uruguay, and Argentina.

PENTECOSTAL ASSEMBLIES OF THE WORLD, INC.

This body is the oldest "oneness"—that is, Jesus Only—organization in the United States. It was officially founded in 1907, but takes its place in the Apostolic-Pentecostal movement that traces its origins "directly back to the Day of Pentecost, A.D. 33." The catch phrase "Jesus Only" is based on the Word of God (The Holy Bible, King James Version), which tells of the death, burial, and resurrection of Jesus Christ. The goal of the Pentecostal Assemblies of the World, Inc., is to spread that message, the gospel, to all people.

From the beginning, this body has been interracial. It remains that way, significantly, to this day. Its leadership is in some cases white and in others black. So committed to inclusiveness is Pentecostal Assemblies of the World, Inc., that it does not keep records of membership along racial lines.

This denomination hosts two major conferences annually to which its constituents come from all over the world to worship God and fellowship with one another. It is headed by a presiding bishop who spiritually guides its members. There is also an executive board, including an assistant presiding bishop, a general secretary, a general treasurer, and lay directors. The organization's administrator and staff handle its business affairs.

Membership is approximately one million in the U.S. The number of churches here is about 1,600 and overseas about 1,000. This body is heavily concentrated in urban areas on both coasts (such as Chicago, Detroit, and Indianapolis). Its churches serve in all 50 states.

The Aenon Bible College, located in Indianapolis, exists to train ministers and lay members. The college has affiliate institutes all over the U.S. and two foreign affiliates in Liberia—the Samuel Grimes Bible Institute and the Haywood Mission.

PENTECOSTAL CHURCH OF GOD

This body, with its headquarters in Joplin, Missouri, was organized in Chicago on December 30, 1919. The name Pentecostal Assemblies of the U.S.A. was used until the general convention on February 22, 1922, when it was changed to Pentecostal Church of God. For a number of years "of America" was a part of the name, but this was dropped in 1979.

Evangelical and Pentecostal in doctrine and practice, the church is an active member of both the National Association of Evangelicals and the Pentecostal Fellowship of North America. The doctrines of salvation, divine healing, baptism in the Holy Spirit (with the evidence of speaking in tongues), and the second coming of Christ are strongly emphasized.

Officers include general superintendent, general secretary, director of world missions, director of home missions, director of Indian missions, director of Pentecostal ladies auxiliary, district superintendents, district presbyters, and district secretary-treasurers. A general convention meets biennially; most of the districts have annual conventions.

In 1992 there were 1,170 churches with a constituency of 101,786 in 42 states; 2,262 churches and outstations with 200,000 members in 32 other countries. There are 81 resident Bible schools and Christian schools in other countries, with a student enrollment of 4,951. The church owns and operates Messenger College, Messenger Publishing House, and Messenger Towers, all in Joplin, Missouri.

PENTECOSTAL FREE-WILL BAPTIST CHURCH, INC.

As the name suggests, this is a Pentecostal group that came into existence in 1959 through the merging of three Free-Will Baptist conferences in North Carolina. The doctrine is a mixture of Baptist and Pentecostal beliefs, including regeneration through faith in the shed blood of Christ, sanctification as a second definite work of grace (subsequent to regeneration), Pentecostal baptism of the Holy Spirit, divine healing, and the premillennial second coming of Christ. Heritage Bible College was established in September 1972.

Officials include general superintendent, general secretary, and general treasurer. A general meeting composed of lay and ministerial representatives is held biennially in August.

There are 11,757 members in 148 churches in eastern North Carolina. Mission work is carried on in nine foreign countries; Bible institutes are operated in Mexico, the Philippines, and Venezuela.

PENTECOSTAL HOLINESS CHURCH, INTERNATIONAL

This church was organized in 1898 at Anderson, South Carolina, by a number of Holiness associations; at the time it was called the Fire-Baptized Holiness Church. In the same year, in Goldsboro, North Carolina, another group was organized as the Pentecostal Holiness Church. The two bodies united in 1911, and a third body, the Tabernacle Pentecost Church, joined them in 1915. There are 137,313 members in 1,582 churches in the U.S., and 241,225 members in foreign mission fields. Principal strength is in the Carolinas, Virginia, Oklahoma, Florida, Texas, and California.

The theological standards of Methodism prevail, with certain modifications. The denomination accepts the premillennial teaching of the Second Coming and believes that provision was made in the atonement for healing of the body. Divine healing is practiced, but not to the exclusion of medicine. Three distinctive experiences are taught: two works of grace—justification by faith and sanctification—and Spirit baptism, attested to by speaking in other tongues. Services are often characterized by "joyous demonstrations."

A general executive board of nine members is elected by a quadrennial conference for a four-year term; members are limited to two consecutive terms in any one office. There is a general superintendent, two assistant general superintendents, a secretary-treasurer, and five board members who represent geographical areas and the church at large. Foreign mission work takes place in 71 countries.

Emmanuel College and Oklahoma City Southwestern College are four-year accredited colleges. There is a children's home at Falcon, North Carolina; a children's convalescent center at Bethany, Oklahoma; and two homes for the aged—at Falcon and at Carmen, Oklahoma.

UNITED PENTECOSTAL CHURCH, INTERNATIONAL

This church was founded in 1945 by the union of the Pentecostal Assemblies of Jesus Christ and the Pentecostal Church, Inc. Both of those bodies were formed by Oneness Pentecostals, who withdrew from the Assemblies of God in 1916.

The United Pentecostal Church, International teaches water baptism in the name of Jesus Christ and the baptism of the Holy Spirit. A Holiness code includes disapproval of secret societies, mixed bathing, cutting of women's hair, worldly amusements, home television sets, and immodest dress.

Government is congregational, with a general conference that meets annually. A general superintendent, two assistants, and a secretary-treasurer are members of a general board that consists of superintendents, executive presbyters, and division heads.

The church has 500,000 members in the U.S. and Canada, 3,700 churches, and 7,600 ministers. A foreign missions program supports 287 full-time missionaries in 74 foreign countries, with national workers in 40 countries. Its worldwide membership is 1.5 million.

World Aflame Press, the church's publishing house in Hazelwood, Missouri, publishes books, Sunday school materials, and a wide variety of religious literature. *The Pentecostal Herald* is the official organ of the United Pentecostal Church International, and there are various divisional publications. The church also sponsors "Harvestime," an international radio broadcast, a children's home in Tupelo, Mississippi, and nine endorsed Bible colleges.

PILLAR OF FIRE

The Pillar of Fire originated in the evangelistic efforts of its founder, Alma White. She often preached from the pulpit of her husband, the Reverend Kent White, a circuit-riding Methodist minister in Colorado, when he was on his circuit. Her fervent exhortations on regeneration and holiness, or sanctification, as a second definite work of grace brought her into conflict with the bishops and other leaders of Methodism, and she withdrew to establish the Pentecostal Union in 1901. The name was changed to Pillar of Fire in 1917.

The first headquarters were in Denver, Colorado, but were later moved to Zarephath, near Bound Brook, New Jersey. In Denver (Westminster), the Pillar of Fire operates Belleview Christian College, Belleview Bible Seminary, and Christian elementary and secondary schools. A pioneer Christian radio station, KPOF, which went on the air in 1928, is recognized by the National Religious Broadcasters as "the oldest radio station of the oldest Christian network" in the United States.

At the international headquarters, Zarephath, New Jersey, are WAWZ (1931), serving much of the tri-state area of New York, New Jersey, and Pennsylvania. They also operate Zarephath Bible Seminary and Alma Preparatory School (with a Christian kindergarten through grade 6 program in nearby Bound Brook). and also a publishing house. In Cincinnati, WAKW (1962) serves another tri-state area: Ohio, Kentucky, and Indiana. Eden Grove Academy is a thriving Christian school that has served the community for many decades.

Other schools are operated by the Pillar of Fire in such places as Los Angeles and Pacifica (near San Francisco), California; Seattle; Chicago; and Jacksonville, Florida; London; the Philippines; Liberia; Nigeria; and Malawi.

Pillar of Fire theology is essentially Wesleyan, with emphasis on repentance, justification, second-blessing holiness, premillennialism, future judgment, and the inspiration and authority of the Scriptures. Sacraments include baptism and the Lord's Supper; marriage is a "divine institution."

Alma White became the first bishop of the Pillar of Fire. On her death, authority passed to her elder son, Bishop Arthur K. White. Later her granddaughter, Bishop Arlene White Lawrence, became president and general superintendent. She was succeeded in 1984 by Bishop Donald J. Wolfram. Membership classes are probationary, regular, and full. There are deacons and deaconesses, and both men and women are ordained as ministers. There are also consecrated deaconesses, licensed preachers, missionaries, presiding elders, and bishops.

Much literature has been printed and distributed in the U.S. and elsewhere, and programs broadcast 24 hours a day on the network of Christian radio stations, with a potential audience of close to 30 million people. Mission work is carried on in India, Spain, the Philippines, Great Britain, and several African countries.

PLYMOUTH BRETHREN

Plymouth Brethren is a widely used, but generally unofficial, designation for a loose grouping of churches with early nineteenth-century roots in the British Isles. Within these churches, the common terminology is simply Brethren or assemblies or Brethren assemblies. The name *Plymouth* will be heard infrequently in casual conversation, but never appears in advertising, on signs, or in church bulletins. Outsiders combined the two words when the 1,000-

member congregation in Plymouth, England, attracted notice with its active evangelism. In Great Britain and the Commonwealth countries, the word *Christian* has gradually replaced *Plymouth* for governmental purposes, but this change is less advanced in the U.S. The matter of names is a sensitive issue among Brethren, reflecting a historical emphasis on the unity of all believers. The movement arose in a highly sectarian age when closed Communion was practiced in most denominations. The early Brethren envisioned a basis for Christian unity—not in the ecumenical merging of denominations, but in forsaking denominational structures and names in order to meet simply as Christians, welcoming all who belong to Christ. The designation *Plymouth* Brethren is inconsistent with this concept because it does not encompass all born-again Christians; the term *Brethren* by itself is not resented. The autonomy of the local congregation is another feature of the movement, coupled with the doctrinal understanding that a *church* is not a building, but the gathering of people who meet there.

The weekly hour-long "remembrance meeting" is probably the surest way to identify a Brethren assembly. The centrality of the Communion service is characteristic: In accord with the meaning of "priesthood of all believers," the service is unstructured, with all men, and now often women, of the assembly free to speak. A preacher may serve full-time with a congregation, but will not be identified as clergy or given control of the service.

Under the influence of Anthony Norris Groves, who later became the first missionary, an initial group of believers, meeting in Ireland, realized they could break bread spiritually either with or without the presence of clergy. Thereafter, Brethren have consistently refused to restrict the administration of baptism or the Lord's Supper to ordained ministers, thus effectively eliminating a clergy-laity distinction and the traditional concept of ordination.

They moved quickly to the understanding that the Word of God could be ministered by any brother with spiritual gifts. The sharing of preaching responsibilities among men of the congregation has been both a strength and a weakness of the movement.

The Brethren are committed to all the fundamentals of orthodox Christianity, including the verbal inspiration of Scripture. They strongly emphasize gospel preaching and the necessity for personal conversion. Except for the weekly breaking of bread and the absence of collections at other meetings, their services are much like those of evangelical Baptist or free and Bible churches.

Among U.S. evangelicals, Brethren have had an influence out of proportion to their numbers. Their premillennial theology helped shape evangelicalism, especially in the proliferation of independent churches and mission boards. Many have responded to the Brethren emphasis on plurality of leadership and participatory worship in the local church. Brethren are also characteristically found in leadership positions in interdenominational evangelistic campaigns and the founding and operation of nondenominational Bible schools, colleges, seminaries, and parachurch organizations. They have only one multiple-year college-level institution of their own, Emmaus Bible College in Dubuque, Iowa.

As a result of a division in England in 1848, there are two basic types of assemblies, commonly known as *exclusive* and *open*. Led in the beginning by John Nelson Darby, the exclusive assemblies produced most of the movement's well-known Bible teachers—Kelly, Grant, Mackintosh, and others. They operated on the premise that disciplinary action taken by one assembly was binding on all. As a result, once started, a division continued, until by the end of the century the exclusive Brethren were divided into seven or eight main groups. Recent mergers have reduced that number somewhat, and an important American group has merged with the open assemblies.

Open assemblies were led by George Muller, well known for his orphanages and life of faith. Their strength has always been in evangelism and foreign missions. Lacking the exclusive disciplinary premise, local disputes spread only as far as there was interest and involvement; thus open assemblies have never experienced worldwide division.

Exclusive assemblies were dominant in the nineteenth century, but today there are an estimated 850 open assemblies in the United States, with 250 exclusive groups. The number of members is estimated at 98,000.

Christian Missions in Many Lands, Inc., publishes a missionary magazine and an address list of missionaries who serve overseas. In keeping with Brethren concepts of ministers' and missionaries' direct responsibilities to the Lord, workers are not assigned to specific tasks or locations, nor is responsibility assumed for their financial support. There are no mission boards in the conventional sense.

The Brethren are strongest in Pennsylvania, North Carolina, Florida, Michigan, Illinois, New Jersey, Iowa, and California. Apart from the metropolitan areas of Los Angeles and San Francisco, only scattered assemblies exist in the western half of the U.S.

PRESBYTERIAN

Originating between 1534 and 1560 with the Protestant theological program of John Calvin in France and Switzerland, the Presby-

terian denomination is so named because it is a church governed by presbyters (representatives). This church places great emphasis on the theology of God's sovereignty over the world and people's lives and on people's response to God's authority and will, known through Word and Spirit. More cerebral and verbal than emotional and aesthetic, it values understanding, learning, and propriety. Because of its covenantal understanding of the relation between God and people, it stresses active human responsibility. In the U.S., strongest among people of middle-class Scot and Scots-Irish descent, it has fostered many colleges and exercised cultural influence far beyond its size.

Presbyterianism has two firm and deep roots: One leads to the Greek *presbuteros*, "elder," and has to do with the system of church government of ancient and apostolic times; the other leads to John Calvin and the Protestant Reformation and pertains to the form of government used by all people who call themselves Presbyterian and hold the faith of the Reformed churches.

Calvin (1509–64), from France, was trained in the law. Turning to theology, his keen legalistic mind and lust for freedom from the rigid, confining forms of Roman Catholicism drove him as a fugitive to Geneva, where he quickly grasped the reins of leadership in the Reformed sector. Resolute and often harsh with his opponents, he established his theological system in the Swiss capital, making it, according to Macaulay, the "cleanest and most wholesome city in Europe."

Calvin's whole thought revolved around the concept of sovereignty: "The sovereignty of God in his universe, the sovereignty of Christ in salvation, the sovereignty of the Scriptures, in faith and conduct, the sovereignty of the individual conscience in the interpretation of the Will and Word of God." His system has been summarized in five main points: human impotence, unconditional predestination, limited atonement, irresistible grace, and final perseverance. God, according to Calvin, is the sovereign and eternal ruler of the world; humans are completely dominated by and dependent upon God.

Out of Calvinism came miracles of reform; few have made as many contributions in so many fields at once—education, the building of an intelligent ministry, the liberation of the oppressed and persecuted, and the establishment of democratic forms of government in both church and state. In Calvin's thoughts lay the germ that in time destroyed the divine right of kings. He gave a new dignity to the people and brought representative government to parliaments and church officials. He struck the final blow at feudalism and offered a spiritual and moral tone for dawning capitalism.

Strictly speaking, John Calvin did not found Presbyterianism; he merely laid the foundations upon which it was constructed—in Switzerland, Holland, France, England, Scotland, and Ireland. From France came the Huguenots, and by 1560, there were in that country 2,000 churches of Presbyterian complexion; the people of Holland established the Dutch Reformed Church; British Presbyterians gained courage in their struggle against Mary I ("Bloody" Mary); and from Scotland came the Covenanters and John Knox.

A delegation of Scots sat in the Westminster Assembly of Divines (1643–48) with 121 English ministers, 10 peers, and 20 members of the House of Commons. They resolved to have "no bishop, and no king." That assembly, a milestone in Presbyterian history, met in 1,163 sessions at the call of Parliament to resolve the struggle over the compulsory use of the Anglican *Book of Common Prayer.* Those sessions produced a Larger and a Shorter Catechism; a directory for the public worship of God; a form of government; and the Westminster Confession of Faith, which, built upon the Old and New Testaments, became the doctrinal standard of Scottish, British, and American Presbyterianism.

Dominant in the Westminster Assembly, Presbyterians soon also dominated the British government. Oliver Cromwell completed the ousting of the monarch and established a commonwealth. The commonwealth subsequently crashed, the monarchy returned, the fires of persecution flamed again, and British Presbyterians fled to North America with the Puritans. An attempt to establish episcopacy in Scotland after 1662 sent many Presbyterians out of Scotland into Ireland, where economic difficulties and religious inequalities then drove them on to America. From 1710 until mid-century, between 3,000 and 6,000 arrived annually, settling at first in New England and the middle colonies.

Those British and Scots-Irish spread Presbyterianism throughout North America. But there were Presbyterian congregations in the colonies long before their arrival. One such group was worshiping in Virginia in 1611; others were underway in Massachusetts and Connecticut in 1630. Long Island and New York had congregations by 1640 and 1643, respectively. Francis Makemie, an Irish minister, ranged the coast from Boston to the Carolinas, planting churches. Six groups were united in the first presbytery in Philadelphia in 1706, and by 1716 it had become a synod made up of four presbyteries; it held its first meeting in 1717. (See PRESBYTERIAN CHURCH [U.S.A.] for further history of Presbyterians in America.)

ASSOCIATE REFORMED PRESBYTERIAN CHURCH

This is a continuing synod of the former Associate Reformed Presbyterian Church, a body of Covenanter and Seceder origins and traditions. (*Covenant* here refers to the Reformed branch of the church. The Associate Presbyterian Church of North America, in distinction, is of *Seceder* origin; the Associate Reformed Church is a result of the union of the two groups.) Feeling that the distance that separated it from its fellow members in the North was too great, the synod of the Carolinas withdrew from the Associate Reformed Church in 1822 to form the Associate Reformed Synod of the South. Following the creation of the United Presbyterian Church in 1848 (which this group never joined), it dropped the phrase "of the South," thereby becoming the Associate Reformed Presbyterian Church. It became a general synod in 1935.

The standards of the Westminster Confession are followed. For some years the only music in this church was the singing of psalms; this was modified in 1946 to permit the use of hymns. Foreign mission fields are located in Pakistan, Mexico, and the Middle East. *The Associate Reformed Presbyterian* is published monthly at Greenville, South Carolina; Erskine College and Erskine Theological Seminary are in Due West, South Carolina; there is an assembly ground, Bonclarken, at Flat Rock, North Carolina; and three retirement centers are supported. Membership totals 38,763 in 197 churches, most in the Southeast.

BIBLE PRESBYTERIAN CHURCH

On June 11, 1936, during the fundamentalist-modernist controversy, a group of about 300 people, led by J. Gresham Machen of Princeton Theological Seminary, met in Philadelphia to form a new church that would be true to the Bible. The name chosen was Presbyterian Church of America, and Dr. Machen was unanimously elected the first moderator.

A year later it became apparent that the new church was actually composed of two groups with views so divergent as to make continued unity impossible. Therefore, on September 6, 1938, one group formed the Bible Presbyterian Church; the other retained the name Presbyterian Church of America, but was denied its use by the courts and called itself the Orthodox Presbyterian Church.

In 1941, the Bible Presbyterians joined with other like-minded churches to found the American Council of Christian Churches, in opposition to the National Council of Churches; in 1948 the International Council of Christian Churches was formed to provide a worldwide association (membership in 1988 included 490 denominations from 100 nations).

The word *Bible* is included in the name of this church to emphasize its Bible-based position. It is thoroughly fundamentalist, subscribing to the Westminster Standards (the Confession of Faith, the Shorter and Larger catechisms), and is strongly Reformed. It opposes all forms of the social gospel and liberation theology and refuses to cooperate with those who compromise such doctrines as the inerrancy and infallibility of the Bible, the virgin birth and deity of Christ, his blood atonement and bodily resurrection, and his literal coming again. It continues to oppose the policies of both the National Council of Churches of Christ in the U.S.A. and the World Council of Churches because of their "departure from historic Christianity."

Properties of the local church are guaranteed to the church itself. Local congregations may call their pastors "without interference" from presbyteries or synods. Any church may withdraw at any time "for reasons sufficient to themselves." The work of the church is carried on through independent agencies rather than denominational boards. Among its approved agencies are Faith Theological Seminary, Shelton College, and two Independent Boards for Presbyterian Missions, one Foreign, the other Home. Presbyteries and synods are meetings for edification and fellowship rather than administration. Membership totals about 10,000 in the U.S. and Canada, and some 47 missionaries serve in 11 foreign mission fields.

CUMBERLAND PRESBYTERIAN CHURCH

An outgrowth of the great revival of 1800, the Cumberland Presbyterian Church dates its origin from February 4, 1810, in Dickson County, Tennessee, where three Presbyterian ministers—Finis Ewing, Samuel King, and Samuel McAdow—constituted a new presbytery. They objected to the doctrine of predestination in the Westminster Confession of Faith; they also insisted that Presbyterian standards for ordination of the clergy be more flexible, in view of the extraordinary circumstances that then existed on the American frontier. The General Assembly was organized in 1829.

A union with the Presbyterian Church (U.S.A.) in 1906 was only partially successful. A considerable segment of the membership, to whom the terms of union were unsatisfactory, perpetuated the Cumberland Presbyterian Church as a separate denomination.

This church reports 92,240 members in 782 congregations, located for the most part in Southern and border states, with some congregations in Indiana, Illinois, Michigan, Iowa, New Mexico, Arizona, and California.

The church sponsors missionaries in Colombia, Japan, Hong Kong, and Liberia in West Africa. It supports Bethel College in McKenzie, Tennessee; Memphis Theological Seminary; and a children's home in Denton, Texas. Denominational headquarters and a resource center are located in Memphis, Tennessee.

EVANGELICAL PRESBYTERIAN CHURCH

Established in March 1981, the Evangelical Presbyterian Church (EPC) is a conservative denomination of nine geographical presbyteries—eight in the U.S. and one in Argentina. From its inception with 12 churches, the EPC has grown to nearly 180 churches with an inclusive membership of over 56,000. It is presbyterian in polity (governance by elders), with the courts of the church being the Session (local), the Presbytery (regional), and the General Assembly (national).

Reformed in doctrine, presbyterian in polity, and evangelical in spirit, the EPC places high priority on church planting along with world missions. World Outreach missionaries numbering almost 50 serve the church's mission at home and abroad. High priority is also placed on developing its women's ministries and youth ministries.

The Westminster Confession and its catechisms are the church's doctrinal standards. Unlike other conservative Presbyterian bodies, it includes chapter 34, "Of the Holy Spirit," and chapter 35, "Of the Love of God and Missions" in the Confession. The historic motto "In essentials, unity; in nonessentials, liberty; in all things, charity" catches the irenic spirit of the EPC.

To the broader world, the General Assembly speaks its mind on particular issues through position papers. To date, position papers on the Holy Spirit, abortion, the value of and respect for human life, the ordination of women as elders, homosexuality, and capital punishment have been adopted.

The Evangelical Presbyterian Church is a member denomination of the National Association of Evangelicals, World Evangelical Fellowship, and the World Alliance of Reformed Churches. Observers attend the North American Presbyterian and Reformed Council (NAPARC) and the Reformed Ecumenical Council.

ORTHODOX PRESBYTERIAN CHURCH

This church was organized June 11, 1936, in protest against what were believed to be modernistic practices by the Presbyterian Church in the U.S.A. The dissenters, led by J. Gresham Machen, refused to disband a foreign missionary society they had formed. They were suspended from the Presbyterian Church in the U.S.A.

and organized the Presbyterian Church of America, but an injunction was brought against the use of that name by the parent body, and in 1938 the name was changed to Orthodox Presbyterian Church.

The Westminster Confession and the Larger and the Shorter Catechism are accepted as subordinate doctrinal standards or creedal statements. Strong emphasis is laid on the infallibility and inerrancy of the Bible (the writers of the books of the Bible were "so guided by Him that their original manuscripts were without error in fact or doctrine"); original sin; the virgin birth, deity, and substitutionary atonement of Christ; his resurrection and ascension; his role as judge at the end of the world and the consummation of the kingdom; the sovereignty of God; and salvation through the sacrifice and power of Christ for those "the Father purposes to save." Salvation is "not because of good works [but] in order to do good works."

The church constitution contains the creedal statement, the form of government, the book of discipline, and the directory for the worship of God. The church has published *Trinity Hymnal,* probably the only hymnal designed as a worship supplement to the Westminster Confession of Faith. Following the presbyterian system of government, a general assembly, meeting annually, appoints committees that conduct work in home and foreign mission, Christian education, and general benevolence. The church supports a seminary in Philadelphia. With 19,094 members in 168 congregations and 24 missions, it is a constituent member of the North American Presbyterian and Reformed Council. Membership is spread throughout the country, with concentration in eastern Pennsylvania, New Jersey, and southern California.

PRESBYTERIAN CHURCH IN AMERICA, THE

Organized at a constitutional assembly in December 1973, this church was first known as the National Presbyterian Church, but in 1974 became the Presbyterian Church in America (PCA). It had separated from the Presbyterian Church in the United States (PCUS, southern) in opposition to a long-developing theological liberalism that denied the deity of Jesus Christ and the inerrancy and authority of Scripture. Whereas the PCA denied women positions in church offices, the PCUS not only permitted women to serve in such offices but also began to force all churches to comply. There was also opposition to the PCUS affiliation with the National and the World Council of Churches, which they believed supported the radical left position and social activism. In addition, as conservatives, the Southern church opposed the movement toward merger with the more liberal United Presbyterian Church in the U.S.A.

PRESBYTERIAN CHURCH (U.S.A.)

The PCA made a firm commitment to the Westminster Confession of Faith and the Catechisms, doctrinal standards that express the distinctive Calvinist or Reformed tradition and that have been significant in Presbyterianism since 1645.

The PCA maintains the historic polity of Presbyterian governance: rule by presbyters (or elders) and the graded courts, the session governing the local church; the presbytery for regional matters; and the general assembly at the national level. It views seriously the position of the parity of elders, making a distinction between the two classes—teaching elders and ruling elders.

In 1982, the Reformed Presbyterian Church, Evangelical Synod (RPCES), joined the PCA, bringing with it Covenant College on Lookout Mountain, Georgia, and Covenant Theological Seminary in St. Louis, Missouri.

The PCA headquarters is in Atlanta, where work by three program committees is coordinated—Mission to the World, Mission to North America, and Christian Education and Publication. The office of Stated Clerk is responsible for the administration of the General Assembly. Other agencies are the PCA Foundation; the Insurance, Annuities and Relief Board; and Investors Fund. Ridge Haven, the conference center, is located close to Rosman, North Carolina.

The PCA is one of the fastest growing denominations, with 1,126 churches and missions throughout the U.S. and Canada. As of December 1992, more than 197,591 communicant members have been augmented by almost 45,000 noncommunicant members.

PRESBYTERIAN CHURCH (U.S.A.)

Following formal separation that began during the Civil War and lasted for 122 years, the two largest American Presbyterian churches were reunited on June 10, 1983, in a historic Communion service celebrated by some 15,000 persons in the Georgia World Congress Center in Atlanta and by many more on a nationwide television link. The creation of the new Presbyterian Church (U.S.A.) came during the simultaneous general assemblies of the former denominations—United Presbyterian Church in the U.S.A. (UPCUSA, the "national" church), and Presbyterian Church in the United States (PCUS, the "Southern" church). The Reverend J. Randolph Taylor, pastor of Myers Park Presbyterian Church in Charlotte, North Carolina, was elected the new group's first moderator.

A General Assembly Council was created to oversee the work of combining functions from the UPCUSA offices in New York and the PCUS offices in Atlanta; it began meeting at once to tackle the problems of merging budgets, creating a single ministerial candidacy system, and deciding locations of the new denomination's administrative offices, among many other concerns. The timetable for these processes, while subject to the will of the council, anticipates completion in a decade.

Origins of the new church go back to the first American presbytery founded in Philadelphia in 1706. Since then, the two churches' histories have flowed in sometimes separate but always parallel streams until the reunification in 1983.

American Presbyterians met in a general synod in 1729 and adopted the Westminster Confession of Faith, together with the Larger and the Shorter Catechism, "good forms of sound words, and systems of Christian doctrine." The same synod denied civil magistrates any power over the church and banned the persecution of anyone for religious faith.

Free in the new land and fired with their Scots-Irish and Covenanter backgrounds, Presbyterians quickly began to procure trained ministers. William Tennent, Sr., organized a "log college" in a cabin at Neshaminy, Pennsylvania, with three of his four sons as his first pupils. This family school grew into the most important Presbyterian institution of higher learning in the colonies. From it came the College of New Jersey (later Princeton University) and a stream of revivalistic Presbyterian preachers who played leading roles in the Great Awakening of the early eighteenth century.

Prominent among them were William Tennent, Jr., and his brother Gilbert, who met and followed British revivalist George Whitefield in preaching an emotional "new birth" revivalism, which conflicted with the old creedal Calvinism. The camp-meeting revival, born as a Presbyterian institution, grew out of that Great Awakening enthusiasm. But Presbyterian objection to emotional revivalism went deep, and in 1740, it split the church. Preachers on the "old side" opposed revivalism, while those of the "new side" endorsed it, claiming that less attention should be paid to college training of ministers and more to recruiting regenerated common men.

The two sides quarreled until they reunited in 1757. The next year, in the first united synod, there were 94 ministers in the colonial Presbyterian Church, 200 congregations, and 10,000 members. One of the ablest of the new-side preachers was John Witherspoon, president of Princeton, a member of the Continental Congress and the only member of the clergy to sign the Declaration of Independence.

Witherspoon may have been instrumental in the general synod's decision to call upon Presbyterian churches to "uphold and promote" the resolutions of the Continental Congress. The Scots-Irish accepted the Revolution with relish; their persecution in England and Northern Ireland had made them solid anti-British dissenters. Their old cry "No bishop and no king" was heard back in England—statesman Horace Walpole supposedly remarked that "Cousin America" had run off with a Presbyterian parson.

Presbyterians moved swiftly to strengthen their church after the colonial victory at Yorktown; the synod met in Philadelphia in 1788 while the new nation's constitution was being drafted in the same city. The national administrative body of American Presbyterianism was known as a presbytery from 1706 to 1716, as a synod from 1717 to 1788, and as a general assembly from 1789 to the present.

From 1790 until 1837, membership in the Presbyterian Church in the U.S.A. (as it was called at that time) increased from 18,000 to 220,557, due to the revivalism sweeping the country and to the plan of union with the Congregationalists. Under that plan, Presbyterian and Congregational preachers and laypeople moving into the new western territory worked and built together. Preachers of the two groups preached in one another's pulpits, and members held the right of representation in both the congregational association and the presbytery. The plan worked well on the whole, absorbing the fruits of the national revivals and giving real impetus to missionary work at home and abroad.

Those years promised to be an era of Presbyterian expansion. Marcus Whitman drove the first team and wagon over the South Pass of the Rockies into the great Northwest. After him came hosts of Presbyterian ministers and laypeople, building churches, schools, colleges, and seminaries. Between 1812 and 1836, Princeton, Allegheny, Auburn, Columbia, Lane, McCormick, Union (Virginia), and Union (New York City) theological seminaries were created; missionary and educational societies were begun as well.

Then came disagreements between "Old School" and "New School" Presbyterians over matters of discipline and the expenditure of missionary money. The General Assembly of 1837 expelled four New School synods, which promptly met in their own convention to form a new General Assembly. The Presbyterian Church in the U.S.A. (PCUSA) remained split between New School advocates, who wanted to continue to work with Congregationalists, and those of the Old School, who were suspicious of Congregational theology.

In 1810, even before the Old School–New School division, the Cumberland presbytery had broken away to form the Cumberland Presbyterian Church after a dispute over the educational qualifications of ministers, and antislavery sentiment began to increase. In 1846, the Old School assembly regarded slavery as no bar to Christian communion, but in that same year, the New School condemned the practice strongly. By 1857, several Southern New School synods had withdrawn to form the United Synod of the Presbyterian Church. The greater schism came in 1861, following the outbreak of the Civil War, when 47 Southern presbyteries of the Old School formed the Presbyterian Church in the Confederate States of America. In 1867, following the war, the United Synod and the Confederate churches merged to form the Presbyterian Church in the United States (PCUS); the synod of Kentucky joined in 1869; the synod of Missouri in 1874. But the Northern-Southern separation continued until the reunion of 1983; however, the two assemblies were exchanging "fraternal salutations" throughout the nineteenth century.

The Southern Church

The Presbyterian Church in the United States (PCUS), initially Old School in doctrine, continued to develop its own style of faith and practice. Presbyterians in the South had long made special contributions to the nation. In Virginia and North Carolina, they were calling for American independence well before the Boston riots, and Mecklenburg Presbytery in North Carolina was the first ecclesiastical body in the colonies to approve the Declaration of Independence.

Presbyterian civic leaders brought law and order to many parts of the South before colonial officials could assume such duties, and the ministers taught school before the establishment of public school systems. Presbyterians were prominent during both the French and Indian War and the American Revolution, and with Baptists they laid the political, spiritual, moral, and intellectual foundations for the famous Jeffersonian Act for Establishing Religious Freedom, the Virginia statement that preceded similar ones in the Constitution and elsewhere.

The PCUS church government developed parallel to that of the Northern churches. Offices were gradually centralized in Atlanta under the General Assembly Mission Board; mission work was always undertaken on a worldwide scale, a special source of pride to Southern Presbyterians. In 1982, just prior to reunion, PCUS members numbered 814,931 in 2,704 churches, with 61 presbyteries (17 already functioning as "united" with UPCUSA presbyteries) and seven synods. There were 6,077 ordained ministers on the rolls. Church-supported seminaries were Austin, Columbia, Louisville, and Union (Richmond), as well as the Presbyterian School of Christian Education, a unique institution. Several secondary schools and mission schools, as well as colleges, children's homes, and homes for the elderly also were supported.

PRESBYTERIAN CHURCH (U.S.A.)

The National Church

The Old School and New School bodies of the Presbyterian Church in the U.S.A. (PCUSA) had held separate assemblies since 1837, but were united in 1870 on the basis of the Westminster Confession. Most of the Cumberland churches joined them in 1907; the Welsh Calvinist Methodists joined in 1920.

In the decades from 1920 until 1950, an emphasis on theology was seen in a liberal-conservative struggle. There was also an emphasis on unity, evident in the proposed merger with the Protestant Episcopal Church, which did not take place, and the accomplished merger with the United Presbyterian Church of North America (UPCNA) in 1958.

The UPCNA had been formed exactly a century earlier by a merger of the Associate Presbyterian Church with the Associate Reformed Presbyterian Church. Their doctrines, traditions, and institutions were preserved in the new church's presbyterian style of government by local sessions, presbyteries, synods, and general assembly.

The UPCNA doctrine rested on the Westminster Confession, with a few modifications, one of which amended its chapter on the power of civil magistrates. A 1925 confessional statement of 44 articles contained the substance of Westminster, but restricted divorce to marital infidelity, denied infant damnation, extended the sacraments to all who professed faith in Christ and led Christian lives, and withdrew the old protest against secret societies. It also abandoned the exclusive use of psalms, maintained belief in the verbal inspiration of the Scriptures, affirmed the sufficiency and fullness of the provisions of God for the needs of Christ, emphasized the renewing and sanctifying power of the Holy Spirit, and held that salvation is free to all sinners.

There were no insurmountable differences when the UPCNA and the PCUSA merged in 1958 to become the United Presbyterian Church in the U.S.A. (UPCUSA); there were only the usual disagreements between conservatives and liberals. On the whole, all found agreement in the Westminster Confession, their accepted doctrinal statement.

But the Westminster Confession was more than 300 years old, and many had come to believe that a new statement was needed to proclaim the gospel in twentieth-century language. So in 1967, after eight years of work, a special committee presented a draft of the first new major doctrinal statement since 1647 to the General Assembly, and it was ratified.

257

The UPCUSA now had a *Book of Confessions* with nine creeds: the Nicene Creed of 325 C.E., the Apostles' Creed of the second century, the Scots Confession of 1560, the Heidelberg Confession of 1647, the Shorter Catechism of 1647, the 1934 Theological Declaration of Barmen, and the Confession of 1967. These were grouped together in the *Book of Confessions* to trace the development of the great Christian affirmations, especially in the Reformed tradition; to make clear the common beliefs of most of the world's Christians; and to offer common ground for unity.

The brief (4,200 words) Confession of 1967, avoiding the confusing terminology of the Westminster Confession, stressed the concepts of love, sin, eternal life, and especially the work of reconciliation in God, Christ, and the church. Christ-centered, it generally merely repeated the Westminster tenets in modern speech. Some opposition persisted, on the ground that the new document watered down the Westminster Confession, but most United Presbyterians accepted the document as reflecting true Presbyterianism and as offering a wide theological base on which all Presbyterians could stand together.

The UPCUSA eventually reorganized its offices into three agencies based in New York City. The Program Agency sends missionaries, supports education and human ministries, and aids in church development and disaster relief, among other functions. The Vocation Agency develops new ministries and helps people prepare for the ministry. The Support Agency works in communication, research, and finance. The General Assembly Mission Council coordinated all three until its termination at the time of the 1983 merger.

In 1982, on the eve of reunion, the UPCUSA had 2,351,119 members nationwide and 15,178 ordained ministers. Its 8,975 churches were grouped in 151 presbyteries and 15 synods; 17 of the presbyteries were joint "union" bodies with similar units in PCUS.

The New Church

The new Presbyterian Church (U.S.A.) created in 1983 had a total of 3,166,050 members and 21,255 ministers nationwide, in 11,679 churches, organized into 195 presbyteries and 20 synods. (The former "union" presbytery pairs are now counted as one, and two pairs of synods in overlapping areas have already consolidated.) Since the boundaries of synods and presbyteries in Southern states now overlap, the number will doubtless be reduced further as these regional bodies move to consolidate their functions. The former UPCUSA had churches nationwide, which explains the existence of its synods and presbyteries in the Southern states alongside those of the former PCUS.

Always interested in education, the new church now has an expanded network of schools. There are 70 Presbyterian-related colleges, 11 seminaries, and six secondary schools in the U.S. The church has operated two book publishing companies, now united in Louisville as the Westminster John Knox Press. The church's official periodical is the monthly *Presbyterian Survey,* published in Louisville. The national headquarters was dedicated in that city on October 28–29, 1988. Although some departments are located elsewhere, the offices in Louisville represent the marriage of the old national church's offices from New York and the Southern church's from Atlanta.

Under the Presbyterian system of government, each congregation has a local session made up of elders, with the pastor as moderator. The session governs the local church, receiving and disciplining members as well as acting for the church's welfare. Presbyteries, made up of congregations in a local district, examine, ordain, and install ministers; review reports from sessions; and hear any complaints. The synods, occupying larger boundaries, review the presbytery records, organize new presbyteries, and help administer denominational matters. The highest judicial body is the general assembly, which meets yearly and is made up of lay and clergy delegates elected by their presbyteries on a proportional plan of representation. The general assembly settles all matters of policy and doctrine referred to it by the lower governing bodies, establishes new synods, appoints agencies and commissions, and reviews all appeals. Its decisions are final, except that it cannot, of itself, amend the church's constitution. There are two officers of the general assembly: A stated clerk (the chief executive officer of the church) is elected for four years and may be reelected; a moderator is chosen each year to preside over the meetings and often speaks for the church during the year.

While Presbyterians are found throughout the U.S., about 40 percent of the 2,805,548 members live in the area of the former PCUS—the South. The most populous synod is the Synod of the Trinity (Pennsylvania and West Virginia), with about 8 percent of the members. Membership is greatest in large cities, with concentrations in Ohio, Pennsylvania, New York, Virginia, North Carolina, Florida, Texas, Illinois, and New Jersey.

REFORMED PRESBYTERIAN CHURCH OF NORTH AMERICA

The first minister of the body of direct Covenanter lineage came to the colonies in 1752 from the Reformed Presbytery of Scotland. Most of the early membership merged with the Associate Presbytery in 1782, but a small group reorganized in 1798, under the name *Reformed Presbytery.* A synod was constituted at Philadelphia in 1809, only to split into Old Light and New Light groups in 1833; the dispute concerned citizenship and the right of Old Light members to vote or participate in public affairs. The general synod of the Reformed Presbyterian Church (New Light) imposed no such restriction. This restriction was finally removed in 1964, and members are free to participate in civil government and vote on issues and for candidates committed to Christian principles of civil government. In 1969, the Reformed Church merged with the Associate Presbyterian Church of North America.

Special emphasis is given to the inerrancy of Scripture, the sovereignty of God, and the Lordship of Christ over every area of human life. The government is thoroughly Presbyterian, except that there is no general assembly. Members use only the Psalms in their worship services; no instrumental music is permitted. Members cannot join secret societies.

Home missionaries work in seven states under a Board of Home Missions and Church Extension; foreign missionaries are stationed in Japan, Cyprus, and Taiwan. Geneva College is located at Beaver Falls, Pennsylvania, and a theological seminary at Pittsburgh. The church operates one home for elderly persons. The denomination is a member of the National Association of Evangelicals and of the North American Presbyterian and Reformed Council. There are 5,174 members in 68 congregations and six mission stations. Strength in the U.S. lies in western Pennsylvania and eastern Kansas.

SECOND CUMBERLAND PRESBYTERIAN CHURCH IN THE UNITED STATES

This church, originally the Colored Cumberland Presbyterian Church, was organized in 1869 by the 20,000 black members of the pre–Civil War Cumberland Presbyterian Church, and later gained the full approval of the general assembly of the church, held in 1969. The first three presbyteries were established in Tennessee, where the first, the Tennessee Synod, was organized in 1871.

In doctrine, this church follows the Westminster Confession, with four reservations: (1) There are no eternal reprobates; (2) Christ died for all humankind, not for the elect alone; (3) there is no infant damnation; (4) the Spirit of God operates in the world coextensively with Christ's atonement, so "as to leave all men inexcusable."

There are 16 presbyteries and four synods, with 15,500 communicants in 143 congregations. The Alabama Synod comprises nearly one-fourth of the constituency. The church's ministers are trained at the Cumberland Presbyterian Church college in McKenzie, Tennessee, and at its seminary in Memphis. Serious conversation continues concerning unification with the Cumberland Presbyterian Church.

REFORMED

This family of Protestants stands squarely in the tradition of Calvinist thinking about Christian meaning. It makes a great deal of the theological dimension of church life, stressing the sermon and sound doctrine. More rationalist than pietist, its conservatism takes the form of strict theological orthodoxy. It is not fundamentalist, however, inasmuch as it systematically correlates a wide range of Christian teachings, rather than listing doctrines one by one and ranking them for priority.

Of European origin, it bases its theology on the Belgic, Heidelberg, and Dort confessions. Its roots lie mostly in the Netherlands but extend to Germany, Hungary, and France to a smaller degree. In the U.S., the immigration of Calvinists from Holland to the upper Midwest has provided its largest population and the strength of its leadership.

When the Belgic Confession was written in 1561 as the creedal cornerstone of the Reformed churches in Belgium and Holland, the "Churches in the Netherlands which sit under the Cross" gave thanks to God in the preface of that document: "The blood of our brethren . . . crieth out." There was real cause for crying out at that time, as the Reformation spread during the Netherlands' long struggle against Catholic Spain. The Dutch Reformed Church was cradled in cruelty.

The Reformation-founded churches called Reformed, as distinguished from those called Lutheran, originated in Switzerland under Zwingli, Calvin, and Melanchthon. They were called Reformed in Switzerland, Holland, and Germany; Presbyterian, in England and Scotland; Huguenot, in France; and various national names, for others in Bohemia and Hungary.

As they moved overseas to the American colonies, they formed into four groups: from Holland, (1) the Reformed Church in America, and (2) the Christian Reformed Church; from the German Palatinate, (3) the Reformed Church in the United States, later known as the Evangelical and Reformed Church, now merged with the Congregational Christian churches in the United Church of Christ; and from Hungary, (4) the Free Magyar Reformed Church in America. All were and still are Calvinist and conservative, basing their doctrine generally on the Heidelberg Catechism, the Belgic Confession, and the Canons of the Synod of Dort. They use a modified presbyterian form of government.

CHRISTIAN REFORMED CHURCH IN NORTH AMERICA

With a membership of 311,202 in 979 churches, this Reformed group originated in Michigan in 1847 and was affiliated with the Reformed Church in America from 1850 until 1857, when it found itself in disagreement with the parent church on matters of doctrine and discipline. A conference held at Holland, Michigan, effected the separation of the True Holland Reformed Church, which, after a series of changes in name, became the present Christian Reformed Church in North America. Emigration from Holland brought several other groups into the new organization, rapidly increasing its membership.

The Christian Reformed Church today is largely English-speaking, although the Dutch, Spanish, French, Navajo, Zuni, Korean, Chinese, and Vietnamese languages are used in some of the churches. Doctrine shows no important differences from accepted Reformed standards; the three historic formulas of unity are accepted: the Belgic Confession, the Canons of Dort, and the Heidelberg Catechism. Organization bears the usual Reformed characteristics, including 46 classes that meet every four months (in some cases every six months), but with no intermediate or particular synods between the classes; a general synod made up of two ministers and two elders from each classis meets annually.

Christian Reformed Home Missions provides guidance and financial assistance to some 200 new and established churches that maintain ministries among the Navaho, Zunis, African Americans, Asian Americans, Hispanic Americans, and on many university campuses; 200 foreign missionaries are stationed in Japan, China, France, Nigeria, the Philippines, Australia, Russia, and many countries in

Latin America and Africa. The Christian Reformed World Relief Committee carries on a worldwide relief program. The "Back to God Hour" radio program, broadcast from a chain of stations in the U.S. and abroad, reaches Europe, Africa, and Asia as well as South America; a television ministry also broadcasts in the U.S. and Canada. There are five colleges—Calvin College and Seminary, Grand Rapids, Michigan; Dordt College, Sioux Center, Iowa; Trinity International University, Palos Heights, Illinois; Redeemer Reformed College, Hamilton, Ontario; and King's College, Edmonton, Alberta. A publishing house in Grand Rapids provides literature for the church and its agencies, as well as educational material for many other churches. Closely associated with the church are unique Christian school societies made up of parents who serve and support a national educational program.

HUNGARIAN REFORMED CHURCH IN AMERICA

Work in the U.S. among Hungarian Reformed people began in 1891. With the breakup of the Austro-Hungarian Empire and the impoverishment of the Reformed Church in Hungary, the church in Hungary transferred jurisdiction of its U.S. churches to the Reformed Church in the United States in an agreement reached at Tiffin, Ohio, in 1921. Three of the original congregations refused to accept the agreement. Together with four other congregations they united to form the Free Magyar Reformed Church in America in 1924 in Duquesne, Pennsylvania, a fully independent, autonomous church. The church's name was changed in 1958 to Hungarian Reformed Church in America.

The church's polity is a combination of Synod-Presbyterian elements gradually developed in Hungary from the mid-sixteenth century. At present it is made up of three classes—New York, Eastern, and Western—which form a Synod headed by an elected bishop and a chief lay curator. Doctrinal standards are those of the Heidelberg Catechism and the Second Helvetic Confession. The synod meets every two years, and a constitutional General Synod is held every four years.

There are 31 congregations with 8,600 baptized members in New Jersey, New York, Connecticut, Pennsylvania, Ohio, Michigan, Florida, California, Texas, the District of Columbia, and Ontario, Canada.

The church is a constituent member of the World Alliance of Reformed Churches, the World Council of Churches, and the National Council of Churches of Christ in the U.S.A.

NETHERLANDS REFORMED CONGREGATIONS

With 26 congregations and 9,462 members in North America, this Reformed body is associated with 162 like-minded congregations and 90,000 members in the Netherlands. It supports several home and foreign missions and 11 schools with 2,286 students.

In 1907, a number of churches in the Netherlands that had seceded earlier from the Reformed state church united to form the Gereformeerde Gemeenten. In American, these congregations were joined by a number that broke away from the Christian Reformed Church over doctrinal differences.

Three Reformed forms of unity are subscribed to: the Belgic Confession of Faith, the Heidelberg Catechism, and the Canons of Dordt. This body stresses the classic doctrines of the Reformed tradition.

PROTESTANT REFORMED CHURCHES IN AMERICA

Three consistories and the pastors of the Classis Grand Rapids East and Grand Rapids West of the Christian Reformed Church were deposed from that church as the result of a disagreement over the doctrine of common grace (Arminianism). The debate began in 1923; the dissenters formally organized as the Protestant Reformed Churches in America in 1926.

They stand for particular grace for the elect alone and hold to the three Reformed confessions—the Heidelberg Catechism, the Belgic Confession, and the Canons of Dordrecht—as the basis of their belief in the infallible Word of God. In government they are Presbyterian, subscribing to the 87 Articles of the Church Order of Dordrecht. A general synod meets annually in June.

A theological seminary is maintained at Grand Rapids, Michigan. The Reformed Free Publishing Association publishes a bimonthly periodical, *The Standard Bearer*; a monthly publication, *Beacon Lights,* is issued by the young people's federation. There are 4,700 members in 21 churches in Michigan, Illinois, Iowa, Wisconsin, Minnesota, Colorado, California, Washington, North Dakota, South Dakota, Texas, New Jersey, and Canada. Several home mission fields and two foreign fields—Jamaica and Singapore—are supported.

REFORMED CHURCH IN AMERICA

As early as 1614, what is now known as the Reformed Church in America had an unorganized membership along the upper reaches of the Hudson River in the area of Fort Orange (Albany), New York. There were no regularly established congregations or churches, but members were numerous enough to require the services of Reformed lay ministers, two of whom came from Holland in 1623 as "comforters of the sick." By 1628 the Dutch in New Amsterdam had a pastor of their own, Jonas Michaelius, and an organized collegiate church, the oldest church in the middle colonies and the oldest church in America with an uninterrupted ministry.

When the English took possession of New Amsterdam in 1664, Dutch churches were thriving in Albany, Kingston, Brooklyn, Manhattan, and at Bergen, New Jersey. When immigration from Holland ceased, perhaps 8,000 Dutch church people were holding services in their own language, served primarily by pastors sent from Holland. It was difficult and expensive to send native-born ministerial candidates to Holland for education and ordination; this issue rent the Reformed Church and was finally resolved by building a college and seminary at New Brunswick, New Jersey—Queen's College, founded by John Henry Livingston. This institution later became New Brunswick Theological Seminary—the first seminary in this country—and Rutgers University.

A sharp controversy over the authority of the Classes of Amsterdam resulted in complete independence for the Dutch churches in America. A general body and five particular bodies were created, a constitution was drawn up in 1792, and the General Synod was organized in 1794. Both names—Dutch Reformed Church in North America and Reformed Dutch Church in the United States of America—were in use in 1792. In 1819 the church was incorporated as the Reformed Protestant Dutch Church, and in 1867 it became the Reformed Church in America.

A large majority of the ministers and laypeople of the Reformed Church supported the American Revolution. Two generals, Philip Schuyler and Nicholas Herkimer, were members of the Reformed Church. As the Dutch became more and more Americanized, the English language gradually became accepted in the churches, but not without a struggle.

A second emigration from the Netherlands began in the middle of the nineteenth century, bringing entire congregations with their pastors. One group, led by Albertus van Raalte, established a community called Holland in western Michigan. Van Raalte and his group became part of the Reformed Church in America in 1850. Another colony, led by Hendrick Scholte, settled in Pella, Iowa, and, except for a small dissenting group, merged with the Reformed Church in America in 1856.

North American mission work began in 1786, although work among Native Americans had started much earlier. Needy churches in New York, Pennsylvania, and Kentucky, were assisted by missionaries from the classis of Albany until 1806, when the General Synod assumed administration of all missionary agencies, in cooperation with the American Board of Commissioners for Foreign Mission. In 1832 the Board of Foreign Missions was created; it continued to work through the American Board until 1857, when it began to operate independently. Insisting on seven years of college and seminary training for its ministers, the church in 1828 established the Education Society of the Reformed Church in America, later the Board of Education of the General Synod.

The explicit statements and principles of the Belgic Confession, the Heidelberg Catechism, and the Canons of the Synod of Dort are still the doctrinal standards of the Reformed Church in America. The mild and gentle spirit of the confession, with its emphasis on salvation through Christ, is a central theme; the primacy of God's power in human life is at the heart of the preaching, as it is at the heart of the Canons of Dort; and the Heidelberg Catechism, based on the three-fold division of the Epistle to the Romans, is employed in many Christian doctrine classes. The divine authority of the Scriptures is important. Worship is semi-liturgical, with an optional liturgy; only the forms for baptism and the Lord's Supper, the two recognized sacraments, are obligatory.

The government of the church is essentially presbyterian. The governing body in the local church is the consistory, made up of elders, deacons, and the pastor, who is always president. Elders are charged with the guidance of the spiritual life of the church, and deacons are in charge of benevolences, but they generally meet and act as one body. A number of churches in a limited area are grouped into a classis, which has immediate supervision of the churches and clergy within its bounds. The classis is composed of elder delegates from each congregation and the ministers in the area. Classes are grouped into regional synods, which supervise the planning and programming of the churches within the area. The highest legislative and judicial body of the church is the General Synod, which meets once a year. It is composed of clergy and elder delegates from each classis; the size of the delegation depends on the size of the classis.

The various program and service functions of the denomination are supervised by a 60-member General Synod Council, which is subdivided into seven committees. Each of the denomination's classes has a representative on the council. Denominational staff are located at the Interchurch Center in New York City and at several regional centers throughout the U.S. and Canada.

The Reformed Church has a strong mission history and is at work in some 20 countries. Through ethnic/racial councils in North America, the denomination relates to African Americans, Pacific and Asian Americans, Hispanic Americans, and Native Americans. The denomination has two theological seminaries (New Brunswick, in New Jersey, and Western, in Holland, Michigan) and three colleges (Central, in Pella, Iowa; Hope, in Holland, Michigan; and Northwestern, in Orange City, Iowa). Membership in 1992 stood at 194,416 active-confirmed members in 968 churches, with the greatest numerical strength in Michigan, New York, New Jersey, Iowa, and California.

REFORMED CHURCH IN THE UNITED STATES

This body originated with Swiss and German immigrants who arrived in this country in the 1700s; it operated under the auspices of the Dutch Reformed Synod of South and North Holland, but separated from that synod in 1793. Since 1869 it has been known as the Reformed Church in the United States. In 1934, most of its churches merged with the Evangelical Church to become the Evangelical and Reformed Church; and in 1957, with Congregational and Christian churches, to become the United Church of Christ.

One group, the Eureka Classis in South Dakota, refused to become a part of the united church. In 1986 the Eureka Classis divided into four classes and organized as the Synod of the Reformed Church in the United States. The doctrines are those set forth in the Heidelberg Catechism. There are 37 churches, with an inclusive membership of 4,176 baptized and communicant members and 39 active ministers. Primary strength is located in the Dakotas and California.

ROMAN CATHOLIC CHURCH

For the first 1,500 years of Christianity's history, the Western world was almost solidly Roman Catholic. In the eleventh century, Eastern Christianity went its independent way to form Eastern Orthodoxy in a number of national churches. Then the Protestant Reformation of the sixteenth century disrupted the unity of the Western church, leaving Europe divided among Roman Catholic, Lutheran, Anglican, Anabaptist, and Reformed, with the prospect of still further divisions as denominationalism increased.

The Roman Catholic Church dates its beginning from the moment of Christ's selection of the apostle Peter as guardian of the keys of heaven and earth and chief of the apostles, and it claims the fisherman as its first pope. During the second, third, and fourth centuries its claim to the theological primacy of Rome was reinforced by practical developments in the church and Western society. It gained temporal authority and power when it arose as the only body strong enough to rule after the fall of Rome in 410 C.E. A house of terror, ravaged first by Goths, Vandals, and Franks, then by Saxons, Danes, Alemanni, Lombards, and Burgundians, Europe found its only steadying hand in the church. Without the church, anarchy would have been king from Britain to the Bosphorus.

The first mention of the term *catholic* (universal) was made by Ignatius about 110–115 C.E., but the first real demonstration of its authority came in Rome as it won the barbarians to its banners while it kept the flame of faith burning in its churches and the candle of wisdom alive in its monastic schools. Augustine (354–430) deeply influenced its theological and philosophical structure and gave the papacy its finest justification and defense. He left it strong enough to grant crowns or deny them to Europe's heads of state.

The church beat back the threats of its enemies at home and afar; it converted the barbarian, defeated the Saracen, and employed the Inquisition against the heretic boring from within. It brought the hopeful interval known as the Peace of God; it also supported chivalry and feudalism, mounted the Crusades, built schools, and created a noble art and literature. For long centuries, the Benedictine monasteries guarded and preserved learning and culture in Europe. That order was founded in 529 in Italy in St. Benedict; since then, more than 4 million men have practiced the Benedictine rule of life. Centuries later in 1209, St. Francis of Assisi established the Franciscan Order, and at about the same time, St. Dominic began his Order of Friars Preachers (Dominicans). Catholic thought was profoundly influenced by the writings of Thomas Aquinas (1225–74), a Dominican who integrated Aristotelian philosophy with faith

Inevitably there arose temptations of power within and prosperity from the outside. Then came the Reformation. Roman Catholic scholars readily admit that there were corrupt individuals within the church and reform was necessary. Indeed, reform was underway even before the Reformation; Martin Luther was a reformer within the church before he broke away. Erasmus and Savonarola wrote and preached against the corruption and worldliness of certain Roman Catholic leaders and laypeople, but they stayed within the church. That these reformers had a case is not denied by Roman Catholic historians or scholars; they do, however, maintain that while priests and bishops, and even popes, may err, the one true church cannot err, and Luther was wrong in rebelling. But rebel he did, and the Roman church suffered its most fateful division.

There were also other reasons for the revolt: the growth of nationalism and secularism; ambitious political princes and rulers, who wanted no interference from the church; the Renaissance, with its revival of Greek and Roman pagan influences. All those forces worked together to produce the Reformation. The Counter Reformation, focused in the Council of Trent (1545–63), was effective in halting the spread of new Protestantism in Europe and won back some areas to the Roman Catholic Church and faith; one of its chief instruments was the Society of Jesus (Jesuits), an educational and missionary order founded by Ignatius of Loyola in 1534.

But long before Luther's time, Roman Catholics had reached America. The first diocese on this side of the Atlantic was established in Greenland in 1125; bishops were in residence there until 1377. Priests came with Columbus from Catholic Spain in 1492; missionaries came with Coronado and other early Spanish explorers. Most perished, but one established the first permanent parish in America at St. Augustine, Florida, in 1565.

French explorers, *voyageurs*, and colonizers—Cartier, Joliet, Marquette, and others—were Roman Catholics, generally accompanied by missionary groups such as the Recollects, Jesuits, Sulpicians, Capuchins, and secular clergy. New France became a vicariate apostolic in 1658, with Bishop Laval at its head. The See of Quebec (1675) had spiritual jurisdiction over the vast province of France in North America, reaching down the valley of the Mississippi to Louisiana.

In 1634 Roman Catholics founded Maryland; later they were restricted by law in Maryland and most other colonies, and the restrictions were not lifted until after the Revolution. In the face of these restrictions, and in view of the fact that most colonial immigrants were Protestants, the Roman Catholic Church grew slowly. In 1696, only seven Catholic families were in New York, and 80 years later they were still traveling to Philadelphia to receive the sacraments. In 1763 they were fewer than 25,000 Catholics in a population of 2.2 million, and they were under the jurisdiction of the vicar apostolic of London.

Among the signatures on the Articles of Confederation, the Declaration of Independence, and the Constitution, are found those of three Catholics—Thomas Fitzsimmons, Charles Carroll of Carrollton, and Daniel Carroll. The Revolution brought them religious as well as political freedom; religious equality became law with the adoption of the Constitution in 1787.

There was no immediate hierarchal superior in the U.S. when the war ended, and the vicar apostolic in London refused to exercise jurisdiction over the "rebels." After long investigation and delay and an appeal to Rome, the Reverend John Carroll was named Superior, or perfect apostolic, of the church in the 13 original states. At that time, 15,800 Catholics resided in Maryland, 700 in Pennsylvania, 200 in Virginia, and 1,500 in New York, unorganized and with no priests. At the turn of the century, there were about 150,000 Roman Catholics in 80 churches; by 1890 there were 6,231,417—a growth due primarily to the flood of emigration from the Catholic countries of Europe.

Baltimore became the first American diocese in 1789, and an archdiocese in 1808; other dioceses and archdioceses were formed as the church expanded. Three plenary, or national, councils were held at Baltimore in 1852, 1866, and 1884. Archbishop John McCloskey of New York became the first American cardinal in 1875, and Archbishop James Gibbons of Baltimore was elevated to the same rank in 1877.

The Civil War and two world wars failed to disturb the work of the church or interrupt its growth; indeed, World War I produced one of the ablest hierarchal Roman Catholic agencies in the country—the National War Council, now known as the United States Catholic Conference. There were 18,608,003 Catholics in the U.S. in 1926. In 1993 the Roman Catholic Church, the largest church in the U.S., reported 59,221,000 members in approximately 19,860 churches. About 23 percent of the American people identified themselves as Roman Catholics.

The faith and doctrine of Catholicism are founded upon "that deposit of faith given to it by Christ and through his apostles, sustained by the Bible and by tradition." Thus the church accepts the Apostles' Creed, the Nicene-Constantinople Creed, the Athanasian Creed, and the Creed of Pius IV, also called the Creedal Statement of the Council of Trent.

Roman Catholics believe in seven sacraments. *Baptism,* necessary for membership in the church, is administered to infants and adults by pouring or immersion; anointing with the holy chrism in the form of a cross follows baptism. *Confirmation* is by the laying on of hands; the ordinary minister of this sacrament is the bishop, but priests also may confirm. The laity may receive the *Eucharist* in the forms of bread and wine; the body and blood of Christ are considered actually present in the eucharistic elements. Through the sacrament of *reconciliation,* postbaptismal sins are forgiven. *Anointing of the sick* is for the seriously ill, injured, or aged. The sacraments of *holy orders* is for the ordination of deacons, priests, and bishops. *Marriage* is a sacrament that "cannot be dissolved by any human power"; this rules out remarriage after divorce. Members are required to attend Mass on Sundays and on obligatory holy days, fast and abstain on certain appointed days, confess at least once a year, receive the Holy Eucharist during the Easter season, contribute to the support of the church, and strictly observe the marriage regulations of the church.

The central act of worship is the Mass; its two principal parts are the liturgy of the World and the liturgy of the Eucharist. From the third century until 1963, the Western church prescribed Latin as the liturgical language; now the entire Mass is recited in the vernacular by both priest and people. Many Catholics also participate in devotions such as benediction, the rosary, stations of the cross, and novenas.

The government of the Roman Catholic Church is hierarchical, but lay members of the parishes assume much responsibility. The trend since Vatican Council II (1962–65) is toward more and more lay participation. At the head of the structure stands the pope, who is also Bishop of Rome and "Vicar of Christ on earth and the Visible Head of the Church." His authority is supreme in all matters of faith and discipline.

Next is the College of Cardinals. Although laypeople once were appointed as cardinals, the office has been limited to priests since 1918. Many cardinals live in Rome, acting as advisers to the pope or as heads or members of the various congregations or commissions that supervise the administration of the church. When a pope dies, cardinals elect the successor, and hold authority in the interim. The Roman Curia is the official body of administrative offices through which the pope governs the church; it is composed of congregations, tribunals, and curial offices.

In the U.S. there are nine active cardinals, 42 archbishops (six are also cardinals), 351 bishops, and more than 51,000 priests; there are 36 archdioceses and 162 dioceses. An archbishop is in charge of an archdiocese and has precedence in that province. Bishops, appointed by Rome, usually upon suggestions from the U.S. hierarchy, are the ruling authorities in the dioceses, but appeals from their decisions may be taken to the apostolic delegate at Washington, and even to Rome. The parish priest, responsible to the bishop, is assigned by the bishop or archbishop and holds authority to celebrate Mass and administer the sacraments, with the help of such other priests as the parish may need.

The clergy of the church also include deacons. Since the restoration of the Permanent Deaconate in 1967, more than 10,840 men have completed the training course and been ordained deacons. Most of these men are married and over 35. They are empowered to preach, baptize, distribute Holy Communion, and officiate at weddings. Most deacons support themselves in secular jobs and exercise their ministry during weekends and evenings.

Seminarians study for orders in seminaries. Some 6,000 men are in diocesan and religious-order seminaries. The usual course covers a period of eight years—four years of philosophy and four years of theology. Those in religious orders also spend one or two years in a noviate.

In 1993 there were 33,476 diocesan or secular priests in the U.S., and 17,576 who belong to religious orders and congregations. Add to these the 6,260 lay brothers and 94,022 sisters engaged in religious work, and their importance in the overall task of the church becomes clear. The official *Catholic Directory* lists a total of 131 religious orders of priests and brothers (about one third for brothers only), and more than 400 for women.

These orders differ widely in their work. Some are "contemplative," the members remaining in monasteries or cloistered convents. Those in active or mixed religious orders engage in teaching care of the sick, missionary work, writing, or social work. Brothers and sisters are required to take vows of poverty, chastity, obedience but are not ordained; they engage primarily in educational, philanthropic, and charitable work.

Besides religious orders and congregations, Catholics may join secular institutions whose members also observe poverty, chastity, and obedience but do not wear distinctive garb or live together in a community. Before receiving approval as secular institutes engaged in apostolic work, these groups may operate as approved "pious unions." Worldwide membership in these institutes and unions exceed 15,000. Some members are also ordained priests.

Three ecclesiastical councils form an important part of the Catholic system: (1) The general, or ecumenical, council is called by the pope or with his consent; it is composed of all the bishops, and its actions on matters of doctrine and discipline must be approved by the pope; (2) the plenary, or national, council is made up of the bishops of a given country; its acts, too, must be submitted to the Holy See; (3) provincial and diocesan councils make further promulgation and application of the decrees passed by the other councils and approved by the pope.

Pope John XXIII summoned all the bishops of the church to the twenty-first ecumenical council, the Second Vatican Council; it met from 1962 to 1965. Following Pope John's death, Pope Paul VI reconvened the council, which stimulated liturgical reform, encouraged Catholic participation in the ecumenical movement, updated many church practices, and inaugurated the idea of collegiality among the bishops.

In 1968 Paul VI reaffirmed the official church position against any form of artificial birth control. Many theologians, priests, and lay-people protested this, voicing opposition to the encyclical *Humanae Vitae;* the hierarchies of such countries as France, Canada, Belgium, Holland, Switzerland, Austria, and West Germany interpreted the papal position in the light of freedom of the individual conscience.

With the most centralized government in Christendom, the Holy See at Rome has representatives in many countries of the world. Roman Catholic churches have been established in 217 countries, with a total membership of more than 950 million. The majority of Italians, Spanish, Irish, Austrians, Poles, Latin Americans, Belgians, Hungarians, Southern Germans, Portuguese, French, and Filipinos are baptized Roman Catholics. The Society for the Propagation of the Faith is the overall representative missionary body. The U.S. has sent about 7,500 missionaries to 110 foreign countries.

Education has been a primary concern of American Catholics since the establishment of a classical school at St. Augustine, Florida, in 1606. As of 1993 there were 7,065 elementary parochial and private schools in this country with about 2 million students, and 1,377 Catholic high schools with 634,000 students. More than 660,000 students attend 231 Catholic colleges and universities, including Notre Dame, Fordham, Georgetown, Boston College, St. Louis, Marquette, Loyola, and Villanova.

Almost every diocese publishes a weekly newspaper; more than 400 Catholic newspapers and magazines are published in the U.S. and Canada. Some of the largest and most influential periodicals are *The National Catholic Reporter, Commonweal, America, Columbia, U.S. Catholic, St. Anthony Messenger, Catholic Digest, Catholic World, Ligourian, The Wanderer, Twin Circle,* and *The National Catholic Register.*

The National Conference on Catholic Charities helps to coordinate charity and welfare work on state and national levels; work is also conducted by several religious orders whose members devote full time to the relief of the poor in homes or institutions, and many dioceses have bureaus of charity. The Society of St. Vincent de Paul is perhaps the largest and most effective charitable organization; numerous others—Little Sisters of the Poor, Sisters of Charity, Daughters of Charity of the Society of St. Vincent de Paul, Sisters of Mercy, the Third Order of Franciscans—are active among the poor in Catholic hospitals, orphanages, and homes for the aged. There are nearly 700 homes for the aged and 244 orphanages. More than 50 million patients are treated annually in 624 general and special hospitals; one of every three beds in the nation's private hospitals is provided by the Catholic hospital system.

Members of the Catholic hierarchy are also members of the United States Catholic Conference, which operates as a clearing-house for information. This conference facilitates discussion of all policies that affect the interests and activities of the church; it unifies, coordinates, and organizes social welfare, education, and other ac-tivities. All bishops in the U.S., its territories, and possessions have a voice in this conference.

Parish councils composed of laypeople, created to aid the priest in the management of the parish, have consultative powers; new dioce-san senates, composed of priests, assist the bishop in setting policies in the diocese.

While most Roman Catholics belong to the Latin Rite, at least 20 groups of churches, with an estimated 10 to 12 million Catholics worldwide, belong to the Eastern Rite. These Catholics hold identi-cal doctrinal beliefs and recognize the authority of the pope, but differ in language, liturgy, customs, church laws, and tradition. Gen-erally, they follow one of five historic rites: Byzantine, Alexandrian, Antiochian, Armenian, or Chaldean; the main bodies are Catholic Copt, Ethiopian Catholic, Syrian, Catholic Armenian, Malabar Catholic, and Maronite.

Some 518,000 Eastern Rite Catholics, mostly Ukrainians and Ruthenians, live in the U.S. All these rights are jurisdictionally related to one or another of the Eastern Patriarchs.

The Roman Catholic Church today finds itself in an era of change, tension, and dissension. Pope John XXXIII and Vatican II brought about new programs and approaches in the fields of ecumenism, religious liberty, the liturgy, Scripture studies, and social action. Before Vatican II, Catholics were forbidden to attend meetings of the World Council of Churches; now Catholic observers attend council sessions, and bishops of the Church have entered into theo-logical dialogue with several larger Protestant denominations.

The number of Spirit-filled Catholics, that is, those who believe in and claim charismatic gifts, such as speaking in tongues, healing, interpretation, and prophecy, is some 300,000. Many more have had some measure of contact with what is broadly called charismatic Catholicism.

Dissension is a common feature in contemporary Church life. Some of the most troublesome issues have to do with clerical celibacy, birth control, abortion, patriarchy and hierarchy in the church, and the official stands of the church on political and economic matters.

The present Pope, John Paul II, from Poland, is the first non-Italian pope since the 1520s. A true internationalist in itinerary and linguistic skills, he is a solid traditionalist in matters of doctrine and practice, notably on family and gender issues. With respect to social and political concerns, he qualifies as a progressive. The mixture of "liberal" and "conservative" in him seems to mirror many tensions in this global Christian community. These are indeed tense and critical times for this historic church.

SALVATION ARMY

William Booth, an ordained minister in the Methodist New Connexion in England, regretfully left the pulpit of that church in 1861 to become a freelance evangelist. This step led him, in 1865, to dedicate his life to the poverty-stricken unchurched masses in the slum areas of London's East End. He first planned to supplement the work of the churches, but this proved impractical; many converts did not want to go where they were sent, and often when they did go, they were not accepted. Moreover, Booth soon found that he needed the converts to help handle the great crowds that came to his meetings. He began his work in Mile End Waste under the name Christian Mission; in 1878 the name was changed to the Salvation Army.

Booth first organized his movement along lines of Methodist polity, with annual conferences at which reports were made and programs planned. But when the name was changed, the whole organization became dominated by the new title. Articles of War (declaration of faith) were drawn up, and soon the mission stations became corps, members became soldiers, evangelists became officers, and converts were called seekers. Booth was designated as General, and his organization was gradually set up on a military pattern, which provided a direct line of authority and a practical system of training personnel for effective action. He reasoned that it was "just as valid to build an army of crusaders to save souls as it has been to send armies to recover a sepulchre."

The work spread quickly over England, Scotland, and Wales and was officially established in the United States in 1880 by a pioneer group under the direction of George Scott Railton. Once committed to a policy of expansion, Booth lost no time in sending pioneering parties in different directions. They reached Australia and France in 1881; Switzerland, Sweden, India, and Canada in 1882; New Zealand and South Africa in 1883; and Germany in 1886. Today the Salvation Army works in 93 lands with approximately 25,000 officers; preaches the gospel in some 127 languages at 14,600 evangelical centers; and operates more than 5,088 social institutions, hospitals, schools, and agencies. The general membership numbers about 1,500,000.

The Army conducts its religious and social programs in all 50 states, preaching the gospel and effecting the spiritual, moral, and physical reclamation of those who come under its influence through 10,013 centers of operation, including 4,884 service extension units. These are administered by more than 4,250 officers, assisted by about 27,326 employees.

Administratively, the Army is under the command of a General. The primary unit of the Army is the corps, of which there may be several in a city. Each corps is commanded by an officer, ranging in rank from lieutenant to major, who is responsible to divisional headquarters. A number of corps make up each of the 38 divisions in the U.S., with the work of each division under the direct supervision of a divisional commander. Divisions are grouped into four territories—Eastern, Central, Southern, and Western—with headquarters in West Nyack, New York; Des Plaines, Illinois; Atlanta, Georgia; and Rancho Palos Verdes, California. Territorial commanders are in charge of each territory, and the four territorial headquarters are composed of departments to facilitate all phases of Army work.

The national headquarters in Alexandria, Virginia, is the coordinating office for the entire country, and the national commander is the chief administrative officer, official spokesman, and president of all Salvation Army corporations in the U.S. Property and revenues are in the custody of a board of trustees, or directors, and citizens' advisory boards assist in interpreting the work of the Army to the general public.

Within the structure of the Army, converts who desire to become soldiers (members) are required to sign the Articles of War, after which, as members, they give volunteer service. The function of officers, who are commissioned to full-time Salvation Army service, is similar to that of ministers of other churches.

Basic training for each officer is a two-year-in-residence course at one of the Army's four schools in Suffern, New York; Chicago; Atlanta; and Rancho Palos Verdes. The chief source of officer candidates is the Salvation Army corps. A soldier who has served actively for at least six months may make application and, if accepted, may enter the School for Officers' Training, where the curriculum, in addition to formal study, includes field experience as well as orientation in all possible areas of Salvation Army service. The officer graduates from the school as a lieutenant and, following additional study, is eligible to attain the rank of captain, major, lieutenant colonel, colonel, or commissioner.

The motivating force of the Salvation Army is the religious faith of its officers and soldiers, and the fundamental doctrines of the organization are stated in the 11 cardinal affirmations of its Foundation Deed of 1878. These statements document the Army's recognition of the Bible as the only rule of Christian faith and practice; God as the Creator and Father of all humankind; the Trinity of Father, Son, and Holy Ghost; Jesus Christ as Son of God and "Son of man"; sin as the great destroyer of soul and society; salvation as God's remedy for human sin and the ultimate and eternal hope made available through Christ; sanctification as the individual's present and maturing experience of a life set apart for the holy purposes of the kingdom of God; and an eternal destiny that may triumph over sin and death.

While the Salvation Army has a dual function of church and social agency, its first purpose is salvation "by the power of the Holy Spirit combined with the influence of human ingenuity and love." Its social services are merely a means of meeting the needs of the "whole person," putting the socially disinherited—the needy both physically and spiritually—into a condition to be uplifted.

The work of the Army in the U.S. includes 119 adult rehabilitation centers, aiding almost 41,000 annually. Nearly 185,000 are served annually in 89 medical facilities; 49 camps provide camping facilities for more than 98,000 children, mothers, and senior citizens. The Army maintains more than 272 boys' and girls' clubs, with more than 100,000 members; 339 canteens, serving about 3,524,663 in emergencies; family service bureaus, serving 11,400,000 persons. About 150,000 persons make life-changing spiritual decisions under the Army's ministry each year. There are also hotels and lodges for men and women, missing person bureaus, day-care centers, alcoholic care facilities, correctional service bureaus for prisoners and their families, programs for homeless persons, and other allied services. These services are given without respect to race, color, creed, or condition; the whole work is financed largely through voluntary subscriptions, federal funds, and annual appeals.

SCHWENKFELDER CHURCH

Caspar Schwenckfeld von Ossig (1489–1561), a Silesian nobleman baptized and raised in the Roman Catholic Church, experienced a spiritual awakening in 1519. Disappointed in his hope to help reform the Catholic Church from within, he played a leading role in the Reformation, advocating wider reading of the Bible by laypeople, urging the need for power, guidance, and leading of the Holy Spirit and preaching that the sacramental consuming of the Lord's Supper is a mystical partaking of Christ as food for the soul—but that the food is really bread. This interpretation of the Lord's Supper, together with his insistence on complete separation of church and state, led him into disagreement with Lutheranism.

He founded a number of spiritual brotherhoods whose members in time came to be known as Schwenkfelders. Nearly 200 persons arrived in the U.S. in 1734, and the first formal society was organized in 1782. The body has disappeared in Europe but persists in the U.S., with 2,489 members in five local congregations, located within a 50-mile radius of Philadelphia.

All theology, the members hold, should be constructed from the Bible, but the Scriptures are considered dead without the indwelling Word. Christ's divinity was progressive, his human nature becoming more and more divine without "losing its identity"; faith, regeneration, and subsequent spiritual growth change human nature; but justification by faith must not obscure the positive regeneration imparted by Christ; thus the theology is Christocentric.

In polity the body is congregational; each church is incorporated, self-sustaining, and conducts its affairs through its districts or local conference. A general conference composed of all the churches meets twice a year to develop the larger program of education and missions. The general conference sponsored the founding of the Perkiomen School at Pennsburg, Pennsylvania, in 1892; a majority of its board of trustees are still members of Schwenkfelder churches. Schwenckfeld Manor, low-rent housing for elderly persons, is located at Lansdale, Pennsylvania.

SOCIAL BRETHREN

This body was organized in Illinois in 1867 by a small group of persons from various denominations who held quite orthodox doctrines but disagreed with those denominations in certain matters of interpretation of Scripture, discipline, and decorum. In 1983 it reported three associations, each meeting annually; a general assembly that meets biennially; 26 churches in Illinois, Michigan, and Indiana; and 1,165 members. Recently two churches and a mission were organized in the Philippines.

The confession of faith emphasizes the infinite power, wisdom, and goodness of God, in whom are united three persons of one substance, power, and eternity: the Father, the Son, and the Holy Ghost; the authority and consistency of the Scriptures, comprising the Old and the New Testament, as containing all things necessary to salvation, "so that whatsoever is not read therein nor may be proved thereby is not required of any man that it should be believed as an article of faith or thought to be requisite or necessary to salvation"; regeneration and sanctification through Christ; eternal salvation of the redeemed; and eternal punishment for apostasy.

The ordinances of baptism and the Lord's Supper are for true believers only; baptism may be by sprinkling, pouring, or immersion. Lay members of the church have the right of suffrage and free speech, but ministers are called to preach the gospel, not political speeches. Polity is a fusion of Baptist and Methodist structures and customs. The work of the Social Brethren, aside from efforts in mutual aid and assistance, is largely evangelistic.

SPIRITUALIST

This movement is known popularly for its mediums, séances, and clairvoyance. Ouija boards, table tipping, spirit rappings, and conversations have attracted thousands of persons anxious to communicate with their departed loved ones. But Spiritualism offers genuine religious bases and connotations as well as psychic experiments. The movement has become a church. The National Spiritual Alliance (NSA) has a declaration of Principles:

1. We believe in Infinite Intelligence.
2. We believe that the phenomena of Nature, both physical and spiritual, are the expression of Infinite Intelligence.
3. We affirm that a correct understanding of such expression, and living in accordance therewith, constitute true religion.
4. We affirm that the existence and personal identity of the individual continue after the change called death.
5. We affirm that communication with the so-called dead is a fact scientifically proven by the phenomena of Spiritualism.
6. We believe that the highest morality is contained in the Golden Rule. . . .
7. We affirm the moral responsibility of the individual and that he makes his own happiness or unhappiness as he obeys or disobeys Nature's physical and spiritual laws.
8. We affirm that the doorway to reformation is never closed against any human soul, here or hereafter.
9. We affirm that the practice of Prophecy, as authorized by the Holy Bible, is a divine and God-given gift, reestablished and proven through mediumship by the phenomena of Spiritualism.

The teaching of God as love is central in Spiritualism; the Lord's Prayer is used in both public worship and private séances. Christ is recognized as a medium; the annunciation was a message from the spirit world, the transfiguration was an opportunity for materialization of the spirits of Moses and Elias, and the resurrection was evidence that all people live on in the spirit world.

The soul is often called the astral body; at death the material body dissolves, and the soul, as the body of the spirit, progresses through a series of spheres to a higher and higher existence. In two lower spheres, persons of bad character or sinful record are purified and made ready for higher existences. Most of the departed are to be found in the third sphere, the summer land; beyond this are the philosopher's sphere, the advanced contemplative and intellectual sphere, the love sphere, and the Christ sphere. All reach the higher spheres eventually; Spiritualists do not believe in heaven or hell or that any are ever lost.

Services or séances are held in private homes, rented halls, or churches. Most Spiritualist churches have regular services with prayer, music, selections from the *Spiritualist Manual,* a sermon or lecture, and spirit messages from the departed. Churches and ministers are supported by freewill offerings; mediums and ministers also gain support from classes and séances in which fees are charged. Attendance at church services is invariably small; one authority estimates the average congregation at 20 to 25. But membership cannot be estimated on the basis of church attendance; for every enrolled member, at least 15 are not enrolled but are interested in the movement and in attending services. A membership total of more than 180,000 has been reported, but this is not comprehensive or inclusive of all who use the services of the church.

Administration and government differ slightly in the various groups, but most have district or state associations and an annual general convention. All have mediums, and most have ministers in charge of the congregations. Requirements for licensing and ordination also differ, but a determined effort is being made to raise the standards of education and character in the larger groups.

NATIONAL SPIRITUAL ALLIANCE OF THE U.S.A.

This body was founded in 1913 by G. Tabor Thompson and has its headquarters at Lake Pleasant, Massachusetts, where it was incorporated. Holding general Spiritualist doctrines, the alliance stresses paranormal and impersonal manifestations and intercommunication with the spirit world. Salvation is held to be through the development of personal character: "One reaps as he sows, yet . . . all things are working together for good and evolution obtains perpetually in all persons."

Local churches of the alliance elect their own officers and choose their own ministers. A three-day convention is held annually, at which delegates from all the churches elect national officers—president, secretary, and treasurer. An official board of directors steers the missionary work of ministers and certified mediums; college training is not required, but a minister must have passed a course of study arranged by the alliance. Mediums may baptize, but only ministers may officiate at ceremonies of ordination and marriage. Work of the alliance involves benevolent, literary, educational, musical, and scientific activities. There are 3,230 members and 34 churches in central Massachusetts and Connecticut.

NATIONAL SPIRITUALIST ASSOCIATION OF CHURCHES

Organized in Chicago in 1893, the National Spiritualist Association of Churches is the orthodox body of American Spiritualism. Influential far beyond its immediate membership, this association furnishes literature for the whole Spiritualist movement. Advocating higher qualifications for mediums and ministers, it supports a seminary, the Morris Pratt Institute, where a great deal of work is done by correspondence. A national director of education oversees a training course for members, licentiates, lecturers, mediums, and ordained ministers. An annual legislative convention is held, and officers are elected triennially. Members number 2,883 in 137 churches. In 1994, the Association established an educational center in Lily Dale, New York.

SWEDENBORGIAN CHURCH, GENERAL CONVENTION OF

The theology of the Churches of the New Jerusalem, commonly called Swedenborgian, is based on the teachings of Emmanuel Swedenborg. Born in Stockholm in 1688, Swedenborg was a scientist distinguished in the fields of mathematics, geology, cosmology, and anatomy before he turned seriously to theology. Although certain he was divinely commissioned to teach the doctrines of the "New Church," Swedenborg himself never preached or founded a church. His followers, however, felt that the need for a separate denomination was implicit in the New Revelation.

The New Church as an organization arose in London in 1783 when Robert Hindmarsh, a printer, gathered a few friends to discuss the writings of Swedenborg; they formed a general conference of their societies in 1815. The first Swedenborgian Society in America was organized at Baltimore, Maryland, in 1792, and in 1817 the General Convention of the New Jerusalem in the U.S.A. was established.

The Churches of the New Jerusalem exist in three main bodies: the General Convention of the New Jerusalem in the U.S.A., the older U.S. body; the General Church of the New Jerusalem, which broke from the older group in 1890; and the General Conference in England.

The Faith and Aims of the church state that the "Lord Jesus Christ has come again, not in a physical reappearance, but in spirit and in truth; not in a single event only, but in a progressive manifestation of his presence among men." Tokens of his coming appear in the burst of scientific development, the rise of the spirit of inquiry, the progress toward political and intellectual freedom, and the deepening sense of national and international responsibility that has characterized the last 150 years. The coming of the Son of Man is the "direct and sole work of the Lord." Word of this was given by Emanuel Swedenborg to his followers.

The doctrines of the General Convention of the New Jerusalem are set forth in its liturgy:

1. That there is one God, in whom there is a Divine Trinity; and that He is the Lord Jesus Christ.
2. That saving faith is to believe in Him.
3. Every man is born to evils of every kind, and unless through repentance he removes them in part, he remains in them, and he who remains in them cannot be saved.
4. That good actions are to be done, because they are of God and from God.
5. That these are to be done by a man as from himself; but that it ought to be believed that they are done from the Lord with him and by him.

The societies are grouped into a general convention that meets annually. Each society is self-regulating, with ministers and general pastors (in charge of state associations). Services are liturgical, based on the *Book of Worship* issued by the General Convention. The convention now has 2,073 members active in 47 societies. A theological school is in Newton, Massachusetts, and the Swedenborg Foundation in New York City distributes Swedenborg's writings.

The General Church of the New Jerusalem accepts the full divine authority of those writings, acknowledging that they are not really *Swedenborg's*, but rather are "from the Lord alone." There is no fixed constitution; polity is based on "essential unanimity" in free council and assembly. There are ministers, pastors, and bishops, the latter being chosen by a general assembly that meets every three or four years; 2,143 members are reported in 21 organized circles and 15 groups. There is a theological school, a college, and a secondary school. Headquarters is at Bryn Athyn, Pennsylvania, where a cathedral has been built.

THEOSOPHY

Theosophy is the universal perennial philosophy that is thought to underlie all religions; thus it draws from both Eastern and Western philosophy and religious teaching. The term itself antedates the establishment of the Theosophical Society and was first used to describe the system of philosophy espoused by Ammonias Saccas in the second century.

Chief founder of the modern theosophical movement was Helena Petrovna Blavatsky, who was born in Russia in 1831 and traveled over the world in search of "a knowledge of the laws which govern the universe." She arrived in the U.S. in 1872 and, with Henry Steel Olcott and William Q. Judge, founded the Theosophical Society of New York in 1875. Her aim was "to form a nucleus of the Universal Brotherhood of Humanity, without distinction of race, creed, sex, caste, or color; to encourage the study of comparative religion, philosophy, and science; and to investigate the unexplained laws of nature and the powers latent in man."

Blavatsky brought out the teachings of the great thinkers of various religions, sciences, and philosophies, both ancient and current at that time. Proceeding from the premise that God is immanent in the hidden forces of nature and that people can attain perfection through their own powers, she described God as impersonal—the Absolute Principle of pantheistic Hinduism, the Tao of Taoism, the Godhead of Christianity. Each person is a part of God, and within each is a divine potential; therefore, all are related.

She held that all religions stem from a hierarchy that includes Jesus, Buddha, and other master thinkers who have experienced a series of rebirths, or reincarnations, ultimately to attain divinity. Reincarnation is a central theme in Theosophy; it is the method through which persons rid themselves of all impurities and unfold their inner potentials through varied experiences. Closely connected with the concept of reincarnation is that of *karma,* the law of cause and effect; each rebirth, then, is seen as the result of actions, thoughts, and desires brought from the past.

Olcott and Blavatsky left New York in late 1878, on their way to India. They established the headquarters of the society at Adyer, near Madras in southern India, in 1882. When Blavatsky died in 1891, Annie Besant took over leadership of the movement, with Olcott as president, until his death in 1907. During that period, conflicts developed between Besant and the leaders of other Theosophical groups in Europe and the U.S. In 1895, William Q. Judge, one of the three founders and president of the American society, established an independent Theosophical Society in America; those loyal to Besant worked in the society whose headquarters was in India. Other splits developed in the years that followed, and the fragmentation is still evident, but the basic teachings of Blavatsky still hold in all groups.

No accurate report of membership seems possible among these groups, but it is estimated that there are some 40,000 Theosophists worldwide, perhaps 5,000 in the U.S. The Theosophical Society was the first group to bring out the philosophy behind occultism. Its influence, thanks to the current interest in Eastern philosophy and religion, is felt in many other occult groups unconnected with any Theosophical Society.

TRIUMPH THE CHURCH AND KINGDOM OF GOD IN CHRIST (INTERNATIONAL)

Founded in Georgia in 1902 by E. D. Smith, this church teaches that all "justified" believers are cleansed from sin through the shed blood of Christ; entire sanctification is an instantaneous, definite work of second grace obtained through the faith of the consecrated believer; Christ will come a second time; and baptism by fire is a scriptural experience also obtainable by faith. Doctrine, summarized in seven steps, leads one to eternal life.

General overseers, or bishops, are the chief officers of the body. The chief executive is known as the chief apostle. The church meets quadrennially in an International Religious Congress; at other times the work of the church is carried on by state, county, and local officers. There are 54,000 members in 496 churches, most in the Southeastern United States, but with some in Liberia and the Philippine Islands.

UNITARIAN UNIVERSALIST ASSOCIATION

In May 1961, the Unitarian and Universalist churches in the U.S. and Canada were consolidated as the Unitarian Universalist Association of Congregations in North America, one of the most influential liberal churches. The two bodies had separate and interesting origins and history.

Unitarians often claimed that their thought reaches back into the early Christian centuries, before the concept of Trinitarianism developed. Unitarianism as we know it today, however, began with the Protestant Reformation, among Anti-Trinitarians and Socinians. The movement spread from independent thinkers and Anabaptists in Switzerland, Hungary, Transylvania, Holland, Poland, and Italy to England. There it found champions in such leaders as Newton, Locke, and Milton, but no attempt was made to organize the movement until late in the eighteenth century.

American Unitarianism, however, developed independently, when members of the liberal wing of the Congregational Church in eastern Massachusetts, who asked that they not be required to subscribe to a creed, were branded as Unitarian. The first organized church to turn to Unitarianism as a body, however, was not a Congregational church but the Episcopal King's Chapel in Boston in 1784.

In the second half of the eighteenth century, many older and larger Congregational churches that moved toward Unitarianism were known as Liberal Christian. The split within Congregationalism came into the open in 1805 with the appointment of Henry Ware as professor of theology at Harvard; it was confirmed in 1819 when William Ellery Channing of Boston preached his famous Baltimore sermon outlining the Unitarian view. Channing defined the true church in these words: "By his Church our Savior does not mean a party bearing the name of a human leader, distinguished by a form or an opinion, and on the ground of this distinction, denying the name and character of Christians to all but themselves. . . . These are the church—men made better, made holy, virtuous by his religion—men who, hoping in his promises, keep his commands."

In accordance with its charter, the American Unitarian Association (1925–61) considered itself devoted to certain moral, religious, educational, and charitable purposes, which may be as enlightening to the non-Unitarian as an analysis of its religious or doctrinal statements:

1. Diffuse the knowledge and promote the interests of religion that Jesus taught as love to God and love to man;
2. Strengthen the churches and fellowships that unite in the association for more and better work for the kingdom of God;
3. Organize new churches and fellowships for the extension of Unitarianism in our own countries and in other lands; and

4. Encourage sympathy and cooperation among religious liberals at home and abroad.

Organization was liberally congregational; independent local churches were grouped in local, county, district, state, and regional conferences and were united in an international association for purposes of fellowship, counsel, and promotion of mutual interests. At the time of the merger, there were four Unitarian seminaries, two preparatory schools, 386 churches, and approximately 115,000 members. Foreign work is now conducted through the International Association for Religious Freedom, with headquarters at Oxford, England; the International Association has correspondents in 65 countries.

Universalists find evidence of their thinking and philosophy in many cultural streams; Universalism has much in common with several religions throughout the world. Having roots in both pre-Christian and contemporary world faiths, yet within the Christian frame of reference, Universalists claim roots in the early Christian Gnostics, Clement of Alexandria and Theodore of Mopsuestia, Anabaptists, and the seventeenth- and eighteenth-century German mystics. American Universalism has its direct origin in the work of George DeBenneville, a lay theologian; John Murray, a British anti-Calvinist; and Hosea Ballou, an original Universalist thinker.

DeBenneville, the English-educated son of French Huguenot *émigrés,* studied medicine in Germany and in 1741 came under the influence of the early Brethren, Friends of God, and German Pietists in Pennsylvania. He preached his gospel of universal salvation as he practiced medicine among the settlers and Native Americans.

In 1759, James Relly of England wrote *Union,* in which he opposed the Calvinistic doctrine of election of the few. Relly's conviction of universal salvation deeply influenced John Murray, a Wesleyan evangelist who came to New Jersey in 1770 and found groups of universalist-minded people scattered along the Atlantic coast. He became minister to one such group in Gloucester, Massachusetts, and later served briefly as a Revolutionary War chaplain in the armies of Washington and Greene. His Independent Christian Church of Gloucester became the first organized Universalist church in America in 1779. One of its charter members was Gloster Dalton, an African American.

The Universalists met at Philadelphia in 1790 to draft their first declaration of faith and plan of government. They condemned war, but approved settling disputes out of course, abolition of slavery and education of black persons, testimony by affirmation rather than by oath, and free public education. This Philadelphia declaration was adopted by a group of New England Universalists in 1793.

At about the same time, Hosea Ballou, a schoolteacher and itinerant preacher in Vermont, was ordained in the Universalist ministry. He broke radically with Murray's thought, in 1805 publishing the *Treatise on Atonement*, which gave Universalists their first consistent philosophy. Ballou rejected the theories of total depravity, endless punishment in hell, the Trinity, and miracles. Humankind, said Ballou, was potentially good and capable of perfectibility; God, being a God of infinite love, recognized humanity's heavenly nature and loved the human race as God's own offspring. The meaning of the atonement was not found in bloody sacrifice to appease divine wrath, but in the heroic sacrifice of Jesus. And Jesus was not God but a Son of the universal God, who revealed the love of God and wanted to win all persons to that love. This avowedly Unitarian-Universalist statement of theology deeply influenced American Universalism.

Universalists were active very early in reform movements for prison inmates and working women; they opposed slavery from their earliest days, stood for separation of church and state, and have maintained a continuing interest in the fields of science, labor, management, civil rights, and human concern. Medical workers were placed in German refugee centers; international student work-camp teams served underprivileged children and refugee youths in Europe. They fed children in Japan; developed community centers in India; provided child care for black children in Virginia; supported a social center at an interracial public housing development in Chicago; and worked in various state mental hospitals.

They founded several colleges and universities—Tufts, St. Lawrence, Lombard (now linked to the University of Chicago), Goddard, California Institute of Technology, Akron, Dean Junior College, and Westbrook Junior College. At the time of the merger, there were 68,949 members in 334 churches.

In the new Unitarian Universalist Association, neither body seems to have lost any of its original ideology, theology, or purpose. Except for matters of organization and government, the churches involved will continue as they have through the years; no minister, member, or congregation "shall be required to subscribe to any particular interpretation of religion, or to any particular religious belief or creed." The aims of the association were set forth in 1985 in a revised statement.

The Principles and Purposes of the member congregations of the Unitarian Universalist Association covenant to affirm and promote:

(a) The inherent worth and dignity of every person;
(b) Justice, equity, and compassion in human relationships;
(c) Acceptance of one another and encouragement to spiritual growth in our congregations;
(d) A free and responsible search for truth and meaning;
(e) The right of conscience and the use of the democratic process within our congregations and in society at large;
(f) The goal of world community with peace, liberty, and justice for all;
(g) Respect for the interdependent web of all existence of which we are a part.

In recent years the Association has been heavily involved in numerous causes and concerns: the issue of racial and cultural diversity in what have been historically white congregations; the rise of feminist consciousness; scholarship in church history and process theology; inner-city ministries; and the rights of gay, lesbian, and bisexual persons.

A general assembly, with clergy and lay representatives, is the overall policy-making body, meeting annually. The elected officers of the Association—moderator, president, two vice-moderators, secretary, and treasurer—all elected for four-year terms, together with 24 other elected members, constitute a Board of Trustees, which appoints the executive and administrative officers and generally carries out policies and directives. Members of this board have the usual powers of corporate directors as provided by law; they meet four times a year, between regular meetings of the general assembly.

A series of committees is appointed to facilitate and coordinate the Association's work. Under the general assembly, there are a nominating committee, program and business committees, and a commission on appraisal; under the Board of Trustees, an executive committee, ministerial fellowship committee, finance committee, and investment committee.

Among the most notable and successful achievements of the Association are its publishing house, Beacon Press, which produces fifty new titles each year and is one of the most distinguished independent publishing houses in the U.S.; a periodical, *The World,* circulated six times a year to more than 110,000 member families; the Unitarian Universalist Service Committee, which provides leadership and materials in the field of social change; and a religious education curriculum that ranks as one of the best in the U.S.

Continental headquarters are in Boston; 23 district offices have been established in regional or geographical areas; there were

204,000 adherents in 1,020 congregations in 1993. Principal strength lies in the Northeast, the Midwest, and the Pacific West Coast.

UNITED CHURCH OF CHRIST

Four churches of real importance in American history constitute the United Church of Christ: the Congregational Churches, the Christian Church, the Evangelical Synod, and the Reformed Church. The first two bodies merged in 1931 to become Congregational Christian Churches; they were joined in 1957 by the merged Evangelical and Reformed churches. The union was complete when the constitution was adopted at Philadelphia in July 1961. So important are the backgrounds of these denominations, each of which has a long life of its own, that attention is given to them following a description of the current body.

On July 8, 1959, at Oberlin, Ohio, representatives of the Congregational Christian Churches and the Evangelical and Reformed Church, upon merging into the United Church of Christ, adopted this statement, understood as a "testimony rather than a test of faith":

We believe in God, the Eternal Spirit, Father of our Lord Jesus Christ and our Father, and to his deeds we testify:

He calls the worlds into being, creates man in his own image and sets before him the ways of life and death.

He seeks in holy love to save all people from aimlessness and sin.

He judges men and nations by his righteous will declared through prophets and apostles.

In Jesus Christ, the man of Nazareth, our crucified and risen Lord, he has come to us and shared our common lot, conquering sin and death and reconciling the world to himself.

He bestows upon us his Holy Spirit, creating and renewing the Church of Jesus Christ, binding in covenant faithful people of all ages, tongues, and races.

He calls us into his Church to accept the cost and joy of discipleship, to be his servants in the service of men, to proclaim the gospel to all the world and resist the powers of evil, to share in Christ's baptism and eat at his table, to join him in his passion and victory.

He promises to all who trust him forgiveness of sins and fullness of grace, courage in the struggle for justice and peace, his presence in trial and rejoicing, and eternal life in his kingdom which has no end.

Blessing and honor, glory and power be unto him. Amen.

This statement is not intended to set forth doctrinal positions (the doctrines and theological positions of the four churches now within the United Church of Christ remain as they were), or to stand as a substitute for the historic creeds, confessions, and covenants of the churches involved. It is not binding upon any local church in the denomination. But it does stand as a tribute to the faith, charity, and understanding of the merging groups.

Equally impressive is the understanding and cooperation evident in the governmental provisions of the constitution. The United Church of Christ represents a union of congregationalism and presbyterianism—"It establishes congregationalism as the rule for the local congregation and presbyterianism as the basis for organization of the connectional life of the churches" (Harold E. Fey). The constitution is explicit: "The autonomy of the local church is inherent and modifiable only by its own action. Nothing . . . shall destroy or limit the right of each local church to continue to operate *in the way customary to it.*"

Beside the local church stand associations, conferences, and the general synod. Local churches in a geographical area are grouped into an association, which is concerned with the welfare of the churches within its area: It assists needy churches; receives new churches into the United Church of Christ; licenses, ordains, and installs ministers; adopts its own constitution, bylaws, and rules of procedure; and is made up of the ordained ministers and elected lay delegates of the area. Associations meet regularly and are related to the general synod through their conferences.

Associations are grouped into conferences, again by geographical area, with the exception of the Calvin Synod, a nongeographic, acting conference (made up of churches from the Hungarian Reformed tradition). The voting members of a conference are ordained ministers of associations in the conference and lay delegates elected from local churches. A conference acts on requests and references from the local churches, associations, general synod, and other bodies. It meets annually, and its main function is to coordinate the work and witness of its local churches and associations, to render counsel and advisory service, and to establish conference offices, centers, institutions, and other agencies.

The General Synod is the highest representative body; it meets biennially and is composed of 675 to 725 delegates chosen by the conferences, together with ex-officio delegates—the elected officers of the church, members of the Executive Council, the moderator, and assistant moderators. The conference delegates are clergy and laity, in equal numbers; there are also associate delegates, with voice but with no vote. The General Synod nominates and elects the officers of the church (president, secretary, director of finance/treasurer) for four-year terms and a moderator and two assistant moderators to preside over the next session of the General Synod for one year only. (The duties are quite similar to those of a moderator among Presbyterians.)

The major boards, commissions, councils, offices, and "other instrumentalities" of the church are established by the General Synod. They include the United Church Board for World Ministries, which works cooperatively with the Division of Overseas Ministries of the Christian Church (Disciples of Christ), made up of 225 ministers and laypeople; the United Church Board for Homeland Ministries, also with 225 ministers and laypeople; the Office for Church in Society; the Office for ministers and laypeople; the Office for Church Life and Leadership; the Commission for Racial Justice; the Stewardship Council, which is responsible for program development, information, promotion, and audiovisual resources; and the Coordinating Center for Women in Church and Society. Pension and relief activities are administered by a nonprofit corporation, which reports annually to the General Synod. Two committees—nominating and credentials—also are appointed by the General Synod, which is authorized to appoint any necessary committees.

An Executive Council of 44 voting members and 10 ex-officio members (ministers and laypeople) is elected by the General Synod to act for the Synod between its meetings. It recommends salaries for officers of the church as part of a national budget, has responsibility for the church's publications, prepares the agenda for all meetings of the General Synod, and appoints committees not otherwise provided; it also submits to the General Synod "any recommendation it may deem useful" for the work of the church.

The United Church of Christ has old and deep roots in both the congregational tradition of English Protestantism and its German sources. That movement in England and colonial America enjoyed clear identity until the American Revolution, but lost membership to the Unitarian exodus, and its relative standing among denominations fell as frontier conditions began to give shape to Americanized religious patterns. The Evangelical and Reformed tradition brought to the United Church of Christ varieties of German confessional Protestantism and a sizable membership with a progressive outlook. The Congregational Christian Churches contributed an indigenously American, even a frontier and Southern form, to the stream. While some local congregations in both bodies declined to enter the merger, there are today 1,555,382 members in 6,264 churches in the United Church of Christ.

The national church holds membership in the National Council of Churches of Christ in the U.S.A., in the World Council of Churches, and in the World Alliance of Reformed Churches. Since 1985, the

United Church of Christ has enjoyed an ecumenical partnership with the Christian Church (Disciples of Christ). Both denominations are active in the Consultation on Church Union. Long ecumenical despite American Congregationalism's early career as an established church, the United Church of Christ remains a leader in cooperative Christianity, especially through its ministries in education, social action, and service. The words of John Robinson as he bade the Pilgrims Godspeed in 1619 endure as a keynote to this denomination's life: "God hath yet more truth and light to break forth from His Holy Word."

Congregational Church

Congregationalism has been an issue in Christianity from the beginning; it began, as has been suggested, "without a name and with no sense of its destiny." Even before the Reformation, dissenting groups of church people in England were "seeking a better way" than that of the established church. As the Reformation developed, dissent took corporate form in the Puritan movement, of which Congregationalism was the most radical wing.

It was generally believed that Congregationalism arose from separationism, a movement that began in the days of Queen Elizabeth I and held that to attempt to reform the Church of England from within was hopeless; the only course for a true Christian was to separate completely from the Church of England. Recent historians, however, believe that although Robert Browne and other separatists developed ideas identical with those of early Congregationalists, the two groups were wholly distinct: Members of the former were perfectionists and refused to cooperate with other branches of the church; those of the latter group were as cooperative as possible without giving up their principles.

John Robinson, one of the most influential early Congregational leaders, first entered church history as a separatist. In 1609 he fled persecution in England and settled at Leiden in the Netherlands, with the exiled congregation from Scrooby in Nottinghamshire. There he met William Ames, Congregationalism's first great theologian, and Henry Jacob, its first great pamphleteer and organizer, who also were fugitives from the ecclesiastical courts of Britain. And they converted Robinson from rigid separatism to congregationalism.

For twelve years Robinson and his congregation enjoyed peace and freedom under the Dutch. But haunted by the conviction that their children would not grow up as English people, a large part of the company sailed for America in 1620 aboard the historic *Mayflower*. In a hostile new world, with the wilderness before them and the sea at their backs, they helped lay the foundations of the American commonwealth; the democratic ideals of their Plymouth colony, worked out slowly and painfully, were the cornerstone of the structure that gave the U.S. its free state, free schools, and free social and political life.

Other Congregational churches were established at Barnstable, Salem, and elsewhere along the Massachusetts coast. Between 1630 and 1640, 20,000 Puritans arrived at Massachusetts Bay, and it was inevitable that the "Bay People" who came directly from England and the "Plymouth People" from the Netherlands should join forces to establish an all-powerful theocratic government.

Church and commonwealth were that theocracy's two instruments. It was a stern and, at times, intolerant regime. Suffrage was limited to church members; Anne Hutchinson and Roger Williams were banished; Baptists were hauled into court; four Quakers were hanged on Boston Common. It was a dark but comparatively short period that ended with the Act of Toleration in 1689.

In 1636 Thomas Hooker led a company of 100 to what is now Hartford, Connecticut; the freeman's constitution drawn up by Hooker and his associates became the model for the American Constitution. Objecting to the rigidity of current church worship, Congregationalists such as Jonathan Edwards of Northampton played leading roles in the Great Awakening, which began in 1734; that revival was marked not only by the eloquence of George Whitefield but also by the vigorous writings and preaching of Edwards, whose books are now regarded as American classics.

Emerging stronger than ever from the Revolution, in which it played a great part, during the next century Congregationalism was concerned with five significant developments: higher education, missions, the Unitarian separation, the formation of a national council, and the production of a uniform statement of belief. In the field of education, this church had already made tremendous contributions: It founded Harvard in 1636; Yale (1707) was a project for the education of its clergy; Dartmouth (1769) developed from Eleazer Wheelock's school for Native Americans. These, with Williams, Amherst, Bowdoin, and Middlebury, were among the first colleges in New England. By 1953, 48 colleges and ten theological seminaries with Congregational Christian origin or connection had been established in the U.S.

Interest in missions among Congregationalists began the day the Pilgrims landed at Plymouth. The Mayhews, David Brainerd, and John Eliot were soon at work among Native Americans. Eliot spent seven years mastering their language and translated the Bible and published a catechism in 1653, the first book to be printed in their language. By 1674 there were 4,000 "praying Indians" in New England, with 24 native preachers.

When the wagon trains went West, the families of Congregational ministers and missionaries were prominent. Manasseh Cutler, a preacher from Hamilton, Massachusetts, was instrumental in framing the famous Northwest Territory Ordinance of 1787; other ministers led the founding of Marietta, Ohio, the first permanent settlement in the Northwest Territory.

The American Board of Commissioners for Foreign Missions, organized in 1810, was concerned at first with both home and foreign missionary work. On it served not only Congregationalists but also representatives of Presbyterian, Dutch Reformed, and Associate Reformed churches. The young men who had participated in the famous "haystack" meeting at Williams College were the first to be ordained. Missionaries were sent to more than 30 foreign countries and American territories, including Hawaii, where within 25 years Congregational missionaries taught a whole nation of people to read and write and laid the foundations of a constitutionally democratic government.

The rise of denominationalism worked against the complexion of the American Board, and by mid-century all non-Congregationalists had withdrawn to go their separate ways. The Board was no longer interdenominational.

Moving westward, Congregational missionaries from New England came into contact with Presbyterians from the middle and Southern states. To avoid competition and duplication of effort, a plan was developed under which ministers and members from both churches were exchanged and accepted on an equal basis. Adopted in 1801, the plan eventually worked to the advantage of Presbyterians; it was discontinued in 1852, leaving Presbyterians stronger in the West, though Congregationalists had a virtual monopoly in New England.

But the plan did much to inspire new Congregational missionary work. In 1826 the American Home Missionary Society was founded, and in 1846 the American Missionary Association, which was active in the South before the Civil War, was started. It was especially effective toward the end of that conflict, with its "contraband" schools for black persons, one of which became Hampton Institute.

Meanwhile, differences of opinion between theological liberals and conservatives were developing within the church. Strict Calvinists and Trinitarians were opposed by Unitarians, and a famous sermon by William Ellery Channing at Baltimore in 1819 made a division inevitable. The American Unitarian Association was established in 1825, and almost all of the older Congregational churches in eastern Massachusetts went Unitarian; only one Congregational church was left in Boston. Debate and legal action over property and funds were not concluded until about 1840.

In spite of Unitarian defection, Congregationalism continued to grow until a national supervisory body became necessary. A council held at Boston in 1865 was so effective that a regular system of councils was established. Following conferences between the associations into which the churches had grouped themselves, the first of these national councils was called at Oberlin, Ohio, in 1871. Known as the General Council of the Congregational Christian Churches, it met biennially and acted as an overall advisory body for the entire fellowship.

The council of 1913 at Kansas City, Missouri, adopted a declaration on faith, polity, and wider fellowship that has been accepted by many churches as a statement of faith. While it did not in any way modify the independence of local churches, it did give a new spiritual unity to the church.

The "wider fellowship" was taken seriously; unity and cooperation across denominational lines have been outstanding characteristics of Congregationalism. Christian Endeavor, the largest young people's organization in Protestantism, was founded in 1881 by a Congregationalist, Francis E. Clark; by 1885 it had become interdenominational, known all over the world as the United Society of Christian Endeavor.

In 1924 the Evangelical Protestant Church of North America joined the National Council of Congregational Churches in the Evangelical Protestant Conference of Congregational Churches; the comparative closeness of the two mergers—with the Christian Churches and the Evangelical and Reformed Church—again witnesses to the widening fellowship and vision of Congregationalists. Into the most recent merger they brought 47 church-related (not church-*controlled*) colleges; 11 theological seminaries; foreign mission stations in Africa, Mexico, Japan, the Philippines, India, Ceylon, Greece, Lebanon, Syria, Turkey, Korea, and Micronesia; and home missionaries in every state in the U.S. along with Puerto Rico.

Christian Churches

The Christian Churches, like the Congregational, were born in protest against ecclesiasticism and the denial of individual freedom. Actually, there were three revolts.

The first was in 1792, when James O'Kelly, a Methodist minister in Virginia, withdrew from that church in protest when the superintendency developed into an episcopacy; he especially objected to the power of bishops to appoint ministers to their charges. O'Kelly and his followers organized under the name Republican Methodist, later changed to Christian; the new church insisted that the Bible be taken as the only rule and discipline and that Christian character be made the only requirement for church membership.

Abner Jones, convinced that "sectarian names and human creeds should be abandoned," left the Vermont Baptists in 1801 to organize First Christian Church at Lyndon, Vermont. This was done from a desire to secure a wider freedom of religious thought and fellowship. Like O'Kelly, Jones insisted that piety and character be the sole test of Christian fellowship.

In the Great Awakening that swept Tennessee and Kentucky in 1801, a great deal of preaching either ignored the old emphasis on doctrines of various denominations or directly contradicted them. Barton W. Stone, accused of anti-Presbyterian preaching, led a number of Presbyterians out of the Synod of Kentucky to organize a Springfield presbytery, which was discontinued as its members gradually came to accept the ideology of James O'Kelly and Abner Jones and adopted the name *Christian*. Stone, an ardent revivalist, was deeply influenced by the preaching of Alexander Campbell and led many of his followers and churches into the Disciples of Christ. But the majority of his Christian Churches remained with the original Christian body.

The groups under O'Kelly, Jones, and Stone engaged in a long series of conferences that resulted in agreement on six basic Christian principles:

1. Christ, the only head of the Church.
2. The Bible, sufficient rule of faith and practice.
3. Christian character, the measure of membership.
4. A right, individual interpretation of the Scripture, as a way of life.
5. "Christian," the name taken as worthy of the followers of Christ.
6. Unity, Christians working together to save the world.

No council or other body in the Christian Church has ever drawn up any other creed or statement. Its interpretation of Bible teaching might be called evangelical, but no sincere follower of Christ is barred from membership because of difference in theological belief. Open Communion is practiced. Baptism is considered a duty but is not required; immersion is still generally used in churches from this tradition, but any mode may be employed.

The union of the Congregational and Christian churches was thoroughly democratic, leaving each group free to continue its own forms of worship and its own polity and doctrine. Adhering strictly to the congregational idea, each local church was at liberty to call itself either Congregational or Christian, and the same choice was found in the self-governing district and state associations into which the churches were organized.

Evangelical Church

The Evangelical Synod originated when six ministers of Lutheran and Reformed churches in the Evangelical United Church of Prussia met at Gravois Settlement near St. Louis in 1840 to form the Evangelical Union of the West. Two ministers had been sent by the Rhenish Missionary Society and two by the Missionary Society of Basel; the others were independent, one coming from Bremen, the other from Strasbourg.

The Evangelical Union of the West was a cooperative ministerial association until 1849, when the first permanent organization was established. As the movement spread east and northwest among German-speaking Lutheran and Reformed peoples, headquarters was established at St. Louis, and a new name, German Evangelical Synod of North America, adopted. A series of amalgamations with four other bodies—German, Evangelical Church Association of Ohio, German United Evangelical Synod of the East, Evangelical Synod of the Northwest, and United Evangelical Synod of the East— resulted in the formation of the Evangelical Synod of North America, giving it a membership of 281,598 at the time of the merger with the Reformed Church in the U.S.

Reformed Church in the U.S., The

The Reformed Church in the U.S. originated in the flood tide of German immigrants to Pennsylvania in the eighteenth century. More than half the Germans there in 1730 were Reformed; the congregations were widely separated along the frontier and, lacking ministers, often employed schoolteachers to lead the services. Three pastors— Johann Philip Boehm, George Michael Weiss, and Johann Bartholomaeus Rieger—were deeply influenced by Michael Schlatter, who had been sent to America by the (Dutch Reformed) Synod of South and North Holland. In 1747, they organized with him a coetus (synod) in Philadelphia, directly responsible to, and in part financially supported by, the synod in Holland. It declared its independence in 1793, taking the name German Reformed Church; in that year it reported 178 congregations and 15,000 communicants. The word *German* was dropped from the name in 1869, and thereafter the denomination was called the Reformed Church in the United States.

Reformed church missionaries went across the Alleghenies into Ohio and south into North Carolina. In 1819 an overall synod divided the country into eight districts, or classes, and an independent Ohio classis was formed in 1824. Franklin College (now Franklin and Marshall) was founded at Lancaster, Pennsylvania, with the support of Benjamin Franklin; a theological seminary was opened at Carlisle and later moved to Lancaster; an academy that later became Marshall College was established in 1836. The Synod of Ohio established a theological school and Heidelberg University at Tiffin, Ohio, in 1850. In 1836 the mother synod in the East and the Ohio synod were united into a general synod, which functioned until the merger with the Evangelical Synod of North America in 1934.

Difficulties arose in the early years of the nineteenth century. Older Germans preferred the use of the German language; second-generation members demanded English. And inevitably in a church of such mixed membership, there was conflict between conservatives and liberals. Some churches withdrew to form a separate synod, but returned in 1837 when wiser heads prevailed and compromises were made. District synods of both German-speaking and English-speaking congregations were created, and two Hungarian classes from the Old Hungarian Reformed Church were added in 1924.

By 1934 the boards of the church were directing widespread home missions and foreign missionary work in Japan, China, and Mesopotamia. There were 12 institutions of higher learning, three theological seminaries, and three orphanages. The 348,189 members were largely concentrated in Pennsylvania and Ohio.

The Evangelical and Reformed Church was the product of a union established at Cleveland, Ohio, on June 26, 1934, by two bodies with basic agreements in doctrine, polity, and culture—Evangelical Synod of North America and Reformed Church in the United States.

Few difficulties were encountered in reconciling the doctrines of the two bodies when the union was finally accomplished. Both churches were German Calvinistic. The Reformed Church had been based historically on the Heidelberg Catechism; the Evangelical Synod, on the Heidelberg Catechism, the Augsburg Confession, and Luther's Catechism. These three standards of faith were woven into one in the new constitution of the Evangelical and Reformed Church: "The Holy Scriptures of the Old and New Testaments are recognized as the Word of God and the ultimate rule of Christian faith and practice."

The doctrinal standards of the Evangelical and Reformed Church are the Heidelberg Catechism, Luther's Catechism, and the Augsburg Confession. They are accepted as an authoritative interpretation of the essential truth taught in the Holy Scriptures.

Wherever these doctrinal standards differ, ministers, members, and congregations, in accordance with the liberty of conscience inherent in the Gospel, are allowed to adhere to the interpretation of one of these confessions. However, in each case the final norm is the Word of God.

Two sacraments—baptism, usually administered to infants, and the Lord's Supper—are accepted. Confirmation, generally before the thirteenth or fourteenth year; ordination; consecration; marriage; and liturgical burial are considered rites. Although hymns and forms of worship were provided for general use, a wide freedom of worship is practiced. Most congregations make regular use of the Apostles' and Nicene Creeds.

Church polity, when this church joined the Congregational Christian Churches in 1957, was modified presbyterian; each local church was governed by a consistory, or church council, elected from its own membership. Local churches formed 34 synods, each made up of a pastor and a lay delegate from each charge. The synod met twice a year and had jurisdiction over all ministers and congregations; examined, licensed, and ordained all pastors; and elected its own officers—a procedure quite different from that of the Congregational Christian Churches.

The Evangelical and Reformed Church was a thriving church when the details of union were being worked out. In 1959 there were 810,000 members in 2,740 churches, eight colleges, three theological schools, and two academies; foreign missionaries in India, Japan, Hong Kong, Iraq, Africa, and Honduras; and a widespread home missionary work among the people of the Ozarks, Native Americans, Volga Germans, Hungarians, and the Japanese.

UNITED HOLY CHURCH OF AMERICA, INC.

A pentecostal church organized at Method, North Carolina, in a meeting held by Isaac Cheshier in 1886, this body was successively called Holy Church of North Carolina, Holy Church of North Carolina and Virginia, and finally, in 1918, United Holy Church of America, Inc. Its purpose is to establish and maintain holy convocations, assemblies, conventions, conferences, public worship, missionary and school work, orphanages, manual and trade training, and religious resorts, both permanent and temporary.

Articles of faith contain statements of belief in the Trinity, the record of the revelation of God in the Bible, redemption through Christ, justification with instantaneous sanctification, baptism of the Holy Spirit, divine healing, and the ultimate reign of Christ over the earth. Baptism by immersion, the Lord's Supper, and foot washing are observed as ordinances.

This fellowship believes in tongues speaking and views Spirit baptism as normative, although it shares the position held by many Pentecostal groups that speaking in tongues is not required for full membership, full discipleship, or spirit baptism.

The chief officer is the president; the board of bishops supervises the general work of the church. There were 50,000 members in 470 churches in 1970.

UNITY SCHOOL OF CHRISTIANITY

In 1886, Charles Fillmore, bankrupt and crippled, and his wife, Myrtle, seriously ill with tuberculosis, discovered a way of life based on affirmative prayer. This approach is offered today in the Unity School of Christianity as a curative in many areas beyond physical healing. Unity Schools is not a church or a denomination, but a nonsectarian religious educational institution devoted to demonstrating that following the teaching of Jesus Christ is a practical, seven-day-a-week way of life. "The true church is a state of consciousness in man."

The Fillmores held that "whatever man wants he can have by voicing his desire in the right way into the Universal Mind." They studied Christian Science, the Bible, Transcendentalism, New Thought, Quakerism, Theosophy, Rosicrucianism, Spiritism, and Hinduism; out of their studies came an ideology built on ancient truth and concepts, but moving in a new direction.

Unity teaches that God is "Principle, Law, Being, Mind, Spirit, All Good, omnipotent, omniscient, unchangeable, Creator, Father, Cause and Source of all that is." The "meeting ground of man and God" is Mind. According to Unity, the Trinity is most commonly described as mind, idea, and expression. "The Father is Principle, the Son is the Principle revealed in creative plan. The Holy Spirit is the executive power of both Father and Son carrying out the creative plan." Jesus Christ is "Spiritual man . . . the direct offspring of Divine Mind, God's idea of perfect man." Human beings are children of God, with potential for Christ consciousness. It is through Christ, or the Christ consciousness, that the human gains eternal life and salvation. Salvation means the attainment of true spiritual consciousness, becoming like Christ. This transformation takes place not in any hereafter, but "here in this earth" through a process of unfolding and regeneration. A person suffers no final death, but changes into increasingly better states until finally becoming like Christ. Members of Unity believe that all people will have this experience.

Unity has been described as "a religious philosophy with an 'open end,' seeking to find God's truth in all of life, wherever it may be." It has no strict creed or dogma; it finds good in all religions and teaches that we should keep our minds open to receive that goodness. Unity teaches that reality is ultimately spiritual and that realization of spiritual truth will illumine, heal, and prosper us. Cultivation of health-conducive emotions such as love, confidence, and joy is encouraged. Overcoming health-inhibiting emotions such as anger, hatred, and despair is also encouraged. It has no rules concerning health but concentrates on spiritual goals, knowing that healthful living habits will follow. Some Unity students are vegetarians in the interest of health; many are not.

Prayer and meditation are suggested for every human want and illness. The Unity way of prayer and meditation involves relaxation and affirmation of spiritual truth to develop the consciousness of the individual and silent receptivity to Divine Mind for whatever the seeker needs. The Bible is used constantly and is highly valued, but is not considered the sole or final authority in faith and practice; people must be in direct, personal communion with God, not dependent upon such secondary sources as the Scriptures.

The Association of Unity Churches, an independent but related organization of ministers and licensed teachers, evolved out of the work of the founding generations. The Association ordains ministers, provides educational and administrative support, and is self-supporting through its more than 600 member churches. Unity School trains the ministers in a two-year program. It also educates teachers and offers retreat programs.

Unity School's central work is done through what is called Silent Unity. A large staff in Unity Village, near Kansas City, Missouri, is available to pray with people day and night; workers answer telephone calls and letters—an average of one million calls and nearly two million letters annually. This service of prayer and affirmation offers help on every conceivable problem; each case or call is assigned to a member of the staff, who suggests the proper affirmations. The whole staff joins in group prayer and meditation several times a day. All calls and requests are answered; there is no charge for this service, but love offerings are accepted. Most calls come from members of various Christian churches; correspondents are never asked to leave the churches to which they belong.

Some 75 million copies of booklets, brochures, and magazines are published annually and used by many who never contact headquarters or become members of a Unity church. About 20 new audio cassettes and several video cassettes are produced annually.

VOLUNTEERS OF AMERICA, INC.

Volunteers of America (VOA) is a Christian church and social-welfare organization founded and incorporated in New York in 1896 by Ballington Booth and Maud Booth. Its mission is to reach and uplift all people, bringing them to the immediate knowledge and active service of God.

Today VOA is one of the nation's largest multipurpose human-care agencies, offering more than 400 programs in 200 communities across the U.S. Its programs are geared to assisting persons in need, such as the elderly, youth, substance abusers, offenders and ex-offenders, and homeless persons.

Volunteers of America is governed by both a religious body, the Grand Field Council, and a corporate body, the National Board of Directors. The Council is made up of all VOA ministers and represents the membership of the organization. The Council is responsible for framing the articles of incorporation, constitution, bylaws, and regulations and for electing its president. The National Board of Directors consists of 31 members and is responsible for the direction and effective functioning of the organization.

The chief officer of Volunteers of America, Inc., elected for a five-year term, is president of the corporation as well as head of the church. The president appoints vice presidents and directors to the national staff. The national office, in Metairie, Louisiana, provides technical and administrative support to local VOA service units.

WESLEYAN CHURCH, THE

Until 1968 this body was called Wesleyan Methodist Church of America. At the time of its founding in 1843, it represented a protest against slavery and the Methodist episcopacy, predating by one year the historic division of the Methodist Episcopal Church and Methodist Episcopal Church, South. With the slavery issue settled by the Civil War, other differences—entire sanctification and the issue of the liquor traffic—seemed important enough to continue its separate existence.

In June 1968, the Wesleyan Methodist Church merged with the Pilgrim Holiness Church to become the Wesleyan Church. The

Pilgrim Holiness Church, founded in 1897, was close in doctrine and polity to the Church of the Nazarene and thus close to Methodism and in agreement with Wesleyan doctrines; there was no change in doctrinal emphases when the two churches joined.

The time-honored teaching of entire sanctification is still central. Candidates for church membership are required to disavow the use, sale, or manufacture of tobacco and alcoholic beverages and to refrain from membership in secret societies.

From a total constituency of 313,000, there are 119,406 members in 1,684 churches in the North American General Conference, with areas of greatest strength in Indiana, Michigan, Ohio, and North Carolina. An enlarging evangelistic and missionary activity is directed from Indiana. In 1988, missionaries from 28 districts were at work in many countries of Asia, Africa, the Caribbean, Latin America, and, most recently, in Europe. Four liberal arts colleges, one Bible college, and a seminary foundation are supported.

WORLDWIDE CHURCH OF GOD

The Worldwide Church of God (formerly the Radio Church of God) began its work in 1933 under the leadership of Herbert W. Armstrong. After Armstrong's death in 1986, Joseph W. Tkach became Pastor General.

The mission statement of the church is to proclaim the gospel of Jesus Christ around the world and to help members grow spiritually. Unaffiliated with other religious bodies, it describes itself as nonpolitical.

Its Statement of Beliefs affirms belief in one God, who is the Father, the Son, and the Holy Spirit. Concerning human nature, the inspiration of the Scriptures, Christ's bodily resurrection, and baptism, the church holds traditional positions, and it takes a strong stand against bearing arms and the taking of human life. It rejects the concept of everlasting conscious torment in hell for the unsaved.

The Lord's Supper, or Passover of Jesus Christ, is observed annually as a memorial of the death of Jesus. The sabbath (Friday sunset to Saturday sunset) is observed as a day of worship. Seven annual holy days are observed, and certain "unclean" meats are avoided.

A worldwide ministry, with churches in 124 countries and territories, is carried out from the headquarters in Pasadena, California. The church supports Ambassador College in Big Sandy, Texas, a four-year liberal arts college that stresses Christian values. Church membership is 99,000 with 67,000 in the United States.

Since 1934, the church has published *The Plain Truth*, a magazine now read by more than 5 million people each month. The syndicated television and radio program, "The World Tomorrow," airs on 148 television and radio stations around the world.

APPENDIX A:

Fourteen Kinds of Evangelicalism in America

Subcultural Evangelical Group	Major Emphasis	Symbols
1. Fundamentalist	Personal and ecclesiastical separationism; biblicism	Bob Jones University; American Council of Christian Churches; *Sword of the Lord*
2. Dispensational	Dispensational hermeneutics; pretribulaytionalism and premillenarianism	Dallas Theological Seminary; Moody Bible Institute: *Moody Monthly*; Moody Press
3. Conservative	Cooperative evangelism; inclusive of all evangelical groups; broad theological base	Wheaton College; Trinity Seminary; Gordon-Conwell Seminary; *Christianity Today;* Billy Graham; The Zondervan Corp.; National Association of Evangelicals
4. Nondenominational	Unity of the Church; restoration of NT Christianity	Milligan College
5. Reformed	Calvinism (some with a decidedly Puritan flavor); covenant theology and hermeneutics	Calvin College and Seminary; Westminster Seminary; Covenant Seminary; Reformed Seminary; Francis Schaeffer
6. Anabaptist	Discipleship; poverty; Peace movement; Pacifism	Goshen College; Reba Place Fellowship; John Howard Yoder
7. Wesleyan	Arminianism; sanctification	Asbury College and Seminary; Seattle Pacific College
8. Holiness	The second work of grace	Lee College; Nazarene Church
9. Pentecostal	Gift of tongues	Church of God; Assemblies of God

10.	Charismatic	Gifts of the Holy Spirit	Oral Roberts University; Melodyland School of Theology
11.	Black	Black consciousness	National Association of Black Evangelicals
12.	Progressive	Openness toward critical scholarship and ecumenical relations	Fuller Seminary
13.	Radical	Moral, social, and political consciousness	*Sojourners; The Other Side; Wittenburg Door*
14.	Mainline	Historic consciousness at least back to the Reformation	Movements in major denominations: Methodist, Lutheran, Presbyterian, Episcopal, Baptist

APPENDIX B:

Hunter's Four Traditions of Evangelicalism

1. Baptist tradition
   Southern Baptist Convention; American Baptist Churches of the USA
   Disciples of Christ
   (many) Churches of Christ
   Plymouth Brethren
   Independent Fundamentalist Churches of America
   Independent Fundamentalist Bible Churches
   Seventh Day Adventist
   World Wide Church of God
   Church of God International

2. Holiness-Pentecostal tradition
   (a) Holiness
       Churches of God in North America
       Church of God (Anderson, Ind.)
       Wesleyan Church
       Church of the Nazarene
       Church of Christ (Holiness) USA
   (b) Pentecostal
       Church of God (Cleveland, Tenn.)
       Church of God of Prophecy
       Full Gospel Church Association
       Assemblies of God

3. Reformed-Confessional tradition
   Christian Reformed Church
   Orthodox Presbyterian Church
   Presbyterian Church in America
   Lutheran Church—Missouri Synod
   Evangelical Lutheran Synod
   Association of Evangelical Lutheran Churches

4. Anabaptist tradition
   Mennonite Church
   General Conference Mennonite Church
   Brethren in Christ Church
   Evangelical Mennonite Church
   (churches of the) Evangelical Friends Alliance

APPENDIX C:

Pentecostal Bodies*

Holiness-Pentecostal Denominations
    Apostolic Faith
    Church of God
    Church of God (Cleveland, Tenn.)
    Church of God in Christ
    Church of God in Christ, International
    Church of God of Prophecy
    Church of God of the Mountain Assembly
    Congregational Holiness Church
    International Pentecostal Church of Christ
    (Original) Church of God
    Pentecostal Fire-Baptized Holiness Church
    Pentecostal Free Will Baptist Church, Inc.
    Pentecostal Holiness Church, International
    United Holy Church of America

Baptistic-Pentecostal Denominations
    Assemblies of God
    Bible Church of Christ, Inc.
    Christian Church of North America, General Council
    Elim Fellowship
    Full Gospel Assemblies, International
    Full Gospel Fellowship of Churches and Ministers, International
    Independent Assemblies of God, International
    International Church of the Foursquare Gospel
    Open Bible Standard Churches
    Pentecostal Church of God

Unitarian (Oneness) Pentecostal Denominations
    Apostolic Faith Mission Church of God
    Apostolic Overcoming Holy Church of God
    Bible Way Church of Our Lord Jesus Christ, World Wide, Inc.
    Church of Our Lord Jesus Christ of the Apostolic Faith
    United Pentecostal Church, International

*The above typology for Pentecostal Bodies was supplied to Constant H. Jacquet, Jr., late editor of the *Yearbook of American and Canadian Churches,* by Dr. H. Vinson Synan, Asst. Gen. Supr., International Pentecostal Holiness Church. According to Dr. Synan, "Holiness-Pentecostal" bodies are those that teach the three-stages theory of Christian experience (i.e., conversion, sanctification, baptism of the Holy Spirit). "Baptistic-Pentecostal" denominations are those that teach a two-stage theory (i.e., conversion and baptism of the Holy Spirit). "Unitarian-Pentecostal" bodies deny the traditional concept of the Trinity and teach that Jesus Christ alone is God.

APPENDIX D:

Headquarters of Denominations

Adventist
Seventh Day Adventist: 12501 Old Columbia Pike, Silver Spring, MD 20904.
Advent Christian Church: 14601 Albemarle Road, P.O. Box 23152, Charlotte, NC 28212
Church of God (General Conference): P.O. Box 100, Oregon, IL 61061
Amana Church Society: Box 103, Middle, IA 52307
American Ethical Union: 2 W. 64th St., New York, NY 10023
American Evangelical Christian Churches: 64 South St., Indianapolis, IN 46227
American Rescue Workers: 2827 Frankford Ave., P.O. Box 4766, Philadelphia, PA 19134
Anglican Orthodox Church: P.O. Box 128, Statesville, NC 28677
Apostolic Christian Church (Nazarene): P.O. Box 151, Tremont, IL 61568
Apostolic Christian Church of America: Dale R. Eisenmann, 6913 Wilmette Ave., Darien, IL 60559
Apostolic Faith Mission of Portland Oregon: 6615 S.E. 52nd Ave., Portland, OR 97206
Apostolic Overcoming Holy Church of God: 1120 N. 24th St., Birmingham, AL 35234
Baha'i: 536 Sheridan Road, Wilmette, IL 60091
Baptist
American Baptist Association, 4605 N. State Line Ave., P.O. Box 901, Texarkana, TX 75503
American Baptist Churches in the U.S.A., P.O. Box 851, Valley Forge, PA 19482
Baptist Bible Fellowship, International: P.O. Box 191, Springfield, MO 65801
Baptist General Conference: 2002 S. Arlington Heights Rd., Arlington Heights, IL 60005
Bethel Ministerial Association: 7055 S. Manker Dr., Indianapolis, IN 46227
Central Baptist Association: Larry Browder, Rt. 1, Timbertree Rd., Kingsport, TN 37660
Conservative Baptist Association of America: P.O. Box 66, Wheaton, IL 60187
Duck River (and Kindred) Associations of Baptists: Clerk, Marvin Davenport, 65 Davenport Road, Auburntown, TN 37016
Free Will Baptist: P.O. Box 5002, Antioch, TN 37011-5002
General Association of Regular Baptist Churches: 1300 N. Meacham Rd., Schaumburg, IL 60195
General Baptist: 100 Stinson Dr., Poplar Bluff, MO 63901
General Conference of the Evangelical Baptist Church, Inc.: 1601 E. Rose St., Goldsboro, NC 27530

Landmark Baptist: Dr. I. K. Cross, P.O. Box 848, Bellflower, CA 90706

National Baptist Convention of America: Pres., E. Edward Jones, 1450 Pierre Ave., Shreveport, LA 71103

National Baptist Convention U.S.A., Inc., Pres., Dr. T. J. Jemison, 915 Spain St., Baton Rouge, LA 70802

National Missionary Baptist Convention of America: 719 Crosby St., San Diego, CA 92113

National Primitive Baptist Convention of the U.S.A.: P.O. Box 2355, Tallahassee, FL 32301

North American Baptist Conference: 1 S. 210 Summit Ave., Oakbrook Terrace, IL 60181

Primitive Baptist: Elder W. H. Cayce, S. Second St., Thornton, AR 71766

Progressive National Baptist Convention, Inc.: 601 50th St., N.E., Washington, DC 20019

Reformed Baptist: J. Zens, P.O. Box 548, St. Croix Falls, WI 54024

Separate Baptists in Christ: Rev. Jim Goff, 1020 Gagel Ave., Louisville, KY 40216

Seventh Day Baptist General Conference: P.O. Box 1678, Janesville, WI 53547

Southern Baptist Convention: 901 Commerce St., Nashville, TN 37203

United Baptist: Omer E. Baker, 8640 Brazil Rd., Jacksonville, FL 32208

United Free Will Baptist: Kinston College, 1000 University St., Kinston, NC 18501

Berean Fundamental Church: P.O. Box 397, North Platte, NE 69101

Bible Fellowship Church: Pastor W. B. Hottel, 404 W. Main St., Terre Hill, PA 17581

Bible Protestant Church: Exec. Sec., Harold E. Haines, P.O. Box 43, Glassboro, NJ 08028

Bible Way Church, World Wide: 1130 New Jersey Ave., N.W., Washington, DC 20001

Brethren

Dunkers

  Brethren Church: 524 College Ave., Ashland, OH 44805

  Church of the Brethren: 1451 Dundee Ave., Elgin, IL 60120

  Fellowship of Grace Brethren Churches: Grace Theological Seminary, Winona Lake, In 46903

  Old German Baptist Brethren: Elder Clement Skiles, Rt. 1, Box 140, Bringhurst, IN 46903

River Brethren

  Brethren in Christ Church: General Sec., R. Donald Shafer, Brethren in Christ Church Offices, P.O. Box 290, Grantham, PA 17027

  United Zion Church: Sec., Rev. J. Paul Martin, Box 212D, Rt. 1, Anneville, PA 17003

United Brethren

  Church of the United Brethren in Christ: 302 Lake St., P.O. Box 650, Huntington, IN 46750

  United Christian Church: Elder Henry C. Heagy, R.D. 4, Lebanon Co., PA 17042

Buddhist Communities
    Buddhist Churches of America: 1710 Octavia St., San Francisco, CA 94109
Christadelphian: Norman D. Zilmer, 1000 Mohawk Dr., Elgin, IL 60120
Christian and Missionary Alliance: 350 N. Highland Ave., Nyack, NY 10960
Christian Catholic Church: Dowie Memorial Dr., Zion, IL 60099
Christian Church (Disciples of Christ): P.O. Box 1986, 222 S. Downey Ave., Indianapolis, IN 46219
Christian Church of North America: 1294 Rutledge Rd., Transfer, PA 16154
Christian Church and Churches of Christ: 4210 Bridgetown Rd., Cincinnati, OH 45211
Christian Congregation: Supt., Rev. Ora Wilbert Eads, 804 W. Hemlock St., La Follette, TN 37766
Christian Union: P.O. Box 27, Greenfield, OH 45123
Christ's Sanctified Holy Church: S. Cutting Ave. & E. Spencer St., Jennings, LA 70546
Church of Christ (Holiness) U.S.A.: 329 E. Monument St., Jackson, MS 39202
Church of Christ, Scientist: Christian Science Center, 175 Huntington Ave., Boston, MA 02115
Church of God
    Church of God (Anderson, Ind.): Box 2420, Anderson, IN 46011
    Church of God (Apostolic): St. Peter's Church of God, 11th & Hickory St., Winston-Salem, NC 27101
    Church of God, Inc., (Original): P.O. Box 3086, Chattanooga, TN 37404
    Church of God (Cleveland, Tenn.): P.O. Box 2430, Cleveland, TN 37320
    Church of God (Seventh Day, Denver, Colo.): P.O. Box 33677, Denver, CO 80233
    Church of God (7th Day, Salem, W. Va.): 70 Water St., Salem, WV 26426
    Church of God (New Testament Judaism): P.O. Box 1207, Jerusalem Acres, Cleveland, TN 37311
    Church of God (Huntsville, Ala.): 1207, #2, Willow Brook S.E., Huntsville, AL 35802
    Church of God and Saints of Christ: c/o Bishop James R. Grant, 10703 Wade Park Ave., Cleveland, OH 44106
    Church of God by Faith: 3220 Haines St., Jacksonville, FL 32206
    Church of God, Holiness: 170 Ashby St., N.W., Atlanta, GA 30314
    Church of God in Christ: 938 Mason St., Memphis, TN 38126
        Church of God in Christ (International): 1905 Columbia Ave., Philadelphia, PA 19121
        Church of God of Prophecy: Bible Place, Box 2910, Cleveland, TN 37320
Church of Illumination: Beverly Hall, Clymer Rd., Quakertown, PA 18951
Church of Jesus Christ: P.O. Box 1414, Cleveland, TN 37311
Church of Our Lord Jesus Christ of the Apostolic Faith, Inc., 2081 Adam Clayton Powell Blvd., New York, NY 10027

Church of the Living God

Church of the Living God (Christian Workers for Fellowship): 430 Forest Ave., Cincinnati, OH 45229

House of God, Which Is the Church of the Living God: Bishop A. H. White, 6107 Cobbs Creed Pkwy., Philadelphia, PA 19143

Church of the Nazarene: 6401 The Paseo, Kansas City, MO 64131

Churches of Christ: Ed., Furman Kearley, *Gospel Advocate*, P.O. Box 167, Monahans, TX 79756

Churches of Christ in Christian Union: 1426 Lancaster Pike, Box 30, Circleville, OH 43113

Churches of God, General Conference: P.O. Box 926, Findlay, OH 45839

Community Churches, International Council of: 11995 S. LaGrange Rd., Suite C, Mokena, IL 60448

Congregational Bible Churches, Inc., P.O. Box 265, Hutchinson, KS 67501

Congregational Christian Churches (National Association): P.O. Box 1620, Oak Creek, WI 53154

Congregational Holiness Church: 3888 Fayetteville Hwy., Griffin, GA 30223

Congregational Holiness Churches, Inc.: P.O. Box 573, Abilene, KS 67410

Conservative Congregational Christian Conference: 7582 Currell Blvd., Ste. 108, St. Paul, MN 55125

Divine Science: 1819 E. 14th Ave., Denver, CO 80218

Episcopal/Anglican

African Orthodox Church: c/o Rt. Rev. James A. Ford, 137 Alston St., Cambridge, MA 02139

Episcopal Church, The: 815 Second Ave., New York, NY 10017

Reformed Episcopal Church: 2001 Frederick Rd., Baltimore, MD 21228

Evangelical Church, The: Gen. Supt. John F. Sills, 3000 Market St., N.E., Ste. 528, Salem, OR 97301

Evangelical Congregational Church: P.O. Box 186, Myerstown, PA 17067

Evangelical Covenant Church: 5101 N. Francisco Ave., Chicago, IL 60625

Evangelical Free Church of America: 1515 E. 66th St., Minneapolis, MN 55423

Foursquare Gospel, International Church of the: 1910 W. Sunset Blvd., Ste. 200, Los Angeles, CA 90026

Friends (Quaker)

Friends General Conference: 1216 Arch St., Philadelphia, PA 19107

Friends United Meeting: Gen. Sec., Stephen Main, 101 Quaker Hill Dr., Richmond, IN 47374

Religious Society of Friends (Conservative): Ray Treadway, North Carolina Yearly Meeting, 710 E. Lake Dr., Greensboro, NC 27401

Grace Gospel Fellowship: 2125 Martindale S.W., Grand Rapids, MI 49509

Hindu Communities

Vedanta Society: 34 W. 71st St., New York, NY 10023

Independent Fundamental Churches of America: P.O. Box 810, Grandville, MI 49468

Jehovah's Witnesses: 25 Columbia Heights, Brooklyn, NY 11201

Judaism
    Agudath Israel of America (central address of "ultra-orthodox"): 5 Beekman St., New York, NY 10038
    American Jewish Committee: 165 E. 56th St., New York, NY 10022
    Federation of Reconstructionist Congregations and Hauvurot: Church Road and Greenwood Drive, Wyncote, PA 19095
    Lubavitcher: Lubavitcher World Headquarters, 7700 Eastern Parkway, Brooklyn, NY 11213
    Union of American Hebrew Congregations (Reform): 838 Fifth Ave., New York, NY 10021
    United Synagogues of America (Conservative): 155 Fifth Ave., New York, NY 10010

Latter-Day Saints
    Church of Christ (Temple Lot): Temple Lot, P.O. Box 472, Independence, MO 64051
    Church of Jesus Christ (Bickertonites): Sixth & Lincoln, Monongahela, PA 15063
    Church of Jesus Christ of Latter-day Saints (Strangite): Elder Vernon D. Swift, P.O. Box 552, Artesia, MN 88210
    Church of Jesus Christ of Latter-day Saints: 150 E. North Temple St., Salt Lake City, UT 84150
    Reorganized Church of Jesus Christ of Latter-day Saints: Box 1059, Independence, MO 64051

Lutheran
    Apostolic Lutheran Church of America: Sec., James Johnson, Rt. 1, Box 462, Houghton, MI 49931
    Church of the Lutheran Brethren of America: Box 655, Fergus Falls, MN 56537
    Church of the Lutheran Confession: 460 75th Ave., N.E., Minneapolis, MN 55432
    Evangelical Lutheran Church in America: 8765 W. Higgins Rd., Chicago, IL 60631
    Evangelical Lutheran Synod: Rev. Alf Mereseth, 106 S. 13th St., Northwood, IA 50459
    Free Lutheran Congregations: 3110 E. Medicine Lake Blvd., Minneapolis, MN 55441
    Lutheran Church, Missouri Synod: 1333 S. Kirkwood Rd., St. Louis, MO 63122
    Protestant Conference (Lutheran): Sec., Rev. Gerald Hinz, P.O. Box 86, Shiocton, WI 54170
    Wisconsin Evangelical Lutheran Synod: 2929 N. Mayfair Rd., Wauwatosa, WI 53222

Mennonite
    Beachy Amish Mennonite Churches: Ervin N. Hershberger, R.D. 1, Meyersdale, PA 15552
    Church of God in Christ, Mennonite: 420 Wedel St., P.O. Drawer 230, Moundridge, KS 67107

Conservative Mennonite Conference: Sec., David I. Miller, 9910 Rosedale-Milford Center Rd., Irwin, OH 43029

Evangelical Mennonite Church: 1420 Kerrway Ct., Fort Wayne, IN 46805

Fellowship of Evangelical Bible Churches: 5800 S. 14th St., Omaha, NE 68107

General Conference Mennonite Church: 722 Main St., Box 347, Newton, KS 67114

Hutterian Brethren: Rev. Paul S. Gross, Rt. 1, Box 6E, Reardon, WA 99029

Mennonite Brethren Churches, General Conference of: Exec. Sec., Marvin Hein, 4812 E. Butler Ave., Fresno, CA 93727

Mennonite Church: 528 E. Madison St., Lombard, IL 60148

Old Order Amish Church: Raber's Bookstore, Rt. 1, Baltic, OH 43804

Old Order (Wisler) Mennonite Church: Henry W. Riehl, Rt. 1, Columbiana, OH 44408

Reformed Mennonite Church: Glenn M. Gross, 906 Grantham Rd., Mechanicsburg, PA 17055

Unaffiliated Mennonite: Ed., *Mennonite Yearbook*, 616 Walnut, Scottdale, PA 15683

Methodist

African Methodist Episcopal Church: Sec., Rev. Cecil W. Howard, P.O. Box 183, St. Louis, MO 63166

African Methodist Episcopal Zion Church: Sec., Rev. Earle E. Johnson, P.O. Box 28232, Charlotte, NC 28232

Christian Methodist Episcopal Church: Sec., W. Clyde Williams, 201 Ashby St., N.W., Atlanta, GA 30314

Congregational Methodist Church: Sec., Rev. Frank Gilmore, P.O. Box 9, Florence, MS 39073

Evangelical Methodist Church: 3000 W. Kellogg Dr., Wichita, KS 67213

Free Methodist Church of North America: 770 N. High School Rd., Indianapolis, IN 46214

Fundamental Methodist Church, Inc.: 1034 N. Broadway, Springfield, MO 65801

Primitive Methodist Church, U.S.A.: Sec., Rev. William H. Fudge, 1045 Laurel Run Rd., Wilkes-Barre, PA 18702

Reformed Methodist Union Episcopal Church: Fred H. Moore, 115 St. Margaret St., Charleston, SC 29403

Southern Methodist Church: Pres., W. Lynn Corbett, P.O. Box 132, Orangeburg, SC 29115

Union American Methodist Episcopal Church: Rev. David M. Harmon, 774 Pine St., Camden, NJ 08123

United Methodist Church, The: Council on Ministries, 601 W. Riverview Ave., Dayton, OH 45406

Metropolitan Community Churches: 5300 Santa Monica Blvd., Ste., 304, Los Angeles, CA 90029

Missionary Church: 3901 S. Wayne Ave., Fort Wayne, IN 46807

Moravian

    Moravian Church in America *(Unitas Fratrum)*: P.O. Box 1245, Bethlehem, PA 18016

    Unity of the Brethren: Sec., Dorothy E. Kocian, 107 S. Barbara, Waco, TX 76705

Muslim

    The Islamic Center of Washington: 2551 Massachusetts Ave., N.W., Washington, DC 20008

New Apostolic Church of North America: 3753 N. Troy St., Chicago, IL 60618

Old Catholic

    Liberal Catholic Church: Rt. Rev. Lawrence J. Smith, 9740 S. Ayers Ave., Evergreen Park, IL 60642

    Mariavite Old Catholic Church: 2803 10th St., Wyandotte, MI 48192

    North American Old Roman Catholic Church: 4200 N. Kedvale Ave., Chicago, IL 60641

    Old Roman Catholic Church in Europe and America (English Rite): St. Mary Magdalene Church, 2820 N. Lincoln Ave., Chicago, IL 60657

    Polish National Catholic Church of America: 1002 Pittston Ave., Scranton, PA 18505

Open Bible Standard Churches, Inc.: 2020 Bell Ave., Des Moines, IA 50315

Orthodox (Eastern)

    Albanian Orthodox Archdiocese in America: 529 E. Broadway, South Boston, MA 02127

    American Carpatho-Russian Orthodox Greek Catholic Church: 312 Garfield St., Johnstown, PA 15906

    Antiochian Orthodox Catholic Archdiocese of North America: 358 Mountain Rd., Englewood, NJ 07631

    Bulgarian Eastern Orthodox Church: 550-A W. 50th St., New York, NY 10019

    Eastern Orthodox Catholic Church in America: 1914 Hwy 17-92, Fern Park, FL 32730

    Greek Orthodox Archdiocese of North and South America: 8-10 E. 79th St., New York, NY 10021

    Romanian Orthodox Episcopate of America: 2522 Grey Tower Rd., Jackson, MI 49201

    Russian Orthodox Church in the U.S.A.: St. Nicholas Patriarchal Cathedral, 15 E. 97th St., New York, NY 10029

    Russian Orthodox Church Outside Russia: 75 E. 93rd St., New York, NY 10028

    Serbian Eastern Orthodox Church in the U.S.A. and Canada: P.O. Box 519, Libertyville, IL 60048

    Syrian Orthodox Church of Antioch: 49 Kipp Ave., Lodi, NJ 07644

    Ukrainian Orthodox Churches: P.O. Box 495, S. Bound Brook, NJ 08880

Pentecostal

    Assemblies of God, General Council of: 1445 Boonville Ave., Springfield, MO 65802

APPENDIX D

Elim Fellowship: Carlton Spencer, 7245 Colby St., Lima, NY 14485
Independent Assemblies of God, International: 8504 Commerce Ave.,
San Diego, CA 92121
International Pentecostal Church of Christ: Box 439, London, OH 43140
Pentecostal Assemblies of the World, Inc.: 3939 Meadows Dr., Indianapolis, IN 46208
Pentecostal Church of God: 221 Main St., Joplin, MO 64801
Pentecostal Free-Will Baptist Church, Inc.: P.O. Box 1568, Dunn, NC
28334
Pentecostal Holiness Church, International: P.O. Box 12609, Oklahoma
City, OK 73157
United Pentecostal Church, International: 8844 Dunn Rd., Hazelwood,
MO 63042
Pillar of Fire: Zarephath, NJ 08890
Plymouth Brethren: P.O. Box 294, 218 W. Willow, Wheaton, IL 60187
Presbyterian
Associate Reformed Presbyterian Church: One Cleveland St., Greenville,
SC 29601
Bible Presbyterian Church: Haddon Ave. & Cuthbert Blvd., Collinswood,
NJ 08108
Cumberland Presbyterian Church: 1978 Union Ave., Memphis, TN 38104
Evangelical Presbyterian Church: 29140 Buckingham Ave., Ste. 5,
Livonia, MI 48154
Orthodox Presbyterian Church: 2345 Willow Brook Dr., Huntington
Valley, PA 19006
Presbyterian Church in America: 1852 Century Pl., Ste. 190, Atlanta,
GA 30345
Presbyterian Church (U.S.A.): 100 Witherspoon St., Louisville, KY 40202
Reformed Presbyterian Church of North America: Clerk, Louis D. Hutmire, 7418 Penn Ave., Pittsburgh, PA 15208
Second Cumberland Presbyterian Church in the United States: 226
Church St., Huntsville, AL 35801
Reformed
Christian Reformed Church: Clerk, Leonard J. Hoffman, 2850 Kalamazoo
Ave., S.E., Grand Rapids, MI 49560
Hungarian Reformed Church in America: Bishop Andrew Harsanyi, P.O.
Box D, Hopatcong, NY 07843
Netherlands Reformed Congregations: Pres. Dr. J. R. Beeke, 2115
Romence Dr., N.E., Grand Rapids, MI 49503
Protestant Reformed Church: 16511 S. Park Ave., South Holland, IL
60473
Reformed Church in America: 475 Riverside Dr., New York, NY 10027
Reformed Church in the United States: Clerk, Rev. Steven E. Work, 2350
Leigh Ave., San Jose, CA 95124
Roman Catholic Church: U.S. Catholic Conference, 1312 Massachusetts
Ave., N.W., Washington, DC 20005
The Salvation Army: 615 Slaters Lane, P.O. Box 269, Alexandria, VA 22313

Schwenkfelder Church: Pennsburg, PA 18073
Social Brethren: Rev. John Hancock, R.R. 3, Box 221, Harrisburg, IL 62946
Spiritualist
  National Spiritual Alliance of the U.S.A.: Sec., Beth Armstrong, 239
    Washington St., Keene, NH 03431
  National Spiritualist Association of Churches: Pres., Joseph H. Merrill,
    P.O. Box 128, Cassedega, FL 37206
Swedenborgian Church, General Convention of: 139 E. 23rd St., New York,
  NY 10010
Theosophy: Theosophical Publishing House, 306 W. Geneva Rd., Wheaton,
  IL 60189
Triumph the Church and Kingdom of God in Christ (International): Rt. Rev.
  Zephaniah Swindle, Rt. 1, Box 1927, Shelbyville, TX 75073
Unitarian Universalist Association: 25 Beacon St., Boston, MA 02108
United Church of Christ: 700 Prospect Ave., Cleveland, OH 44115
United Holy Church of America, Inc.: 825 Fairoak Ave., Chillum, MD 20783
Unity School of Christianity: Unity Village, MO 64065
Volunteers of America: 3813 N. Causeway Blvd. Metairie, LA 70002
Wesleyan Church, The: P.O. Box 50434, Indianapolis, IN 46250
Worldwide Church of God: 300 W. Green St., Pasadena, CA 91129

APPENDIX E:

Glossary of Terms

Absolution: The remission of guilt by a priest, following confession.

Adoration: An act of homage to God.

Advent: The coming of God in Christ, or the incarnation. May refer to the second coming.

Affusion: The pouring or sprinkling of water in baptism.

Allah: In Islam, the name of the Supreme Being, or all-powerful God.

Anathema: Anything cursed or despised.

Anchorite: A monk or zealous one who lives in isolation.

Annunciation: The announcement by the angel Gabriel to the virgin Mary that she was to be the mother of Christ.

Anointing: The act of consecrating candidates for baptism, or the sick, by the application of oil (as in the Anointing of the Sick).

Antichrist: The one against Christ, to be destroyed at Christ's second coming.

Antinomianism: The doctrine that the gospel does away with prescribed moral laws so that the Christian is not bound by them.

Apocalyptic: Literally, pertaining to the revelation of the end time.

Apocrypha: A group of writings from the period near the beginnings of Christianity. Part of the Catholic Scriptures regarded by many Protestants as noncanonical or not authoritative, but worthy of study for their religious and historical value.

Apostolic: Of or pertaining to the apostles, the 12 men Jesus sent forth with authority.

Apostolic Succession: The doctrine of an unbroken line of succession in the episcopacy, from the apostles to the present time, maintained in Eastern, Roman, and Anglican churches.

Arminian: The spiritual heirs of Arminius (1560–1609), a Dutch Protestant theologian, in support of freedom of the will. Arminius denied the later Calvinist doctrine of unconditional limited atonement and irresistible grace.

Athanasian: The belief of Athanasius (293–373) a defender of the orthodox view of the divinity of Christ. He opposed and won over Arius at the Council of Nicaea; Arius held that Christ was created by, but was essentially different from, the Father.

Atonement: The reconciliation of the sinner with God through the sufferings and death of Jesus Christ.

Autocephalous: Ecclesiastically self-controling, or having jurisdiction as an independent head. *Autocephali* was a term applied in early Christian times to bishops who recognized no ecclesiastical superior.

Autonomous: Self-governing, or independent, as in a local congregation.

Ban, The: A sentence that amounts to excommunication or outlawry by the church, upon those guilty of an act or speech forbidden by the church.

Baptism: The ceremonial application of water to a person by sprinkling, immersion, or affusion, as a sign of the washing away of sin, of rebirth or new life, and of admission into the church as commanded by Christ in Matthew

317

28:19. Spirit baptism in some denominations is a baptism by the Holy Spirit, not with water.

Born Again: The experience of a second birth in the Spirit.

Byzantine: Related to the city of Byzantium (Constantinople), a historic center of Eastern Orthodoxy.

Calvinists: Those holding the doctrinal or theological outlook of John Calvin (1509–64), typically in Presbyterian and Reformed churches.

Canon: The books admitted to the Bible as authoritative—39 in the Old Testament, 27 in the New.

Catechism: The form or guide used in instruction of candidates for church membership, preceding baptism. A book containing items for such instruction.

Catholic: Universal, common. Refers to the whole church.

Catholicos: The title given to the chief bishop of a church, usually in the East.

Celibacy: The state of being unmarried and abstaining from sexual relations; a requirement for Roman Catholic priests and the members of some orders.

Cenobite: Person in a religious order who lives in a separate cell, but shares a common life with other such persons.

Chalice: A cup containing the sacramental wine used at Communion services.

Charisma: Spiritual giftedness (in Greek, *grace*) enabling one to manifest an unusual ability for the benefit of others.

Chastity: The state of refraining from sexual relations in order to consecrate one's sexuality to spiritual ends. A vow in many religious orders.

Chrism: An ungent, usually olive oil or balm, used in Orthodox, Anglican, and Roman Catholic churches for anointing at baptism, confirmation, ordination, or consecration services, and sometimes for the sick.

Christocentric: With Christ as the center. Usually refers to the orientation of a theological system.

Christology: A systematic teaching about Christ, the meaning of his life and his place in the divine revelation and redemption.

Collect: A brief prayer, highly stylized. In Roman and Anglican liturgies, a prayer read before the Gospel and Epistle.

Communicant: A church member who participates in the Lord's Supper.

Communion: The Lord's Supper. "Open" Communion is open to all Christians; "closed" Communion is closed to all except those of a particular faith or belief. The word is also used occasionally as a synonym for "denomination."

Communion of Saints: The spiritual union of all people in the Christian community, including the dead.

Confession: A statement of the beliefs of a religious body, similar to a creed. Also an admission of sin, either privately or as a sacrament in the Roman Catholic Church.

Confirmation: The initiatory rite by which persons are inducted into the church. In some churches, a sacrament.

Congregational: The church polity that makes the authority of the local congregation supreme within its own area.

Consecrate: To set apart as sacred certain persons, animals, places, objects, or times.

APPENDIX E

Consubstantiation: The theory that, following the words of institution in the Lord's Supper, the substantial body and blood of Christ join sacramentally with the bread and wine (which remain unchanged), the union remaining only until the purpose of the consecration is fulfilled. Applied sometimes to Lutheran doctrine, but not actually accepted by Lutherans.

Contrition: Sorrow for sin.

Conversion: Religiously, a radical spiritual and moral change, commonly attending a change of belief and involving profoundly altered spirit and conduct—"a change of heart."

Covenant: Sacred relationship between God and an individual or a people. The Latin term *testament* is a translation of the Greek word for *covenant*—hence "Old Testament" and "New Testament." A central theme especially in Calvinist thought.

Creed: A statement of belief that summarizes the central doctrines affirmed by a body of Christians. Often recited by the congregations as part of worship.

Deacon: The principal lay officer in some denominations, especially Baptist. Its origin is often identified with the appointment of the Seven in Acts 6:1-6.

Decalogue: The Ten Commandments, found in Exodus 20.

Deism: A form of Christianity in which God's existence or will is in universal natural law rather than through revelation.

Diocese: The territory of a church under the jurisdiction of a bishop.

Dispensationalism: The concept that God deals with the world in specific time periods, or "dispensations," usually seven in number, each having one major purpose and accomplishment.

Doctrine: What is taught as the belief of a church.

Dogma: Belief generally regarded as necessary for salvation.

Ecclesiastical: Pertaining to the church. From the Greek *ecclesia* (assembly).

Ecumenical or Oecumenical: General, universal, representing the whole Christian church.

Ecumenical Councils, The: The seven early church councils: Nicaea in 325, Constantinople in 381, Ephesus in 431, Chalcedon in 451, Constantinople (II) in 553, Constantinople (III) in 680, and Nicaea (II) in 787.

Election: God's choice of an individual or a people for salvation. The basis of the Jews' calling to be the chosen people and of the doctrine of predestination.

Encyclical: A letter sent to local churches, usually a communication from the pope, but more recently used in a broader sense, to report the actions or findings of a church conference.

Episcopal: Having to do with bishops, or governed by bishops. From the Greek *episcopos.*

Eschatology: Study of the last things, involving the final coming and triumph of Christ and God's rule, and sometimes the resurrection.

Esoteric: Restricted to an inner circle, from the custom in the Greek Mystery religions, and explaining advanced doctrines only to the fully initiated.

Eucharist: Holy Communion, or the Lord's Supper. From the Greek *eucharisteo* in 1 Corinthians 11:24 (to give thanks).

319

Evangelical: Loyal to the gospel of Christ. Used in history to distinguish those kinds of Christianity that stress evangelism, personal conversion, and authority-mindedness.

Excommunication: Exclusion from the religious fellowship of the church, either permanent or temporary.

Extreme Unction: *See* Anointing.

Fall, The: Estrangement from God through sin, as symbolized by the disobedience of Adam and Eve.

Fasting: Going without food, or certain foods, for a specified period, as an act of discipline toward a life of purer service to God.

Feast Day: A day in the church calendar set aside for celebration—for feasting, not fasting—such as Christmas or Easter or a remembrance day for saints or heroes in church history.

Foot Washing: The practice of washing the feet, observed regularly by some Protestant bodies, and on special occasions by many Catholic Christians. To emulate Jesus' washing his disciples' feet in John 13.

Fornication: Sexual intercourse outside marriage.

Free Will: The power to choose between good and evil, without compulsion or necessity.

Fundamentalism: The movement within conservative Protestantism that requires belief in certain fundamental teachings, most of which have to do with the inerrancy of the Bible and the divinity of Jesus. In contrast to modernism, which interprets the Bible in accordance with more modern scholarship and scientific knowledge.

General Confession: A public, congregational confession of sin; among Roman Catholics, a confession in which the individual sums up past sins; among Protestants, a part of worship recited in unison by pastor and congregation, modeled on historic Roman Catholic and Anglican forms.

Genuflection: The act of bending one knee—in worship, upon entering the sanctuary, or when approaching the altar, as a gesture of reverence or adoration—a custom dating from the early church, usually found in Roman Catholic and some Episcopal churches.

Glossolalia: Speaking in tongues, as a manifestation of baptism with the Holy Spirit. The religious phenomenon described in the account of Pentecost in Acts 2. *See also* Tongues, Gift of

Grace: God's favor or unmerited love; a gift received from God.

Heterodox: Not orthodox; contrary to accepted teachings.

Hierarchy: The body or organization empowered to administer sacred things. Denotes the centralization of authority in church teaching and leadership.

Holiness: Negatively, removal from what is sinful; positively, consecration to God. Also a family of Protestants for whom sanctification, the gift of and calling to righteousness, is a distinguishing mark.

Holy Orders: The power granted the ecclesiastical leaders of the church, especially among Catholic bodies, to perform the acts proper to the ministry.

Immaculate Conception, The: The dogma that when the virgin Mary was conceived in her mother's womb, she was preserved from all stain of original sin.

Immanence: The position, as opposed to transcendence, that God is present in the world.

Immersion: Baptism by submerging the candidate in water.

Immortality: Life exempt from death.

Incarnation: God's becoming a human being in the historical person of Jesus Christ.

Indulgence: In the Roman Catholic Church, a remission "of the temporal punishment due to sins, the guilt of which has already been remitted." Granted only when penance is shown.

Inerrant: The quality of being truthful or without fault. When applied to the text of the Bible by some Christians, the claim that the text is error-free in all aspects.

Infallibility: Possessing definitive and incontestable authority, as applied to the pope or to Scripture.

Inspiration, Verbal: Signifying the supernatural influence upon the writers of the Scriptures by which authority was given their work.

Judgment, Judgment Day: The act of judging by God on the last day, when rewards and punishments will be declared.

Justification: Gaining righteousness from a belief in Jesus Christ, rather than by one's own merit. Being accepted and forgiven by God.

Kiss of Peace, or Holy Kiss: A religious greeting or ceremony, usually during the Eucharist.

Laity: Often taken to mean those members of the church who are not clergy; in actuality, the whole body of Christian people, all lay men and lay women.

Laying On of Hands: A rite of consecration or blessing, sometimes associated with ordination or with healing.

Litany: Form of prayer, made up of a series of petitions and offered by the leader, with congregational responses.

Liturgy, Liturgical: Literally, the "work of the people"; therefore, the public worship of the people of God. More narrowly, a prescribed form of worship as used in Roman Catholic, Orthodox, Anglican, and Lutheran services.

Logos: Christ as the Word of God, a teaching highlighted in John's Gospel.

Love Feast: A common meal of Christians, often culminating in the Eucharist and sometimes called agape.

Mass: The central worship service of the Roman Catholic Church, celebrating the Holy Eucharist.

Medium: A person through whom messages from the spiritual world are sent, as in Spiritualism.

Metropolitan: In an Eastern church, a bishop who has provincial as well as diocesan power.

Modernist: *See* Fundamentalist.

Monophysitism: The doctrine that Christ's human nature is absorbed in his divine nature.

Monotheism: Belief in only one God, as opposed to polytheism or pantheism.

Mysticism: Knowledge of God by immediate experience; a direct and intimate consciousness of divine reality.

321

Nestorian: A follower of Nestorius, a fifth-century Syrian patriarch of Constantinople condemned for teaching that Christ was two persons, divine and human. Still found in Iran, Iraq, and South India.

Nicene: Pertaining to Nicaea, where the Nicene Creed was adopted at the famous council of 325, temporarily settling the controversy concerning the persons of the Trinity; properly called the Niceno-Constantinople Creed.

Nonconformist: One who does not accept, or dissents from, the Church of England, by belonging to another denomination.

Ordinance: A religious rite or ceremony used in preference to sacrament in nonliturgical churches.

Orthodoxy: Belief in a doctrine or practice considered correct or sound.

Pacifism: Dedication to peace, usually entailing refusal to participate in or support the cause of war.

Passover: The Jewish festival commemorating the time when the angel of death "passed over" Israelite homes but required the death of all Egyptian firstborn.

Patriarch: In the Old Testament, the chief of a tribe in Israel; in Christianity, a bishop in a principal center in the East, such as Alexandria or Antioch.

Peace Churches: Churches that historically have held a pacifist position, such as Friends, Brethren, and Mennonites.

Penance: Actions indicative of conversion or contrition, sometimes including fasting or abstinence. In the Roman Catholic Church, a sacrament.

Pentecostalism: The experience of baptism with the Holy Spirit, often accompanied by speaking in tongues and other charismatic gifts.

Perfection: The complete love of God with one's whole being, a doctrine taught by John Wesley.

Pietism: Specifically, a German Lutheran movement of the seventeenth and eighteenth centuries, in the interest of spiritual renewal. Generally, a term used to designate those movements in Christianity that emphasize zeal for missions and the personal, spiritual, and practical, rather than the institutional, formal, and intellectual aspects of faith.

Plenary: Full, complete; a plenary council is attended by all its qualified members.

Polity: The particular form or system of government used by a denomination.

Postmillenarianismi: Belief that the return will come at the end of the millennium.

Predestinarian: A believer in predestination—that each person's eternal destiny is fixed by divine decree.

Premillennialism: Belief that the personal visible return of Christ will precede his reign for a thousand years on earth.

Presbytery: A church court or assembly having the ecclesiastical or spiritual rule and oversight of a district; the district itself.

Reconciliation: The process of being brought back into fellowship with God after a life of estrangement from God.

Redemption: God's deliverance from sin and death through the sacrificial atonement of Christ.

Regeneration: A new birth, re-creation, a radical renewal of life, or conversion.

Religious: Those Roman Catholics who are members of a religious community.

Remission of Sin: Pardon or forgiveness of sin.

Repentance: Conversion to God from a sinful life. A person's act of turning.

Reprobation: The divine decree concerning those who do not attain salvation.

Revelation: God's self-disclosure, as in historical events or in Scripture.

Ritual: A form or office of worship.

Sabbatarian: One who believes that the seventh day should be observed as the Lord's day, or regards Sunday as a day of abstinence from work and amusement.

Sacerdotal: A religious system in which the priestly order has special or sacred powers.

Sacrament: A "visible sign of an invisible grace, instituted by Christ." The Roman Catholic Church observes seven sacraments—the Eucharist, baptism, confirmation, penance, holy matrimony, holy orders, and anointing of the sick; in Protestantism, the first two (and sometimes penance).

Sacramentals: Certain practices or objects, such as the sign of the cross or the use of holy water or candles, symbolizing spiritual reality.

Salvation: Deliverance from sin and death by God's act.

Sanctification: The work of the Holy Spirit beyond justification, toward holiness of life.

Second Coming: The second advent of Jesus, his return to the world to mark the end of history, or this era of history.

See: The jurisdiction of a bishop

Speaking in Tongues: *See* Glossolalia; Tongues, Gift of.

Synod: An ecclesiastical council either of regular standing or appointed as needed; in Presbyterian churches, a body between the presbyteries and the general assembly.

Tongues, Gift of: An ecstatic utterance induced by religious excitement. *See also* Glossolalia.

Total Depravity: The condition created by the Fall, every human faculty having an innate evil taint.

Transcendence: The absolute exaltation of God above the universe and its limitations.

Transfiguration: Change in form or appearance, such as the transfiguration of Jesus (Mark 9:2-10).

Transmutation: The change from one nature, substance, or form to another.

Transubstantiation: The doctrine that after consecration of the elements, the substance of Christ's body and blood is present in the Eucharist.

Trinitarian: A believer in the Trinity—that there is a union of Father, Son, and Holy Ghost in one divine nature.

Triune: Having the quality of three-in-oneness; a reference to the Trinitarian God.

Unction: Anointing with oil, as in the case of sickness or imminent death. (Extreme unction, a sacrament, is now designated as "anointing of the sick.")

Uniate: Persons or churches acknowledging the supremacy of the pope but maintaining their own liturgies or rites.

Unitarian: The theology that insists upon the unity of God, denying the doctrine of the Trinity.

Universalism: Universal salvation, the view that somehow God will redeem all, including those who do not follow Christ.

Unleavened Bread: Bread made without yeast, necessary for Jewish Passover and often used in Christian Communion services.

Venerable: Anglican title for archdeacon; Catholic title for one who has reached a particular point in the process of beatification; title of honor for one of unusual sanctity, as the Venerable Bede.

Venial Sin: In Roman Catholic doctrine, a slight offense that does not require the sacrament of penance; a sin that is not mortal (meriting eternal death).

Venite: "Oh come," Latin version of Psalm 95, used frequently in the service of Morning Prayer.

Versicle: Literally, "little verse," a short statement followed by a congregational or choral response.

Vestment: Article of clothing worn by a religious official.

Vicar: Incumbent of a parish; member of the clergy who serves as the deputy or substitute for another.

Vocation: The calling to serve God in one's work and life; for some, entailing ordination.

Vulgate: Latin version of the Bible, translated by Jerome (d. 420).

Warden: Official of an ecclesiastical institution entrusted with the temporal affairs or the protection of property in a parish.

Western Church: Term of Christianity in Europe or America; for Roman Catholicism; as opposed to Eastern Orthodoxy.

Whitsunday: "White Sunday," or Pentecost, Christian festival on the seventh Sunday after Easter.

Yahweh: Divine name in the Hebrew Scriptures.

Zionism: Modern movement that sought the colonizing of Jews in Palestine. Historically, the return of Jews to their homeland. The forming of the state of Israel in 1948 was in part a result of the Zionist movement.

BIBLIOGRAPHY

GENERAL

Ahlstrom, Sydney E. *A Religious History of the American People.* New Haven: Yale University Press, 1972.

Albanese, Catherine L. *America: Religions and Religion.* Belmont, Calif.: Wadsworth Publishing Co., 1981.

Backman, Milton V., Jr. *Christian Churches of America: Origins and Beliefs.* New York: Scribner's, 1983.

Bedell, Kenneth B., ed. *Yearbook of American and Canadian Churches.* Nashville: Abingdon Press (annual).

Bednarowski, Mary Farrell. *American Religion: A Cultural Perspective.* Englewood Cliffs, N.J.: Prentice-Hall, 1984.

Bellah, Robert N., et al. *Habits of the Heart.* Berkeley: University of California Press, 1986.

Bowden, Henry W. *Dictionary of American Religious Biography.* 2nd ed. Westport, Conn.: Greenwood Press, 1993.

Butler, Jon. *Awash in a Sea of Faith: Christianizing the American People.* Cambridge: Harvard University Press, 1990.

Carroll, Jackson W., et al. *Religion in America: 1950 to the Present.* New York: Harper & Row, 1979.

Cherry, Conrad, ed. *God's New Israel.* Englewood Cliffs, N.J.: Prentice-Hall, 1971.

Clark, Elmer T. *The Small Sects in America.* Nashville: Abingdon Press, 1949.

Douglas, Mary, and Steven M. Tipton. *Religion and America.* Boston: Beacon Press, 1983.

Frazier, E. Franklin. *The Negro Church in America.* Bound with Lincoln, C. Eric. *The Black Church Since Frazier.* New York: Shocken Books, 1973.

Gaustad, Edwin Scott. *A Documentary History of Religion in America.* 2 vols. Grand Rapids: Eerdmans Publishing Co., 1982–83.

———. *Dissent in American Religion.* Chicago: University of Chicago Press, 1973.

———. *Historical Atlas of Religion in America.* rev. ed. New York: Harper & Row, 1976.

Handy, Robert T. *A Christian America: Protestant Hopes and Historical Realities.* 2d ed. New York: Oxford University Press, 1984.

———. *A History of Churches in the United States and Canada.* New York: Oxford University Press, 1976.

Hatch, Nathan O. *The Democratization of American Christianity.* New Haven: Yale University Press, 1989.

Herberg, Will. *Protestant-Catholic-Jew.* reprint ed. Chicago: University of Chicago Press, 1984.

Hill, Samuel S. *The South and the North in American Religion.* Athens: University of Georgia Press, 1980.

Hudson, W. S. *The Great Tradition of American Churches.* New York: Peter Smith, 1963.

———. *Religion in America.* 3rd ed. New York: Scribner's, 1981.

Hughes, Richard T., and C. Leonard Allen. *Illusions of Innocence: Protestant Primitivism in America* Chicago: University of Chicago Press, 1988.

Janes, Janet W., ed. *Women in American Religion.* Philadelphia: University of Pennsylvania Press, 1980.

Kennedy, Robert G. *American Churches.* New York: Crossroad Press, 1982.

BIBLIOGRAPHY

Lincoln, C. Eric. *The Black Church Since Frazier.* Bound with: Frazier, E. Franklin. *The Negro Church in America.* New York: Schocken Books, 1973.

———, ed. *The Black Experience in Religion.* Boston: Beacon Press, 1974.

———, ed. *The Black Experience in Religion.* Garden City, N.Y.: Doubleday, 1974.

Lincoln, C. Eric, and Lawrence H. Mamiya. *The Black Church in the African American Experience.* Durham, N.C.: Duke University Press, 1990.

Lippy, Charles H., and Peter W. Williams. *Encyclopedia of American Reli-gious Experience.* 3 vols. New York: Scribner's, 1987.

Marty, Martin E. *A Nation of Behavers.* Chicago: University of Chicago Press, 1976.

———. *Modern American Religion.* Vol. I: *The Irony of It All.* Vol II: *The Noise of Conflict.* Chicago: University of Chicago Press, 1991.

———. *Pilgrims in Their Own Land.* Boston: Little, Brown, 1984.

———. *The Public Church: Mainline-Evangelical-Catholic.* New York: Cross-road Press, 1981.

———. *Righteous Empire: Protestantism in the United States.* New York: Scrib-ner's, 1986.

Mead, Sidney E. *The Lively Experiment: The Shaping of Christianity in America.* New York: Harper & Row, 1963.

———. *A Nation with the Soul of a Church.* New York: Harper & Row, 1975.

Melton, J. Gordon. *The Encyclopedia of American Religions.* 3 vols. Tarrytown, N.Y.: Triumph Books, 1991.

Miller, William Lee. *The First Liberty.* New York: Alfred A. Knopf, 1986.

Montgomery, William E. *Under Their Own Vine and Fig Tree: The African-American Churches in the South, 1865–1900.* Baton Rouge: Louisiana State University Press, 1993.

Moore, R. Laurence. *Religious Outsiders and the Making of America.* New York: Oxford University Press, 1986.

Mullin, Robert Bruce, and Russell E. Richey, eds. *Reimagining Denomination-alism.* New York: Oxford University Press, 1994.

Nelsen, Hart, et al., eds. *The Black Church in America.* New York: Basic Books, 1971.

Neuhaus, Richard John. *The Naked Public Square.* Grand Rapids: Eerdmans Publishing Co., 1984.

Noll, Mark A. *A History of Christianity in the United States and Canada.* Grand Rapids, Mich.: Eerdmans Publishing Co., 1992.

Noll, Mark A., et al., ed. *Eerdmans Handbook to Christianity in America.* Grand Rapids: Eerdmans Publishing Co., 1983.

Piepkorn, Arthur C. *Profiles in Belief: The Religious Bodies of the United States and Canada.* 4 vols. New York: Harper & Row, 1977–79.

Raboteau, Albert J. *Slave Religion: The "Invisible Institution" in the Antebellum South.* New York: Oxford University Press, 1978.

Roof, Wade Clark, and William McKinney. *American Mainline Religion.* New Brunswick, N.J.: Rutgers University Press, 1987.

Rosten, Leo. *A Guide to the Religions of America.* St. Louis: Bethany Press, 1963.

Ruether, Rosemary Radford, and Rosemary Skinner Keller, eds. 3 vols. *Women and Religion in America.* San Francisco: Harper & Row, 1981.

Sernett, Milton C., ed. *Afro-American Religious History: A Documentary Wit-ness.* Durham, N.C.: Duke University Press, 1985.

Smith, H. Shelton; Handy, Robert T.; and Loetscher, Lefferts A. *American Christianity: An Historical Interpretation with Representative Documents.* 2 vols. New York: Scribner's, 1960–63.

Smith, James W., and A. Leland Jamison. *Religion in American Life.* 4 vols. Princeton, N.J.: Princeton University Press, 1961.

Tuveson, Ernest Lee. *Redeemer Nation: The Idea of America's Millennial Role.* Chicago: University of Chicago Press, 1968.

Wilmore, Gayraud S. *Black Religion and Black Radicalism: An Interpretation of the Religious History of Afro-American People.* 2d ed. Maryknoll, N.Y.: Orbis Books, 1983.

Wilson, John F., and John M. Mulder, eds. *Religion in American History.* Englewood Cliffs, N.J.: Prentice-Hall, 1978.

Wuthnow, Robert. *The Restructuring of American Religion: Society and Faith Since World War II.* Princeton, N.J.: Princeton University Press, 1988.

DENOMINATIONAL

Adventist

Beckford, James A. *The Trumpet of Prophecy: A Sociological Study of Jehovah's Witnesses.* New York: Wiley, 1975.

Doan, Ruth A. *The Miller Heresy, Millennialism and American Culture.* Philadelphia, Pa.: Temple University Press, 1987.

Froom, Le Roy E. *The Prophetic Faith of Our Fathers.* 4 vols. Washington, D.C.: Review & Herald Publishing, 1946–54.

Gaustad, Edwin S. *The Rise of Adventism: Religion, and Society in Mid-Nineteenth Century America.* New York: Harper & Row, 1974.

Hasel, Gerard F. *Old Testament Theology: Basic Issues in the Current Debate.* Grand Rapids: Eerdmans Publishing Co., 1972.

Herndon, Booton. *The Seventh Day: The Story of the Seventh-Day Adventists.* New York: McGraw-Hill, 1960.

Neufeld, Dan F., ed. *Seventh-Day Adventist Encyclopedia,* rev. ed. Washington, D.C.: Review & Herald Publishing, 1976.

Numbers, Ronald L., and Jonathan M. Butler, eds. *The Disappointed: Millennialism in the Nineteenth Century.* Bloomington: Indiana University Press, 1987.

Spalding, Arthur W. *Origin and History of Seventh-Day Adventists.* 4 vols. Washington, D.C.: Review & Herald Publishing, 1961.

White, Ellen G. *The Desire of Ages.* Mountain View, Calif.: Pacific Press Publishing, 1940.

———. *The Great Controversy Between Christ and Satan.* Mountain View, Calif.: Pacific Press Publishing, 1927.

Baptist

Ammerman, Nancy T. *Baptist Battles: Religious Change and Social Conflict in the Southern Baptist Convention.* New Brunswick, N.J.: Rutgers University Press, 1990.

Baker, Robert A. *The Southern Baptist Convention and Its People, 1607–1972.* Nashville: Broadman Press, 1974.

Brackney, William H., ed. *Baptist Life and Thought: 1600–1980: A Source Book.* Valley Forge, Pa.: Judson Press, 1983.

———. *The Baptists.* New York: Greenwood Press, 1988.

Cox, Norman W. *Encyclopedia of Southern Baptists.* Nashville: Broadman Press, 1958–82.

Fitts, Leroy, *A History of Black Baptists.* Nashville: Broadman Press, 1985.

Gaustad, Edwin S., ed. *The Bible, Church Order, and the Churches*. New York: Arno Press, 1980.

Higginbotham, Evelyn Brooks. *Righteous Discontent: The Women's Movement in the Black Baptist Church, 1880–1920*. Cambridge: Harvard University Press, 1993.

Jackson, Joseph H. *A Story of Christian Activism: A History of the National Baptist Convention, U.S.A., Inc.* Nashville: Townsend Press, 1980.

Leonard, Bill J., ed. *Dictionary of Baptists in America*. Downers Grove, Ill.: InterVarsity Press, 1994.

———. *God's Last and Only Hope: The Fragmentation of the Southern Baptist Convention*. Grand Rapids, Mich.: Wm. B. Eerdmans, 1990.

Lumpkin, William L. *Baptist Confessions of Faith*. Valley Forge, Pa.: Judson Press, 1969.

Maring, Norman H., and Winthrop S. Hudson. *A Baptist Manual of Polity and Practice*. Valley Forge, Pa.: Judson Press, 1963.

McBeth, Leon. *The Baptist Heritage*. Nashville, Tenn.: Broadman Press, 1987.

McLoughlin, William G. *New England Dissent, 1620–1833: Baptists and the Separation of Church and State*. Cambridge: Harvard University Press, 1971.

Olson, Adolf. *A Centenary History*. Chicago: Baptist Conference Press, 1952 (Baptist General Conference of America).

Rosenberg, Ellen M. *The Southern Baptists: A Subculture in Transition*. Knoxville: University of Tennessee Press, 1989.

Torbet, Robert G. *A History of the Baptists,* rev. ed. Valley Forge, Pa.: Judson Press, 1963.

Washington, James Melvin. *Frustrated Fellowship: The Black Baptist Quest for Social Power*. Macon, Ga.: Mercer, 1986.

Wood, James E., Jr., ed. *Baptists and the American Experience*. Valley Forge, Pa.: Judson Press, 1976.

Woyke, Frank. *Heritage and Ministry of the North American Baptist Conference*. Oakbrook Terrace, Ill.: North American Baptist Conference, 1979.

Brethren

Bittenger, Emmert F. *Heritage and Promise*. Elgin, Ill.: Brethren Press, 1970.

Durnbaugh, Donald F. *The Brethren in Colonial America*. Elgin, Ill.: Brethren Press, 1967.

———, ed. *The Brethren Encyclopedia*. 3 vols. Philadelphia/Oak Brook, Ill.: Brethren Press, 1983–84.

Sappington, Roger E. *Brethren and Social Policy 1908–58*. Elgin, Ill.: Brethren Press, 1961.

———. *The Brethren in the New Nation*. Elgin, Ill.: Brethren Press, 1976.

Christian Science

A Century of Christian Science Healing. Boston: Christian Science Publishing Society, 1966.

DeWitt, John. *The Christian Science Way of Life*. Boston: Christian Science Publishing Society, 1971.

Eddy, Mary Baker. *Science and Health with Key to the Scriptures*. Boston: Christian Science Board of Directors, 1980.

Gottschalk, Stephen. *The Emergence of Christian Science in American Religious Life*. Berkeley: University of California Press, 1973.

Judah, J. Stillson. *The History and Philosophy of the Metaphysical Movements in America*. Philadelphia: Westminster Press, 1967.

Peel, Robert. *Mary Baker Eddy: The Years of Discovery.* New York: Holt, Rinehart & Winston, 1977.

————. *Mary Baker Eddy: The Years of Trial.* New York: Holt, Rinehart & Winston, 1971.

————. *Christian Science: Its Encounter with American Culture.* New York: Holt, Rinehart & Winston, 1958.

Thomas, Robert David. *"With Bleeding Footsteps": Mary Baker Eddy's Path to Religious Leadership.* New York: Alfred E. Knopf, 1994.

Church of God

Brown, C. E. *When the Trumpet Sounded.* Anderson, Ind.: Warner Press, 1951. (History of Church of God, Anderson, Ind.)

Callen, B. L., ed. *The First Century* [Church of God (Anderson, Ind.)]. 2 vols. Anderson, Ind.: Warner Press, 1979.

Conn, Charles W. *Like a Mighty Army Moves the Church of God, 1886–1955.* Cleveland, Tenn.: Church of God Publishing House, 1955.

Crews, Mickey. *The Church of God: A Social History.* Knoxville: University of Tennessee Press, 1990.

Davidson, C. T. *Upon This Rock.* 3 vols. Cleveland, Tenn.: White Wing Press, 1973–76.

Diary of Ambrose Jessup Tomlinson. Homer A. Tomlinson, ed. 3 vols. Queens Village, N.Y.: Church of God World Headquarters, 1949–55.

Frodsham, S. H. *With Signs Following.* Springfield, Mo.: Gospel Publishing House, 1941.

Riggs, R. M. *The Spirit Himself.* Springfield, Mo.: Gospel Publishing House, 1949.

Stone, James. *The Church of God of Prophecy: History and Polity.* Cleveland, Tenn.: White Wing Publishing House, 1977.

Tomlinson, Homer A. *The Shout of a King.* Queens Village, N.Y.: The Church of God World Headquarters, 1968.

Church of the Nazarene

Laird, Rebecca. *Ordained Women in the Church of the Nazarene: The First Generation.* Kansas City, Mo.: Beacon Hill Press, 1993.

Parker, J. F. *Mission to the World.* Kansas City, Mo.: Nazarene Publishing House, 1983.

Purkiser, W. T. *Called unto Holiness: The Second Twenty-Five Years.* Kansas City, Mo.: Nazarene Publishing House, 1983.

————, ed. *Exploring Our Christian Faith.* Kansas City, Mo.: Beacon Hill Press, 1966.

Redford, M. E. *The Rise of the Church of the Nazarene.* Kansas City: Nazarene Publishing House, 1951.

Smith, Timothy L. *Called unto Holiness: The Story of the Nazarenes, The Formative Years.* Kansas City, Mo.: Nazarene Publishing House, 1962.

Taylor, Richard S. *Life in the Spirit.* Kansas City, Mo.: Beacon Hill Press, 1966.

Churches of Christ

Harrell, David E., Jr. *Quest for a Christian America: The Disciples of Christ and American Society to 1866.* Nashville: Disciples of Christ Historical Society, 1966.

————. *The Social Sources of Division in the Disciples of Christ, 1865–1900.* Atlanta/Athens: Publishing Systems, 1973.

Hooper, Robert E. *Crying in the Wilderness: A Biography of David Lipscomb.* Nashville: David Lipscomb College, 1979.

Hughes, Richard T. *Reviving the Ancient Faith: The Story of Churches of Christ in America.* Grand Rapids: Wm. B. Eerdinans, 1996.

Hughes, Richard T. *The American Quest for the Primitive Church.* Urbana: University of Illinois Press, 1988.

West, Earl Irvin. *The Search for Ancient Order.* 3 vols. Indianapolis: Religious Book Service, 1950, 1964, 1979.

Disciples of Christ

Beazley, George G., Jr. *The Christian Church (Disciples of Christ): An Interpretive Examination in the Cultural Context.* St. Louis: Bethany Press, 1973.

Crain, James Andrew. *The Development of Social Ideas Among the Disciples of Christ.* St. Louis: Bethany Press, 1969.

Garrison, W. E., and A. T. DeGroot. *Disciples of Christ: A History.* St. Louis: Bethany Press, 1958.

Garrison, Winifred E. *Heritage and Destiny.* St. Louis: Bethany Press, 1963.

Harrell, David Edwin, Jr. *Quest for a Christian America: The Disciples of Christ and American Society to 1866.* Nashville: Disciples of Christ Historical Society, 1966.

Humbert, Royal, ed. *A Compend of Alexander Campbell's Theology.* St. Louis: Bethany Press, 1961.

Lair, Loren E. *The Christian Churches and Their Work.* St. Louis: Bethany Press, 1963.

McAllister, Lester G., and William E. Tucker. *Journey in Faith.* St. Louis: Bethany Press, 1975.

Teegarden, Kenneth L. *We Call Ourselves Disciples.* St. Louis: Bethany Press, 1976.

Whitley, Oliver R. *The Trumpet Call of Reformation.* St. Louis: Bethany Press, 1963.

Wrather, Eva Jean. *Alexander Campbell and His Relevance for Today.* Nashville: Disciples of Christ Historical Society, 1955.

———. *Creative Freedom in Action: Alexander Campbell on the Structure of the Church.* St. Louis: Bethany Press, 1968.

Episcopal

Albright, Raymond W. *History of the Protestant Episcopal Church.* New York: Macmillan, 1964.

Holmes, Urban T., III. *What Is Anglicanism?* Wilton, Conn.: Morehouse-Barlow, 1982.

Konolige, K. and F. *The Power of Their Glory.* n.p.: Wyden Books, 1978.

Krumm, John McGill. *Why I Am an Episcopalian.* Boston: Beacon Press, 1957.

Pittenger, W. Norman. *The Episcopal Way of Life.* Englewood Cliffs, N.J.: Prentice-Hall, 1957.

Pritchard, Robert W. *A History of the Episcopal Church.* New York: Morehouse, 1991.

Woolverton, John F. *Colonial Anglicanism in North America 1607–1776.* Detroit: Wayne State University Press, 1984.

Evangelicals

Balmer, Randall. *Mine Eyes Have Seen the Glory: A Journey into the Evangelical Subculture of America.* New York: Oxford University Press, 1989.

BIBLIOGRAPHY

Dayton, Donald W. and Johnston, Robert K., eds. *The Variety of American Evangelicalism.* Knoxville: University of Tennessee Press, 1991.

Hunter, James Davison. *American Evangelicals.* New Brunswick, N.J.: Rutgers University Press, 1984.

————. *Evangelicalism: The Coming Generation.* Chicago: University of Chicago Press, 1987.

Kelly, Dean M. *Why Conservative Churches Are Growing.* New York: Harper & Row, 1972.

McLoughlin, William G. *Revivals, Awakenings, and Reform.* Chicago: University of Chicago Press, 1978.

Noll, Mark, David Bebbington, and George Rawlyk. *Evangelicalism: Comparative Studies of Popular Protestantism in North America, the British Isles, and Beyond, 1700–1900.* New York: Oxford University Press, 1994.

Quebedeaux, Richard. *The Young Evangelicals: Revolution in Orthodoxy.* New York: Harper & Row, 1974.

Smith, Timothy L. *Revivalism and Social Reform.* rev. ed. Baltimore: Johns Hopkins University Press, 1980.

Sweet, Leonard I., ed. *The Evangelical Tradition in America.* Macon, Ga.: Mercer University Press, 1984.

Wells, David F., and John D. Woodbridge, eds. *The Evangelicals: What They Believe, Who They Are, Where They Are Changing.* Nashville: Abingdon Press, 1975.

Friends

Bacon, M. *Quiet Rebels.* New York: Basic Books, 1969.

Bolding, K. E. *Evolutionary Potential of Quakerism.* pamphlet. Wallingford, Pa.: Pendle Hill Publications, 1964.

Brinton, Howard H. *Friends for 300 Years.* Wallingford, Pa.: Pendle Hill Publications, 1965.

Comfort, W. W. *The Quaker Way: Just Among Friends.* Philadelphia: American Friends Service Committee, 1968.

Cooper, C. W., ed. *Break the New Ground: Seven Essays by Contemporary Quakers.* Philadelphia: Friends World Committee, 1969.

Hall, Francis. *Friends in the Americas.* Philadelphia: Friends World Committee, 1976.

————. *Quaker Worship in North America.* Richmond, Ind.: Friends United Press, 1979.

Hamm, Thomas D. *The Transformation of American Quakerism.* Bloomington: Indiana University Press, 1988.

Jonas, G. *On Doing Good.* New York: Scribner's, 1971.

Russell, Elbert. *The History of Quakerism.* New York: Macmillan, 1943; Richmond, Ind.: Friends United Press, 1980.

Sheeran, Michael. *Friendly Persuasion.* Philadelphia: Friends World Committee, 1984.

Fundamentalism

Ammerman, Nancy T. *Bible Believers.* New Brunswick, N.J.: Rutgers University Press, 1988.

Dollar, George. *A History of Fundamentalism in America.* Greenville, S.C.: Bob Jones University Press, 1973.

Marsden, George M. *Fundamentalism and American Culture: The Shaping of Twentieth-Century Evangelicalism, 1870–1925.* New York: Oxford University Press, 1980.

————. *Reforming Fundamentalism: Fuller Seminary and the New Evangelical-ism.* Grand Rapids: Eerdmans Publishing Co., 1987.

Russell, Charles Allyn. *Voices in American Fundamentalism: Seven Biographical Studies.* Philadelphia: Westminster Press, 1976.

Sandeen, Ernest. *The Roots of Fundamentalism: British and American Millenni-alism, 1800–1925.* New York: Oxford University Press, 1970.

Weber, Timothy P. *Living in the Shadow of the Second Coming: American Premillennialism, 1875–1925.* New York: Oxford University Press, 1979.

Jehovah's Witnesses

Beckford, James A. *The Trumpet of Prophecy: A Sociological Study of Jehovah's Witnesses.* Oxford: Basil Blackwell, 1975.

Jehovah's Witnesses in the Divine Purpose. New York: Watch Tower Black Tract Society, 1959.

Harrison, Barbara G. *Visions of Glory.* New York: Simon & Schuster, 1978.

New World Translation of the Holy Scriptures. New York: Watch Tower Bible & Tract Society, 1961.

Penton, James. *Apocalypse Delayed.* Toronto: University of Toronto Press, 1985.

Judaism

Donin, Rabbi Hayim Halevy. *To Be a Jew.* New York: Basic Books, 1973.

Eban, Abba. *My People.* New York: Random House, 1984.

Eisen, Arnold M. *The Chosen People in America: A Study in Jewish Religious Ideology.* Bloomington: Indiana University Press, 1983.

Elazar, Daniel. *Community and Polity.* Philadelphia: Jewish Publication Society, 1976.

Encyclopedia Judaica. 16 vols. Jerusalem: Encyclopedia Judaica, 1972.

Feingold, Harold. *Zion in America.* New York: Twayne, 1974.

Finkelstein, Louis. *The Jews: Their History, Culture and Religion.* 2 vols. 3d ed. New York: Harper & Row, 1949; Shocken Books, 1970.

Glazer, Nathan. *American Judaism.* Chicago: University of Chicago Press, 1957.

Hertzberg, Arthur. *The Jews in America.* New York: Simon and Schuster, 1982.

————. *Judaism.* New York: George Braziller, 1961.

Isaacson, Rabbi Benjamin, and Deborah Wigoder. *The International Jewish Encyclopedia.* Englewood Cliffs, N.J.: Prentice-Hall, 1973.

Karp, Abraham J. *The Jewish Way of Life.* Englewood Cliffs, N.J.: Prentice-Hall, 1962.

Kushner, Harold. *To Life! A Celebration of Jewish Thinking and Being.* Boston: Little Brown, 1993.

Liebman, Charles S. *The Ambivalent American Jew.* Philadelphia: Jewish Publi-cation Society, 1973.

Neusner, Jacob. *The Way of Torah.* Belmont, Calif.: Wadsworth Publishing Co., 1979.

Prager, Dennis and Telushk, Joseph. *The Nine Questions People Ask About Judaism.* New York: Simon and Schuster, 1981.

Rosenthal, Gilbert. *The Many Faces of Judaism: Orthodox, Conservative, Recon-structionist, and Reform.* Edited by S. Rossel. New York: Behrman House, 1978.

Roth, Leon. *Judaism: A Portrait.* New York: Viking Press, 1961.

Silberman, Charles E. *A Certain People.* New York: Summit, 1985.

Sklare, Marshall. *America's Jews.* New York: Random House, 1971.

————. *Conservative Judaism: An American Religious Movement.* New York: Random House, 1972.

BIBLIOGRAPHY

———. *The Jew in American Society.* New York: Behrman House, 1974.
Steinberg, Milton. *Basic Judaism.* New York: Harcourt, Brace, 1947.
Wallach, Michael, E. *Jewish Year Book.* New York: Hartmore (annual).
Waxman, Chaim. *America's Jews in Transition.* Philadelphia: Temple University Press, 1983.
Wouk, Herman. *This Is My God.* New York: Doubleday, 1959.

Latter-Day Saints (Mormons)

Allen, James B., and Glen M. Leonard. *The Story of the Latter-Day Saints.* Salt Lake City: Deseret Book Co., 1976.
Anderson, Nels. *Desert Saints: The Mormon Frontier in Utah.* Chicago: University of Chicago Press, 1966.
Arrington, L. J. *Great Basin Kingdom: An Economic History of the Latter-day Saints.* Cambridge: Harvard University Press, 1958.
———. *Brigham Young: American Moses.* New York: Knopf, 1985.
Arrington, L. J., and Davis Bitton. *The Mormon Experience: A History of the Latter-Day Saints.* New York: Alfred A. Knopf, 1979.
Backman, Milton V., Jr. *Eyewitness Accounts of the Restoration.* Orem, Utah: Grandin Press, 1983.
Barlow, Phillip L. *Mormons and the Bible.* New York: Oxford University Press, 1991.
Bushman, Richard L. *Joseph Smith and the Origins of Mormonism.* Urbana: University of Illinois Press, 1984.
England, Eugene. *Brother Brigham.* Salt Lake City: Bookcraft, 1980.
Hansen, Klaus J. *Mormonism and the American Experience.* Chicago: University of Chicago Press, 1981.
Hill, Donna. *Joseph Smith: The First Mormon.* Garden City, N.Y.: Doubleday, 1977.
Hill, M. S., and J. B. Allen, eds. *Mormonism and American Culture.* New York: Harper & Row, 1972.
O'Dea, Thomas F. *The Mormons.* Chicago: University of Chicago Press, 1957.
Richards, Legrand. *Marvelous Work and a Wonder.* Salt Lake City: Deseret Book Co., 1972.
Shipps, Jan. *Mormonism: The Story of a New Religious Tradition.* Urbana: University of Illinois Press, 1985.
Smith, Joseph. *The Book of Mormon.* Salt Lake City: Deseret Book Co., 1972.
———. *The Doctrine and Covenants.* Salt Lake City: Deseret Book Co., 1971.
———. *The Pearl of Great Price.* Salt Lake City: Deseret Book Co., 1971.
———. *History of the Church of Jesus Christ of Latter-Day Saints.* ed. B. H. Roberts. 7 vols. Salt Lake City: The Church of Jesus Christ of Latter-Day Saints, 1932–51.
Smith, Joseph Fielding, comp. *Teachings of the Prophet Joseph Smith.* Salt Lake City: Deseret Book Co., 1961.
Talmage, James E. *Articles of Faith.* Salt Lake City: Deseret Book Co., 1971.

Lutheran

Albeck, Willard D. *Studies in the Lutheran Confessions.* Philadelphia: Fortress Press, 1968.
Arden G. Everett. *Augustana Heritage.* Rock Island: Augustana Press, 1963.
Bergendoff, Conrad. *The Church of the Lutheran Reformation.* St. Louis: Concordia Publishing House, 1967.
Bodensieck, Julius, ed. *The Encyclopedia of the Lutheran Church.* Philadelphia: Fortress Press, 1965.

BIBLIOGRAPHY

Dillenberger, John, ed. *Martin Luther: Selections from His Writings*. Garden City, N.Y.: Doubleday, 1961.
Ebeling, Gerhard. *Luther: An Introduction to His Thought*. Philadelphia: Fortress Press, 1970.
Groh, John E., and Robert H. Smith, eds. *The Lutheran Church in North America*. St. Louis: Clayton Publishing House, 1979.
Kerr, H. T., ed. *A Compend of Luther's Theology*. Philadelphia: Westminster Press, 1943, 1966.
Lowe, Ralph W. *The Lutheran Way of Life*. Englewood Cliffs, N.J.: Prentice-Hall, 1966.
Nelson, E. Clifford, ed. *The Lutherans in North America*. Philadelphia: Fortress Press, 1980.
Neve, H. T., and B. A. Anderson, eds. *The Maturing of American Lutheranism*. Minneapolis: Augsburg Publishing House, 1968.
Scherer, James A. *Mission and Unity in Lutheranism*. Philadelphia: Fortress Press, 1969.
Schlink, Edmund. *Theology of the Lutheran Confessions*. Philadelphia: Muhlenberg Press, 1961.
Schmidt, John. *The Lutheran Confessions: Their Value and Meaning*. Philadelphia: Muhlenberg Press, 1956.
Tappert, Theodore G., ed. *The Book of Concord: The Confessions of the Evangelical Lutheran Church*. Philadelphia: Muhlenberg Press, 1959.
———. *Lutheran Confessional Theology in America 1840–1880*. Library of Protestant Thought. New York: Oxford University Press, 1972.
Tietjen, John H. *Memoirs in Exile*. Minneapolis: Fortress Press, 1990.
Watson, Philip S. *Let God Be God!* Philadelphia: Muhlenberg Press, 1948.
Wentz, Abdel Ross. *A Basic History of Lutheranism in America*. Philadelphia: Fortress Press, 1964.
———. *The Lutheran Church in American History*. Philadelphia: United Lutheran Publication House, 1933.
Wentz, Frederick K. *Lutherans in Concert*. Philadelphia: Fortress Press, 1969.
Wolf, R. C. *Documents of Lutheran Unity in America*. Philadelphia: Fortress Press, 1966.

Methodist

The Book of Discipline of The United Methodist Church. Nashville: The United Methodist Publishing House, 1992. New edition to be published in 1996.
Bucke, Emory S., ed. 3 vols. *History of American Methodism*. Nashville: Abingdon Press, 1964.
Cobb, John B., Jr. *Grace & Responsibility: A Wesleyan Theology for Today*. Nashville: Abingdon Press, 1995.
George, Carol V. R. *Segregated Sabbaths: Richard Allen and the Emergence of Independent Black Churches, 1760–1840*. New York: Oxford University Press, 1973.
González, Justo L., ed. *Each in Our Own Tongue: A History of Hispanic United Methodism*. Nashville: Abingdon Press, 1991. (Also available in Spanish as *En nuestro propria lengua*.)
Guillermo, Artemio R., ed. *Churches Aflame: Asian Americans and United Methodism*. Nashville: Abingdon Press, 1991.
Harmon, Nolan B. *Understanding The United Methodist Church*. rev. ed. Nashville: Abingdon Press, 1977.
Heitzenrater, Richard P. *Wesley and the People Called Methodists*. Nashville: Abingdon Press, 1995.

Keller, Rosemary S., ed. *Spirituality and Social Responsibility: The Vocation Vision of Women in The United Methodist Tradition.* Nashville: Abingdon Press, 1993.

Lakey, Othal Hawthorne. *The Rise of "Colored Methodism": A Study of the Background and the Beginnings of the Christian Methodist Episcopal Church.* Dallas: Crescendo Book Publications, 1972.

Langford, Thomas A., ed. *Doctrine and Theology in The United Methodist Church.* Nashville: Kingswood Books, 1991.

McEllhenney, John G., ed. *United Methodism in America: A Compact History.* Nashville: Abingdon Press, 1992.

Maddox, Randy L. *Responsible Grace: John Wesley's Practical Theology.* Nashville: Kingswood Books, 1994.

Noley, Homer, ed. *First White Frost: Native Americans and United Methodism.* Nashville: Abingdon Press, 1991.

Norwood, Frederick A., ed. *A Sourcebook of American Methodism.* Nashville: Abingdon Press, 1982.

————. *The Story of American Methodism.* Nashville: Abingdon Press, 1974.

Outler, Albert C., ed. *John Wesley.* New York: Oxford University Press, 1964.

Outler, Albert C., and Richard P. Heitzenrater, eds. *John Wesley's Sermons: An Anthology.* Nashville: Abingdon Press, 1991.

Richardson, Harry V. *Dark Salvation: The Story of Methodism as It Developed Among Blacks in America.* New York: Doubleday, 1976.

Richey, Russell E. *Early American Methodism.* Bloomington: Indiana University Press, 1991.

Richey, Russell E., Kenneth E. Rowe, and Jean Miller Schmidt, eds. *Perspectives on American Methodism: Interpretive Essays.* Nashville: Kingswood Books, 1993.

Rowe, Kenneth E., ed. *United Methodist Studies: Basic Bibliographies.* 3rd ed. Nashville: Abingdon Press, 1992.

Shockley, Grant S., ed. *Heritage and Hope: The African American Presence in United Methodism.* Nashville: Abingdon Press, 1991.

Tuell, Jack M. *The Organization of The United Methodist Church.* rev. ed. Nashville: Abingdon Press, 1989.

Walls, William Jacob. *The African Methodist Episcopal Zion Church: The Reality of the Black Church.* Charlotte, N.C.: A.M.E. Zion Publishing House, 1974.

Wesley, John. *The Works of John Wesley.* 11 vols. to date of projected 35. Richard P. Heitzenrater, general editor; Frank Baker, textual editor. Nashville: Abingdon Press, 1976.

Williams, Colin W. *John Wesley's Theology Today.* Nashville: Abingdon Press, 1960.

Moravian

Fries, Adelaide. *Records of the Moravians in North Carolina.* 10 vols. Raleigh: State Dept. of Archives, 1968.

Gollin, Gillian Lindt. *Moravians in Two Worlds.* New York: Columbia University Press, 1967.

Hamilton, J. T., and K. G. Hamilton. *History of the Moravian Church: The Renewed Unitas Fratrum from 1722–1957.* Bethlehem, Pa.: Interprovincial Board of Christian Education, 1967.

Lewis, Arthur J. *Zinzendorf, The Ecumenical Pioneer: A Study of the Moravian Contribution to Christian Mission and Unity.* London: SCM Press, 1962.

Thorp, Daniel B. *The Moravian Community in Colonial North Carolina.* Knoxville: University of Tennessee Press, 1989.

BIBLIOGRAPHY

Weinlick, John R. *The Moravian Church Through the Ages.* Bethlehem, Pa.: Interprovisional Board of Christian Education, 1966.

Old Catholic

Anson, Peter. *Bishops at Large.* London: Faber & Faber, 1964.

Moss, C. B. *The Old Catholic Movement.* New York: Morehouse-Barlow, 1964.

Pruter, Fr. Karl. *A History of the Old Cathlic Church.* Scottsdale, Ariz.: St. Willborod's Press, 1973.

Pruter, Fr. Karl and Melton, J. Gordon. *The Old Catholic Sourcebook.* New York: Garland, 1983.

Orthodox

Benz, Ernst. *The Eastern Orthodox Church: Its Thought and Life.* Trans. Winston, Richard, and Clara Winston. Chicago: Aldine Publishing Co., 1963.

Bespuda, Anastasia. *Guide to Orthodox America.* Tuckahoe, N.Y.: Saint Vladimir's Press, 1965.

Bogolepov, Alexander A. *Toward an American Orthodox Church: The Establishment of an Autocephalous Orthodox Church.* New York: Morehouse-Barlow, 1963.

Bratsiotis, Panagiotis. *The Greek Catholic Church.* Notre Dame/London: University of Notre Dame Press, 1967.

Bulgakov, Sergius. *The Orthodox Church.* Milwaukee: Morehouse Publishing Co., 1935.

Constantelos, Demetrios J., *The Greek Orthodox Church.* New York: The Seabury Press, 1967.

Emhardt, Chancy, et al. *The Eastern Church in the Western World.* Milwaukee: Morehouse Publishing Co., 1928.

LeGuillou, M.J. *The Spirit of Eastern Orthodoxy.* New York: Hawthorne Books, 1962.

Meyendorff, John. *The Orthodox Church: Its Past and Its Role in the World Today.* Tuckahoe, N.Y.: St. Vladimir's Press, 1981.

Salutos, Theodore. *The Greeks in America.* Cambridge, Mass.: Harvard University Press, 1964.

Schmemann, Alexander. *The Historical Road of Eastern Orthodoxy.* New York: Holt, Rinehart & Winston, 1963.

Ware, Timothy. *The Orthodox Church.* Baltimore: Penguin Books, 1964.

Zernov, Nicholas. *Eastern Christendom: A Study of the Origin and Development of the Eastern Orthodox Church.* New York: G. P. Putnam's Sons, 1961.

Pentecostal

Anderson, Robert Mapes. *Vision of the Disinherited.* New York: Oxford University Press, 1979.

Bartelman, Frank. *What Really Happened at Azusa Street.* Northridge, Calif.: Voice Christian Publications, 1962.

Bennett, Dennis J. *Nine O'clock in the Morning.* Plainfield, N.J.: Logos International, 1970.

Bloch-Hoell, Nils Egede. *The Pentecostal Movement: Its Origin, Development, and Distinctive Character.* New York: Humanities Press, 1964.

Blumhofer, Edith L. *Aimee Semple McPherson Everybody's Sister.* Grand Rapids: Eerdman Publishing Co., 1993.

———. *Restoring the Faith: The Assemblies of God, Pentecostalism, and American Culture.* Urbana: University of Illinois Press, 1993.

BIBLIOGRAPHY

Burgess, Stanley M., and Gary B. McGee, eds. *Dictionary of Pentecostal and Charismatic Movements.* Grand Rapids: Zondervan, 1988.

Clark, E. T. *The Small Sects in America.* Nashville: Abingdon Press, 1949.

Cunningham, Robert C. *Filled with the Spirit.* Springfield, Mo.: Gospel Publishing House, 1972.

Durasoff, Steve. *Bright Wind of the Spirit.* Englewood Cliffs, N.J.: Prentice-Hall, 1972.

Gaver, Jessyca Russell. *Pentecostalism.* New York: Universal Publishing & Distribution Corp., 1971.

Gee, Donald. *Concerning Spiritual Gifts.* Springfield, Mo.: Gospel Publishing House, 1972.

Harper, Michael. *As at the Beginning: The Twentieth-Century Pentecostal Revival.* Plainfield, N.J.: Logos International, 1971.

Harrell, David Edwin, Jr. *All Things Are Possible: The Healing and Charismatic Revivals in Modern America.* Bloomington: Indiana University Press, 1975.

Harris, Ralph W. *Spoken by the Spirit.* Springfield, Mo.: Gospel Publishing House, 1973.

Hollenweger, Walter. *The Pentecostals: The Charismatic Movement in the Churches.* Minneapolis: Augsburg Publishing House, 1972.

Menzies, William W. *Anointed to Serve: The Story of the Assemblies of God.* Springfield, Mo.: Gospel Publishing House, 1971.

Moon, Elmer Louis. *The Pentecostal Church.* New York: Carlton Press, 1966. (A history of the Pentecostal Church of God in America, Inc.)

Nichol, John Thomas. *The Pentecostals.* Plainfield, N.J.: Logos International, 1971.

Paris, Arthur Ernest. *Black Pentecostalism: Southern Religion in an Urban World.* Amherst: University of Massachusets Press, 1982.

Patterson, J.O.; Ross, German O.; and Atkins, Julia Mason. *History and Formative Years of the Church of God in Christ with Excerpts from the Life and Works of Its Founder-Bishop C. H. Mason.* Memphis: Church of God in Christ Publishing House, 1969.

Poloma, Margaret M. *Assemblies of God at the Crossroads.* Knoxville: University of Tennessee Press, 1989.

Sherrill, John. *They Speak with Other Tongues.* Old Tappan, N.J.: Fleming H. Revell, 1964.

Synan, Vinson. *The Holiness-Pentecostal Movement in the United States.* Grand Rapids: Eerdmans Publishing Co., 1972.

———. *The Old-Time Power.* Franklin Springs, Ga.: Advocate Press, 1973.

Williams, Melvin D. *Community in a Black Pentecostal Church.* Pittsburgh: University of Pittsburgh Press, 1974.

Presbyterian

Armstrong, Maurice W.; Loetscher, Lefferts A.: and Anderson, Charles A. *The Presbyterian Enterprise.* Presbyterian Historical Society Publications. Philadelphia: Westminster Press, 1956.

Briggs, C. A. *American Presbyterianism.* New York: Scribner's, 1885.

Calvin, John. *Institutes of the Christian Religion.* Philadelphia: Westminster Press, 1960.

Coalter, Milton J., ed. *The Presbyterian Predicament.* Louisville: John Knox Press, 1990.

Davies, A. Mervin. *The Presbyterian Heritage.* Richmond: John Knox Press, 1965.

Drury, C. M. *Presbyterian Panorama.* Philadephia: Westminster Press, 1952.

Jamison, Wallace N. *The United Presbyterian Story, 1858–1958.* Pittsburgh: Geneva Press, 1958.

Lingle, Walter W., and John W. Kuykendall. *Presbyterians: Their History and Beliefs.* Richmond: John Knox Press, 1978.

Loetscher, Lefferts A. *A Brief History of the Presbyterians.* Philadelphia: Westminster Press, 1978.

———. *The Broadening Church.* Philadelphia: University of Pennsylvania Press, 1954.

Longfield, Bradley J. *The Presbyterian Controversy.* New York: Oxford University Press, 1968.

Melton, Julius. *Presbyterian Worship in America.* Richmond: John Knox Press, 1967.

Murray, Andrew E. *Presbyterians and the Negro: A History.* Philadelphia: Presbyterian Historical Society, 1966.

Slosser, Gaius J., ed. *They Seek a Country: The American Presbyterians.* New York: Macmillan, 1955.

Thompson, R. E. *A History of the Presbyterian Churches in the United States.* American Church History Series. New York: Scribner's, 1895.

Trinterud, Leonard J. *The Forming of an American Tradition.* Philadelphia: Westminster Press, 1949.

Reformed

American Calvinistic Conference. *The Word of God and the Reformed Faith.* Grand Rapids: Baker House, 1942.

Bratt, James D. *Dutch Calvinism in North America.* Grand Rapids: Eerdmans, 1984.

Brouwer, Arie R. *Reformed Church Roots.* New York: Reformed Church Press, 1977.

Brown, W. D. *History of the Reformed Church in America.* New York: Board of Publication of the Reformed Church in America, 1928.

DeJong, Gerald F. *The Dutch Reformed Church in the American Colonies.* 1978.

Erskine, Noel Leo. *Black People and the Reformed Church in America.* Lansing, Ill.: Reformed Church Press, 1978.

Hageman, Howard. *Our Reformed Church.* 11th ed. Lansing: RCA Distribution Center, 1976.

Vanden Berge, Peter M., ed., *Historical Directory of the Reformed Church in America, 1628–1978.* Grand Rapids: Eerdmans, 1978.

Roman Catholic Church

Abbott, Walter M., S. J., ed. *Documents of Vatican II.* New York: American Press, 1966.

Bokenkotter, Thomas W. *A Concise History of the Catholic Church.* Garden City, N.Y.: Doubleday, 1979.

Catholic Almanac. Huntington, Ind.: Our Sunday Visitor Press (annual).

Dolan, Jay P. *The American Catholic Experience.* New York: Doubleday, 1985.

———. *The Immigrant Church: New York's Irish and German Catholics, 1815–1865.* Baltimore: Johns Hopkins University Press, 1975.

Ellis, John Tracy. *American Catholicism.* 2d ed. Chicago: University of Chicago Press, 1969.

Gillard, John T. *The Catholic Church and the American Negro.* Baltimore: St. Joseph's Society Press, 1928; New York: Johnson Reprint Corporation, 1968.

Greeley, Andrew. *The American Catholic.* New York: Basic Books, 1977.

BIBLIOGRAPHY

Hardon, John A., S. J. *Modern Catholic Dictionary.* Garden City, N.Y.: Doubleday, 1980.

Hennesey, James, S. J. *American Catholics.* New York: Oxford University Press, 1981.

Holmes, J. Derek, and Bernard W. Bickers. *A Short History of the Catholic Church.* New York: Paulist Press, 1984.

Kennelly, Karen, ed. *American Catholic Women: A Historical Exploration.* New York: Macmillan, 1989.

Kung, Hans. *The Church.* New York: Sheed & Ward, 1967.

McAvoy, Thomas T. *A History of the Catholic Church in the United States.* Notre Dame, Ind.: University of Notre Dame Press, 1969.

McBrien, Richard P. *Catholicism.* Minneapolis: Winston Press, 1980.

McKenzie, John L. *The Roman Catholic Church.* Garden City, N.Y.: Image Books, 1971.

New Catholic Encyclopedia. New York: McGraw-Hill Book Co., 1967.

O'Brien, David J. *The Renewal of American Catholicism.* New York: Paulist Press, 1972.

————. *Public Catholicism.* New York: Macmillan, 1989.

Official Catholic Dictionary. New York: P. J. Kenedy & Sons (annual).

Weaver, Mary Jo. *New Catholic Women.* New York: Harper and Row. 1985.

Spiritualist

Bach, Marcus. *They Have Found a Faith.* Indianapolis: Bobbs-Merrill, 1946.

Braden, Charles S. *These Also Believe.* New York: Macmillan, 1949.

Hill, J. A. *Spiritualism: Its History, Phenomena and Doctrine.* New York: Doubleday, 1919.

Moore, R. Laurence. *In Search of White Crows.* New York: Oxford University Press, 1993.

Nelson, G. L. *Spiritualism and Society.* New York: Shocken Books, 1969.

The Spiritualist Manual. Washington, D.C.: National Spiritualist Association of the U.S.A., 1944.

Swedenborgian (Churches of the New Jerusalem)

Barrett, B. F. *The Question, What Are the Doctrines of the New Church? Answered.* Germantown, Penna.: Swedenborg Publication Association, 1909.

Smythe, J. K. *Gist of Swedenborg.* Philadelphia: J. B. Lippincott Co., 1920.

Swedenborg, Emmanuel. *Complete Works.* Boston: Houghton Mifflin, 1907.

Unitarian Universalist

Ahlstrom, Sydney E. and Carey, Jonathan S., eds. *An American Reformation: A Documentary History of Unitarian Christianity.* Middletown, Conn.: Wesleyan University Press, 1985.

Cassara, Ernest. *Hosea Ballou.* Boston: Beacon Press, 1961.

Commager, Henry Steele. *Theodore Parker.* Boston: Little, Brown, 1936.

Howe, Daniel Walker. *The Unitarian Conscience.* Cambridge: Harvard University Press, 1970.

Hutchison, William R. *The Transcendentalist Ministers.* New Haven: Yale University Press, 1959.

Kring, Walter D. *Henry Whitney Bellow.* Boston: Skinner House, 1979.

Miller, Russell E. *The Larger Hope.* Boston: Unitarian Universalist Association, 1979.

Persons, Stow. *Free Religion.* New Haven: Yale University Press, 1947.

BIBLIOGRAPHY

Wilbur, Earl Morse. *A History of Unitarianism in Transylvania, England, and America.* Cambridge: Harvard University Press, 1952.

Williams, George H. *American Universalism.* Boston: Universalist Historical Society, 1971.

Wright, George H. *The Beginnings of Universalism in America.* Boston: Beacon Press, 1955.

———. *The Liberal Christians.* Boston: Beacon Press, 1970.

———, ed. *A Stream of Light.* Boston: Unitarian Universalist Association, 1975.

United Church of Christ

Atkins, G. G. *History of American Congregationalism.* Boston: Pilgrim Press, 1942.

Burton, C. E. *Manual of the Congregational and Christian Churches.* Boston: Pilgrim Press, 1936.

Horstman, J. E., and H. H. Werrnecke. *Through Four Centuries.* St. Louis: Eden Publishing House, 1938.

Horton, Douglas. *The United Church of Christ.* New York: Thomas Nelson, 1962.

Rouner, Arthur A., Jr. *The Congregational Way of Life.* Englewood Cliffs, N.J.: Prentice-Hall, 1960.

Stanley, A. Knighton. *The Children Is Crying: Congregationalism Among Black People.* New York: Pilgrim Press, 1979.

Williams, D. D., and R. L. Shinn. *We Believe: An Interpretation of the United Statement of Faith.* New York: United Church Press, 1966.

Zikmund, Barbara Brown. *Hidden Histories.* 2 vols. New York: United Church Press, 1984, 1987.

Unity

Bach, Marcus. *The Unity Way.* Lee's Summit, Mo.: Unity Books, 1982.

Cady, H. Emilie. *Lessons in Truth.* Lee's Summit, Mo.: Unity Books, 1896.

D'Andrade, Hugh. *Herald of the New Age.* New York: Harper & Row, 1974.

Fillmore, Charles R. *Talks on Truth.* Lee's Summit, Mo.: Unity Books, 1926.

———. *Dynamics for Living.* Lee's Summit, Mo.: Unity Books, 1967.

Freeman, J. D. *The Story of Unity.* Lee's Summit, Mo.: Unity Books, 1972.

Index

341

INDEX